THE EDUCATION
OF A
PUBLIC MAN

THE EDUCATION
OF A
PUBLIC MAN

My Life and Politics

HUBERT H. HUMPHREY

Edited by Norman Sherman

1976
Doubleday & Company, Inc.   Garden City, New York

Some of this material first appeared in the following periodicals: "My Father," copyright © 1966 by Hubert H. Humphrey, November 1966 issue of *The Atlantic Monthly;* "My Marathon Talk with Russia's Boss," copyright © 1959 by Hubert H. Humphrey, January 12, 1959, issue of *Life* magazine; adapted material from *Beyond Civil Rights,* copyright © 1968 by Hubert H. Humphrey. Adapted by permission of Random House, Inc.

PHOTO CREDITS
Humphrey family photographs: 1; 2; 3; 4; 5; 6; 7; 8; 9; 10; 11; 12; 13; 14; 15; 20; 21; 31. Photo by Driscoll: 16. Time-Life Picture Agency © Time Inc.: 17 (photo by Paul Schutzer). United Press International: 18; 23; 24; 25; 26; 27; 28; 30. Marty Nordstrom, Black Star: 19; 29. Photo Lab USIS India, New Delhi: 22.

ISBN: 0-385-05603-6
Library of Congress Catalog Card Number 75-36628
Copyright © 1976 by Hubert H. Humphrey
All rights reserved
Printed in the United States of America
First Edition

I dedicate this book to my family, with love and appreciation. It is their book, too.

To the memory of my father, mother, and brother Ralph.

To Muriel, my partner (and sweetheart), who has made my way easier, my life fuller, and without whom I could not have reached out to be what I wanted to be.

To my sisters, Frances and Fern, and to my children, Nancy, Skip, Bob, and Doug.

All of them have helped me, sharing me with my public responsibilities in a generous and tolerant spirit.

CONTENTS

viii CONTENTS

BOOK THREE   NEXT DOOR TO POWER

FOREWORD

"If you are never more than you have been, you will be a foot-note in American history. But if you will tell honestly what you have seen and felt and learned for a quarter of a century of American life, people may read you a hundred years from now."

When my friend who was to edit this book said that to me in 1969, I was insulted and put off by what I considered gross impertinence. After all, I thought, I have been senator and Vice President and the Democratic candidate for President, and I am proud of what I have accomplished.

But as I thought about it, the idea of candor for history appealed to me. I wanted someday to write about my life, but I had read so many books by political leaders that were ego trips, sanitized, banal, that I hesitated. Writing for a future audience seemed an implicit defense against the pitfalls of a self-serving, self-justifying reconstruction of history. Maybe an honest book could be written.

You must judge whether I have succeeded. To the extent that I have, this book may have merit and be worthy of your attention even now, clearly not so much for what it tells about me, but for what it may tell about our government and our country.

As much as I would like and as much as I have tried, I cannot proclaim that everything in this book is historically accurate. Others may recall differently things I have written about. All political leaders, if not simply all men, want to be seen and remembered in the best possible light. This is, then, just one man's view of himself and of America. It is as accurate as I can recall events of my lifetime, as true to those recollections as I can describe.

Oral history has become a standard technique in recent years, and this is really a kind of oral history of myself. Beginning in 1969 shortly after I left the Vice President's office, I began to record my thoughts about people and events in my lifetime, of things I myself had done.

I was aided in this by several people who researched my files going back to my student days and who produced a series of questions for me to answer. Other associates of mine raised questions about periods and events in which they were involved. As I responded to all these questions, my memory would be jogged and I would add other stories.

Ultimately, the tapes were transcribed and edited. As I read the edited transcripts, I would dictate more to fill in the holes, and finally, of course, there was my scrutiny of the manuscript to make sure that each word was as I wanted it.

I thought the process would be quick and easy. It was not. To find the time to dictate was tough enough, but to create the conditions for reflection and to decide what went in and what came out were even more difficult. When the conditions were right, generally on vacations or back home in Minnesota, I dictated and edited; when they weren't, I put the book aside, sometimes for many months at a time. If history was the object, there seemed no reason to rush.

The prologue—covering thirty-six hours around election day 1968—is a little out of the ordinary and probably deserves some special description. Norman Sherman, then my press secretary, who had spent most of those hours with me or close by gave me notes of what went on, what was talked about. In February of 1969, when those memories were still fresh, he urged me to describe what that time had been like not in political terms, but in human ones. I sat alone one Sunday night in my study at home and, using those notes, recalled what my thoughts were. It was an unpleasant experience, as recollection of defeat must be, but an interesting one.

Obviously, the prologue does not reflect everything I thought, but I think it does reflect my moods and something of what I thought. In retrospect, I was much more unhappy about some people and much more generous about others than I would be today. But I have let it all stand.

I think it is useful, probably even important, to remind people of the obvious fact that no matter how high a man may rise in this democracy, he functions with the human emotions and limitations that we all share.

I have enjoyed my life, its disappointments outweighed by its pleasures. I have loved my country in a way that some people consider sentimental and out of style. I still do, and I remain an optimist, with joy, without apology, about this country and about the American experiment in democracy. I hope my story tells you why.

PROLOGUE

A DAY OF WAITING

"I have done my best. I have lost. Mr. Nixon has won. The democratic process has worked its will, so now let's get on with the urgent task of uniting our country."

In a lifetime of thousands of speeches and millions of words, those were the hardest ones I have ever had to speak.

They came at the end of the longest day of my life, the day during which 73 million citizens cast their ballots for me or for someone else for President of the United States. It was a day when every minute lingered, when time was suspended, when suddenly there was nothing more to do after months on a treadmill, when finally fatigue overwhelmed me.

Yet it was so special and tense a day. It was a day of schoolboys' dreams, a day almost all men in public life in America include in their fantasies. A day of harshest reality, of total success or total failure. At its end, no matter what the margin, I might be President-elect of the United States or I would be out of public service for the first time in a quarter of a century.

Election Day, for the candidate, can only be solitary self-confinement in the midst of madness, and my thoughts alone, euphoric one moment, depressed the next, kept me company that day.

The day had begun in California, and then we flew on to Minnesota to vote and await the results . . .

The Secret Service log describes the day so starkly:

> (12:01 a.m. The Vice President and party were at the residence of Mr. Lloyd Hand, 507 North Sierra Drive, Beverly Hills, California.)

. . . Dancing with Muriel is as much fun now as it was the first time, twenty-five years ago. She has been a wonderful partner. I love her more than ever . . .

. . . It's a joyous party, like a victory party. Too soon, though. I doubt we can win. But the weekend has been so great, we're really coming on. Fifty-five thousand people in the Houston Astrodome on Sunday, Johnson at his best, really laying it on for me, and Monday in Los Angeles, big and enthusiastic mobs of people. And tonight's telethon was wonderful, too. Maybe it will be enough. Probably it won't. We needed a few more days. The momentum was with us.

. . . Jesse Unruh isn't here, and I'm glad. He was never really for us. He cozied up to every element in his state that was anti-Johnson and anti-Humphrey, while I was fighting for my political life and the Democratic party. He proved so often that he can't be trusted . . .

> (1:47 a.m. The Vice President, accompanied by Mrs. Humphrey, departed the Lloyd Hand residence, with George Hickey driving and DSAIC Walter Coughlin riding in the front seat.)

. . . Muriel is so lovely. I couldn't have managed this year without her. We've given it everything we had. She'd be good in the White House—good for the country. People love her.

. . . I've climbed that damned ladder of politics, and every step has been rough. I've slipped so many times and almost fallen back. I wonder what it would have been like with money enough and money early, when it really counts? That top rung is never going to be mine. My fingernails are scraping it, but I don't have a grip. Yet maybe, maybe we can make it. It's so damn close. I am so tired.

(2:10 a.m. The Vice President and party arrived at the Los Angeles International Airport and boarded TWA charter, after chatting briefly with various members of the press.)

. . . How many interviews with the same questions, the same answers, the same smile. I like the reporters, but I'm glad I'm done. These last four years with them have been rough, these past months impossible. "When are you going to be your own man, when are you going to be your own man, what do you really think about Vietnam?" If you lie, they believe you. If you're honest, you're evasive.

. . . I can carry California. I've *got* to or I'm dead. Gene McCarthy could have helped. I thought we had an understanding, but he didn't deliver. Maybe he couldn't. God knows the pressure would have been great not to. And when he did speak out, it was late and halfhearted.

. . . A compromise peace plank at the convention would have helped in California, helped everywhere. I wanted one so badly. I cleared one with Rusk. I cleared it with Rostow. Johnson must have okayed it. Why he sent Marvin Watson out to Chicago to kill it, I'll never know.

. . . Chicago was a disaster anyway. It was awful. How can you be fair in a thing like that? Should I have kicked Daley beyond what I believed? Trying to be fair, I looked weak.

(2:25 a.m. The Vice President and party were airborne aboard TWA charter enroute to Minneapolis, Minnesota.)

. . . The last take-off. I wonder how many times we've done this since March 31. One hundred fifty times. Two hundred? Got to get some rest . . . God, what a year to run. The Tet offensive, the primaries and McCarthy, riots and backlash, the assassinations, Wallace, Chicago. No money when we needed it. No party spirit for so long.

. . . No matter what we did in September, it didn't seem to come out right. We were broke. Then, that convention was so late—no time to heal wounds. I wanted to be loyal to the President. My guts, my heart wouldn't let me do it any other way. I just couldn't yield to his critics . . . No, Governor, I won't resign as Vice President. How many times did I say that, even to Lyndon's "friends."

. . . And every time I'd make a statement with some little twist that was my own, it would get shot down in Washington. Maybe twice. The President was impossible on the war. Such a fury when I showed him my task-force report on Vietnam. That was July. He said the same things in October.

. . . I had a choice. Break with the President and be denounced as irresponsible. Or muddle through. Really no choice if I wanted to be President. And I do, how badly I do.

. . . I have got to get some rest.

(7:41 a.m. The Vice President and party arrived Minneapolis, Minnesota, and were met by a crowd of approximately 1,500 persons and various members of the press. The weather was cold with a heavy drizzle.)

. . . What a crowd, what a glorious crowd. Look at them. That's what it's all about. Man, they make the juices flow. These people in Minnesota have given me so much. I've got to win. I'm *home*, I'm really home. They love Muriel. Look at them. I can't let them down.

. . . It's like '48 when I came home from Philadelphia. Not a patronage job among them. Believers. True believers. What a special place this is.

(7:55 a.m. The Vice President and Mrs. Humphrey departed the Minneapolis-St. Paul Airport enroute to Waverly, Minnesota (Marysville Township, Minnesota). Special Agent Shanahan drove the Vice President, with ASAIC Burke riding in the front seat.)

. . . Campaigns are kind of crazy. Those cars stretched out behind us. Press buses. Staff people. Hangers-on. It's a traveling circus with no county fair to go to. I guess I love it. Wait till our neighbors see this bunch at the town hall. There isn't room for thirty people inside and there must be a couple of hundred trailing along. Squeeze and shove. What a show! I hope my neighbors forgive the stampede.

(9:05 a.m. The Vice President and Mrs. Humphrey arrived
Marysville Township, Minnesota, where they voted at the
Township Hall.)

. . . This is it. What an odd feeling. Almost schizophrenic, voting for yourself for President. Different from voting for senator
or mayor. Stand still and pray. *Please, God,* let our efforts be
successful.

. . . We've come so far so fast. We are going to make it . . .
No, we aren't. Stop thinking that. I am so tired again.

(9:28 a.m. The Vice President and Mrs. Humphrey departed
Marysville Township enroute to their residence in Waverly,
Minnesota.)

. . . The ground is really wet. Must have rained hard. I wonder how the crops around here have been. I've got to ask Harold.
The house looks so warm and inviting.

(9:31 a.m. The Vice President and Mrs. Humphrey arrived
at their residence in Waverly, Minnesota.)

. . . We are alone. I am alone.

When we woke up later that gray day, neither Muriel nor I
talked much. I was less tired though still almost aching with fatigue and the letdown. I thought less about the campaign and
personalities, and possibly to cheer myself up, began to think
more about what I might do as President.

. . . Clark Clifford would make a fine Secretary of State. He's
surprised people with his views on the war. He's been really
good at the White House. I have a feeling he hasn't liked me.
But he's so able—so sound. I'd appoint him right off the bat.
He's first-rate.

. . . I need Cy Vance to come back. I'd want him to replace
Clifford at Defense. He's got those funny little glasses in front of
a beautiful mind. Got to be careful not to surround myself with
just Johnson men. Those two are okay. It has to be a new administration, my administration. Johnson picked some good people.

. . . Vietnam is a mess. I'm sure, pretty sure, that we were right going there, but we've got to get out. Fast. It's ripping the country apart. We've got to start withdrawing troops. I'd do that quickly.

. . . Wonder why Johnson shot me down when I said that troops would be withdrawn in 1969? I was right. I got the information from the White House. Ruined my credibility, made me look like a damn fool. It hurt. Never really recovered from that.

. . . I think we can do something about the black revolution, too. We really got along pretty well in the black community, even with the militants. Someday we'll get credit for what we started. It's messy now, maybe for another ten, twenty years, but the country's strong enough to take it. It'll be better for it.

. . . I can deal with the Russians. Nixon can't. He doesn't really understand the nature of communism, doesn't understand its strengths or its weaknesses. He doesn't know where or how to challenge them. We've got to get arms control or we're going to blow ourselves to hell. Why don't more people believe that? I'd like to do something there. For the country. For Adlai, too. I wish he'd lived for this year.

(4:25 p.m. The Vice President, accompanied by Norman Sherman, Harold Chapman (caretaker), and the local sheriff, Darryl Wolf, departed his Waverly residence enroute to Buffalo, Minnesota. The Vice President drove the car himself.)

. . . You get to be a captive in high public office. Little things like never driving yourself. Funny, both Kennedy and Johnson liked to drive their own cars when they got away from the White House for a couple of days of rest.

. . . I wonder how Ed Muskie is doing. What a job he's done. What a wonderful guy! If nothing else works out, at least I got to know Ed and Jane so much better. Muskie or Agnew. What a choice. I really will give Ed responsibility. He'll run the domestic end, and I'll get us out of Vietnam.

. . . I wonder if I should have blown the whistle on Anna Chennault and Nixon. He must have known about her call to Thieu. I *wish* I could have been sure. Damn Thieu. Dragging his feet this past weekend hurt us. I wonder if that call did it. If Nixon knew. Maybe I should have blasted them anyway.

(4:45 p.m. The Vice President and party arrived at Buffalo, Minnesota, where they visited the following stores and chatted briefly with various people: Buffalo Cleaners, Wagners Drug Store, and Burkland's.)

. . . There's so much space out here. Harlem's so crowded. The cities are so packed. There must be as many people on a block in Harlem as there are in all of Buffalo. Probably more. None of our traditional liberal answers is good enough. Conservatives are worse. Got to move in new directions, new cities, industry out here. Hough, Lawndale, Watts, Harlem, how do you solve it? But it's got to be solved.

. . . I like these people here. Open. Straight. We're so lucky! Life seems so uncomplicated. I suppose it isn't, particularly. Problems are different, solvable. Like my Doland.

. . . I wish my dad had lived to see this day. He'd have been so proud. And helpful. A wise man, and a decent one. I wonder what made him that different from most of the people around him. He gave me so much, I've really missed him all these years.

(5:15 p.m. The Vice President and party departed Buffalo, Minnesota.)

. . . Henry Kissinger should be in the White House. I hope he'll come. Sam Huntington, too. He's been really helpful. That Boston bunch is bright. I can understand why John Kennedy used them. I can do without Arthur Schlesinger. Glad his books are better than his politics.

. . . John Kennedy really brought something special to politics, to the White House. I don't have it, whatever it was he had. But neither does Nixon. I think I can be a healer. We need goodwill and understanding now. Muriel and I could lift the spirit in our own way. We could really open up the White House. And politics.

(5:35 p.m. The Vice President and party arrived at the Triple H Ranch in Lake Waverly.)

. . . The press in Washington are like birds on a wire. When one flies, they all fly. Most of them liked us. Most of them probably voted for me today. But I could never satisfy them. They thought of me as a liberal, but my loyalty to Johnson was more than they could take. "Humphrey's going to lose. Ignominious defeat. Thirty-five electoral votes. Behind Wallace." Even when things changed it took them two or three weeks to believe it.

(6:45 p.m. The Vice President, accompanied by Mrs. Humphrey, departed Waverly enroute to the residence of Mr. Dwayne Andreas, Excelsior, Minnesota, for dinner and to await the election returns. They were driven by SA Shanahan, with ASAIC Lawson riding in the front seat.)

. . . I wonder what Daley will produce. "Don't upset Daley." It was like a political catechism. We should have gone into Illinois more. I've been telling everyone that for weeks. We probably should have worked more with Daley and young Adlai. I've got to carry Illinois. I'll need more than Cook County to do it. Those downstate crowds were pretty enthusiastic. We've really poured the money in there these last couple of weeks.

. . . Wallace may hurt us downstate. That whole lousy movement may cost me the election. Going to cost the country more. Hate. Hate. Hate. So much of it from the right and left this year!

(7:23 p.m. The Vice President and Mrs. Humphrey arrived at the residence of Mr. and Mrs. Dwayne Andreas.)

. . . Dwayne and Inez have been good to us and for us. We're really like one big family, their kids and our kids. What'll happen to them in the White House: Nancy, Skip, Bob, Doug? They never really liked politics. It took me away so much, never gave them back much. This year has been different. They've worked hard. And well. I've got to be closer to them, however this turns out.

. . . The food looks great. But it all tastes the same. I really don't want to eat. God, I am nervous. They're all more nervous. How can I sit still? The polls are beginning to close. So many things we could have done differently. All or nothing in a couple of hours. I'm not listening.

. . . Those first results look pretty good. Stay calm. We're going to carry New England all right. Abe Ribicoff really had no stomach for my coming into Connecticut. Hardly close enough at the beginning of that day to get in the same picture with me. Crowds were tremendous, big, enthusiastic. Abe was following so close at the end of the day. We carried Connecticut. That's what counts tonight. Dempsey and Bailey came through.

. . . It's going to be close. Close. Close. Which way? New York looks good. So does Pennsylvania. I doubt we can make it in New Jersey. Dick and Betty Hughes worked their hearts out for us. Dick wanted that vice presidency so badly. He's a good trouper. Disappointment and all, he really put out for us. But some of the boys just doublecrossed both of us.

(10:25 p.m. The Vice President and Mrs. Humphrey departed the Andreas residence to the Leamington Hotel in Minneapolis, Minnesota, with SA Shanahan driving and SAIC Weaver riding in the front seat.)

. . . You owe so much to so many people in politics. For every phony there are so many good folks. Big ones, like Ted Kennedy. He had so many reasons not to help, but he really gave. I remember how he shook in Boston when he got up to speak. What guts! I really like Ted and Joan. And George McGovern. He's a gentleman. He stood up for me at the convention. George and Eleanor and their family—good neighbors and friends.

. . . And the President. He did every specific thing we asked him to in the border states, in Texas. It was a tough year for him. He wasn't easy to get along with.

. . . Ladybird was. I love her. She's a wonderful, warm human being. Been so good to Muriel and me. And a super politician. She really is something special.

(11:05 p.m. The Vice President and Mrs. Humphrey arrived at the Leamington Hotel and proceeded to the Summit Suite.)

. . . That crowd is going to crush us. They're so damned enthusiastic. I can see it. But I don't feel it. Strange. Usually I do.

It's contagious. It jazzes me up. Not now. They're looking at me like I'm President. I'm not. Oh, God, I'm not going to be either. I'm so nervous. I've got to get upstairs where it's quiet.

. . . That Maryland vote is really encouraging. Border states are awful. Imagine a guy like Wallace getting so many votes. North. South. Everywhere. Such an ugly part of American politics.

. . . We're losing. We're losing.

. . . It's gone.

. . . But a lot better than the gloom boys thought I'd do. Small joy. I've got to go downstairs and talk to the people. What am I going to say? Maybe there's still a chance. Can't give up.

. . . Those people are our friends. I can't keep them waiting any longer. They've been patient . . . faithful . . . loyal. How much I owe them! I'm up where the glory is, they're down there doing the drudge work. Day after day, campaign after campaign. They've given me so much. I've failed them.

(2:15 to 2:35 a.m. The Vice President made brief statement in the Hall of States. He returned to suite and retired for the night.)

. . . Look at all the press. Got to be careful, not too enthusiastic; whatever I say will stay with me forever. The people need a pep talk, though. Can't tell them it'll take a miracle to pull this out. Can't tell them it's over. They want hope, not facts. So do I.

I know it's gone. I want to be alone—away from it all—just get to bed.

. . . How will I ever be able to sleep?

I awoke at eight o'clock the next morning, dressed, and sat in the living room of the suite listening to the latest returns. Alone, no family, no staff around, and as the returns from Missouri, Illinois, and California came in, I knew for certain it was all over. I could no longer pretend or hope that something might happen that would make me President of the United States. I had to prepare for the gruesome ritual of concession.

I ordered my own breakfast from room service and waited thirty minutes for it to come. Now family, friends, staff wandered into the suite, sleepy-eyed, depressed, with nothing much to say.

. . . Daley on the phone. "Don't give up. Votes are not all in. Can still carry Illinois." Decent gesture. Trying to make me feel good. Probably means it. I still like him. A proud man. I understand him.

. . . Congratulations, Dick. Mr. President. Congratulations. He's gracious. That's about it. To lose to Nixon. Ye gods! No warmth, no strength, no emotion, no spirit. No heart. Politics of the computer. Probably if I had more of it, I'd be President.

(10:55 a.m. The Vice President, accompanied by Mrs. Humphrey, departed the suite and proceeded to the Hall of States, where he presented a brief statement.)

. . . This is the worst moment of my life. What a disappointment to have failed. We could have won it. We should have won it. I owe everybody so much. There are some who didn't produce. Who didn't help as they could have. Got to hide the bitterness.

. . . Look at Muriel. What a woman! What a wife! She wants to cry. She's got guts, courage. We'll carry this off with dignity. No cry-baby act. No complaining.

(11:20 a.m. The above party returned to their suite on the 14th floor.)

. . . I've got to get out to Waverly. I need to get away. I'm numb . . . I am heartbroken.

(2:30 p.m. The Vice President and Mrs. Humphrey departed the Leamington Hotel via Line Limousine, driven by SA Shanahan, with SAIC Weaver in the front seat. The follow-up car was worked by DSAIC Coughlin and SA's Taylor, Thomas, Welch and Ciatti.)

. . . Who knows? Maybe Nixon is right for the country now. Give it time to catch its breath. There's been such misery ever since John Kennedy's death. I just can't believe Nixon's right. There's so much to do. Now—not later.

. . . What am I going to do? There isn't anything I want to do. I wanted to be President.

(2:42 p.m. The above party arrived at the Lincoln Del Restaurant.)

. . . I was ready. I'd really trained for the presidency. I know government. We had such great plans. We could have changed things. Damn it, I love this country. We could have done so much good.

. . . Corned beef sandwich in a delicatessen with Freddy Gates. Not the way I planned it. People are so nice here. I'd never have gotten anywhere in politics without the Jewish community.

. . . I feel so empty.

. . . I could have gotten us out of that bloody war. I'd have taken chances for peace. Nixon won't. Play it cool. Oh, I suppose he wants out as much as I do. Maybe he'll do what has to be done. God, I hope so.

(3:48 p.m. Vice President and Mrs. Humphrey departed the Lincoln Del Restaurant in Ford Motor Company Lincoln, with SA Shanahan driving and SAIC Weaver riding in the front seat. The follow-up car was worked by SA's Faison, Clockadale, Curtis, Massa and DSAIC Coughlin.)

. . . I could cry. Never quite felt like this. I did some things *so* badly. You make such stupid mistakes in a campaign. Maybe another week would have done it. We were coming on so fast. Why, why, why did we start so far back? What's the use?

(4:30 p.m. The Vice President and party arrived at the Triple H Ranch in Waverly, Minnesota. There were no additional activities on this date.)

And that, as honestly as I can reconstruct it, was my longest day, at the end of my longest year. I look back with regret that I failed—myself, the people who gave me so much in time, money, energy, spirit; regret that I missed the chance to implement, as President, the ideas and ideals so many of us had struggled for.

But I also look back with some pride. I was given the nomination of my party for the presidency of the United States. No finer honor could come to a man than that, particularly after a long political career that had not been without controversy.

I had tried to speak out as forthrightly as possible in those circumstances about the issues that confront our country. I satisfied my conscience, even if I was not able to satisfy all my fellow Democrats, either on my right or on my left.

I take some solace in feeling that 1968 was simply not the year when the American people wanted liberal leadership so much as they wanted a respite from anxiety and frustration. There were many mistakes made in my campaign, some by me personally, some by our Democratic organization. Had we done things differently, we might have won. I think we would have, but why waste time on regrets, when there is so much else to remember.

BOOK ONE

"IN THE MIDDLE OF THIS GREAT BIG CONTINENT"

1. PRAIRIE LAND, PRAIRIE PEOPLE

In 1906, Lily, South Dakota, had a population of 175 people. Two of those people were my father and mother.

He was twenty-five years old, a druggist, one of five children of a Minnesota farmer whose Quaker traditions and family went back to the Revolutionary War period in America.

She was six years younger, a country teacher in a one-room school, the daughter of Norwegian immigrants who had herself been born in Kristiansand, Norway, and only recently come to America. She had ten brothers and sisters.

They, Hubert Humphrey and Christine Sannes, were married in April 1906 in the Highland Lutheran Church in Lily.

That marriage was to last for almost forty-three years, until my father's death. They had four children: Ralph, Fern, Frances, and me.

That is my family and who I am.

The kind of public man I am has been overwhelmingly shaped by two influences: the land of South Dakota and an extraordinary relationship with an extraordinary man, my father.

I learned about the land—learned to love it—from a man of the sea. My maternal grandfather, Guttorm Andreas Sannes, was a captain in the Norwegian Merchant Marine come aground in South Dakota. A wiry six-footer with a goatee, he had begun as a cabin boy at twelve and traveled across the seas—to Russia,

Cuba, and China. At age thirty-eight, with a wife and two children, he followed an immigrant's dream to the United States.

Here he hoped to be a riverboat captain on the Missouri River, combining his love of seas and ships with the riches of a new land; but, like other immigrants, he had received only part of the truth.

The Missouri was filled with sandbars and was not really navigable for the riverboats of his dreams, so Grandfather Sannes, now called Andrew, turned instead to the soil. He settled first near Sioux Falls and then moved, in 1889, homesteading near Lily, in north-central South Dakota, where many members of his family settled and where he farmed until he died, in 1929.

Grandfather Sannes was a religious man, who looked upon his land and cattle with a kind of reverence. As a steward of the land, he would not exploit it. Before such ideas were commonplace, he was an instinctive conservationist, rotating his crops and always leaving some of his land fallow.

Added to his religious mission was a frugal nature. As a boy, working in the fields under his direction, I would rake up around the tied shocks of grain, gathering the grain that had fallen so that there would be no waste. And as he cared for his cattle and his land, so he cared for machinery. He treated the equipment with loving concern, repairing every minor breakdown, protecting the machinery in sheds, as few farmers did. (He had one old wagon which shone like new for almost forty years.)

My grandmother, Tomina Sannes, was a loving woman, too, laboring in her kitchen, her garden, and when necessary, in the barn and in the fields. Surrounded by her children and grandchildren, she was a woman of joy and good humor. I loved her so much!

Christmas and summers on the farm were very special. Christmas meant cousins and aunts and uncles coming by horse-drawn wagon, filling the house with sounds of carols and conversation and laughter, filling themselves with chicken and ham and canned vegetables from the garden and home-baked pies and cookies. Good harvest years and bad, Christmas remained the same.

When I was very young, I'd hang up my Christmas stocking a second time, hoping for a refill of fruits and candy and a toy.

The second day, there would be a corn cob or a couple of pieces of coal from a less beneficent Santa Claus. Grandma would explain the obvious moral about greed and, after a couple of tries, I stopped, having learned my lesson.

Summers for a town boy meant hard work, but also fun in the out-of-doors, riding the hay wagon, driving the cattle from pasture to the barn, feeding the chickens. There was the freedom to run through the fields, scaring up pheasants, playing hide-and-seek around the barn, pursuing dogs and cats.

One summer I saw, in awe and childish wonderment, the effects of a tornado: wagons and machinery picked up and hurled across the countryside; cattle lifted from the pasture into neighboring fields, stunned but not killed; and straw driven into fence posts and into the bark of trees, sticking out like porcupine quills.

I learned then something that is never far out of mind as I work on agricultural legislation: that farmers are always puppets of the weather. It determines when they plant, when they harvest, when they work, and their profit. It enters constantly into conversation; it dominates their thoughts. Life was not only hard, it was capricious.

To live, not just survive, required good spirits and hope, and Grandmother Sannes supplied those. Like most other farm women, she kept part of the money she got from selling eggs. "Egg money" was a traditional and acceptable family embezzlement and permitted the wife to buy things, sometimes frivolous, to make a hard life in rural America more livable.

Grandmother bought wallpaper to add some color and pattern to the plain interior of the house, and the dinner table had napkins and occasionally new dishes—all because of "egg money." She also bought candy for her grandchildren. When I gorged myself on candy corn and jelly beans, I savored not only their sweetness, but Grandmother's little game, too.

My paternal grandfather, John Humphrey, was born on a farm in Ohio in 1850, but his family were Yankees who had lived in Massachusetts and Connecticut since the mid-1700s. When he was five, the family moved to Minnesota to another farm near Union Lakes.

When he married, in 1872, he and his wife farmed for another five years. Then, defeated by a series of bad crops and locusts, they moved on to Oregon with two young children. A third child was born in 1879—my Uncle John—and a fourth, my father, was born in 1882. When he was about six months old, the family moved back to Minnesota to farm once again, this time near Elk River. Grandfather Humphrey was a dairy farmer; he also raised potatoes and small grain.

My grandmother, Adeline Humphrey, was also born in Ohio. Her family were Pennsylvania Quakers who had been in the United States since the late-seventeenth century, arriving about 1690. Her family moved from Ohio to Indiana to Minnesota, where she was a schoolteacher when she married my grandfather.

I did not know my paternal grandmother, but she was apparently a remarkable woman for her time. Her sons remembered her delight in literature and music. She read and exposed them to Victor Hugo, Dickens, Scott, Bret Harte, Mark Twain, Thackeray, Lowell, and Hawthorne. More importantly, she had Quaker strength and commitment, which her family absorbed. Her son John recalls her as "unselfish, unsparing of her strength and energy in behalf of others, even to the last. Like her father before her, she was a free, fearless, analytical thinker, of positive temperament and quick decision."

I did know my father well, however, and the same description might have been made of him.

2. NEVER A PILL
WITHOUT AN IDEA

My father was a man in love his whole life. He had an unshakable faith in his own strength, in other people, and in this country. He had a sense of wonder about the United States that rubbed off on all of us, the kind of love and obligation that was true of a lot of immigrants. Though mother was born in Norway, and my father in Oregon, it was father who used to speak about our country with the reverence of the immigrant.

"Just think of it, boys," he said once, "here we are in the middle of this great big continent, here in South Dakota, with the land stretching out for hundreds of miles, with people who can vote and govern their own lives, with riches enough for all if we will take care to do justice."

Repeating these words now gives them the sound of a Fourth of July speech, but my father meant them and felt them. It never occurred to him to hold back his feelings or to hesitate about the things he valued. What he felt, he felt wholeheartedly, without trying to protect himself with reserve, suspicion, or emotional caution.

He was a missionary with a sense of humor, and undoubtedly he was a romantic. When his friends would josh him about his talk about the good society, and education, and about his politics, he would say, "Before the fact is the dream."

He believed that man is inspired by his dreams, that he is on earth in order to make his dreams come true. There was never a question that work and dreams were both necessary parts of his life, his children's lives or, really, of all lives.

In such small towns, parents and children knew each other well. There were no divided worlds of home and work, of children and adults, each force existing separately from the other. It was natural for children to learn the lessons of life in their most useful form—by observation and participation.

In our cities today it often takes a special effort to get the whole family together. Parents at work and in their social lives are often strangers to their children, and the children semi-strangers to them.

I was at my father's elbow constantly, watching him, listening to him, eventually, of course, debating with him. It was the finest legacy he could have left me. As a result, my life has been a fortunate one, my joy and happiness more than any man should expect.

I have had a part in the drama of our age. I have been in the councils of the great and powerful. But these events have had meaning and purpose because I had the priceless good fortune of spending earlier times, almost every day of my childhood, working at the side of a wise and sensitive man for whom idealism was not simply a creed, but a way of life.

My father attended the public schools of Minnesota: elementary school in Elk River, and then high school at St. James, Minnesota, where his elder brother, my Uncle Harry, was principal.

He graduated from the Drew School of Pharmacy in Minneapolis and moved on to his first drugstore, with a partner, in Lily, South Dakota, in 1903. The prairie land of South Dakota was still largely unbroken when he settled there.

In the ten years after 1900, the population of South Dakota increased tremendously,[1] as the Indian lands and railroad grants were made available to settlers. Trade centers like Lily appeared overnight. And most were to disappear almost as quickly.

People, stores, and towns came and went. A place name on the map might mean one business—a general store, a grain elevator, a drugstore, a farm equipment supplier—or several. If business was bad, if personal problems became great, or if disease or whimsy struck, people moved on, businesses closed, and the town disappeared, leaving an empty structure or two at a lonely crossroad on the wide, flat land.

In the thirty-plus years from the turn of the century until the depression and drought struck hard at South Dakota, there arose 573 new trade centers. During the same period, 398 disappeared —almost all of them centers with fewer than four businesses.

After a couple of years, when the store in Lily failed to produce, my father moved to Granite Falls, Minnesota, to try again. It was there, in February 1907, that my brother Ralph was born. When the drugstore burned down four years later, my family moved once again, this time to Wallace, South Dakota.

I was born there in 1911, in a room over the drugstore. By 1915, we had moved again, this time to Doland, about fifty miles away. Fortunately we settled down, and I spent the remaining years of my childhood there.

My childhood was happy—much of the summertime on the farm, many hours of winter out-of-doors, skating and sliding on the snow, and all of the time being part of a family filled with love and warmth, concerned with people and ideas.

I sound Pollyanna-ish when I speak of my childhood, my family, and Doland, but I think it is real and not simply nostalgia. Doland, as small as it was and as much as it resembled hundreds of other little midwestern towns was, I think, different.

Like other towns, the schools and the church were the central influences, but there was a special independence and pride and intellectual ferment. There was a sense of community, a brightness of spirit that was rare.

Our school won academic honors; our athletic teams beat towns much bigger. We had a municipal power plant, street lights on Main Street, a community park, the big water tower (we called it a standpipe then) long before others did.

I think it was an accident of history that a few men of inquiring minds somehow came together and projected their intensity onto the community. My dad, along with Rev. Albert Hartt, and the local general practitioner, Doc Sherwood, would have stood out in much larger cities. Their energies compressed in a smaller sphere gave power to the whole town.

We were not, however, without our social strata, our haves and have-nots. Shantytown was a small area where the poorer families lived, and mother was uneasy that I had friends there. My father always encouraged us to know everyone.

One day, a friend of mine and I went into the drugstore. I said, "Dad, Jonathan here doesn't have any shoes, and his feet are so cold, they're blue." My father took one look, pushed the NO SALE key on the cash register, took out some money, and walked Jonathan down the street to buy him woolen socks and a pair of sturdy boots.

My father did that kind of thing in a way that was not an act of charity—simply a matter of elemental justice and fairness. (Years later, during the depression, when he canceled thirteen thousand dollars' worth of debts at our drugstore—money we sorely needed to pay our own bills—he shrugged it off with the same humane attitude. He coupled it with a business rationalization: "Hubert, if they owe us money they can't pay, they'll be too embarrassed to come into the store. This way, at least, they feel easier about coming in.")

When I was ten, my father decided the time had come; I would wash dishes and make sodas. I was too short to reach the counter and pull the spigots, so he built a little ramp behind the fountain, and I worked—and listened—from there.

In that ice-cream parlor atmosphere, I heard things that further shaped my life and attitudes toward people and ideas. At night, Dad would sit down with the local lawyer, the doctor, a minister, the bankers, and the postmaster, to discuss and argue the issues of the day. In his store, there was eager talk about politics, town affairs, and religion—just as there was around our dinner table. (They used to say about Dad, "He never sells you a pill without selling you an idea.") I've attended several good universities, listened to some of the great parliamentary debates of our time, but have seldom heard better discussions of basic issues than I did as a boy standing on a wooden platform behind a soda fountain.

I've been told often that I talk too long and too frequently. But I was infected then with the excitement of good discussions. Dialogue and conversation, as I listened and learned, meant having something to say but drawing out others; being passionately concerned with the people and the issues but tempering that passion with respect for those who thought differently.

In Doland, Dad was a Democrat among friends and neighbors who took their Republicanism—along with their religion—very seriously. And while he was a kind man, in political debate he gave everything he had, and that could be considerable. A druggist in a tiny town in the middle of the continent, American history and world affairs were as real to him as they were in Washington, D.C., 1342 miles away (I know the mileage because a sign in Doland says so).

He subscribed to the *Christian Science Monitor,* the New York *Herald Tribune,* the Minneapolis *Journal,* the St. Paul *Dispatch,* and the Watertown (S.D.) *Public Opinion.* Time after time, when he read about some political development in Washington or London or Berlin, he'd say, "You should know this, Hubert. It might affect your life someday."[2]

There was nothing casual about my father's interests. Sometimes if he found something that fascinated him, he would wake us out of a sound sleep and read it to us. Only partly in jest, he occasionally would say, "Stay out of bed as long as you can. Most people die there. You are only alive when you are awake."

His compulsion to make every hour a waking one became a family joke. When he insisted on talking late at night after work, my weary mother would suggest we go to bed. He would give her an affectionate squeeze and urge her to "sleep for all of us."

When Dad discovered a field of art or learning, he plunged into it as though he were the original discoverer. During the 1920s, for example, he became interested in classical music. He'd drive three hundred miles in his car to Minneapolis to hear a symphony orchestra. Suddenly the drugstore would be full of wind-up Victrolas, Edison Phonographs (the "Phonograph with a Soul"), and piles of R.C.A. Red Seal records. He brought home a beautiful console, and later would come into the living room with dozens of records from the store. He'd pretend he had no choice because they hadn't sold.

He was the Sol Hurok of Doland. If he heard of a concert scheduled within a couple of hundred miles, he would try to arrange an appearance in our "opera house." The Doland Opera House was on the second floor above a clothing store run by Uncle Gus and Aunt Sophie Thurn.

It had permanent, hardwood, fold-up seats for about one hundred fifty people on the main floor and another fifty or so in the balcony. We thought it elegant. On weekends, Tom Mix and Harry Carey movies played. It was the home of town meetings, farmers' conventions, and the high school class play.

Traveling theatrical companies, part of the American scene then, would play there. Dad had the ticket board in the store and got free tickets for his efforts. When the troupe arrived, Dad would always drag our furniture up to the stage as part of the set, leaving a half-barren house for my patient mother.

In the 1930s, when he discovered opera, his record library filled with his favorites, most of them recorded by the Metropolitan. He bought books on opera and studied them as though he were a music student at Juilliard.

After we moved to Huron, he encountered poetry. Innocent and unashamed, unconcerned about what was intellectual or sophisticated, he read everything from Edgar Guest to Longfellow to Keats and Shelley and Wordsworth.[3]

But culture never quite had equal billing with politics, and my political training began in Doland. When most of the town wanted to sell the municipally owned power plant to a private utility, Dad was against it.[4] He was a city councilman then, and he fought the idea tooth and nail. I was twelve years old and he would take me to the evening meetings of the council, install me in a chair by a corner window, and then do battle, hour after hour.

As the evening wore on, I'd doze off only to be waked when Dad hit a peak of oratory. Ultimately, he lost the fight, but he did it in a way that brought him respect. His independence, outspoken way, and good spirits prevented controversy from becoming angry. Though he was a Democrat and town rebel in a politically orthodox town, people liked him enough to elect him mayor. Of the 660 people in Doland, only a dozen or so were Democrats. The equation was simple: Republicanism was synonymous with respectability and Protestantism. As a boy, I felt that to be a Democrat was to be, if not pagan, at least less than holy.

The "good folks" logic was rigid: Democrats were Irish; Irish were Catholic; and if you were Democratic, Irish, and Catholic, it was a prima facie case that you could not be respectable, upstanding, or in touch with the True God. Even if you were neither Irish nor Catholic but still Democratic, their logic leapt over reason and heaped you in with that suspicious lot.

My mother, however, was quite acceptable by community standards. She was a pretty, petite five-foot-three young woman with dark brown hair and twinkly blue eyes. She was Republican, respectable, upstanding, and God-fearing, and she and my father disagreed for a long time on churches as well as on politics. She was a strict churchgoer and for a long time he was not, having been influenced in his youth by the work of Robert Ingersoll, the "Great Agnostic."

I attended church as a boy, primarily at mother's insistence, but also because I liked it and because Julian Hartt, the minister's son, was a close friend. In 1922, on the day Ralph and I were baptized, my father, then forty, joined the church. Like poetry, opera, and classical music, the Methodist Church got the full Humphrey treatment. Dad was soon on the church board and taught Sunday school, drawing the biggest, most enthusiastic adult classes in the county.

While he accepted the Christian theology totally, his emphasis was on the social imperatives of religion. A heavenly city, according to Dad, could be created on earth through good works.

His own good works did not end when his class was over. In an evangelical spirit, he would bring home three or four or more people for Sunday dinner* and more talk.

Mother was a superb cook and she'd pile up plates of chicken and mashed potatoes and vegetables. Her specialties were breads (she won bakery prizes at county and state fairs) and sweets: homemade marshmallows; jellies, jams, and preserves; and cinnamon rolls thick with homemade caramel.

Outside, however, things were not quite so sweet.

---

* In the rural Midwest, dinner is at noon or thereabouts, supper at night, and lunch is something served in between.

3. THE BANKS CLOSED EARLY

Although farm prices rose slightly after 1921, the farmers were caught in a vise of high costs and low prices. And drought made life and economic conditions even worse.

As the land and profits dried up, banks began to fail. In this, we were ahead of our time in South Dakota, presaging the acute banking failure throughout the Midwest.

Banks were almost like the trade centers, appearing and disappearing. The movement of people and the opening of lands had created a euphoric banking climate. Little towns had three and four banks. (In 1921 in Massachusetts, there was one bank for every 12,345 people; in South Dakota, one for every 921 people.) There were 631 banks in South Dakota in 1911, but the number had fallen to 587 by 1920, and during the next decade a third of those failed.

Doland itself had two banks, failing within a few months of each other in 1926.* After that, my father kept his money either in cash, government bonds, or goods for his store. By 1930 the government bonds were gone, and our cash was limited as our sales diminished.[1]

My father told me how the Federal Reserve Board tightened up credit around 1921 and 1922, requiring greater reserves for the local banks. Farmers and businessmen in the Midwest had to

* I lost all the money I had saved from peddling newspapers and magazines—about one hundred forty dollars—in the Doland Security State Bank.

pay up their loans or were not permitted to refinance them. As a result, there was a general liquidation of assets, causing a small recession in our part of the country.

My teen-age years filled me with the impression that the Federal Reserve and the big banks of the East were the enemies of the farmer and the small businessman. Most of the people in the Dakotas, with the exception of a few rock-ribbed Republicans, believed that the economic system was stacked against them, that Wall Street (and that name was enunciated in an almost mystical way) milked the Midwest of its capital and manipulated the credit structure to the disadvantage of the "people." They saw a solid and hostile phalanx of banks, railroads, and utilities lined up against them.

If Wall Street was distant, its effects were immediate and real. Small banks closed not because they were poorly managed, but because they could no longer meet the increased demands of the larger banks, which were calling their loans or insisting on requirements that could not be met.

Politics is filled with paradox and irony, and I saw then my first inexplicable example. The Dakotas were strongly Republican. Republican leadership, both at home and nationally, supported almost without question national bank policies that strangled local banks.

Yet local bankers, always respected men of the community, to their last gasp staunchly praised Republican leadership, even as they called loans from farmers and businessmen who couldn't pay. All of them, it seemed, continued to vote Republican and treated Democrats as the enemy.

What this anomalous situation did spawn, however, was a Republican mutation. Out of this midwestern social and political conservatism grew some indigenous radical and liberal movements. Strangely, while some were ultimately absorbed by the Democratic party, all were the offspring of Republican respectability: the Progressive party of Robert La Follette in Wisconsin, the sometime radical Minnesota Farmer-Labor party, the Non-Partisan League of the Dakotas, and variations of Teddy Roosevelt's Bull Moose party.

The first senator I ever heard speak was Peter Norbeck, a South Dakota Republican, later labeled by Senator George Moses of New Hampshire as a "Son of the Wild Jackasses." He, along with Charles McNary of Oregon, William Borah of Idaho, Hiram Johnson of California, and George Norris of Nebraska, spoke for agrarian America and added a distinctly dissident strain to the Republican party.

The 1927 financial collapse in South Dakota was the beginning of the depression for the Midwest, and there was really no recovery from it before the nation plunged into "The Great Depression." Many of the banks that closed in 1926 and 1927 did not reopen until after the bank moratorium of 1933.

During the 1920s, the United States was still a rural country, with relatively few enormous cities. But it was dominated in many ways by powerful, urban financial interests that were also entrenched in the political life of our nation: the railroads, the private utilities, the banks of New York, Boston, Philadelphia, Chicago, and San Francisco. In a sense, all of them were the tools by which super banking structures controlled the flow of credit and dominated the operations of the Federal Reserve System.

The effects were awesome. Many previously well-to-do people were economically bereft; many a farmer lost everything as banks called in loans and mortgages, compelling first the sale of livestock and then the land. The economy, as well as the human spirit, was depressed further. Businesses that depended on a healthy farm economy died. And the control of one's own life, the fruits of one's labor, seemed the passive toys of distant forces.

Farmers, in weariness and frustration, complained to Dad that grain prices always seemed down at harvest time, voicing suspicions that traders in Chicago and Minneapolis were manipulating the market. In fact, as the farmers hauled their grain to market in horse-drawn wagons, the prices on wheat and oats and barley and rye (and later on corn) would drop precipitously.

A farmer could not hold his production off the market until he could get a better price, since there was no on-the-farm storage then, no government programs of crop loans. Just as he was dependent on the whims of weather, the farmer was also dependent on and often the victim of economic forces he could not control.

Though we were not farmers, when they lost so did we.

4. THE LOSS OF HOME

The first time I ever saw my father weep, I was sixteen years old and he was forty-five. It is something I have never forgotten not just because it moved me deeply, but because what followed was so typical of my father's approach to life.

The place we lived in was the kind of home every lucky child has in his life—not just a house but a warm nest for all the excitement and love of growing up.

It wasn't a showplace but it was a pretty good house, as good as any in Doland. It was a two-story, squarish place with white siding and a big screened-in front porch, rooms with hardwood floors, a big basement and two bathrooms, beautiful shade trees on the front lawn, and a plum and apple orchard in the back. A cement driveway led up to a garage, and behind it was a tool shed we turned into a chicken house.

When I came home from high school one day in 1927, my mother was standing next to Dad and a stranger, under a big cottonwood on the front lawn. She was crying. Both men looked solemn, and I wondered what was wrong. Mother said, "Dad has to sell the house to pay our bills." My father talked to the man for a short time, signed a paper, and then the man went away. Afterward, Dad wept.

He was a broad-shouldered man almost six feet tall, with big strong hands, a jutting chin, and that high forehead his children inherited. His rimless glasses sometimes gave him a professorial

look, but he was usually so jolly and vigorous that the most no-
ticeable thing about him was seemingly inexhaustible zest. He
just couldn't be passive about anything and was seldom sad. Seeing my father's tears shook me.

At that moment, I began to have an adult's awareness of the
possibilities for pain and tragedy in life. Other people in town
suffered similar losses of home and happiness. One neighbor and
close friend, the president of Security State Bank, Fred Gross,
committed suicide.

But our tears dried. We moved to a smaller house, which we
rented. Distress in a small town like Doland had no protection of
anonymity. It seemed then such total and public humiliation, but
my father never looked back.

He showed not a discernible ounce of acrimony, apology, or
defeatism, and I don't think he felt any. He plunged on. Some
people who enjoy the sunshine of living are unprepared for the
storms. When they are shocked or hurt, they withdraw and cover
up. Not my father. Right up to the time he died, in November
1949, he had an undiminished appetite for life, accepting the bitter, enjoying the sweet.

Desperate for more business, it was during this time that Dad
took a short course in veterinary medicine to learn how to use
serums and vaccines. Sick cattle, hogs, and poultry took us from
behind the counter and out into the country. I frequently went
with my father and learned from him.

Hog cholera was a constant problem, and we would go from
farm to farm vaccinating hogs for ten cents apiece plus the cost
of the serum. Dad taught farmers how to care for their sick hogs
and cattle and chickens, how to recognize the symptoms, how to
do the vaccinations themselves.

We had one hundred sets of animal syringes in the store, one
for virus, one for the serum, and we loaned them to the farmers
free. Keeping them clean and sterile was my job, and I made
sure the serums did not get contaminated. Until the day I left
for the University of Minnesota, I sometimes traveled alone,
sometimes with my dad, helping farmers vaccinate cattle for
anthrax, hogs for cholera, and poultry for a variety of ailments.

But whatever the demands of drugstore, vaccinations, and
Sunday school, Dad's interest in politics was still prime.

In 1928 he was a delegate to the Democratic National Convention. He and a friend drove to Houston, Texas, in the friend's Chevrolet, piling themselves and their suitcases proudly into the car with all of us standing around. They were two small-town Americans off to nominate a presidential candidate.[1]

When Dad returned, filled with the drama of the convention, he poured out every detail of every speech, every fight, every personality. He showed off his souvenirs as if they were holy relics: his delegate badge, Al Smith posters, and a little brown Al Smith derby made of cardboard.

Smith was as different from us as any man could be, but Dad said he was a progressive who would be a fine President for the people. His identification with Smith was extraordinary, but as he recounted events of the convention, he became even more excited about the man who nominated Smith: someone named Franklin Roosevelt. Dad was certain that this Roosevelt would one day be President of the United States.

Since there were so few Democrats, it may not have been such an honor to run the Democratic campaign in our county. But to Dad (and me) it seemed an appointment of national significance. With his typical enthusiasm, he dashed about the county trying to convince everyone that Al Smith was the man.

But Smith was too different. The parochialism and some ingrained prejudices of our region surfaced. Crosses burned on a little hill a half mile west of Doland, the highest land around—a Ku Klux Klan reminder of the "dangers" of a Catholic President.

Smith was everything that created Spink County suspicion: a Democrat, Catholic, Irish, wet, and to top it off, a man with a New York accent. All of that was too much for our townspeople and farmers, who found Herbert Hoover comfortable. They recalled favorably his excellent work in food relief after World War I, and they respected him as a reasonable, moderate Republican in Calvin Coolidge's Cabinet. It didn't hurt, either, that he was from Iowa.

Dad's only hangup about Smith was on prohibition—the ban on drinking, which both my parents supported, my mother more intensely than my father. Nevertheless, Dad argued vehemently for Smith, and every customer in the drugstore heard his views before receiving change or parcel.* But his persuasiveness did not equal his enthusiasm, and Hoover carried Spink County as he carried the country.

By the time Dad had finished reading the news accounts of Smith's defeat, he was already looking to the day he could campaign for Franklin Roosevelt.

While I had already begun to share my father's fixation on politics, I was still a typical high school senior,† learning my lines for the class play, concerned about the glory of our school on the athletic field, convinced that my generation, particularly I, could make things right in the rest of the world. Though debts and disaster cast a pall over our family and town, I somehow never doubted that I'd get to college.

In the spring of 1929 we talked often about where I should go —leaving unspoken the difficulties of doing so. At a time when the clutch of family was strong and a few miles a long distance, my mother urged Dakota Wesleyan in Mitchell, South Dakota.

It was only ninety-five miles away, several of the teachers in Doland were Wesleyan graduates, and my brother Ralph had been a student there for the previous two years. Besides, it was a Methodist school, and that pleased Mother.

Brookings State College, also close and cheap, seemed to be an alternative, but my father strenuously lobbied for the University of Minnesota, and I applied. His brothers, John and Harry, had studied there, and I think my father regretted that he had not. In a sense, if I attended the University of Minnesota it would fulfill vicariously his own lost hope. Beyond that, I'm sure he felt that experience in a city somewhat larger and a touch more cosmopolitan than either Brookings or Mitchell was important.

That summer, I was accepted at the university, and prepared for my first real move away from home.

---

* Years later, whenever some small-town businessman said he couldn't take an open stand for me because of "business," I'd smile to myself, recalling my father.

† My pattern of life was set even then. In a little high school, if you have the energy you can do almost everything. It has been said that I "played football, basketball, ran the half mile, acted in school plays, played baritone horn in the band, and was graduated as the class star debater, top student, and valedictorian." I sometimes wonder what would have happened had I gone to a large high school.

5. "DON'T EVER ADMIT THAT YOU DON'T KNOW HOW TO DANCE"

My father drove me to Minneapolis in his new Model A Ford, a shiny green car of which we were both terribly proud. It was the car's first long trip,* and we had to drive slowly to break it in. We did the three hundred miles from Doland to Minneapolis at 25–35 miles an hour, and after many hours on the road, registered at a hotel in downtown Minneapolis where they had elevators. (If you grow up in a small town with buildings rarely over two stories high, an elevator is an exciting device.)

The next morning, we drove to the university, and no country boy was ever more wide-eyed. I first saw Folwell Hall, a massive, block-long classroom building of four or five stories, red brick, with little turrets and false chimneys. Later someone described the bizarre architecture as Beer Barrel Renaissance, but at the time it seemed the most glorious work of man. I thought that the whole town of Doland could fit inside.

As we drove through the campus, other big buildings—such as Northrop Auditorium—just added to the thrill. Walking into the Administration Building and seeing all the post office boxes, I thought, again in terms of Doland, "Wow, there are more post office boxes than in our whole town." The city and the university

* And my second trip to Minneapolis. I'd been there briefly with my dad when I was about thirteen years old.

seemed fantastically large, as though I were viewing everything through a giant magnifying glass.

After that first, eye-popping trip through the university, we turned to the more pedestrian task of finding me a place to live. We had been referred by friends to a rooming house about four blocks from the campus. It was run by a wonderful, outgoing, strong-willed woman, Mrs. T. A. Zimmerman, and from the moment we rented the room, Ma Zim looked after me, as she had after many young men.

There is something constant about students' rooms—tiny, drab, bed, bureau, closet, study table—and my room was no different. About ten by twelve feet, it was tucked into the right, rear corner of the first floor, my palace and my cell.

I unloaded my few belongings. Dad then drove me back to the edge of the campus. From there, he would start back to Doland and the store. "Now," he said, "we've driven from Doland to your rooming house to the gates of the university. From here on out, it's on you. This is a big college and you better move in on it."

What a lonely moment! The "big man" from Doland became a little man in a big school in a big city. I moved mechanically down the long block past Folwell Hall to the end of the line of freshmen waiting to register at the Music Building.

After I registered, I came back to the corner where my dad had dropped me, uncertain where I lived. I was afraid to ask for directions, not wanting to act dumb or small-townish. I wandered around, finally spotted Marshall High School and my rooming house across the street.

That first day, Ma Zim—recognizing familiar loneliness and doubts—fed me dinner and talked about the university. Soon she would tease me and advise me, part mother, part older sister, even part father.

Male roomers used to sit on her porch and ogle the girls on their way to Marshall or to the university. In due course, Ma Zim decided the time for looking had ended and I had to find myself a date. Her first step in my education was insisting that I learn to dance, and she had her daughter, Grace, teach me.

When I had overcome a splendid awkwardness and learned a few basic steps, she said, "Now you just go down to the Marigold

Ballroom and get yourself a girl. If she doesn't follow you when you dance, you scold her, and don't ever admit that you don't know how to dance."

The Marigold was for those who liked to dance, but it was also an inexpensive way for young people—lonely, new in town, often from the farm—to meet others. Shy boys and girls trying to be men and women would stand around the dance floor or sit in the booths, hoping to find an exciting companion. Forty-five years later, that ballroom was still there,† and I suppose the same floor play was going on.

With confidence gained at the Marigold, I moved—under Ma Zim's direction—to the college sunlight dances at the Student Union and to my first "girl friend." I remember telling someone in the ingenuousness of my age and the language of my time, "I am awfully sweet on Gloria Bock." Later I added another dancing partner, Mildred Gillespie, from Mountain Iron, Minnesota. They were my best friends, and the sunlight dances and the Common People's Ball were my social life that semester.[1]

As a freshman, I made no great splash. That fall quarter, I took the standard courses: English, chemistry, French, sociology. I was on the freshman debating team, got turned down by the student newspaper, and generally was a good, healthy, normal student, avidly attending football games, avidly skipping convocations, studying some, growing up some.

I missed my family. I went home fairly often, hitchhiking or occasionally riding the Minneapolis and St. Louis Railroad. Trucks hauling grain and cattle and farm supplies moved back and forth steadily between Minneapolis and the rural areas. I'd hook a ride on one when I could. The cabs of the semitrailers, then as now, usually had a sleeping ledge up behind the drivers —and, after a bit of polite conversation, I'd ask permission to climb up and sleep until we got to Doland.

If I had the money I'd ride the M. & St. L. Their tracks west from Minneapolis were bumpy and the trip was usually a tedious and uncomfortable one. But they led home.

Those trips passed through a countryside of darkness. Elec-

† It closed in 1975. I was invited to its last night but unfortunately couldn't make it.

tricity, which brightened cities before the turn of the century, had barely reached into the rural Midwest in 1929. In the stations at the towns there was some electricity, but in the country, between stops, there was a blackness unbroken except for the moon and stars. Occasionally, as the train rolled along, you could see a light, like a flickering candle, moving slowly in the distance —a kerosene lamp undulating with the farmer's body as he moved, probably cursing the darkness, from house to barn.[2]

6. EATING MISTAKES

During my first quarter at the university, my father paid my tuition and I was given about ten dollars a week to live on—a considerable amount of money. But, during the Christmas holiday, Dad said he could no longer afford that. He'd try to help me as much as he could with tuition, but I'd have to earn my board and room and other expenses.

Back in Minneapolis, I discovered that a drugstore was about to open just about a block from where I lived. With my years of drugstore experience, I thought getting a job would be a cinch. But the staff had already been hired, and I was turned down.

Still, Swoboda's Drugstore seemed like the logical place to work, so I invoked a Horatio Alger ploy. I casually snuck down to the basement, where they had boxes of root-beer mugs, sundae and water glasses, and plates to be washed for the fountain. And I started washing. After a couple of days, the manager of the store, Mr. Ed Oelke, came downstairs and asked, "What are you doing down here?" I said, "Well, I just needed a job and nobody would hire me, so I came down and went to work."

My determination got to him. "Well," he said, "as long as you're here, I suppose I better give you a job."

I was paid twenty cents an hour to wash dishes, clean up, and sweep out. I also got a one-third discount on food. I had wanted to work at the fountain, where the people were, and was disappointed to be in the basement; but at least it was income.

The boy who worked the fountain, a kid named Schumacher, knew nothing about mixing the syrups, hardly enough to draw Cokes. I had literally grown up behind a soda fountain and knew the ice cream and soda business. I taught him what I knew, and he protected me on my job. Then we worked out a survival system. I ate mistakes: a mistake in a sandwich or a mistake in a salad. Schumacher would let me know that a sandwich had been sent back and I'd grab it, withdraw to the basement, and pretend to chip ice while I swallowed the food in a gulp or two. He always left a little malted milk in the mixing can instead of serving it all, and we'd drink what was left ourselves. The Schumacher-Swoboda diet wasn't fancy, but it was food and it was free.

I didn't earn much, but it kept me alive until summer, when I went home and back to work in our drugstore. I intended to return to the university in the fall, but business was terrible. Dad said, "I can't have both you and Ralph gone at the same time. I need one of you to help me in the store." Ralph had stayed out during the year I was in Minnesota, and we agreed to switch. Ralph took my job at Swoboda's Drugstore. I stayed at home and helped Dad, but life—after Minneapolis—was dull. There was little to do except suffer as business got worse. I replaced my city dancing partners with a new girl, Caroline Rich, whose family ran the little hotel in town.

At Christmas time, a fifty-dollar check arrived from my Uncle Harry Humphrey, with a note: "This is something to start you back to school." Uncle Harry was chief plant pathologist for the Department of Agriculture. He was determined that I get a good education and kept after me to do so.[1]

At about the same time, I got a call from Ma Zimmerman urging me to come back to school and offering me free room and board if I would wait on tables and clean up around the house.

Dad and I talked about our options. Finally, he said, "Son, you'd better go back to school. There's only one thing to do here, and that's just fade away and go broke."

It was uncharacteristic of him but it was a time of despondency and depression. There'd been no crops since 1927, the banks had closed, and there were no hopeful signs.

After Christmas, I hitchhiked to Minneapolis, made my way to Ma Zim's, unloaded my few belongings, and went over to

Swoboda's. There Ralph was—standing importantly behind the cashier's counter. He'd been promoted. "I've arranged for you to get a job," he said. "You're going to work over in the soda fountain." He seemed never to have known that I had already worked my way up to the fountain before and that I had arranged *his* job. I suffered quietly as he explained that he worked days and that I would work from 6 P.M. until midnight. With the discovery that he also made a nickel more an hour than I, brotherly love was severely strained.

Tuition and fees took all of Uncle Harry's fifty dollars plus most of what little I had saved. I had no money to buy books, so between classes and work, I haunted the library. I even tutored in French with a sliding scale of payment: twenty dollars for an A, fifteen for a B, ten for a C, five for a D.

One day my dad showed up, sat at the counter, and waited for me to finish work. When the store closed, at midnight, I had to clean up, and that took another half hour or so. Then we went down to his hotel. He told me, "Son, if I'm going broke, I'm not going to do it in a little town. I've got to get out of Doland. We can't make it there. I've been to Huron and it's a growing town. I have a place there I can rent."

The idea of leaving Doland was shocking. It had been a happy place for us. Our family grew up there; Dad was a leader in the community. My mother and sisters were comfortable among old friends and near relatives. Dad simply said, "I've just got to go." And he was right.

On one level, my father was a fine example of the prevailing myths of the twenties: Puritan ethic, hard and independent work, boosterism, and success, as God willed it, to those who worked for it. But inevitably these myths could not stand up against the reality of failure everywhere: failure of the land to produce, failure of the institutions of finance and government, the loss of options and—ultimately—of hope.

The last hope was for us to flee, but even to flee required the help of others. We went together to the Minneapolis Drug Company, our major creditor—and a company with whom Dad had been doing business for twenty-five years. To move to Huron required the carrying of current debt, more merchandise, and a loan. Without all three, there could be nothing.

We showed our books to three men at the drug company: Mr. Carlson, George Doerr, and Sewall Andrews. And Dad pledged as collateral his life insurance and his loyalty. Through mutual affection, and a little business acumen, we received merchandise and a line of credit.

Dad went home and started the move. He was living in a room near his new store when Ralph and I arrived, after final exams, in late March 1931. Mother and our sisters had stayed in Doland so that sister Fern could finish the school year. When we saw how hard Dad was working, Ralph and I agreed that we could not leave him alone. Neither of us went back to the university; instead we moved into the basement of the store to save money and time, since we worked late and got up early.

We became one of the first Walgreen agency stores in the United States. Our grand opening, with roses and carnations for the ladies, threatened to be the high point. We rarely did twenty or twenty-five dollars' worth of business in a day. When Dad lowered his prices to attract business, a representative of the Chamber of Commerce visited and indicated that other merchants didn't like his low-pricing practices. The man said, "You're a small merchant in a big town, and you'll never make it here."

It was one of the few times I ever saw my father intensely angry. "Listen," he said, "when you start to pay my bills and feed my family and pay my taxes, you can come in here and tell me how to run this business. Until then, get the hell out of here!" And he reached up, pulled the Chamber of Commerce sign off a ledge, handed it to the surprised visitor, and said, "I don't want to belong to this outfit. Get out!" (That was the last he had to do with them until, when I was elected to office, the Huron Chamber honored me with a dinner.)

In the winter of 1932, I decided that I ought to become a pharmacist if I was going to remain in the drugstore business permanently, a situation that seemed increasingly likely.

I enrolled at the Capitol College of Pharmacy in Denver, Colorado, for an intensive course lasting about six months. I went out to Denver with a purpose in mind and that was to learn all the technical aspects of pharmacy. I proceeded to do that.

I used the same books as a student of a four-year course and learned enough in that six-month period to pass the same exam. I memorized the same formulae and filled the same prescriptions. More importantly, I learned what the human mind can absorb when motivated and when proper techniques of education are used.

7. PILLS, HOGTONE, AND NOSE DROPS

Back in Huron after graduating, the drugstore was my life and it seemed then that it might always be. I was, like Dad, a small-town businessman, and I absorbed certain attitudes from that experience that permanently shaped my political philosophy.

I never got hooked in those chaotic times, as so many people did, on Marxism or other radicalism as a way out of the depression. Had I continued at the university uninterrupted, I might have, but I was involved instead in a business whose purpose was to make a profit, and I frankly liked the system even if we weren't particularly successful.

While I have been called radical, socialist, sometimes Communist, accused of holding wild-eyed economic views, I have really never been anything other than an advocate of a pragmatic free enterprise.

Conservatives say, as though it were their view alone, that "Profits are the fuel that powers our economy. The only way a businessman can stay in business is to make a profit; the only way that government can collect taxes is when there is a profit." It is not illiberal to agree, and I do.

But legitimate questions remain as to what kind of profits are reasonable—whether they arise from exploitation and deceit or from service fairly provided. It is clearly necessary for the government to "intrude" with some safeguards and standards to protect its citizens and to protect the system from abuse.

Big government is a necessary consequence of an urban, industrial, corporate nation. It is an institution whose power must be carefully used, as a countervailing force to other institutions in the private sector, to prevent abuses.

This is not to ignore the fact that there is a great deal of difference between the world of government and the world of commerce and that government is not always right. Too often, unfortunately, the people who draft the rules, regulations, and legislation have little understanding of the problems and expense they create for the governed. Further, as a senator I learned that there is frequently a real difference between the intent of a law and its application.

Some "specialists" in the executive branch seem to think they not only know without question what is best for the people, but have a kind of subtle disdain and occasionally not-so-subtle contempt for both the private-enterprise system on the one hand and the elected representatives of the people on the other.

A certain amount of skepticism is healthy, but democracy itself may die, the victim of patronizing indifference, if the mutual respect between the bureaucracy and the citizenry deteriorates further.

I don't mean to castigate civil servants generally, since most take the idea of service seriously. But a kind of elitism, a professional governmental snobbishness, has grown as bureaucracy has expanded and government programs increased.

Growing up in those hard times, I learned a lot about people. In the early thirties, it wasn't the traditional poor who were in rebellion, but those who had once had something. Now they were mad—ready to march, picket, indeed to destroy.

People who have been poor for an endless time frequently become broken to their status, find it difficult to rebel. The newly poor are different.

One day in Huron hundreds of farmers—irate and recently made radical—marched down the street to hold a mass meeting in Campbell Park, the main park in our community.

As we watched, my father said quietly that while we as a family and a business were poor—money gone, deep in debt, behind in taxes, on the verge of bankruptcy—those marching people still looked upon us as having something. If a revolution were to break out, or even a violent demonstration, we would be among the first attacked, not because we had so much, not because we had ever been well-to-do, but simply because, when people lose everything they have, they turn on those who have a little and are visible.

Later, when the Works Progress Administration (WPA) put some of those people to work, Dad lectured me, "The only reason we're not on WPA is because other people are. They spend part of their income in our store and that's what keeps us going. I want you to have respect for them. We get ours in a second stage, but we're living off government help too."

Isolated as we were, it was clear even then how intimately interconnected people and issues are, how mutually dependent; how government programs never have simple, isolated effects. But theories of government were a passing concern. The store was reality.

We struggled, each of us working as hard as possible, but the struggle often seemed in vain. We were forced into a barter system: a hunk of beef, a few dozen eggs, butter, or potatoes for our goods. We swapped drugs for chickens, plucked and cooked them, made chicken salad, and sold it in sandwiches.[1]

We also began to manufacture our own patent medicines for humans and animals. Our first effort was suggested by a radio ad* for "Master Liquid Hogtone," which claimed that hogs that ate it in their slop were healthy and heavier. Our imitation was "Humphrey's BTV (Body Tone Veterinary)," which we mixed in our basement. I'd fill five 50-gallon steel barrels with the stuff and we'd pay kids a dime for each gallon glass jug they brought in. We'd sterilize the jugs and fill them with BTV. The label made grandiose claims that couldn't pass any modern truth-in-labeling act, but a few swallows accomplished most of what was claimed: it provided minerals and it wormed the hogs.

For people, we made "Humphrey's Chest Oil" for colds and the flu, and "Humphrey's Sniffles," a substitute for Vicks Nose Drops. I felt ours were better. Vicks used mineral oil, which is

---

* The radio station was WNAX of Yankton, South Dakota, where Lawrence Welk got his start.

not absorbent, and we used a vegetable-oil base, which was. I added benzocaine, a local anesthetic, so that even if the sniffles didn't get better, you felt it less.

We put "Sniffles" in one-ounce and half-ounce bottles with a little dropper, and in a great mercantile tradition, the package cost more than the contents.

From time to time, I'd pile bottles of our medicines into Dad's car and peddle them to less enterprising druggists in nearby towns.

We were the farmers' drugstore, but the farmers had no money, and a gloom settled over us like dust. Farmers in need of medicine, which went to them without hesitation, were followed by an influx of nagging, humiliating bill collectors to whom we could pay nothing. I used to see my father, his exuberant spirits momentarily giving in, sitting head in hands, grinding his life and spirit away between unpaid bills and unpaid accounts.

Only the Minneapolis Drug Company was particularly considerate of him and our dilemma. Finally even they, when purchased by McKesson, Robbins, brought pressure on us. My dad and I went to Minneapolis to see our three benefactors once again. That meeting is chiseled still as sharply on my psyche as an epitaph on a headstone.

My dad said: "I owe you a lot of money. Still, I'm not going to kill myself. I'm not going to commit suicide. I've run this store for years. I've bought every dollar of merchandise that I could from you. You've made money off of me, but you've been very considerate of me. So if you need another drugstore, and you feel that I can't run it, well, you go ahead and take it. I'll just go get me a job someplace.

"Now, here are the books. You can see where I buy my stock. You can see that you've gotten 85 per cent or more of the business. And we've done business for thirty-five years, since the first day I was a druggist. If you need this store to make your accounts look better, if McKesson needs it, why, you tell McKesson they can have Humphrey's Drug Store. But if you let me alone and let me run it, and let me still have title to it, I'll pay off every dollar. And I'll have the store and you'll have your money. You make up your mind what you want to do."

Mr. Doerr said, "Well, there's no doubt in my mind what we ought to do, Mr. Humphrey. You run the store. And I'll take the responsibility with McKesson."[2]

So we continued, haltingly, trying to do our best to succeed in a society in which the machinery of government and finance had broken down and the machinery of agriculture had stopped dead. That period left permanent impressions and, indeed, prejudices with me. My attitudes on banking and finance were largely conditioned then. My fear of private debt came out of my father's experiences. My views on the needs of rural America, on agricultural legislation, on soil conservation were all formed in those difficult days.

That period was also to teach me what government can mean to a society, how government can really affect the day-to-day lives of individuals—for the better. It taught me what government can mean in terms of improving the human condition and of improving the human environment. I witnessed how government programs literally rebuilt the territory and again made life tolerable, filling the people with hope.

8. "TOGETHER WE CAN DO THINGS"

My own life became much more tolerable when I met a young woman in 1932. She was a student at Huron College, where I went to dance whenever I could. Muriel Buck was a shapely, attractive girl, shyly charming and independent.

I liked her immediately and was pleased when she started dropping into the drugstore with her friend Betty Halpenny to have an ice cream soda or a Coke. They would dawdle and I would dash around the store trying to look important, stopping to talk as often as I could.

Soon I asked her for a date, and she accepted. But dating was difficult in Huron, because there was almost nothing to do. On Wednesday nights the public dance hall about a mile outside of town was open. A church social, a rare movie at the State Theatre—that was about it.

My working hours were another serious impediment to romance. Our store opened at seven in the morning and stayed open most nights until midnight. When he could, my dad would let me have a night or two off each week, but it was difficult. One of those nights, I devoted to the Boy Scouts at the Methodist Church as scoutmaster of Troop 6, the other frequently to work as president of Beadle County Young Democrats.

When I could get Wednesday night off, I would try to take Muriel dancing. She and I would whirl around the floor, dance after dance, until intermission. We'd buy two bottles of orange pop and go out to the car and talk until the band came back.

The financial crunch soon hit the Buck family, too, and Muriel left college and went to work. We began to see each other more frequently, since she often came into the store after supper to wait for me and to help my dad with his accounts and records.

Finally, after about two years of serious courtship, I bought a small diamond and we were engaged, in December of 1935.

Our engagement was a step up the social ladder of Huron for me. The Humphreys were newcomers and a little "different." The Bucks were straight, respectable, and conservative. They lived in one of the better homes of Huron. Muriel's brothers, Gordon and Merle, were commercial pilots, having their own airplanes—surely a sign of well-being in the late 1920s and early '30s. Muriel's dad, Andrew Buck, in partnership with his brothers, owned several produce houses in South Dakota and western Minnesota which bought the farmers' butter, eggs, poultry, and other perishable commodities. He was a deacon of the Presbyterian Church, a director of the James River Valley Bank, a member of the school board, and known for his generosity to local charities and schools.

They were a part of the tight, thin stratum of what might be called Huron "society." One of the families with whom they associated was the Wheelers, who owned an older, more established drugstore than ours. Even after Muriel and I were engaged, the Bucks other than Muriel continued to trade with the Wheelers, their loyalties strong and unyielding, a quality virtually bred into Muriel, too.

Muriel's mother died young, in 1934, and when Andrew Buck sold his produce houses, themselves becoming victims of the depression, he built a vacation resort* at Big Stone Lake on the Minnesota-South Dakota border.[1] Muriel, in an act of rare independence for those days, took an apartment instead of rooming with a local family.

During the summers, however, she would take leave from her

---

* A midwestern "resort" can be a half-dozen uninsulated cabins with outhouses, and should not be confused with anything elegant. A flat-bottom wooden boat with creaky oars, and a can of worms, completed the décor.

bookkeeper's job with the local private utility corporation and help her father with the cabins at the resort.[2]

When I could, on a summer Saturday night, I would leave Huron about eleven o'clock and hitch a ride the ninety miles to Watertown. Muriel would meet me there in her father's Chevy pickup truck and we would drive together the fifty remaining miles to Big Stone Lake. Though it was often after two o'clock in the morning when we arrived, we'd swim and then talk on into the morning.

The lake was beautiful, and sunrise and sunset particularly so for a couple in love. We would float in a little rowboat fishing for bass or crappies, happy to be alone together. Had it not been for Muriel and her dad, I might never have learned to love the out-of-doors as I do. In the fall, there was duck and pheasant hunting. Grandpa Buck was a crack shot with his 12-gauge, double-barreled shotgun. Muriel would join us on those early-morning treks to the duck blinds and later walking the cornfields as we tried to flush out pheasants. Her 20-gauge shotgun, which was her mother's, is today the favorite hunting gun for our sons.

In August of 1935, my sister Frances was to graduate from George Washington University, and I made the trip to Washington to be there. One night, filled with the excitement of the city and the New Deal atmosphere, I wrote Muriel:

. . . This trip has impressed one thing on my mind, Muriel. That impression is the need of an education, an alert mind, clean living, and a bit of culture which undoubtedly will come with age and learning. I don't necessarily mean more college is necessary, but I need to do more reading, more writing, more thinking, if I ever want to fulfill my dream of being someone in this world. Maybe I seem foolish to have such vain hopes and plans, but Bucky, I can see how someday, if you and I just apply ourselves and make up our minds to work for bigger things, how we can someday live here in Washington and probably be in government politics or service. I intend to set my aim at Congress. Don't laugh at me, Muriel. Maybe it does sound rather egotistical and beyond reason, but Muriel I do know others have succeeded. Why haven't I a chance? You'll help me I know.

Together we can do things I am sure. Never let me get lazy or discouraged. You be my inspirational force, Muriel, and always encourage me in what you feel will be right for me to do. Does all this sound ridiculous to you? Tell me, Bucky—please don't let your love for me blind your quality of reason and judgment.

Washington, D.C. thrills me to my very finger tips. I simply revel and beam with delight in this realm of politics and government. Oh gosh, I hope my dream comes true—I'm going to try anyhow, but first I shall prepare myself for the task by reading and thinking always as a liberal. Roosevelt is a super-man. His speech last night surely baffled the Republicans, in fact they are lost in a sea of uncertainty as to how to attack him. . . .

I was slow in setting the marriage date. There was so little money available and I was virtually married to the drugstore. When Muriel dropped a hint that she might move to California, I reacted quickly. We set the date for September 3, 1936.

Shortly before our wedding, one of the clerks in the drugstore asked for a vacation during the first week of September and my dad said okay. I wrote to Muriel suggesting that we delay our marriage until the vacation was over. I heard immediately from an irate prospective father-in-law, who suggested that I keep the plans as set if I wanted to marry his daughter. I did.

Once again the drugstore intruded. I was working so hard that I neglected to get the marriage license until the last minute. A friendly county official opened the courthouse the night before the wedding.

We were married at eight o'clock in the morning so that the drugstore would not have to be closed during the busiest hours while the family was at the wedding. That morning, my sister Frances, who was one of the bridesmaids, lost her garter and we couldn't leave until she found it. I was still in a fury when we got to the Huron Presbyterian Church and found it already filled with family and friends. I burst out, "My God, we're late!" in an unnecessary announcement audible to the entire congregation. The laughter eased the tension in the church, and Muriel and I were married in a simple ceremony, okay in the eye of God and the law but unrecorded by the traditional photographer since it seemed a frivolous expense.

In Dad's Model A Ford, we took the fifty-dollar wedding present from Muriel's dad and our savings—about thirty dollars—and set off on our honeymoon. We did not, however, leave alone. To save bus fare back to her job in Watertown, my sister Frances rode with us. It was an awkward beginning, but after a couple of hours we were finally alone and continued on to Minneapolis.

We stayed at the Andrews Hotel, not particularly ritzy, but at least a place I knew from my previous visits there with my father. The next day, I took Muriel out to meet Ma Zim, my old landlady, and then we drove up to Duluth and Lake Superior. Superior's North Shore was, and still is, the standard middle-class honeymoon spot in the area. Our only extravagance was taking an old tub of an excursion boat (it sank a couple of years later) out for a cruise on the lake.

With only five days for our honeymoon, we waited until the last minute before starting home. We drove straight through, exhilarated in our love and marriage, but growing more tired by the hour. About eleven o'clock that night, ten miles from home, we hit a cow crossing the road. The stunned cow slipped into the ditch, the radiator of the car was smashed, and we were marooned.†

The two of us pushed the leaking car toward a distant crossroad until someone picked us up and helped us find the farmer whose cow we had struck and then took us into Huron.

We settled into a rented house with dollhouse-sized rooms. But it had a furnace in the basement, unlike most houses around us, and a tiny goldfish pond out back. When the sun struck the pond, the fish glittered as they alternately moved and paused in the water. It was a happy time.

† The cow died soon after and the farmer demanded payment from my father and me. In South Dakota then, anyone who hit a farmer's animal was liable even if the creature was loose and caused the accident. A cow could do no wrong. We paid double damages—for the cow and the car.

9. WITH DAD'S BLESSINGS, WITH MURIEL'S BOUNTY

During the next year, South Dakota wore us down. The depression, the dust storms, and the demands of family on a newlywed couple were finally too much.

Each dust storm left me more depressed. I became ill* when one began, as they always did, west of town. A deep-purple cloud would roll across the flat land, getting darker as it built up with more dirt. It would become a massive black wall, blotting out the sun even at noon so that it was a dully shining disk barely visible.

People walked around holding a wet handkerchief over mouth and nose. The heat was frightful and the dust was everywhere, filtering through the tiniest crack around a window or door, leaving a layer of grime on curtains and furniture.

Outside of town, the topsoil, dried and cracked from the drought, built up like snow against the fences. When the wells went dry, farmers hauled water from the river for the cattle and themselves.

After the dust came the grasshoppers, which literally ate the paint off houses, since the land was so barren. Sometimes I thought it was the end of the world.

It was hard to pull myself away from my dad and the store. When I did, I felt guilty because I wasn't doing my share. When

* To this day, when an excessively high wind whips dust through the air to any significant degree, my throat gets parched and I feel uncomfortable.

I didn't, I felt guilty because I wasn't being an adequate husband. Fortunately, in the tug of war over my loyalty Muriel won.

During the long, dark nights of our first winter together, we would talk of our hopes for a future outside of Huron. We had no plans and only the vaguest of dreams.

We bought magazines about the Caribbean and the Mediterranean, and talked of saving enough for a cruise to learn more about other parts of the world. But mostly we talked of continuing my education. I spoke so often of the joys of the University of Minnesota that Muriel was determined that we go there.

With the strength of her determination, I finally raised the question of my future with my father. One August evening after we had closed the store, we sat in his car outside his house after midnight and I told him how depressed I was, almost physically ill from the work, the dust storms, the conflict between my desire to do something and be somebody and my loyalty to him. In the darkness, I felt his sorrow as well as his understanding. "Hubert, if you aren't happy, then you ought to do something about it."†

I would not have left without Dad's blessings and I could not have left without Muriel's bounty. We had saved little from my salary of fifteen dollars a week, but Muriel, working at the electric company, had managed to save $675.

In September 1937 Dad drove us to Minneapolis in the same Model A Ford that had hit the cow. We left Huron early one morning, my mother and Muriel in the back seat, Dad and I in the front, the sun beating down on the flat prairie land, the two-lane highway stretching due east into the sun.

The land was sere and brown, without the lushness of a good harvest. Grasshoppers had devastated the area in 1935 and 1936, chewing up the crops, gnawing into fence posts, and 1937 had been another dry year. I wondered if those fields would ever be green again.

† My dad had been elected to the South Dakota State Legislature in 1936. He had a promising political career ahead of him. He was being considered by the Democrats for governor. Obviously he could not give serious consideration to such a possibility if I were to leave. The drugstore required at least one of us to be in charge. Then, too, I truly liked the pharmacy—it had been so much a part of my life. The emotional ties were strong, and yet I knew I had to make the break.

It took us more than ten hours to get to Minneapolis, and as we bounced along the highway through little towns that had been a part of me—Cavour, Iroquois, De Smet, Lake Preston, Arlington, Brookings—I watched the gaunt faces of men standing, staring in front of buildings laminated with dust. Life seemed so static. Only the wind seemed to move.

We chattered bravely much of the way, but periodically all of us would drop into silence. For my father and me, there was particular sadness, knowing that I might never return to South Dakota to work with him, knowing he would be restricted still more stringently to the difficult task of keeping the drugstore going.

By the time we reached Mankato, Minnesota, and turned north on Highway 169 up the Minnesota River Valley, the signs of the drought and depression began to disappear. As the dry, brown quality was replaced with green and water, the sadness, too, was replaced with joy and excitement, at least in Muriel and me, for we were launched on a new kind of life.

I hadn't really made up my mind what I wanted to do back in college. I just wanted to get away from the tension, from the gloom, the depression and problems of South Dakota.

I wanted to strike out on my own to have a life with my wife that was separate and distinct. I wanted to learn something, anything new. I had thought some about a future in politics. Beyond the interest that my father had bred into me, I had listened to political speakers in South Dakota, appalled at times at their lack of knowledge. I figured a man with a little information might go a long way.

So I went back to the university and picked courses I thought might be useful and enjoyable. I signed up for twenty-one credit hours when the maximum was fifteen. The dean of students, a venerable old gentleman named Nicholson, called me in and said flatly that my appetite for learning exceeded permissible limits.

I told him that whenever people came into our drugstore and said they wanted three tubes of toothpaste, even if I knew they only needed one, I sold them what they wanted. It was their money and their decision and that's the way I felt about the university. I was paying preciously higher tuition as an out-of-state student and I was in a hurry.

We compromised and I bounded into university life driven to

1. "My grandmother, To-
mina Sannes . . . a woman
of joy and good humor."

2. "My maternal grand-
father, Guttorn Andreas
Sannes, was a captain in
the Norwegian Merchant
Marine come aground in
South Dakota. . . . He followed an immigrant's
dream to the United
States."

3. The author's mother and father around 1910. "He was a Minnesota farmer whose Quaker traditions and family went back to the Revolutionary War period in America. . . . She was a country teacher in a one-room school, the daughter of Norwegian immigrants. . . ."

4. An early boyhood home in Wallace, South Dakota.

5. Hubert Humphrey (left) and brother Ralph, around 1914.

6. "By 1915 we had moved three times, this time to Doland [South Dakota]. . . . I spent the remaining years of my childhood there."

7. The Humphrey home in Doland, 1920. Hubert, with sister Frances and brother Ralph, stands in the foreground.

make up for time lost, to learn everything and to do so immediately.

I'd been gone six years and came back as a contemporary of people who had already become assistant and associate professors. I was able, therefore, to establish something more than a simple student-teacher relationship.

Further, since Muriel and I were married and since all of us—junior faculty and students—were relatively poor, we spent a good deal of time visiting back and forth. Movies and nightclubs were a rare and expensive entertainment. So we talked. And argued. And solved the world's problems.

It is difficult to reconstruct that delicious sense of emancipation. Plunged once again into the world of ideas, I squeezed every minute for all it was worth. And each moment was saturated with the essence of my future life: politics, debate on issues, change in society. It was a joyous time. That period provided me with ideas and direction, and with friends whose imprint remained strong on whatever I have done.

While I have never really had an alter ego, politically or intellectually, the man politically closest to me in that period of my life was Evron Kirkpatrick. Kirk, in 1937, had recently come to the university with a Yale Ph.D. He was an exciting professor, with great interest in practical politics, who was extremely well-read and imaginative about the problems of government.

His influence was not a heavy ideological one but, rather, grew from Socratic methods—of questioning and hot intellectual pursuit, of forcing a student to sharpen and polish his argument under Kirk's and his fellow students' public scrutiny.[1]

I came back to the university quite parochial in background, if not entirely in outlook. Except for my earlier periods in Minneapolis, a couple of trips to Chicago and Washington, and my brief stint in Denver at the Capitol College of Pharmacy, I had spent all my life in South Dakota.

While my father had bred into me an interest in government and certain attitudes toward people and society, I was still a rather unsophisticated product of the agricultural Midwest.

Men like Kirkpatrick offered the seeds of new ideas and the sunlight of wisdom. New ideas and new friends made those university years the most personally productive ones I have ever lived. Muriel and I, away from South Dakota, grew even closer. Since neither of our families could help, money remained a problem. Muriel, looking for a job, was faced with a barrier: married women were not being hired. She took off her wedding ring, and finally found a temporary bookkeeper's job at fifty cents an hour. When she was soon promoted to a full-time job at sixty-five dollars a month, she put her ring back on. Despite my heavy school load, I got a job, too. Once again, it was in a campus drugstore, but now, at least, as a pharmacist.

We lived in a third-floor garret, dingy and cramped, but it looked out on the brightness of Van Cleve Park, where we could see grass and trees and hear kids playing.[2] We had one room, barely large enough for our bed and a desk, a radio, and a hot plate for our coffee pot. We shared a bathroom and kitchen with other tenants, who fortunately soon became good friends.

Undergraduate married couples were rare before the G.I. Bill, but there was another married couple, Don and Pug Williams, in the other room on our floor. We often joined them for sandwiches and cocoa or coffee in the communal kitchen.

During those days, I decided that if you peeled back the hide of a cow, you'd find nothing but hamburger. It was the basic ingredient of almost every meat supper we had—meatballs or meatloaf, goulash or patties. It was nourishing, cheap, and inevitable.

Occasionally, when we were both too tired to cook, we'd buy White Castle hamburgers because they were frequently on sale, three thin ones for a dime. A special occasion would permit one pork chop apiece. We'd vary our diet with waffles made from Bisquick, soaking them in a syrup we made from brown sugar.

On rare evenings when we could relax, we would play "Monopoly" with friends in the kitchen, popping popcorn and drinking root beer. Once every two weeks or so, on a Saturday night, Muriel and I would go downtown, have a drink or two, and dance our legs off. We'd take up more space at a table and on the dance floor than our two-dollar expenditure deserved but, oblivious to hostile stares of waitress and bartender, we lived it up.

During this time, I met Orville Freeman,[3] a man whose friendship has been important to me and whose interests even then paralleled mine. He was an intense, highly competitive young man, and we talked endlessly in argument or agreement about government and politics.

He was no richer than we and often brought his girl friends to our house for a cheap date. If they didn't like popcorn, "Monopoly," or root beer coupled with a lot of talk, they must have found the evenings dull.

Considering the constant economic pressures, those times were strangely happy. During my senior year, I entered every available competition. Not so much for honor as the money. (If they had paid money for becoming Homecoming Queen, I might even have tried that.) I won the Forensic Medal and the William Jennings Bryan prize for the best political science essay,‡ and was sad when I lost the campus oratorical contest.

The real prize of that year was the birth, on February 27, of our first child, Nancy. We moved to a little bigger place, took in a roomer to help pay the rent, and things seemed to be looking up; then, in the latter part of April, Muriel's dad had a heart attack.

Someone had to look after him, and Muriel was the only one who could. We had adjusted to the loss of income when Muriel quit her job to become a mother. I was not sure I could adjust as easily to her absence.

We borrowed a car, piled Nancy, then less than three months old, in a basket in the back seat, and set out for Milbank, South Dakota, 175 miles away. I returned immediately in order not to miss school or work; Muriel and Nancy stayed through the summer nursing Dad Buck.

In June 1939 I was done with my undergraduate work, having finished about three years' work in two. I graduated magna cum laude and made Phi Beta Kappa, but my satisfaction was incomplete. Muriel, still at her dad's side, was unable to be with me.

‡ As soon as I learned I had won a prize, I went to the dean of students to ask for my money immediately. He took a dim view of breaking normal patterns, but gave in to my pleading.

10. INTO HUEY LONG'S SOUTH

A bachelor's degree in political science didn't prepare you for much, so Muriel and I decided I should do graduate work, aiming for a doctorate and a teaching career. While I had a choice of several midwestern universities, I decided to go to Louisiana State University. I had never been to the South, and LSU, where Charles Hyneman, a friend and former professor of Kirkpatrick's, was chairman of the Political Science Department, offered me a $450 fellowship.

I left for Louisiana alone. (Muriel and Nancy were to follow several weeks later, after I'd had a chance to find a place to live.) Out of Chicago, the Illinois Central Railroad ran deeper and deeper into a strange Southland, until it arrived at Hammond, Louisiana, self-proclaimed "Strawberry Capital of the World." From there, I went by bus to Baton Rouge through what seemed a jungle—Spanish moss hanging from the trees and the weather steaming hot. It was a strange, new environment for a South Dakota boy from the dry prairies.

The first few nights, I slept for free in a dirty barracks under the stadium and then moved into a rooming house, where I met thumb-sized cockroaches for the first time. I sat entranced and repelled as they walked up the walls and across the ceilings. (The local folks called them waterbugs and seemed to consider them normal interior décor.)

I left the rooming house to the bugs and moved to a small

apartment on Highland Road, paying about thirty-five dollars a month. Muriel and Nancy, still an infant, finally joined me. And we began together a most difficult and impecunious time. The train fares plus the rent ate up a good part of my year's salary, and Muriel, soon after we arrived, had to get a job typing in the office of the Department of Government.

In addition, she made sandwiches each morning—her ham salad was most popular—and I took them to the university to sell for ten cents. The sandwiches sustained my fellow students, and the few pennies' profit sustained us. It was moonlighting in the middle of the day, but we were desperate. The depression, which was beginning to lift for some other people, still rested heavily on us.

The politics of Louisiana and the atmosphere of the university itself were exotic.

By the time I arrived in Louisiana, the Huey Long machine had crumbled. Long himself had been assassinated. However, through it all, university life and Louisiana politics continued in their normal fashion, a normalcy hard for a square Northerner to comprehend.

Dance bands played in the student-union cafeteria during lunch. It was the sort of entertainment that came rarely to Huron and only occasionally to the University of Minnesota campus but was daily fare at LSU.

And campus politics, fueled by hysteria and enthusiasm, bewildered and amused me. Campus elections were run like major elections, with voting booths and expensive campaigns. The year before I arrived, Russell Long had run for student-government president on a platform that included a promise of a five-cent laundry for shirts. He won, and they built the laundry.

The year I was there, Russ arranged to bring Ted Lewis and his orchestra, at the height of Lewis's popularity, to the campus for a campaign rally for Long's candidate. The students simply had politics in their blood, and they took it seriously, though with exuberance and flamboyance.

But if campus politics amused me, state politics amazed me. The viciousness, the personal vitriol, the character assassination, and the countercharges were an education unmatched by what I learned in class. It was an education, too, that served me well in understanding some of my Senate colleagues when I ultimately got there.[1]

A reform governor, Sam Jones, was elected that year, but the signs of reformation were barely discernible to a trained eye. He was saddled down quickly by the legislative chairmen who were remnants of the Long machine and products of Louisiana rural politics.

Huey Long was a special creature in American politics. I saw him twice before he was assassinated. First, in 1932, in Sioux Falls, South Dakota, when he was campaigning for Franklin Roosevelt. The second time was on my visit to Washington in 1935. I was sitting in the Senate visitors' gallery when Long swept into the chamber—a sudden, compelling, dramatic presence —in white shoes, a cream-colored suit, and an orange tie.

The press had portrayed Long as a flamboyant character and political clown, and his dress seemed to confirm it. That day, his speech did not. His record, as I learned it when I got to Louisiana, did not. He was a radical populist, and sometimes a demagogue. He was surrounded by corruption and a kind of moral looseness. But he had guts. And commitment. Huey Long was a people's politician who fought the "interests." He said, "Louisiana lives in the mud." He tried to change that and the people knew it.

Louisiana state politics had been so dominated by the oil, natural gas, mineral, and timber barons that they paid little in taxes; and as a result, there were few services provided for the people —few hospitals, inadequate educational facilities, no paved roads, few graveled roads.

Long had the tongue of a demagogue, but he had the heart of a compassionate man. He ultimately added to those the muscle of a political despot, benevolent in some instances, vicious in others.

He appealed to the so-called "rednecks," the up-country folk, for support and he gave back to them a better life. He built them roads and hospitals and schools. He took them out of the mud, at least part way.

When Long became governor, Louisiana State University was essentially a land-grant, cow college. By the time he died, it had become a leading university of the South. He moved the college from around the capitol in Baton Rouge out to the open fields of the nearby country, where he built a beautiful new campus. And he made the rich pay for it. For the first time, the industries whose fortunes were made on non-renewable resources of the state paid up a fairer share of the taxes.

The politics of Huey Long are strange to most of us, his ethics and tactics different from ours. He was a political autocrat, with a popular and elected base, with money and power to reward his friends and to destroy his enemies—and he did that ruthlessly. But his most basic corruption didn't lie in building castles and plantations and fortune for himself. His corruption was of a far more pervasive kind in politics: an insatiable desire for publicity, for cheers, for power.

Politics is not an avocation in the South. It is a way of life, and in Huey Long's instance, a way of death.*

Everything you did in Louisiana—study or work—was, in a sense, conditioned by that environment of often corrupt, usually bizarre, southern politics and race relations.

Louisiana taught me something about American life that I barely knew in fact or in theory. A rather conventional northern white liberal, I had never been exposed to black Americans.[2] I had never been truly aware of institutionalized white paternalism.

Northern liberals like myself talked of the Negro as a group, and a group we respected, but none of us ever had as intimate a relationship with blacks, as children or adults, as many Southerners. The hollowness of our affection began to dawn on me slowly in Louisiana and came home full force once I got into public life and tried to deal with the problems of race relations in the North.

I remember a white LSU classmate telling me of his childhood, how he was brought up by a "mammy" who had done more for him than his own mother. He spoke of his "mammy" with what could only be described as filial love. And yet, as an adult, he held virtually all Negroes at arm's length.

I was dismayed by what I saw: the white, neatly painted houses of the whites, the unpainted shacks of the blacks; the

---

* It may be the only time in American history when money was actually raised to build a memorial to the assassin.

stately homes on manicured lawns in the white sections, the open sewage ditches in black neighborhoods. When I discovered the WHITE and COLORED signs for drinking fountains and toilets, I found them both ridiculous and offensive. I remember my naïve reaction: "Why, it's uneconomic." No one, I thought, could view black life in Louisiana without shock and outrage. Yet its importance to me was not only what I saw there and what my reaction was to southern segregation. It also opened my eyes to the prejudice of the North.[3]

My abstract commitment to civil rights was given flesh and blood during my year in Louisiana. But my main purpose there was, of course, to continue my formal education, and I submerged myself in my studies. Toward the end of the school year, I went to Charles Hyneman and told him, in despair, that I had given up hope of getting a master's degree. My adviser was Alex Daspit, a Rhodes scholar and one who was himself working on an advanced degree at Harvard. Daspit and I had locked horns on my thesis. He thought my views of Roosevelt less than objective. I considered them fair, objective, and scholarly.[4]

Resolution of our differences seemed out of the question, and I was relieved to learn from Hyneman that Daspit would soon return to Harvard to finish his own work. By the time my preliminary orals came up in the summer, Daspit was gone and Hyneman, Robert Harris, and Norton Long were my examination committee.[5]

The examination went smoothly except for one wild moment. I thought I was doing well when suddenly Norton Long, who was about the same age as I, said, "Hubert, I've decided I'm going to fail you on this examination." I froze and could barely squeak out, "Why?"

Long said, "Well, if we give you a degree, you'll just as likely as not end up a college professor,† and if we flunk you right now, you are more likely to go back to Minnesota and run for the United States Senate, and you'll amount to something."

I joined in the laughter only slightly.

† In later years I was made vice president of the American Political Science Association, and it was a great pleasure to continue to work in that demanding and exciting discipline.

11. "I'VE GOT A JOB NOW, AND I'M PAYING TAXES"

In June 1940, after finishing my course work for a master's degree, we headed back to Minnesota, where I intended to continue my graduate study. Through William Anderson, the chairman of the Political Science Department, I found a $200-a-month summer job training adult-education teachers under the Work Projects Administration (WPA) program in Duluth. The students were all unemployed people who had a teaching background or suitable training for teaching duties in various WPA education, art, and writers' projects.

The last time I had been in Duluth was on my honeymoon with Muriel, so it was particularly lonesome when she and Nancy stayed in South Dakota to save money. But it was also an exciting summer for me.

My students, many of whom were older than I, had had jobs, lost them, and now the WPA was taking them out of their personal and economic depression and giving them something productive to do. There was a common bond of hope and rebirth. And because I was alone, I worked intensely with them—teaching, talking, learning.

At the end of the summer, Muriel and I and Nancy were back together in southeastern Minneapolis, the area around the University of Minnesota that was to be our home until we went to Washington.

That part of town had built up from the Mississippi River

bank in the nineteenth century, and fine old homes of early residents had turned into rooming houses on quiet, tree-lined streets. It was almost a community set apart from the rest of the city, a community filled with the atmosphere of any university—the rooming houses, bookstores, campus hang-outs, all the intensity of inquiring youth.

I still think of it, in a strange way, as home. My political career was launched there. My ideas of government and politics, though formed by South Dakota, my father, and my earlier education, were refined and organized there. And many of the men who would be my friends and/or advisers during the next quarter of a century lived there.[1]

My decision to stay at the University of Minnesota was a tough one, but an inevitable one—and in retrospect, a wise one. But what I really wanted to do at that time was to go to Princeton, where I had also been offered a scholarship.

That had been my dream, because of my father's identification with Woodrow Wilson's ideas. Princeton, where Wilson had been president, seemed from my earliest years like a shining educational heaven—a political and intellectual ancestral home.

But I was so broke that I feared to take that long a trip, that far away from home, so soon after our Louisiana experience. With wife and child, I wondered how we'd survive in the East.

So we stayed in Minnesota and barely survived there. Professor William Anderson once again came through. He offered me a teaching assistantship that paid six hundred dollars a year.

I knew from our Louisiana experience that we couldn't make it on that money, so I negotiated with Professor Anderson for a heavier teaching load and pay of about eleven hundred dollars a year. At the same time, however, and growing out of my WPA teaching in Duluth, I was offered the job of Twin City director of the Workers' Education Program. It paid about one hundred fifty dollars a month and primarily involved trade unions. I took it instead of the teaching assistantship, though I continued to work toward a Ph.D.

Through that job, I met and worked with the labor leaders of Minneapolis and St. Paul. Without it, I would never have been asked to run for mayor in 1943. And it was there that I ran into my first intense, personal experience with the Communist left.

There were essentially three groups of teachers at that time on WPA: the Stalinist Communists, the Trotskyist bloc, and a third group of everyone else. The Stalinists and Trotskyists hated each other, and when we had teachers' sessions, they'd sit on opposite sides of the room and harass each other. The presence of such an intense Marxist movement in Minnesota may seem strange, but it became, for several reasons, possibly the most active Communist center between the East and West coasts.

Minnesota is a special political place. It has a conservative base, primarily built around the old Yankees who dominated business and finance in the cities, the rural German Catholic population, and large elements of the Scandinavians both urban and rural.

But from that solid and rocky base have blossomed wild flowers of political, social, and economic radicalism. Agrarian radicalism grew more rapidly than the crops through farm depression and difficulties. Labor militance developed from vicious and bloody strikes in the thirties. And a socialist element was transplanted there, arriving with Finnish and other Scandinavian farmers and workers. On the Iron Range of northern Minnesota, the workers, largely eastern and southern European immigrants, hated the bosses—the mining companies—with such intensity (and often with good reason) that a small but militant Communist movement soon flourished.

The farmers looked at the cities as the place where the products of their fields—the literal fruits of their labors—went. They saw the banks, the railroads, the milling interests grow fat as their profits grew thin. They fought the elements of sun, wind, rain, snow, and drought. And in those years when they overcame the elements, they saw, or at least thought they saw, their rightful gain flow inexorably, like the spring runoff, away from their farms.

As a result, the farm areas of the Midwest witnessed a series of farm protests and efforts at rural organization. The Grange, Populism, and the co-operative movement stirred the farmer and affected the politics of Minnesota.[2]

With that mixture of radicalism in the background, I began my duties in early October 1940. I soon discovered that a number of teachers were not working. They were more interested in their own brand of revolution and agitation. They were supposed to work a forty-hour week, ten of teaching and thirty of preparation, for which they were paid about one hundred dollars a month.

My only ideology was that people ought to do their jobs, so I sent out the word that anyone without a full schedule by Thanksgiving would be fired. Only ten people were needed for a class, and with the large, unemployed labor movement in the Twin Cities, that was not difficult. When Thanksgiving came, several of the teachers still had made no effort to fill their schedules, so I fired them.

And they raised unshirted hell. They went from the district director through the state employment office, and then to the Federal Works Administration in Washington. The bureaucracy shook all along the line, and I finally was summoned to the office of Jacob Herzog, the state director of employment for WPA.

Herzog listened to my explanation. Then he reached out and put his hand on my shoulder and said, "I never thought I'd find a man with guts enough to fire anyone on WPA for not working." He stood with me, taking a great deal of the heat himself, and out of that experience we became good friends and, over the ensuing years, strong political allies.

From that job, I moved up to district director of workers' education, then in 1940 to state director of workers' services. The Workers' Service Program had a variety of activities: from recreation programs to vocational education, from classes in parliamentary procedure and public speaking to English grammar and literature.*

With defense activities increasing, jobs were becoming available, but the courses were meant to do more than simply prepare men and women for work. In a sense, our program was an instance of massive group therapy, providing people with a feeling of hope and worth and personal improvement at the same time that they prepared themselves for jobs.

I remember deciding one day that everyone who completed a specific course of study would get a signed certificate as a kind

---

* Once a week, generally Monday, after the end of the work day, I would hold what we called a current-events review. It was attended by dozens of WPA staff people and became a regular feature of the office program.

of diploma. At the time, my only purpose was to make each person know that someone recognized his or her achievement. Subsequently, when I became a political candidate, I met hundreds of people through the state who spoke with pride of the certificate I had signed. In countless homes, the framed certificate had a prominent place on the living-room wall.

There's no doubt that the WPA program had its weaknesses and that there were some people who were not competent. But by and large most people did well when they had a chance on a job.

The people who were criticized so much for being on WPA were the same people who, when they went into private industry, did an amazing job in the defense plants, shops, and schools all over the United States. You sometimes wonder what miraculous changes overcame those "lazy, ne'er-do-well WPA'ers" as they were described in the hostile editorials and cartoons.

A year or so after having been in the program a man came up to me at the First Congregational Church in Minneapolis. He said (and I remember his voice and his words clearly even after twenty-six years), "Mr. Humphrey, do you think the government wasted its money on me? I've got a job now, and I'm paying taxes. And my boy is in the Air Force. He's just been decorated for valor in battle."

I've never forgotten. He was trying to tell me something I have seen and heard many times—then, among the white workers, and more recently, among black hard-core unemployed who were trained under the Poverty Program—that lives that seem hopeless and worthless can change and become productive. I've listened day after day, decade after decade, to political and theoretical arguments about cost per person, waste in government programs, and all the other clichés that come so easily to those who have. None of the arguments makes much sense to me when measured against the human gain—in dignity, sense of community, and even ultimate material benefit for society.

In 1942 I became the divisional director for training and re-employment. My job was, ironically, to liquidate the WPA. We had a vocational training program all over the state of Minnesota, funneling our "graduates" to new jobs through the state and United States employment offices.

The WPA vocational training project used vocational training equipment in many of our high schools, as well as equipment we bought. It was enormously successful. From July 1940 up to January 1942, about eight thousand people, including five thousand in the Twin Cities, were trained and put on jobs.

12. "WE'RE TRYING TO FIND A CANDIDATE FOR MAYOR"

I began 1943 confused and unsure of my immediate direction. I became assistant director of the Minnesota War Manpower Commission but, like many men, I still didn't know whether I'd be called into service or not. In 1940, when the draft began, I had been classified 3A, the status given men who were married and had children. But the war was heating up, the draft situation seemed to be changing, my younger friends were going into service, and I was torn between responsibility to my family and a desire to be a part of our military effort.

Filled with uncertainty, on the new job only a few months, one Sunday in April I went for an aimless walk, which, as it turned out, gave my life direction for the next twenty-five years.

Downtown Minneapolis was just across the Mississippi River from where we lived, and I headed over the bridge on Hennepin Avenue into our main area of hotels, restaurants, and movie houses. Two men I'd met through the WPA Workers' Education Program, George Phillips, president of the Minneapolis Central Labor Union, and George Murk, president of the Musicians Union, stopped me outside of the Nicollet Hotel and we began talking about the mayoral contest.

They were on their way to a meeting and said, "We're trying to find a candidate for mayor." One of them asked, "Would you be interested?"

"Well, I might be. I don't know what kind of support I would get." Our conversation was casual. I thought I might be interested; they thought they might get me a little labor support, and we left it at that.

I was intrigued with the idea. My trip home was much faster than the trip downtown. I had often talked to Evron Kirkpatrick, Ben Lippincott, Earl Latham, Muriel, and more recently to Arthur Naftalin about my running for office, but it was just talk, since I had more work to do on my Ph.D. Further, I had lived in Minneapolis only a few years, mostly as a student, and was not widely known.

I didn't know much about municipal politics and problems from experience, and I had studied virtually nothing about them either. I preferred Congress, but there was a Republican incumbent in the Third Congressional District, where I lived, who looked unbeatable.

I didn't believe then, as I don't believe now, that political defeat is particularly good for one's character, and I had rejected the idea of running for any public office at that time. On a couple of occasions earlier in the year, Judge Vincent Day of Minneapolis had suggested I consider running for mayor. I did not take the conversations too seriously. I thought about it from time to time, but had done nothing to encourage anyone or to prepare for such a race.

Subsequently, I found out that Judge Day had called together a number of people—leaders of the Central Labor Union and some liberal officeholders—to push the idea of my running for mayor, and I suppose the sidewalk conversation with Phillips and Murk was an outgrowth of Day's advocacy. Once an assistant to Governor Floyd B. Olson, he had later, as a state district judge, assumed Olson's leadership mantle with progressives, particularly in the Twin Cities.

I really believe that had I not accidentally met Phillips and Murk that Sunday, I would not have run for mayor of Minneapolis in 1943. I was thirty-two years old, married, a father, on a new job, with an unfinished doctoral degree hanging in abeyance, and broke. A more objective person might have considered it an unpropitious moment to launch a political career.

I considered the idea for a couple of days, talked again to Muriel and my friends, and then leapt, if not lightly at least eagerly, into the fray. I was not an objective person. From the day I filed, there was not quite three weeks to the primary election day. In those weeks I put together the first coalition of my political career.

It was an uneasy one. While my closest friends and advisers came from the university community, my strongest support had to come from the labor movement. Unfortunately, labor leadership didn't like the university crowd, and my academic friends returned their affection in kind.

I liked the labor groups; I worked hard with them in the Workers' Education Program. I went to union meetings, I drank beer with them, and I went to their dances and parties long before any question of running for office and endorsement arose. Because I lived close by the Labor Temple, I'd wander over to meetings just for the discussion and company. Bull sessions with the union members were as much a part of my education as the university. I was at home with them, as they were with me. And this was important—for the liberal movement in Minneapolis was essentially the labor movement. I had helped to organize a Teachers Union on the university campus, so my contacts were more than social.

Neither the Democratic party nor the Farmer-Labor party had much relevance in municipal politics. On the ballot, the mayor's race was non-partisan, and in the recent past had been essentially a contest between a labor-endorsed candidate and a candidate not endorsed by labor. Ordinarily, the non-labor candidate was more closely involved with the Republican party than the labor candidate was involved with either the Democrats or the Farmer-Laborites.

Much of my support came from what might be called, disdainfully by some, courthouse politicians; in this instance exceptional public servants. Three were most helpful: Judge Day, County Commissioner Ralph Dickman, and County Attorney Michael Dillon—who was also Hennepin County chairman of the Democratic party. In addition, I had the support of a number of leaders from the AFL Central Labor Union and the railroad brotherhoods. But this was not solid labor support.

For one thing, a previously endorsed labor candidate who had become a kind of perennial, T. A. Eide, filed again. A long-time leader of a co-operative creamery in the Twin Cities, he had many friends in the labor movement. In the primary there were —besides Eide, the incumbent mayor, a Republican named Marvin Kline, and myself—eight other candidates. Minnesota law permitted anyone who had the ten dollars filing fee and the desire, to enter. The top two candidates would runoff in the general election.

Secondly, the CIO in Minnesota was largely dominated, not in numbers but in power, by left-wing leaders who had not forgotten our arguments in the Workers' Education Program and who found me too much the liberal Democrat without any Marxist ideology.

Some of the leadership were overt and active Communist party members. Others, of course, were not party members but simply militantly left wing. In any case, even as the least of all evils, they would not support my candidacy, though there were several individual CIO leaders who did.

Third, much of the leadership of the Teamsters Union, which was strong in the Twin Cities, opposed me. Up to 1941, the Teamsters were primarily led by the Trotskyist Dunne brothers, Vincent Ray, Miles, and Grant. In October 1941 Ray Dunne and other Teamster-Trotskyist leaders were convicted of violating the Smith Act.[1]

But earlier that year—in midsummer—the International Teamsters Union had decided to depose the Dunnes and their followers. The state labor conciliator, apparently under Governor Harold Stassen's direction, certified the new leadership, giving them legal sanction and thus authority in the union and control over the union treasury. One of the ways the new Teamster leadership paid off the obligation was public support for Mayor Kline.

Basically, the only other bloc support I had came from the Jewish community and particularly from young people about my own age. I also had a good deal of support within the Negro community.[2]

The Jewish and Negro communities combined didn't amount to much in votes, but they counted then and do still for strength beyond numbers. (Both groups have remained constant supporters through my entire political life.) Obviously, I had to reach beyond these limited areas of support—labor, university people, and the minorities—to the wider population.

I began a whirlwind campaign. Just nineteen days before the primary, joined by Evron Kirkpatrick and Arthur Naftalin, I went to the courthouse and filed. Art, a young journalist working for his doctorate in political science, was an ingenious and hard-working staff virtually by himself.

He worked up the issues, wrote radio scripts, and occasionally raised the money to pay for the radio shows.* While the radio broadcasts didn't make me a household word that year, they were tremendously helpful in making me known. In addition, Naftalin was skillful in exploiting every possible free avenue of publicity.

Money wasn't our only problem. Gas rationing was still in effect, and friends used to pool their coupons for gas enough to transport me from one place to another.

I spoke anywhere I could get an audience. I moved, like a political evangelist, from service-club luncheons and business groups to church basements to labor halls. It is only a slight exaggeration to say that wherever a group of people paused, I was there. I enjoyed it (and still do).

As a result of the incredibly hard work of a small group of people,[3] we survived the primary, 13,477 votes behind Kline.

We would run in the general election.

The following six weeks, to the general election, was a continuation of what we had done before, and we came very close. I lost to Marvin Kline by 5,725 votes.

Minneapolis in 1943 was a schizophrenic city of light and darkness, as confused and unsure of its direction as I. During the day, it was a vibrant regional center of finance and transportation, of milling and agriculture.

It was a city of activity and growth dominated by the New England Yankee families who had come early to Minnesota, either directly from New England or, as with much of the west-

---

* Having been in the 1968 campaign, in which we spent over one million dollars during one day for television, I am amused by the recollection of how hard we worked in 1943 to scrounge up twenty-six dollars for fifteen minutes of WLOL radio, one of the smaller stations in Minneapolis.

ward movement, with stopovers in Ohio, Indiana, or some other midwestern state.

They lived then pretty largely in a single area of town: around Lake Calhoun, Lake Harriet, and Lake of the Isles, or in the Kenwood district.

What they wanted was primarily a conservative government— no radicals in office, police who stood on the "right" side in labor disputes, and relatively low taxes.

There were others who felt daytime was for sleeping and came out only when the sun went down. They ran gambling, prostitution, and liquor in a wide-open town. Minneapolis in those days were much like a frontier town with a little bit of sophistication.

There were two major groups involved: the "Syndicate," run by Kid Cann, and the Tommy Banks "Combination." Both were probably carry-overs from bootlegging days of Prohibition. But there was so much action that many people had a part of it.

Little operators and big ones all saw me with a single vision: a reformer who wanted to take away their special treatment, their arrangements. I had come out of the university and was clearly "owned" by no one. I talked of clean government as though I meant it, and I did. They did their best to arrange my defeat, and they did.

They were allied with a minister who was ostensibly anti-liquor, a kind of latter-day Carrie Nation. Liquor and liquor licensing were always major issues, partly because of certain legal restrictions on them, partly because of the "dry" attitudes of many of our citizens. The parson muddled the issue so it was hard to understand what he was really saying. But the end result was always the same. He made it difficult for anyone who wanted to end the corruption and change the liquor situation to get elected.

More distressing to me than the influence of this single man was the infiltration of "bad" money from fringe elements of the liquor, beer, and entertainment industries to their pets within the labor movement. It was not widespread, but it was corrosive, permitting a few men and a little money to influence certain aldermen, and ultimately decisions of the city council.

I had come to the WPA programs with virtually no experience

with organized labor. There was nothing in South Dakota that could have been called a labor movement. But as an idealist I had always believed in the labor movement. The labor movement supported Roosevelt; the labor movement was for better working conditions, for higher wages. It was the voice of the voiceless. I hated to see it sullied or any part of it compromised.

The ultimate shock was that, for the most part, the "good" people of the community didn't really care. As long as their daytime life went on without complication by the city government, they ignored the night life.

Another lesson, which should have been obvious but wasn't, was that being the head of the ticket does not command the support of incumbents. Though their lips might speak words of support, their hands never get the message. When I ran for mayor, there were liberal aldermen who couldn't have cared less about helping, particularly when it appeared that I had no chance. In fact, two years later, when I returned to Margolis' garage on Plymouth Avenue in North Minneapolis—a biennial political headquarters—I found some of my 1943 campaign literature still there, undistributed.

This taught me early why loyalty and reciprocity are so highly valued by politicians. Cronies and retainers who slavishly surround a powerful man, sycophants chorusing his praise, may be disgusting and worthy of derision by outsiders. They may even be galling to the man himself. But in the highly competitive, all-or-nothing world of politics, where it seems there are always more people shooting at you than helping, loyalty, above all else, seems important. Poker-playing friends of Harry Truman, bridge-playing friends of Dwight Eisenhower, even a beer-guzzling buddy of an alderman, provide the protective environment for a political man to be himself, to relax and enjoy the normal diversions of life. Without them, the isolation of even a lowly office becomes intolerable.

After my defeat, Gideon Seymour, then executive editor of the Minneapolis *Star and Tribune* and a civic leader in Minneapolis, asked me to visit with him. He was a rather independent-minded Republican, reasonably liberal and not doctrinaire, who had been a strong Harold Stassen supporter.

I liked Seymour and admired what he was trying to do to

make Minneapolis a better city. I liked him even more as he began to praise me, suggesting that I could have a successful future in Minnesota politics if I would be careful in my choice of associates and the political course I followed.

Then he asked me to join the Republican party, asking, "Which way do you want to go, the way of Floyd Olson or Harold Stassen?" I suggested that those two choices didn't seem to me the only options, and that I intended to remain a Democrat and a liberal.

He countered by saying that you didn't have to be a conservative to be a Republican. Stassen had a liberal reputation, and two congressmen, Richard Gale of the third District and Walter Judd in the fifth, were his examples of liberals within the Republican party.

He pointed out that the Republicans were the majority party in Minnesota, were in the ascendancy, and that a young man looking to his future in politics in Minnesota had better find a home there. When I replied that I would have to take my chances as a Democrat, he said he understood but was sorry that I was going to sacrifice a very promising political career unnecessarily.

It was a tempting, if impossible, option. I wanted to succeed in politics, and my future did indeed seem bleak. Muriel and I had thirteen hundred dollars in debts as a result of the mayoral campaign. I was trying to pay that off (and I ultimately did, by speaking for five-, ten-, or twenty-five-dollar fees to anyone who would pay). But the more formidable obstacle that Seymour noted was the strength of the Republicans and the seemingly insoluble weakness of the Democrats.

13. "WE MUST UNITE"

Something had to be done about our party, and I took the lead. In July, after my defeat, I sent a twelve-page, handwritten letter to Frank Walker, Postmaster General and chairman of the Democratic National Committee, appealing for help in bringing the Minnesota Democratic and Farmer-Labor parties together. I belabored the obvious: Democrats never won in Minnesota, because the vote was split three ways: Republican, Democratic, and Farmer-Laborite. If liberals were going to win any significant election, Democrats and Farmer-Laborites had to work together.[1]

When a perfunctory reply to my letter arrived from the national committee, taking about seventy dollars that Muriel and I had saved I set off for Washington, convinced that I could persuade Frank Walker to help. It did not occur to me that I might not be able to see him.

I had no money for a hotel room, so I stayed just outside Washington with my Aunt Olive and Uncle Harry Humphrey. Each morning, I would take a streetcar downtown to the national headquarters in the Mayflower Hotel. Each morning, I dutifully asked to see the chairman, actually hoping to see anyone at all after I realized the chairman was not eager to see me.

I wrote Muriel: "It looks like a political operation on crutches. They aren't very interested in listening to a young fellow like me." Finally, more in charity than interest, A. C. Carraway, a southern gentleman on Walker's staff, paused in his quiet day to see me. He'd been around a long time and he listened patiently to my story. But nothing happened. After five more days, I left Uncle Harry's, suitcase in hand, aimed for the bus depot. Depressed, I stopped to have a drink at the Willard Hotel on Pennsylvania Avenue. Then, with time to kill, I called an old Huron friend of my dad's, W. W. Howes, who had been an assistant postmaster general under Jim Farley. Howes, by 1943, was an officer of Midcontinent Airlines, and was, as I discovered, still a political operator.

We chatted over the phone about my dad and South Dakota, about my recent campaign, about what I was doing in Washington. When I told him I'd had no luck at the Democratic National Committee, he asked where I was, told me to wait, and shortly appeared. He questioned me in detail about my plan, walked to a public phone, and called Frank Walker. The conversation was brief, to the point, and effective. "The son of one of my closest friends is here and has been trying to see you all week. I want you to see him. Would you send a car over and have him picked up?"

In ten minutes, the Postmaster General's black limousine picked me up. The turnabout in fortune was beyond belief. After five miserable and unsuccessful days of waiting, just before getting on a bus for twelve hundred fifty miles and thirty-six hours of tedium, hanging on to just enough money to feed myself going home, I was suddenly and elegantly about to meet the man it was impossible to see.

The speech I had prepared over and over again slipped momentarily away in the atmosphere of big limousine, big office, and big Cabinet officer. Walker quickly put me at ease, and listened carefully to my plans. He had not seen my letter, but he seemed persuaded by what I said. He promised to be in touch. I went home confident that the fusion would have his support.

On the bus, my thoughts revolved about what we needed to do to take another step toward fusion. After a while, my thoughts drifted to a somewhat more personal problem: I didn't have a job and I didn't have any money. What I did have was a wife and two kids.

Fortunately, there were a number of possibilities. George Rutman, a friend who owned the Stavis Oil Company in St. Paul, offered me a job. One of the local radio stations, WTCN, asked me to broadcast for them. The national CIO, through Sidney Hillman, unlike the local group, was friendly. Hillman offered me a job with the new Political Action Committee. At one point I even looked over a drugstore with the thought of running it. When I arrived home, another option awaited.

Muriel had the happy news that Macalester College in St. Paul wanted me to teach there.* I had, of course, made up my mind to accept the job when I went over to see Dr. Clarence Ficken, the acting president of Macalester. He had only one stipulation: that I not engage in any open political activity while I was on the Macalester payroll. I agreed. I knew then that I would probably run again for mayor of Minneapolis if I wasn't in military service in 1945,† but I also knew that there was no particular reason for active politicking for the time being.

During the summer session of 1943, I taught a course in political philosophy for the civilian and military students. Everyone seemed interested, as I intensely was, not only in American democracy but also in the backgrounds of Italian Fascism, German Nazism, Japanese militarism, and Soviet communism.[2]

I thoroughly enjoyed teaching. I spent much of my time listening and talking with faculty and students in impromptu sessions.[3] In a small way, I became a campus celebrity, giving the commencement address for the Army Air Corps group on three consecutive occasions. They had only a six-week course and voted each time for the instructor they wanted for their speaker.

But teaching, with all its attractions, was a pale second choice. I had ended a mayoral campaign thirteen hundred dollars in debt, barely older but politically wiser. Besides, I was permanently hooked on politics.

I had become a pharmacist as a matter of necessity. Had I had a religious calling, I might have been a minister. Had I finished my Ph.D., I might have remained within the academic world. Instead, having learned in a campaign that I could move an audi-

---

* I was hired to teach the Army Air Corps officers in the 347th Training Detachment.

† I received an automatic draft classification of 2A as a civilian in an essential job.

ence, exciting them about political issues, motivating them to civic action, I combined some aspects of each career into a political life.

Shortly after I began teaching, the national committee wrote that they were, indeed, interested in helping put the two parties together. Walker had delivered. Oscar Ewing, an assistant national chairman (and later a cabinet officer under President Truman) was assigned to help us.

The first fusion meeting, with Ewing present, was held at the St. Paul Hotel. I had invited about twenty-five people, most of whom would be for the fusion, as well as some who might need a little persuading. We agreed to further discussions by a committee of six Democrats and six Farmer-Laborites and me as the swing man.

Many meetings followed. Although neither party had been winning elections and the need for a fusion was obvious, there were so many suspicions and antagonisms that amalgamation came only slowly. Many of the Democratic leaders, largely urban and Irish Catholic, disliked the Farmer-Laborites even more than they disliked the Republicans.

Part of that antagonism began when Roosevelt worked with Floyd Olson, leaving the Minnesota Democrats to flounder as a weak party. They couldn't elect anybody, and what patronage they had kept very few people happy either in the dispensing or the receiving.

The Farmer-Labor party was divided between the traditional agricultural Populists and the left wing, more urban Marxists. The first group, led by former Governor Hjalmar Petersen, opposed the fusion as a matter of principle. They were honest, progressive, principled people who thought of the Democratic party as being one of patronage only and without real ideology.

It is ironic that the legitimate heirs to the Farmer-Labor tradition, opposed to the fusion, were not in power within the Farmer-Labor party. The left-wing group that had parasitically attached itself to that tradition like a lamprey on a lake trout was in power, and unity had become a religion with them. They twisted and turned according to the demands of the Soviet line.

For most of us, the amalgamation was an effort to fashion local political success. For the Communists and fellow travelers the amalgamation had cosmic significance, tied in their mystical way with the war effort, Soviet-American friendship, and the future of Marxism in America.

When things looked rough and Hennepin County Attorney Mike Dillon despaired of ever reaching an understanding, I told him, "They'll negotiate. They'll come in. There's no doubt about it, because it's all for unity, it's all for Roosevelt. As long as the Soviet Union is in the war, this crowd is going to be willing to sell out to anybody—even us."

The classic statement of the struggle came, for me, one night on the sixth floor of the Dyckman Hotel. Elmer Benson, leader of the left-wing Farmer-Laborites, was loudly denouncing Democratic Chairmen Elmer Kelm, me, and the entire negotiation. "Kelm is a Fascist. So is Humphrey. This is absolutely no good. But we must unite." He knew that everything he was doing was wrong from a traditional Farmer-Labor point of view. Nevertheless he'd always end up saying, "But we must unite."

And unite we finally did, after weeks and weeks of meetings at the end of 1943 and the beginning of 1944.

That whole period was a wildly creative one. On any day, the entire proceeding could have fallen apart, one group or another seeking or protecting political power, first co-operative, then difficult, finally compromising, agreeing, consulting.

The pulse of family life stepped up. Our son Robert was born in March; then Muriel's father died. The state political conventions of the two parties were to take place in April.

This was the first of many painful, poignant moments when personal desires would yield to political necessity. Muriel, fourteen days after the birth of our child, went alone, in the lingering days of a South Dakota winter, to bury her father. The day of his funeral, a new political party—the Democratic Farmer Labor party—was born, and I was there as midwife and keynote speaker rather than beside Muriel as husband.

Shortly before the convention, I had taken an examination hoping for a Naval Reserve officer commission. When the notice came soon after the convention that I had been rejected, I tried to become an enlisted man—a pharmacist's mate or an apprentice seaman.

I was embarrassed by again flunking the physical. The reasons seemed to me insignificant: I was color-blind, had a double hernia, and had some calcification and scars on my lungs (probably from drinking unpasteurized, tuberculous milk as a child). I had the hernia repaired, and the other factors would not have had any effect on my ability to function. Those disabilities, if they could be called that, seemed so slight that I pestered the Navy recruiting officer, Rollo Mudge, incessantly.

In July, I was classified 1A-Limited and started the whole routine over, but the Army decided it was too expensive to draft and support men with dependents. Muriel and I had three children, so I was deferred once more.

In mid-December 1944, after the Battle of the Bulge, draft calls got heavy again, and I was called for another preinduction physical, and once more was classified 1A-Limited. I urged the commanding officer at Fort Snelling Induction Center to accept me. I told him it was embarrassing to me to be deferred. My picture had been in the local paper showing me at Fort Snelling, uniform in hand. I had made plans for my family to go out to South Dakota with my parents, and besides, as I said to the colonel, "I'm labeled political and if I don't get in the service it will haunt me the rest of my days.

The colonel listened and then said, "You are not eligible for service. If we need you, we know where to find you."

That fall, I ran the Roosevelt-Truman campaign effort in Minnesota and spent much of the time working for our first DFL candidate for governor, Byron G. Allen.[4]

I loaded up my 1940 Ford V-8 with campaign literature and drove from small town to village to city in every part of the state. Our candidate for governor, Barney Allen, bore the main burden of the campaign, knowing he had little chance to win. He was a real trouper.

In my first experience with the Democratic National Committee, I learned an unchanging lesson: the DNC is always late with the literature. Boxloads of material, begged for earlier, arrived about a week before the election, too late to be of any value except as scrap paper. Earlier that summer, I had attended my first national convention as a delegate.

Politics has an intensity and a rhythm unlike anything else I know. Even the quiescent periods, between elections, are filled with power plays, choices, shifting friendships, new adversaries, constant loyalties.

The convention and election times are wild. Tension builds constantly, with less and less tolerance for mistakes. Soar to the heady heights of victory, fall to the rocky pits of defeat. Then start all over again. Politics, more than most other careers, requires constant attention. Success requires monomania. Politics intrudes on and defines your life style.

National conventions are themselves a most special part of politics, a unique quadrennial experience. Conventions are sleepless and noisy. They are idealism mixed with expedience. They are dramatic and they are dull. Conventions are masses of people moving, always moving, bumping in crowded elevators, crowded corridors, crowded rooms.

When you get home, you talk of the news items, of the famous names, but few people at a convention see much more than a little of the action. You focus on what you are there to do, or on the fortunes of a person or issue that attracts you, or is closest to you.

No one, in fact, sees the convention whole—not the candidates, the chairman, the television eye. Circus-like, part surface, part subterranean, one understands why a news team once remarked of a convention, shaking their heads in despair, disbelief, and amusement, "Somehow it works. . . ."

The convention system in the United States is a complicated, uneven, often confused and sometimes unfair way of selecting national candidates. It has, nevertheless, usually been successful at creating cohesion around generally good men, despite inevitable unhappiness with candidates and platform.

The 1944 convention was no exception. Our Minnesota DFL delegation went to Chicago pledged to support Henry Wallace for re-election as Vice President.

Wallace, a Midwesterner who understood our agricultural problems, was the philosophical saint of the DFL, and we could not understand Roosevelt's dropping him. Our outrage only increased at the pressure put on us, as on others, by Mayor Ed Kelly of Chicago and by Robert Hannegan of Missouri, the Democratic National Chairman.

But it was our first convention as a new party and we held

tough for Wallace, never switching our votes. Even the old-line Democrats like Kelm, who might have liked to go along with President Roosevelt on Mr. Truman, stood with us. No man seemed more closely aligned with the Midwest, with the Populist liberals, Farmer-Laborites, Non-Partisan Leaguers, and ardent New Dealers than Wallace. Senator Truman, on the other hand, was little known to us. What we knew did not attract us very strongly.

Later that year, however, we held a campaign luncheon for Truman. I introduced him to the several hundred people we had gathered in what had become almost a second home for me that year, the Dyckman Hotel. That was the first time most of us had seen or heard Truman up close and he was not overwhelmingly effective. He spoke without force, but it was obvious, in both his public and our private talk, that he was a strong New Dealer. That, of course, was what really counted. We learned to accept him then; we learned to admire him later.

Still, by the time he and President Roosevelt were elected that fall, none of us thought of him as a potential President.

14. I'M THE MAYOR

What I did think about was myself as potential mayor. We had come a long way from the 1943 campaign, when I had learned as much as I could about the formal structure of city government. In the intervening time, I had turned my attention to understanding the people behind the structure, those who caused government to operate. I followed local news more closely than before, figuring out who the real leaders were in the city—in more current terms, "defining the power structure." Then I set out to meet them—bankers, publishers, businessmen of other sorts—and at the same time I strengthened my association with labor.

A second imperative existed. I had to increase the number of people who were interested in my political career. The 1943 effort had essentially been an effort of very few people. We had no personal organization to do the door-to-door, neighborhood politicking particularly necessary in an underfinanced, local campaign.

By spring 1945 we were reasonably ready for our second campaign. The nucleus of friends had been enlarged ideologically, geographically, and socially. I knew much better who governed the city, and how—beyond the letter of the charter. And I also knew some of what had to be done to improve the life in the city.

Rapidly I went from one audience to the other: church group, service club, union. I got into the papers and on the radio somewhat more easily.

By 1945, the aura of corruption seemed to hang more heavily around the incumbent administration and city. There was also increasing concern about the postwar world. All of that helped me, since I was young, untouched by corruption, and proposing ideas for Minneapolis' future.

The concern for what lay ahead was heightened by the news of President Roosevelt's sudden death. Roosevelt had dominated the political consciousness of America for so long that his death was shocking beyond reason. Possibly 40 per cent of the American population knew no other President. People only slightly younger than I, could scarcely remember Herbert Hoover, and Calvin Coolidge not at all.

When radio stations went immediately to hours of somber music, a quiet settled on our campaign headquarters, where we had heard the announcement. We talked softly about what Roosevelt's death might mean for the future. It was less eulogy at that moment than concern. Here we were, the war practically won, talk of the countries of the world joining together in an organization of nations. Soon there would be 13 million servicemen coming home. What about them? We had not yet finally defined the nature of the victory and postwar policy and suddenly Roosevelt was gone. Suddenly Mr. Truman was President.

Roosevelt's death slowed us down briefly but, on June 2, I was elected to my first public office, carrying eleven of the thirteen wards. I won by thirty-one thousand votes. Many of the people who shared that joyous night with Muriel and me, listening to the returns by radio in our home, have continued to share victory and defeat with me ever since.

One who shared that night of celebration and who was quite unlike anyone else there was a man named Fred Gates. He was just a few years older than I, had been born in Chicago of Lebanese immigrant parents, and had less than a high school education.

I met Fred during the 1943 campaign. He had a little penny arcade on Hennepin Avenue with pinball machines and penny movie machines in which you peered into a metal eyepiece and turned the handle on the right side. Existing as he did on the fringe of the fringe, he knew of corruption in and out of city government, of protection money and payoffs, and he didn't like it. But in 1943 he wasn't sure that I, if elected, would put a stop to it. And he therefore would not support me. He thought I might be a momentary political flash, streaking across the sky, going nowhere.

As the 1945 election approached, Freddie came to me with a simple question: If I was elected mayor, was I going to play it straight?

Was Minneapolis going to be a clean town, were all the fixes off, were the police going to be permitted to be policemen rather than household pets for certain operators in town? When I said I intended to play it straight, he said, "Well, I'll help you."

We quickly became the closest friends. From 1945 until 1971, Fred was more important to my political life than any other person. He became a kind of guardian angel and protector, to whom I could turn with any political or personal matter, involving myself, my family, or my friends.

Family and friends meant everything to him, far more than political party or ideology. So long as you stayed within certain bounds of honesty and decency, his only ideology was, "If you're a friend, I'm for you, and if you treat me well, I'll treat you well."

Once we became friends, the one thing Fred seemed to want above all was to see me a success. He bent his whole life to that purpose. His devotion was total, a kind of loyalty in which one person largely loses himself in the life of another. In the early years, he was a one-man intelligence bureau, and the most effective one I've ever seen. He understood the nether world of floating card games and after-hours whiskey joints. He told me more about how things were really run in Minneapolis than the Police Department ever did, and without him I would never have had as good a program of law enforcement in Minneapolis as we developed.

He spent his time making sure I did not inadvertently get caught up in anything that could soil me. After the 1945 campaign, for example, he came into my office with a half-dozen canceled checks. He had given me the checks early in the campaign, when I barely knew him, and I had signed them over to my campaign committee. Now he said, "You're foolish to be accepting checks made out to you from someone you hardly know.

The only thing you know about my background or my connections, I told you. You didn't know if I was tied up with the mob, or whether I was an independent operator, or whether I was just a good citizen trying to be of help. From here on out, when you run for office, you keep an arm's length away from campaign contributions; *never* handle them yourself. Get a committee and a man you can trust. Otherwise, you're in trouble." He tore up the canceled checks.

By the next campaign, he assumed a role that continued until 1970 through state and national campaigns. Whenever we needed campaign money, Fred was at the center, making sure the fund-raising was done well and properly. He kept track of every dime that came in, and even closer track of every one that went out.

As campaign staffs get larger and people who spend are far removed from those who raise the money, carelessness sets in. Money that dribbles in, pours out. Fred, however, was more careful of contributed money than he ever was of his own, and he tried hard to persuade or force others to be that way. He hated waste, and would chastise those who wasted anything from envelopes, paper, stamps, clips, or staples to buttons, posters, and bunting. Over the years, he saved thousands of dollars checking little items as well as major expenses in advertising and printing, telephone calls, and travel expenses.

He was more than the bookkeeper of my political life. Fred also took care of personal politics. On the one hand, he was my political antenna, my listening post. Because he didn't want anything from me and didn't care how I voted in the Senate, he spoke directly and honestly. He would tell me what people were saying, what they wanted, what they thought I was doing, what they hoped I might do. He brought me information that no staff person or potential seeker of favor can do.

On the other hand, he was a goad, reminding me of things I ought to do, of people I ought to call. While I was senator, I never came home to Minnesota without Freddie holding out a list of names who needed a birthday greeting or a condolence message or a get-well note.

Above all, he was an associate with whom I could relax away from the public view, speaking about people or issues or aspirations, aware that he would never violate a confidence, never repeat anything he shouldn't, never take a momentary rage seriously, never a serious concern lightly.

Once, in 1954, several Minnesota political leaders came to me insisting that I get rid of Fred. They said he was bad for my image and bad for the DFL. Freddie was so easy to cast in the bad-guy role. Short, swarthy, often too fat and sometimes ungrammatical, Fred, indeed, added no elegance. But he brought instead loyalty and love and decency, and they were more precious.

When Fred died, in 1971, his funeral was quietly dignified, in keeping with his life as a small businessman who lived in the same unpretentious house for twenty-six years with the same wife. But there were two United States senators there, one of whom had been Vice President of the United States, an incumbent governor of Minnesota, a former governor, four federal court judges, municipal judges, the head of the local/regional FBI office, priests, pastors, professors, business and labor leaders, and hundreds of others.

They came, I think, because he had been a friend, because they loved him too.[1]

15. "WHY WOULD ANYONE SHOOT AT ME?"

Analysts of government describe the municipal structure of Minneapolis as a weak mayor form of government. That may overstate the mayor's role. He has no control over the budget, no power of the purse strings, and no vote in the city council (he does not participate in their deliberations). With one exception, he appoints no city department heads. He appoints the police chief, and thus the quality of law enforcement is as good or bad as he decides.*

For years, Minneapolis had been wide open. Prostitution, gambling, liquor sales to minors and after-hours joints flourished openly in violation of the law. Since responsibility for those conditions rested on the mayor, I had inevitably made law enforcement the central issue of the campaign. I began late in 1944 to seek out people who had indicated, through civic activity or some statement, interest in changing the quality of the Police Department in Minneapolis. Among the various people I talked to, two were of special importance: Bradshaw Mintener, a Republican civic leader and businessman,[1] and Ed Ryan, then a police detective who lived near me in Southeast Minneapolis.

Mintener's value was twofold. He had a lot of information about corruption and he was able to translate my honest interest in doing something about it to other civic leaders.

* While I didn't have any real power as mayor, the assumption of power can be as great as the fact of power.

Ryan was able to confirm information from Fred Gates and Mintener, but even more importantly he gave me hope that the system could be changed.

Some of those I talked to, including police officers who were themselves involved (Ryan was not), indicated that petty graft was widespread. The cop on the beat or a member of the morals squad would be taken care of by a bartender or an owner who was staying open after hours. It wasn't big stuff, but it pointed to considerable corruption at higher levels. I was never able to determine how much money was moving, but it was clear that owners of gambling houses or brothels operated as casually as they would have run a neighborhood grocery—and with better police protection and security. They stood little danger of being robbed or burglarized.

To change that situation, I needed a tough, untouchable man as chief. In searching the Police Department, I found possibly the most effective police officer I have ever known, Eugene Bernath, a homicide detective who spoke with a heavy Swiss accent. His accent never clouded his meaning, however: "You know, Mr. Mayor, you get just the kind of town you want. If the mayor isn't on the take, or if he hasn't any special friends that he wants to protect, the Police Department will enforce the law. It's all what you want. You tell me what you want and that's the way it will be."†

I decided that the choice of chief ought to involve other people. I had set up a Law Enforcement Committee, made up of four people each from labor, business, and the general community, and a chairman. I had involved them in interviewing prospective chiefs and said I was not going to name the chief until they all agreed. And they did not agree for the longest time. It was two o'clock in the morning of July 4, just a few days after I had been sworn in. Twelve of the thirteen members were for Ed Ryan. Only Robert Wishart, head of the Hennepin County CIO, was holding out.

Bob Wishart was a sturdy labor negotiator who built strong unions because he could rally people to whatever banner he was

† When Ed Ryan was selected chief, Gene Bernath became head of the morals squad and later chief of detectives. True to his word, he gave me the kind of city I wanted, an honest one.

carrying. In many ways, he was ahead of his time, sensitive to the injustices imposed upon the poor and the black. His determination to improve their lot led him into the Communist party apparatus. He played the common role of the front man: a friendly, co-operative leader of liberal persuasion who somehow would always lead his followers to pro-Soviet resolutions and attitudes.

Where there was no real revolutionary activity, words took on increased importance, and Wishart was good at finding the words he wanted. But he was not doctrinaire, and apparently became tired of his manipulated and manipulating role. When I met him, he was trying to disengage himself from the Communists. Not quite ready to leave his old associates, he was playing both sides.

I had put him on the committee because I liked him and trusted his basic decency and good sense.‡ But that night in the mayor's office he stood adamantly alone against Ryan. Finally, I asked him to walk with me out of the office into the corridor. "Bob, I know what's bothering you. You figure Ryan worked too closely with the FBI during these past couple of years. I know this bothers some of your friends and maybe some of your union members, but I tell you Ed Ryan is not a witch-hunter, he's not anti-labor. He's honest and I need him and you ought to be for him."

We argued. He squirmed some but said, "All right. I'll go back and recommend him." Wishart barely survived the attacks on him within the Hennepin County CIO Council. He wavered, almost backtracked, finally stood firm.

I needed every bit of firm support I could get. For over a month, the City Council refused to confirm Ryan. They fought other structural changes I wanted to make on the level of inspectors and deputy inspectors. I had ventured into the sacrosanct area of co-operation between some members of the council and the gambling and liquor forces. There were moments during that month when it seemed hopeless to continue the battle. The council had the authority, even if I had the responsibility.

By getting on the radio and mobilizing public pressure, I finally got Ryan confirmed and some of what we needed

‡ Ultimately, I would appoint him to the Board of Public Welfare, where he served well.

changed within the Police Department. (But it was not until my second term, when we had the chance to defeat some of the more recalcitrant aldermen, that we could do what common sense and good police work demanded.)

Law enforcement and the Police Department consumed much of my time during the first year in office. To dramatize my interest, I often rode a squad car late at night. After speaking at a banquet or meeting, I'd find a squad car, ride with the officers, listen to the radio calls, check in at the central headquarters in the basement of the City Hall to see how the calls were being handled.

I had seen little of the grimness and misery that existed in urban areas. What poverty and deprivation I had seen was largely in South Dakota in the midst of settled, rural surroundings. (I never got that close to black poverty in Louisiana.) Miseries hide themselves more easily in the openness and distances of the country. In contrast, the city at night, dark and anonymous, discloses its angry and ugly parts. But the sights that brought gagging revulsion to me had already created a protective indifference in the police. The scenes repeated night after night: the constant drunk, lying dirty and soiled in a doorway, a muscatel wine bottle, "Sneaky Pete," next to him empty; the violent domestic quarrel, the beaten face, eyes virtually disappearing in puffiness; the surly juvenile delinquent, frightened and arrogant at the same time, foul-mouthed and swaggering, eager to fight, quickly depressed when subdued.

Minneapolis mayors had never interfered with the livelihood of those people who ran the prostitution, gambling, and illegal liquor activities. When I closed up the town, there was first surprise, then anger.

One night the anger showed itself clearly and dangerously. I had been at a meeting with several aldermen and offered them a ride to another meeting they had to attend. I asked the police driver, who usually escorted me to my door, to just drop me off and take the aldermen on to their destination.

The street light near my home was out, but I didn't think it significant. I waved good-by to the car and walked quickly to the door, which Muriel had locked from the inside. As she was opening the door, three shots rang out. I ducked inside, wondering aloud, "Why would anyone shoot at me?" Being more aggravated than scared, after calling the police I went back outside to poke around in the bushes to see if I could find footprints or the used shells. It was a dumb thing to do, but I had decided that the shots were intended to scare me, not kill me—unless the gunman had been one of the world's worst shots.

From time to time, so the men knew my interest was real, I'd be at the central headquarters or in a precinct station when the shifts changed, around midnight. I did not interfere in the running of the department, since neither Ryan nor his successor, Glenn MacLean, could have tolerated that, but my presence was an indication that no hanky-panky would be permitted.

There are so many little ways in which police work can become corrupt work. It isn't always the major scandal, the big graft. Everyone, for example, talks about law enforcement. But members of the clergy would come in to see me. The denomination changed, but the message remained the same: "Well, Mayor, so and so is a great fellow. I know he has been picked up for ——. But he has such a nice family and a good job. I hope you won't press charges against him."

Then there were friends of mine in the labor movement who thought that lax law enforcement was good for the city. And members of the business community thought so, too. "It means more jobs. It means more profits. It makes Minneapolis a better convention city." There was an endless little pilgrimage of the most unlikely people to my office and to the chief's, pleading for "just a little more consideration, a little less rigidity." But this is an area of government in which compromise is neither possible nor reasonable. Crime and corruption grow on each other. The payoff is pervasive, corrosive. When a mayor shrugs his shoulders, someone else's hand turns palm up. Fortunately, most people really do want fair and impartial law enforcement, and they made my decisions easy ones.

I had to change habits within the Police Department. For a long time, police had played along with the dominant liquor forces (the Syndicate and the Combination), who illegally held a number of liquor licenses—to the harm of independent operators. For whatever reason, independents were often trapped into a violation, which meant someone got a payoff to quash the charge or the place was shut down for a time or the license was permanently revoked.

Two men who had opposed me during both the 1943 and the 1945 elections (thinking I was a crusader who would close down every tavern, beer hall, and nightclub in town to enhance my political reputation) ran a decent restaurant, the 620 Club, on Hennepin Avenue. The police entrapped them by getting a mature-looking boy who was under twenty-one to buy a drink. When the bartender served the boy, he was arrested. When I heard about it, I called in the arresting officer, who nonchalantly admitted it was a plant. I said to him, "Listen, my name is Humphrey, not Hitler. We don't use that kind of tactics." We dropped the charge and the word went through the department that entrapment was out.

Other habits were harder to break. Police departments have always had some officers who dislike minorities, a problem that has not yet been solved. But in 1945 few were even discussing the problem, much less seeking solutions. In Minneapolis, rampant prejudice was clearly apparent in attitudes toward Negroes and Indians, and to a lesser extent toward Jews.

On one occasion, a traffic policeman in handing out a ticket called the violator a "dirty Jew." I suspended him for fifteen days without pay. I tried with far less success to stop the verbal abuse of Negroes.

I asked the University of Minnesota Center for Continuation Study to set up a course in human relations for our police officers. More importantly, I suppose, I tried to create an environment in the rest of our municipal activities to lessen the impact of police prejudice. I sponsored civil rights legislation and ordinances, and we passed the first enforceable municipal Fair Employment Practices Commission in the nation.

While I tried to change the attitudes of the police by education and chastisement, I tried, too, to upgrade the image that the policemen and their families had of their work. I spoke to the wives of the officers, telling them what I hoped to do—namely, to make ours the most honest and effective police force in the country, taking away the stigma attached to the entire force because of the dishonesty of some. We increased the number of police, raised salaries, and made the Minneapolis department the first one in the United States on a forty-hour week.

At one point, I called in all the people who held bar licenses and told them I needed increased revenues to pay the police more. I proposed to them that their license fees be increased. "I don't want to have a fight. If you run an honest place, you no longer need to worry about a shakedown. You don't have to pay off anybody any more and it's going to stay that way. I want you to go upstairs and testify for an increase in your own license fees from $1,100 to $1,300. I'd rather have you pay a little more at the City Treasurer's office than to pay much more to a mayor or the chief or the cop on the beat or the head of the morals squad." They went upstairs and we got the increased fees and salaries.

I tried one other way of involving the community in police work which had, I think, good effects, both on the policemen and the community. In various neighborhoods, we started a community council of representative citizens. When a patrolman was assigned to a precinct for his six-month probationary period, he knew that the local community council would be asked to evaluate his performance before he became a full-fledged member of the force.

But being mayor is an empty honor if you let the charter limit your work to the Police Department. Neither my glands nor my view of government permitted me to stop with that.

I tried to be the voice of the community, focusing attention on the scope and nature of the problems of our postwar city. I tried to present alternative solutions and to mobilize public support for some of them; above all, I helped try to create a sense of community to push an apathetic and sometimes hostile city government to action. I needed to reach beyond the normal structure of government if I was to do anything useful. I needed the consent and support of the people. And I got it.

A number of mayor's commissions involved the best talent I could find at the university, in business and the professions, and within labor.[2] The commissions were more than window dressing. They raised their own money, published reports, and lobbied for their program in the city council and through the media to the general public.

With so little authority, I needed the commissions as an almost parallel and unofficial form of government. I learned many lessons in democratic procedure and persuasion that I could not have learned as a more powerful mayor.

16. BRINGING A PARTY TOGETHER

Cities in war years, though untouched by bullets and bombs, go through odd and awkward adjustments. Men leave who are in their prime: their twenties, thirties, forties. The men who remain are, for the most part, the young and the old. Marriages and families are delayed or interrupted.

To Minneapolis, crowded already with women left alone, had come many more young women from the rural areas to work at the defense plants, to fill in the jobs from which men had gone to war. Everything hovered in impermanence; no one seemed to be where he had been or where he was going to be. Our train stations filled and emptied and filled again, almost imperceptibly, with waves of uniforms, the dark pews in the waiting rooms becoming home for soldiers and sailors—stretched out asleep, or sitting up, sleepy heads hanging, chins on chests. And along such main streets as Hennepin Avenue, uniformed young men and some women, in desperate exuberance, were burning up leave time at home.

In home after home, a mother, a father, or a wife bereft because a son or husband had been killed, wept through a moment of public recognition and honor to an endless time of private lament. Japanese relocated from their West Coast homes read letters from their Nisei sons who were training at Fort Snelling for service in Europe. Schools like Macalester College and the University of Minnesota took young men untrained for war and made them into military officers.

Underneath the football stands at the university's Memorial Stadium, dedicated to the dead of another war, conscientious objectors like Max Kampelman[1] became voluntary guinea pigs for starvation experiments, eating less and less, running to collapse on treadmills—dreaming of candy bars—so that information gathered there might help fighting men survive.

And when the war was over, everything changed: The conscientious objectors started to eat regularly again; some Japanese-Americans remained in the Twin Cities, some went back West to rejoin families; some of the women went back to the farms, and more remained to welcome and marry the returning veterans. The trains disgorged men on their way home to places in Minnesota, North and South Dakota, eastern Montana, western Wisconsin, northern Iowa. Terminal-leave pay in hand, safe and free, they moved homeward, to cities without sufficient housing, to schools ill-equipped to absorb new kinds of students under the G. I. Bill of Rights, to a society wrestling with readjustment and relocation. And for those who were interested, a society with new political realities.

The years immediately following the war were marked by an increasing conflict between a small but vigorous Communist left and the liberal-labor social-democratic left.

The conflict had, of course, been there before; but the changes in world power, in hoped-for spheres of influence, came so rapidly after the war that the conflict seemed to accelerate—within the labor movement, within the newly formed American Veterans Committee, and within the Democratic party in some states, including Minnesota.

The Communist mind in America, no matter how brilliant or creative, had certain limitations—at least as I saw it in operation from the 1930s on. It had been devoted not to solving America's problems so much as to following Soviet direction. The Stalinists had been concerned about the depravities of Hitler and Mussolini, but changed their views—not on America's needs but on relations between the Soviet Union and Nazi Germany. They had been interested in racial problems in the thirties, but primarily to the extent that those problems could be exploited in an attack on the system. They had been concerned about economic conditions, as many of us were but, again, their aim was to destroy the system, not to heal it.

My disdain for the American Communists grew almost as much out of their flip-flops as from their exploitation of issues and people. The week before the Nazis attacked the Soviet Union, for example, the Farmer-Labor newspaper, *Minnesota Leader,* carried a headline story calling the war an "imperialist war" and condemning Roosevelt for aid to Britain. That was on Wednesday. On Saturday night, Muriel and I were out on a Mississippi River excursion boat, dancing and living it up on a nickel glass of beer, when the German attack on the Soviet Union became known.

When we got in to shore and heard the news, I said to Muriel, "Well, the left wing in this state will change its tune immediately." The next Wednesday, the imperialist war had disappeared and the *Leader* headlines said that the United States must join the war.

The Communists were simply captive totalitarian minds slipping from position to contrary position as extraneous doctrine directed. That separated them from the realities of American politics, for the American people are not dogmatists or doctrinaire, but pragmatists. Ideology is foreign to most Americans. As a result, the Communist appeal had relatively little impact on the workers, the farmers, or the blacks.[2]

But the Communists were often on the right side of a good issue, even if for the wrong reasons. When they found a good issue, an exploitable event, a victimized person, they grabbed the opportunity to ride it. Since it was clear, I think, even to the Communist leaders themselves that they couldn't succeed as Communists, they were pragmatic enough to move in on an established party, trying to get their own people into positions of leadership, where they could pass the resolutions they wanted, direct activities of a political party to their own goals.

What successes they had in Minnesota were the result not of exceptional brilliance but, rather, of a steadfastness, a willingness to stay up later than anyone else, to stall a meeting, to grab onto a social issue with broad appeal, to stay together while they divided others. If the Communists wanted to influence public policy and exercise some influence on public officials, they had to control the DFL party.

Beginning in 1946, the local left wing—some Communists,

some not—began more aggressively to take political pot shots at me. My support of President Truman turned them meanly against me. The meanness boiled into hate when I helped organize the Americans for Democratic Action, an anti-Communist liberal organization particularly offensive to them.

The DFL convention that year was held at the St. Paul Hotel. Muriel and I arrived in time for me to give the keynote speech, unaware of the control the left wing had taken. The sergeants-at-arms appointed by the left would not let Muriel into the hall. Over the objections of the doorkeeper, I had my police-officer driver escort her in. Once inside, we were met with catcalls—"Fascist," "Warmonger,"—boos and hisses. I had arrived at the convention recalling my central role and success at the 1944 fusion convention, self-satisfied as the leading elected DFL'er in the state, and suddenly there were boos. I never got to make my keynote speech.

We had lost control. The left wing was on the move. The war was over. The Soviet Union had taken its stand against the United States. All the spirit of friendship and unity had vanished, and the local comrades had switched their tactics from being loving, gentle, kind unifiers into being ornery, obstreperous, mean dividers and conquerors.

Then I relearned another lesson: Our conventions ran over Saturday and Sunday. Many people had to leave early on Sunday afternoon to drive back home, some of them as much as three hundred miles. Farmers who had a neighbor milk the cows for them on Saturday night and Sunday morning had to get home for the evening milking. City people wanted to get back to their families, to get ready for the next week's work. But the left wing stayed on. They used their old tactic of keeping the convention in session very late. Then, when enough of our people had gone, they modified the state party constitution, increasing the size of the executive committee, filling those offices with their people to get control of the party structure.

When I finally realized what was happening, I went to find Bob Wishart. Bob had by then become something of a friend, but he was still playing with the left wing, unable to make the break. I told him I thought the manipulation going on was a breach of faith and that I was not going to watch the party be

destroyed by the ideologues. We finally agreed that I would select two officers to maintain balance on the executive committee.
I chose Orville Freeman and Eugenie Anderson.[3] Eugenie became one of the vice chairmen and Orv, after some negotiation,
became secretary. The proposal was that he become party treasurer, and he thought it might be a good idea, but I convinced
him that, there being no money in the party and little prospect
of any, what we needed was somebody to keep the records and
somebody who could make statements in the name of the party
as secretary.

We had lost control, but we had two able people in important
positions. I think we got agreement on these two because the left
wing underestimated both of them. Orville was young and unknown to most of them. They did not realize how smart, tough,
and persevering he was. Eugenie was a feminine, soft-spoken
woman. The left figured that they could overwhelm her, but
along with that femininity was a firm, tough-minded quality they
couldn't handle.

But even with the two of them on the executive committee, it
was clear that the party was in the hands of the left. Increasingly, I became their target. Increasingly, we fought back.

One night during that period, I spoke to a small group at the
Curtis Hotel in Minneapolis and said, "We're not going to let the
political philosophy of the Democratic Farmer-Labor party be
dictated from the Kremlin. You can be a liberal without being a
Communist, and you can be a progressive without being a Communist sympathizer, and we're a liberal progressive party out
here. We're not going to let this left-wing Communist ideology
be the prevailing force, because the people of this state won't accept it, and what's more, it's wrong."

The speech made news, and the factional lines were even more
clearly and rigidly drawn than they had been. From that time
through the 1948 convention, a "them and us" psychology
affected everything.

In the spring of 1947, as my term as mayor was ending, I decided it was time to move into high gear to eliminate Communist
influence in the DFL. My own re-election was not jeopardized
by the battles, but the harassment was a tiresome drain on the
growth of a potentially strong political party. It had to stop.

Philip Murray, national president of the CIO, was the person who could help, so I flew to Pittsburgh to see him. The Northwest Airlines DC-4, slow and bouncy, brought me tired to an exhilarating meeting. Murray and I met for five hours that evening at the William Penn Hotel, talking until past midnight.

I told him I was about to take on a number of his local and state leaders, that they twisted to and fro with the Soviet line, that their main objective seemed to be to embarrass President Truman and United States policies, and that I, as a local Democrat, was constantly attacked by them.

Murray's response was direct. He said, in essence, that he had been looking for someone to take the lead, that he understood my position, and that he would co-operate in running the Communist leadership out of the CIO in Minnesota.[4]

With Murray's help on the union level, we could also remove them from power and leadership in the DFL. The most serious impediment to making the DFL the majority party in Minnesota was soon gone.

My re-election campaign gave us another boost. I carried all thirteen wards, winning by fifty thousand votes with solid labor support and virtually all the business groups behind me, too.[5] I was happy as mayor, but clearly it was not a lifetime career.

In the winter of 1947–48, a group of business leaders, most of them Republicans, invited me to a breakfast meeting ostensibly to talk about the city but, in fact, to urge me to remain as mayor and not to run for the Senate.

They pledged their support, including a fund to cover some of the special expenses that being in public office brought with it, a kind of supplement to the mayor's income of six thousand dollars a year, and a small expense account.

None of the men in that room considered their offer corrupting. They said I was doing a good job as mayor and that the city needed continuity.* I refused their offer. It might have been good business. It was certainly bad politics and morally wrong.

By 1948, newspapers in Minnesota had begun to describe me as ambitious, as though it were a sin. I thought lack of ambition

---

* Undoubtedly, though it was unspoken, some of those men also wanted to guarantee Senator Joseph Ball, the Republican incumbent, only nominal opposition.

was sinful and that a politician without it was ready for retirement. I was not ready to retire and I was ambitious to do more
things better, to make democracy and the DFL work.

While many things remained to be done in Minneapolis, I
began to feel restricted, limited to a local scene when my own interests were increasingly national. I had by then helped organize
the national ADA with such people as Walter Reuther, Leon
Henderson, David Dubinsky, Reinhold Niebuhr, and Eleanor
Roosevelt. The Cold War and international events seemed more
compelling than veterans' housing and liquor licenses.

We had actually started planning for 1948 shortly after we had
been whipped in 1946, when the left wing controlled enough
votes and enough leadership to dominate our state DFL convention. They retained control, but our faction determined to out-
think, outorganize, and outvote them.

We packed our supporters into each precinct and county convention and were able to elect our people to delegate and officer
positions. We had begun in Minneapolis' Second Ward, the area
around the University of Minnesota, where most of us lived,
using as our vehicle a group we called the DFL Independent
Voter. We began organizing ADA chapters, too, as an additional
method of finding people whose political philosophy was liberal
but anti-Communist.

Outside the university area within the Twin Cities, we largely
depended on the cleaned-up labor movement, and outstate we
found farmers and farm-co-operative leaders who were not
aligned with the more radical agrarian traditions.

While we had put together a structure for political action in
1944, it was not until 1948 that we were able to really flesh out
the physical structure with widespread citizen participation.

That participation was essential. As strong as the party was
becoming, as strong as I personally seemed, my nomination was
by no means certain. Minnesota politics is not amenable to
bossism.

Many of the traditions and much of the law governing politics
in Minnesota derive from the agrarian radicalism of the early-
twentieth century, and to some extent to the farm reform movements in the late-nineteenth. Its politics, like those of Wisconsin
and especially North Dakota, are less party oriented than most

other states. Until 1974, the Minnesota legislature was elected on a non-partisan basis; municipal elections were non-partisan; there was no registration of voters by party; in a primary, a voter could vote in either party's elections and could shift from party to party in each succeeding primary without forewarning.

And the caucus system leading up to the state convention is wide open. Every other spring, in election years, anyone can attend publicly announced meetings, held locally by neighborhood precincts in the cities, by township in the country, to elect delegates to the county conventions, which in turn select delegates for the district and ultimately the state convention.

State conventions alternated between the Twin Cities and a town outstate. In 1948, we met in Brainerd, a small town in north-central Minnesota. There were placid lakes, birds warbling in pines and birch, squirrels scurrying among the elm and maple minutes from the hall where hundreds of delegates shrilly and angrily contested for control of the DFL party. So intense, so hostile was our battle, that we could have been in the bottom of a coal mine. The outside world didn't exist as we fought and ultimately, inevitably, broke apart.

The remaining left-wingers and their friends walked out and the animosities of that moment continued in some instances for twenty years and more. We stayed, and control was ours.

Orville Freeman became state DFL chairman, Eugenie Anderson became national committeewoman, and I was nominated for the Senate.[6]

Our attention then turned to the Democratic National Convention, to be held in Philadelphia in July.

17. THE BRIGHT SUNSHINE OF HUMAN RIGHTS

In Minnesota, we were called moderates or even right wing by some. But the Minnesota delegation to the National Democratic Convention in 1948 was liberal-left in regular-party terms. Many of us had been active in the formation of the Americans for Democratic Action, and we went to Philadelphia unsure of whom we would support for President.[1]

James Roosevelt, a leader in ADA, had traveled across the country urging the draft of General Dwight Eisenhower, whose party preference was unknown. Eleanor Roosevelt herself had called several times to discuss it, and I had toyed with the idea, saying publicly it was something we might very well pursue. More talk focused on traditional liberals, however, such as Justice William O. Douglas and Senator Claude Pepper of Florida. By the time we got to Philadelphia, we were under pressure as a delegation to support anybody but Harry Truman.

Much of the pressure came from people associated with Franklin Roosevelt, old New Dealers, now new ADA'ers. They felt that their politics were purer and their ideas better than those of Truman's people. This, of course, caused conflict with the Truman supporters, some of whom had also worked for Roosevelt.

The ADA rented a fraternity house at the University of Pennsylvania, and it was there that a number of us[2] gathered from time to time to discuss the nomination, the platform, and the credential fights that are common to all conventions. At one meeting, there were seventy-five or eighty people, many still holding out. After a number of speeches, I suggested that it was ridiculous for us to delay making a commitment, that Truman was the incumbent President, and that no convention was going to reject him. I proposed that we support him, and declared that I, at least, was going to do that. Sol Hoffman, the president of the Upholsterers Union, followed in urging such a course, and others then concurred.

Much of the support for Truman was not highly enthusiastic but was based on the inevitability of his nomination. My support for him had some of that, but I think it had more. I felt that Truman was a good President, that he was in his own style carrying out much of the liberal program of the New Deal.

As his nomination became more certain, the issue of the civil rights plank took over our thoughts.

President Truman himself had helped make civil rights the central issue, though many of his convention supporters opposed moving too far, thus risking offense to the South. Truman had appointed a presidential Civil Rights Commission, which delivered its report in 1947. The report, *We Hold These Truths*, urged broad legislation in the civil rights areas. I, for one, had studied it and believed it. So had most of those in our ADA meetings. What liberals wanted was a platform statement that went beyond the vague statements of earlier conventions and clearly supported the Truman civil rights measures. I became the spokesman, by conviction and by the fact that I served on the platform committee.

Another fact motivated me. The Republicans at their convention just a few weeks earlier had adopted a relatively forward-looking civil rights plank. If we had been mild, the Republicans might have seized the issue by our default. I felt that was ideologically absurd and politically stupid. So I came down hard on the side of a strong civil rights plank, both as a matter of conscience and as an imperative of political pragmatism.

The weekend before the convention and on Monday and Tuesday, the convention's first days, the platform committee met behind closed doors. There, Andrew Biemiller, then a Wisconsin congressman and spokesman for the labor movement, and I, led the fight, which was hot, long, and angry. The party elders argued that we were going to split the party by causing a southern walkout—and thus elect the Republicans. They said the 1944 platform of FDR should be good enough for all Democrats. At one point, the Democratic leader of the Senate, Scott Lucas of Illinois, pointed at me, called me a "pipsqueak," and accused me of wanting to redo Franklin Roosevelt's work and deny the wishes of the current President of the United States.

The arguments and name-calling went on all day Tuesday. Finally, the Humphrey-Biemiller plank was voted down by about seventy to thirty. I explicitly reserved the right to present a minority plank to the floor. Yet there were those in the committee who felt double-crossed when I ultimately led the floor fight.

It was a painful decision to do so. I did not want to tear the party apart. I knew that the traditional thing to do was to make a gesture toward what was right in terms of civil rights, but not so tough a gesture that the South would leave the Democratic coalition. Events on the convention floor, unlike those inside the platform committee, would make our party differences explicit before the entire nation.

The appeal to party loyalty and the desire to avoid anything that would make the election of Harry Truman more difficult gave me real concern. Further, enough people had told me that my own political career would be ruined that I was selfishly concerned about that, too.

But I meant what I was to say in my speech: that the time had arrived for the Democratic party to get out of the shadow of states' rights and walk forthrightly into the bright sunshine of human rights.

For me personally and for the party, the time had come to suffer whatever the consequences.

But it was sobering, nevertheless, since we were opposed by all of the party hierarchy: the President (so we were told); national party Chairman J. Howard McGrath; convention Chairman Rayburn; Senate Democratic Leader Scott Lucas; the platform committee chairman, Senator Francis Meyers of Pennsylvania; and many others. These were not Southerners and they were not racists. They were moderates who wanted to keep the party together and elect Harry Truman President. So did I.

In retrospect, the decision should have been easy. The plank was morally right and politically right. But it was a decision filled with anxiety, and not to be made alone. I went back to our Minnesota delegation and talked it over and over with them. They encouraged me to do what I wanted to do—take the question to the floor. I talked to my labor friends, where I got a mixed reaction. They were more interested in economic than civil rights issues. Finally, I talked to my father, who was again a South Dakota delegate.

At first he, too, was against presenting the plank to the convention. In my fourth-floor room of the Bellevue Stratford Hotel, we went through all the arguments, for and against. Finally, Dad said, "This may tear the party apart, but if you feel strongly, then you've got to go with it. You can't run away from your conscience, son. You've got to go with it."

I asked, "What do you think will happen?" He said quietly and with resignation, implying disaster, "I don't know. But you'll at least have the eight votes of the South Dakota delegation."

Later, I talked at great length with Muriel—not only about the plank and its chances of passage, but about what the consequences of introducing it would be for my career and our future plans. Clearly, it would have grave repercussions on our lives: it could make me an outcast to many people; and it could even end my chances for a life of public service.

But in the face of that threat to our future, Muriel stood firm. As she had so many times in the past, she reassured me that I was doing the right thing, that I had to carry out what I had begun. Her strong faith once again calmed my fears.

In addition to private meetings, there were larger ones—again at the ADA's rented fraternity house, and finally an all-night meeting in my hotel room. It was almost five o'clock Wednesday morning when we decided precisely what to do: we would propose a strong plank but we would introduce it with solid praise for President Truman's civil rights program.

Less than ten hours were available to line up support and for me to work on a speech. Andy Biemiller called Speaker Rayburn, the convention chairman, and told him we were going to offer a minority report on civil rights. Rayburn said the Southerners were going to offer a state's rights one, too. He explained that he thought the defeat of the Southerners' plank would balance off ours and bring victory to the "moderate" administration plank.

As I sat on the platform that afternoon, speech in hand, big yellow Truman button on my suit, I was still filled with doubts about the effect of what I was going to do. I didn't want to split the party; I didn't want to ruin my career, to go from mayor to "pipsqueak" to oblivion. But I did want to make the case for a clear-cut commitment to a strong civil rights program. Sitting near me on the platform was Ed Flynn, boss of the Bronx, and I showed him what we were proposing, almost in an apologetic way.

"Look," I said, "here's what we're asking. It isn't too much. We think we ought to make the fight. I'm sure we don't really have much chance to carry it, but we ought to make the fight. We surely would welcome your advice."

He read the plank, looked at me, and said, "You go ahead, young man. We should have done this a long time ago. We've got to do it. Go ahead. We'll back you."

He promised New York's votes, and said he'd try to bring in Illinois through Colonel Jack Arvey and Pennsylvania through David Lawrence. When we presented our minority plank, I knew we weren't so far behind as we'd thought the night before. Biemiller read the plank and I gave my speech—my first to any such important gathering.[3] Even though I still feared we would lose, I felt that the speech was reaching the heart of the Democratic party, carried across the country as it was by radio.

When I finished, the demonstration in support began. There in the Illinois delegation was Paul Douglas seizing the banner and leading Adlai Stevenson and Colonel Arvey and Richard Daley, a relatively young man and upcoming politician. Soon there was Pennsylvania and then New York and Massachusetts and Connecticut—the whole eastern seaboard—and then California. Ed Flynn was delivering, and the issue itself seemed to persuade others.

A demonstration, when it is organized, is fun to watch; when it is spontaneous, it is even better: the massed bodies surging, pushing through the aisles and in the pit beneath the platform, state signs swaying with the bodies, smiling faces blurred, the few heads you recognize among the many you don't.

Then the voting started on the states' rights plank. It was defeated. We moved to the Humphrey-Biemiller plank. The vote was close from the beginning, the lead shifting through the state roll call. But we were not alone. When it came to South Dakota's turn on the call, my father stood up and said, "I am Hubert Humphrey, Sr. I cast South Dakota's eight votes for the plank." When it came down to Biemiller's Wisconsin delegation, we were moving into the lead—and Wisconsin voted its twenty-four votes for us. I knew then we had won, and jumped to my feet. The auditorium filled with applause and cheers. When the vote was announced, we had indeed won: 651½ votes to 582½.

Delegates from Mississippi, Alabama, and a few other southern states stood up as though to leave—but Speaker Rayburn quickly declared the meeting recessed. When we reassembled two hours later to vote for the presidential nominee, thirty-five southern delegates, led by Governor J. Strom Thurmond of South Carolina, walked from the hall into a rainstorm.

One can explain the victory at that convention in part by conscience, in part by political realism. Ed Flynn and David Lawrence and Jack Arvey and John Bailey of Connecticut probably supported us because they wanted something to attract the votes of liberals, Negroes, minorities, and labor. Maybe they wanted to protect us from the appeal on the left of Henry Wallace's Progressive party. Perhaps there were those in the northern urban wing who hadn't forgotten that the South deserted Al Smith in 1928 and didn't mind offending them in a kind of get-even gesture twenty years later.

As I came to know the party bosses better, I found that they agreed with the spirit, the principle, the rightness of our plank. They reflected, and our victory reflected, a deep current running in the party and in the country that would make the next quarter century one filled with turmoil and triumph.

But, that night, all we knew was that we, a group of young liberals, had beaten the leadership of the party and led them closer to where they ought to have been.

As soon as the convention ended, we took the train home, exhausted but exuberant. I was thirty-seven years old, and not very long from teaching and graduate school. I had taken on our establishment and won. It was a heady feeling. But it confirmed something I felt and hoped. You *could* stand for a principle in politics and you could move an unwilling party toward a necessary goal. How slowly and with what difficulty you kept it moving I was yet to learn.

It took us a day on the train to get home. We arrived on Saturday afternoon at three o'clock at the Great Northern Station in Minneapolis. Like many stations built when railroads were important for passenger transportation, it was cavernous, huge arches in a high-ceilinged waiting room, and that day it was packed with two thousand people, organized by Fred Gates.

My friends, my supporters, our party had gathered: young people, the labor movement, the traditional liberal groups in our state: Farmers Union members, leaders of the Jewish community, and a few Negroes.

Waving homemade signs, they were a cheering, waving, smiling crowd who lifted me to their shoulders for a two-block march to an eighty-car caravan that honked its way down Hennepin Avenue. It was the DFL party on the move.

There was less than two months from our return to the primary election, about three and a half to the general. Orville Freeman organized and directed the campaign while Fred Gates and I traveled, on my first state-wide campaign, to every corner of the state.*

We had little money and I made up for it with travel, talk, determination, and enthusiasm. Politics can often be a grind, but when you are unknown and it appears that you're going to have to get your votes virtually one at a time, it can be overwhelming. We just never let up.

My opponent, Senator Joseph Ball, had been a journalist before being appointed to fill a seat left vacant by the death of Senator Ernest Lundeen. He had been a kind of liberal, broke with his party to support Roosevelt in 1944, but got more conservative to regain ground lost by that act. He and Senator Robert Taft worked closely, and he supported the Taft-Hartley bill, thus enraging labor and providing me with political support.

* There was rarely time for lunch or dinner. Day after day, Freddie would get a chocolate malted milk and an American cheese sandwich on white bread and set it on the back seat in a bag, and I would gulp it all down as we drove on.

On September 14, primary-election day, I carried the Democratic nomination with 204,175 votes against a left-wing Wallace supporter. Ball drew 269,594 for the Republican nomination. Things looked bleak, so we charged ahead even harder.

President Truman seemed to start with even worse problems and, according to the press, nothing good was happening. Yet as I traveled around the state, it appeared to me that an undercurrent of support began to flow—ripple, wave, torrent. He could win. So could I.

We did. Truman carried Minnesota and the nation. I received 729,494 votes to Senator Ball's 485,801. I was United States senator-elect.[4]

In December, before we moved to Washington, I spent a day there to attend the Gridiron Dinner, a prestigious white-tie affair put on by Washington journalists. When I arrived, I laid out my suit and stiff shirt, the wing collar and white tie, and stepped back to admire it.

As I dressed, all went well until I tried to get the collar attached. I couldn't do it, and I got more and more nervous and fumbling. Finally, in desperation, I called for a bell boy and asked him to help me dress. He had no more experience than I and the two of us wrestled with the collar and studs and tie. By the time I was dressed, my spirits, as well as my collar, were slightly wrinkled, but I marched stiffly off to dinner, fearful that if I bent the whole outfit would come apart.

The next day, as I stood outside the hotel waving for a cab, unable to stop one, I thought back to the mayor's car and driver, symbols of the security I had found in the small world I knew.

Suddenly, mingled with a sense that I had arrived was a sense of being alone. In a bizarre, intuitive flash, I knew I would be alone in the Senate, tested and judged not by cab drivers perhaps, but by men of power. I wondered whether I could survive, whether I could take it, whether I would make it.

BOOK TWO

ON THE BANKS OF
THE POTOMAC

18. MY PRINCIPLES OFFENDED, MY PERSONALITY ENRAGED

Washington is a beautiful city filled with monuments and fountains. Verdant parkways and wide streets separate public buildings which, if not always beautiful, are impressive. In the spring, forsythia and dogwood and, briefly, cherry blossoms fill the city with color; later there are roses and azaleas and lilacs.

It is, of course, also filled with history—the White House, the Capitol, Ford's Theatre. Plaques and monuments everywhere tell you of life and death. Here Lincoln was shot and here he died. Here John Hay lived, here Henry Adams, here Stephen Decatur. There was even a plaque in the Roger Smith Hotel, on the tenth floor, that read FRANKLIN D. ROOSEVELT LIVED IN THESE ROOMS WHEN HE WAS ASSISTANT SECRETARY OF THE NAVY, 1916.

In 1949, Washington was also a city more southern than many southern cities, segregated along racial lines as strictly and harshly as almost any place in the country. Its hotels and restaurants, its washrooms and drinking fountains were all part of the old southern pattern: whites here, Negroes there. Soon after I was sworn in as senator, I took a Negro member of my staff, Cyril King,[1] to lunch in the Senators' Dining Room in the Capitol. We were stopped by the embarrassed head waiter, a Negro himself, and told that we could not be served. It had never occurred to me that the color of a senator's guest was anyone else's business, and I insisted that Cyril and I were going to eat together and there. We did, and no guest of mine was ever again questioned. It was clear, however, that there was no sanctuary from segregation in our nation's capital.

Washington was separated, too, along class and economic lines. There were the old families and the "good families": the rich. There were the government civil servants, and there were the servants who were black. Washington had no heavy industry and thus virtually no labor movement of its own. Essentially, its only business was government, tourism, and real estate, plus the mercantile trades that any city must have. In a city that was not a city, a district without home rule, the board of trade and the real estate board became the city government by leave of the House and Senate's District of Columbia committees. Unfortunately, the Washington Board of Trade, which is similar to chambers of commerce elsewhere, was one of the more conservative groups of its kind in the country. And the real estate board was even more conservative than the board of trade.

So the city's physical beauty was marred by a social indifference, by ugly traditions. I knew none of this. To me, viewing it from Minnesota as a senator-elect, it seemed like perfection on the Potomac. I arrived in Washington with all the excitement of a kid in a new neighborhood. How much I was a small-town kid in a big town, how hostile my new neighborhood could be, how imperfect—all were yet to be discovered.

My victory—as the first Democrat elected to the United States Senate since Minnesota had become a state in 1858—clouded my eyes. I had whipped a powerful Republican senator who had the support of virtually all the press and power structure in the state. In Minneapolis, I was mayor, *the* mayor—and I had done a good job. Everybody, it seemed, knew me. I was the center of the political universe.

In Washington, I not only did not have a driver or an official car, I didn't even know the streets. I had to struggle to find my way to work, to seek out meeting rooms in strange hotels where no one knew me.

Late in November, I left Muriel and our children in Minneapolis and went to Washington with Fred Gates and Bill Simms[2]: Bill to start setting up an office and Freddie to help me get settled. The first problem was to find a house to live in. Muriel and I had sold our house in Southeast Minneapolis for about fifteen thousand dollars, and what little equity we had was supposed to be the down payment on a comparably priced house in Washington. Fred and I wandered around looking for an adequate house close to that price. Finally we found a house for twenty-seven thousand dollars in a typical postwar development. What it lacked in shrubbery and lawn it made up for in mud and dust. The amount frightened me, my depression psyche recoiling at so much debt, but there seemed to be no alternative.

Once I bought the house, Muriel had the movers start East with our belongings. Inevitably, the estimate, seven hundred and fifty dollars, was far less than the actual cost of moving, around eleven or twelve hundred dollars. When the truck arrived, I didn't have the additional money and the movers wouldn't unload until I came up with it. I had already borrowed money from my dad for the unexpected down payment on the house, but I called him once again to borrow a couple of hundred dollars more.

By the time the bill got paid and the truck unloaded, Muriel and the kids had arrived by train. She had traveled with Nancy, nine years old; Skip, six; Bob, four; and Doug, ten months, and arrived exhausted in a house full of misplaced furniture, unpacked boxes, and debts. That first day together, we unpacked the dishes, unrolled the rugs, shoved the furniture around amid crying, tired children. We unpacked all day and all night trying to get our house close to orderly.

These simple personal problems foretold other, more difficult problems, for which I was no better prepared. I was relatively young, with little national political experience. Except for Muriel, who was busy with the kids, I had no one politically or personally close in Washington to whom I could turn with confidence for advice. I was the only Democratic senator from the five states in my region, and I was not all that popular with most of the Democratic senators from other parts of the country. How isolated I was had already come home to me before Muriel arrived to share my loneliness.

In January, there was a special session of the outgoing Eightieth Congress. The new senators were up around the Capitol, visiting, getting their offices lined up. I was up there, too, trying to get acquainted, to learn what I could, to get the feel of being a senator. On opening day of the special session, I sat alone in the Senate gallery, both senator-elect and visitor, watching as senior senators introduced the men elected in their states in November. I saw Senator Scott Lucas introducing Paul Douglas, Senator Dennis Chavez of New Mexico introducing Clinton Anderson. I waited, expectantly, watching Senator Ball, whom I would replace, and Senator Ed Thye, with whom I would now serve. They ignored me, and I was about to go back to the hotel when Senator Lister Hill of Alabama spotted me, came up to the gallery, and escorted me to the floor.[3]

The freeze showed in other ways, too. Ordinarily, some arrangements are made to provide incoming senators with temporary office space. I got none, and for nineteen days I used an office lent by Paul Porter, a Washington attorney who had worked with President Truman. With Congress in special session, defeated senators were still using their offices and I could understand the difficulty of finding space. But I couldn't understand why only I, of all the newcomers, had to work in an office downtown, away from everyone else and through the generosity of a private citizen.

I was prepared for the normal political opposition you could expect to encounter. But I was unprepared for what seemed to be a hostile personal reaction. I was a more than normally gregarious person, who wanted to be liked, even though there would be serious disagreements on issues between me and many other senators. But my actions at the Democratic Convention had elicited bitterness and antagonism far beyond what I expected. I was treated like an evil force that had seeped into sanctified halls.

That attitude was made clear, if there had ever been any doubt, when I walked one afternoon from the Senate chamber past a group of southern senators. They ignored me and I moved silently on, but not out of earshot, and one of them, Senator Richard Russell of Georgia, said, obviously for my benefit: "Can you imagine the people of Minnesota sending that damn fool down here to represent them?"

I was crushed. My fight for civil rights was not a personal vendetta against a person or a region; it was a fight on an issue, on a principle that seemed basic to our democracy. I wanted to do well, and I knew that my political intensity, my personal enthusiasm needed a friendly environment to blossom. I was not prepared for the rejection by my peers, nor was I ready for the abuse from letters, editorials, and cartoons that poured in.

Never in my life have I felt so unwanted as I did during those first months in Washington. I was unhappy in the Senate, uncomfortable, awkward, unable to find a place. My principles offended, my personality enraged. I wasn't going to change one and I didn't know how to change the other.

Virtually the only break in those bleak, gray days came when I made a courtesy call on President Truman to reassure him of my loyalty and my support for his programs. After we had chatted for a while and I was about to leave, he said, "Senator, if there's ever anything I can do for you, will you let me know?" I said, "Mr. President, the one thing that would mean more to me than anything political would be to bring my mother and father here to meet you when they come down for my swearing-in." The President called Matt Connolly, his appointment secretary, and said, "Matt, when Hubert's folks come to town, you make arrangements for me to see them."

When my folks arrived, Matt did. We were ushered into the Oval Office for a 2:30 P.M. appointment. The winter sun shone gently in behind Truman, who rose from his desk and quickly walked toward us, grasping my mother's hand in welcome. She was shy, awestruck; in fact, speechless. My dad, somewhat more sophisticated, more experienced in politics, tried to speak, but he, too, was virtually mute. He had never met the President nor had he ever been to the White House before, and his eyes glistened as Mr. Truman soon began to talk about the 1948 campaign, how he had enjoyed this toughest of campaigns.

He talked to my folks about me, saying what parents like to believe about their children. Then he showed us things he had collected and cherished, the political artifacts that fill so many offices in Washington. At one point he stopped near a huge globe that stood near his desk and traced the journeys he had made since he had become President, talking particularly about the Potsdam Conference. He pointed then to the Soviet Union and said, "This is the place of trouble. If only we could get them to understand that we want peace."

He talked about Stalin and his efforts to convince him that our intentions were honorable. He concluded sadly that we were going to have a difficult time with the Russians and that we had better be strong enough to face up to them.

The President then invited us to walk through the White House with him as guide. We covered all the historic downstairs rooms, and then he took us up to the living quarters. My mother seemed to explode in a series of gasps and gulps, her chattering small talk barely coherent.

When we were about to leave, the President said quietly to my proud parents that he knew I would be a great senator. It was a graceful thing to say, and whether Mr. Truman meant it seriously or not was irrelevant to three grateful Humphreys.

President Truman said that being senator was the greatest office in the country, that it was much better than being President. He said how much he had enjoyed the Senate, that the White House was a big jail, how lonely he felt in the presidency cut off from the people.

We had spent not much more than a half hour with him, but he handled the conversation with such grace that it seemed a neighborly afternoon visit that simply went too quickly. As we left the White House and walked to our car, we were quiet, sharing in our own private ways that special moment, glowing inwardly with pride and accomplishment and affection for each other and for Harry Truman.

Surrounded by family again, my days were tolerable and often as happy as ever. My dad and I talked politics and government, he excited by my election, me by the chance once again to savor the filial friendship that was so special between us. The day I was sworn in, he sat in the gallery leaning forward, smiling brightly.

Before he left, several days later, however, he told me that he was not well and that he did not expect to live much longer. He shrugged off my questions and turned instead to talk about the family. He asked me to promise that I would take care of mother and visit her regularly. He said that the drugstore would need my personal attention even while I was in the Senate and that I should work closely with brother Ralph. And then he would say no more.

Later that year, he died of a cerebral hemorrhage,[4] having shared at least a few pleasant moments of my life as a senator. His death meant not only the loss of father and friend, but it took the one man with whom I could have most freely counseled as I tried to understand what moved this new political world and who held the levers that powered its movements.

I was struggling to comprehend a new environment at a strange time. The casualties of war do not end with a cease-fire. The pains of a postwar period are not solely for the losers. People talk of the dark clouds of war, but there are dark clouds in peacetime, too.

The strains of the war, the sacrifices that people make, the controls over prices and wages, the shortages of goods and materials, all of the pain and grief and discomfort that people are put through often result in a kind of political revulsion.

In Britain, Winston Churchill, war leader and national hero, and his conservatives were defeated even as he sat at the Potsdam Conference. In the United States, in 1946, there had been, fortunately, no presidential election, but the Eightieth Congress, elected that year, represented in political terms the letdown and backlash from the intensity of our experience in World War II. Liberals were turned out and the Republicans became the majority party in Congress. Truman found himself besieged from all sides by critics—in the public, in the press, in business, in the Republican party, and even within his own Democratic party.[5]

The mood of the country turned strident and ugly. American history has rhythms of alternating despair and hope. At that moment, both were intensely present and in conflict.

Things got worse following Truman's victory in 1948, a particularly offensive one to the powerful because it was so surprising. The conservatives, rid of Roosevelt, thought Truman would be easy to beat, and they had polls to confirm their prejudices. Dewey was a cinch in their minds, and yet Mr. Truman, virtually violating the laws of nature, was still President. That fact was simply not accepted by big business or by much of the press in an almost psychotic rejection of reality.

The applause and congratulations had barely died down when the opposition settled in to weaken Truman's leadership and destroy him politically. The demagoguery and heightened rhetoric of the 1948 campaign continued, increasing until the day

Truman left office, in 1953. Those years were the culmination of frustration and partisan anger.

The Republicans had been out of the presidency since 1933, and they were desperate to regain political power. Their leadership in the Senate was increasingly critical and cynical, nurturing a negativism in politics that brought forth the worst in people. From 1948 to 1952, there was an irresponsible mood among the conservatives, growing out of defeat and disappointment, out of hatred for the liberal and progressive programs of President Truman, out of a fight to maintain a status quo that no longer really existed. It used the anguish and distress of the Korean War and fed the irrationality of Senator Joseph McCarthy of Wisconsin. He was the worst, but Senators Jenner and Capehart of Indiana and Dworshak of Idaho, Brewster of Maine, Wherry of Nebraska, Mundt of South Dakota, Bridges of New Hampshire, Cain of Washington, and Dirksen of Illinois helped create the mood he exploited best. They all were relentless in their attacks on Truman and the Democratic party. "Communists, radicals, socialists"—they had labels in their hands to libel anyone they didn't like. Liberals, progressives, members of ADA, officials who worked closely with the labor movement—all qualified for assault.

Still, the social revolution that had begun during the New Deal days of Franklin Roosevelt and may have slowed during the war, was once again moving. The election of 1948 had not only returned President Truman to the White House, but it brought a number of progressive, liberal men to the Senate. Control still rested with the conservatives, primarily Republicans and southern Democrats but involving also several northern Democrats. I have never seen the leadership of the Senate more at odds with the apparent mood of the people.

Even that disparity was as nothing compared to the difference between the people and the philosophy of the groups that dominated Washington and legislation in those years: the National Association of Manufacturers, the American Medical Association, the U. S. Chamber of Commerce, the American Farm Bureau, and other, lesser conservative groups.[6]

I found out from experience how strong these groups were; I managed to take them all on within a short time. It wasn't exactly a political death wish; it was just that every time I associated myself with a bill I thought right and important, it turned out to be on their "black list."

When you were cosponsor of the Missouri Valley Authority, it meant that powerful private-utility interests would oppose you. When you were a cosponsor of national health insurance, you engaged the wrath of the American Medical Association and its ancillaries. When you supported the Farmers Union and firm price supports, you became a target of the Farm Bureau, originally a co-operative itself, now largely a conservative organization with powerful allies in the conservative press and in the financial community. When you supported extension of the minimum wage to cover millions of new workers, it meant you attracted the animosity of vast elements of the business and industrial community. When you advocated repeal of the Taft-Hartley Law, you were taking on the entire corporate establishment.

As I look back on that period, I must admit that some of my efforts appeared quixotic, but there are none of them on the issues, on public policy, that I would have done appreciably differently. The issues were right. The votes weren't there. It's tough being beaten so consistently, but at least I had the privilege of knowing early who my natural opponents were outside the Senate.

Within the Senate I also managed to involve myself in some scrapes with the Establishment. I started early to oppose the seniority system. To cap my activities of the early months, I took on Senator Harry Flood Byrd of Virginia, one of the most powerful men of the Senate and the darling of the conservatives throughout the country. The Byrd machine ran the state of Virginia for more than a quarter of a century. There were two kinds of candidates in Virginia during that time: the Byrd candidates and the losers.

In 1949 he was at the zenith of his power, a conservative Democrat who had opposed Franklin Roosevelt and who had himself been considered a possible presidential nominee. Byrd was the chairman of the Joint Committee on Reduction of Nonessential Federal Expenditures, a committee whose sole purpose, as far as I could discover, was to provide patronage jobs for a few Byrd friends and relatives from Virginia. It put out a few reports compiled from other people's old statistical material, and I felt that the committee itself was the most nonessential expenditure of federal funds that I had come across. My evidence of its valueless nature came from members of the American Political Science Association, and I delivered a well-documented speech pointing out the committee's inadequacies. I discovered sadly that the APSA doesn't carry much weight in the Senate of the United States, particularly when it's under conservative control.

Further, I made an egregious error that violated the traditions of the Senate: I attacked Byrd when he was not on the floor. As I discovered later, he was away because of illness in his family, making my error doubly damning. The next day, about twenty-five senators—Republicans and Democrats, including Walter George of Georgia, Robert Taft of Ohio, Pat McCarran of Nevada, and Eugene Milliken of Colorado—stood and launched a bitter counterattack on me for challenging a sinecure of the Senate. I found that when you attack a man like Senator Byrd, you'd better have more than just facts.

The only senator to come to my defense publicly was Millard Tydings of Maryland. His defense wasn't to the issue at hand so much as it was an expression of compassion. He figuratively put an arm around me and said, "Don't be afraid. You have a right as a senator to do what you're doing, and these men ought to treat you with more kindliness and respect." It was the tender, loving care of a father for a sickly, and possibly dying, child.*

I sat through the attacks, absorbing humiliation, until there were no words and no one left to heap scorn on me. I left the chamber and went to the elevator to go back to the Senate Office Building. There, on the elevator, was Senator Byrd. He was not smiling. I said, "Senator, I know when I've been licked," and extended my hand. He took it in what wasn't exactly a friendly handshake, but it at least represented the traditional courtesy of the Senate.

I had barely recovered when, the next day, one of my assistants came to me and said, "I have new material for you from the American Political Science Association. You ought to go back

---

* Paul Douglas, freshman like me, remained silent but in the chamber to provide me moral support.

8. Young Hubert and his dog Rex.

9. The author and Muriel studying. "New ideas and friends made those university [of Minnesota] years the most personally productive ones I have ever lived. Muriel and I grew even closer."

10. On graduation day with friend Orville Freeman (later Secretary of Agriculture). "He often brought his girlfriends to our house for a cheap date . . . popcorn, Monopoly, root beer, and a *lot* of talk."

11. "[Once] . . . the drugstore was my life and it seemed it might always be. . . ."

12. "Little operators and big ones all saw me with a single vision: a reformer who wanted to take away their special treatment, their arrangements. . . . I talked of clean government as though I meant it, and I did."

and open this case up again. This time, you'll be able to gain support." "Listen," I said, "*you* go do it. I wouldn't care if what you have is a newly discovered chapter from the Bible: I'm not about ready to open up another attack on Senator Byrd. I've been walloped, beaten, worked over. I'm the guy who has to take it; all you have to do is hand me the ammunition. The trouble is that you're giving me blanks, and they've got howitzers."

I didn't go on with it. That one day was enough. I found out where the power was in the Senate, and I also found out what you could expect when you challenge that power frontally.†

† The Senate ultimately abolished the committee, in 1975.

19. COMPROMISE IS NOT A DIRTY WORD

In 1949, Senator Richard Russell was the most powerful man in the Senate. He directed a band of a score or so of southern senators in a coalition with about the same number of Republicans led by Senator Robert Taft of Ohio. While Taft more often got the headlines as the Republican leader, Russell was really the master strategist and tactician for the conservative coalition. Even Senator Scott Lucas, who, as majority leader, spoke as though he were in charge, always checked any important or controversial question with Russell, or in his absence with Walter George or Harry Byrd.

The coalition served Taft and the Republicans well. Democratic presidents could be harassed; liberal legislation could be amended, delayed, or killed far more readily with the additional support of the southern Democrats. It was a political arrangement that was convenient, efficacious, and natural, because it cut across regional and party lines, providing a solid conservative phalanx against liberal social, economic, and racial legislation.

Within the Senate, the Republican party, with few exceptions, was either lackluster or mean. The exceptional Republicans, such as Senator Arthur Vandenberg of Michigan, Senator Charles Tobey of New Hampshire, and Senator Irving Ives of New York, were apparently not eager for the leadership role, and it devolved on Taft, who was a fierce partisan, totally loyal to his party. It was said of Taft that he had the best mind in the Senate until he made it up. And he was an excellent student of government, had a kind of integrity, and was straightforward, but I always felt that his main quality of leadership was his political tenacity—his stubbornness and perseverance.

Richard Russell was the real leader and most able of all the conservatives. Smarter than others, shrewd in the ways of the Senate, brilliant in tactics and parliamentary maneuver, and determined that the South have a dominant role in it, he knew that the only way to achieve the objectives he wanted was to have an effective coalition with the Republican conservatives.

Russell was essentially constructive on most matters of foreign policy and on many domestic issues, with the important exception of civil rights. He was an effective and articulate spokesman for rural America and undoubtedly the best-informed man in the Senate on matters of national defense.[1]

His tremendous ability was weakened and corroded by his unalterable opposition to the passage of any legislation that would alleviate the plight of the black man throughout the nation. He was the victim of his region, the victim of a heritage of the past, unable to break out of the bonds of his own slavery.

Had he been able to sense the importance of the human rights issue and the need for constructive civil rights legislation, he might well have been a genuine candidate for the presidency and might have been elected.

The coalition held together only on certain issues, and Russell never pushed it to the breaking point, where partisan loyalties would be stronger than the needs of the moment. Russell and the Southerners used knowledge instead of numbers to have their way in the Senate. They stood together, with a clear but flexible loyalty system, using the seniority system to dominate the committees of the Senate as well as its infrastructure.

In actual numbers, the Southerners were no more numerous than the northern or western liberal Democrats. Politics to a Southerner was a vocation, and he worked hard at it. As a result, coming from a one-party region, he could ordinarily expect to be elected again and again. The liberals, on the other hand, came and went, were elected for a term or two, then were defeated or quit. Those who stayed longer never developed sufficient cohesion to be a bloc force. Northern Democrats, those from the East and the Midwest and the Far West, would often split. They were independent and had little sense of loyalty to either a region or a group.

The concept of loyalty also differed appreciably between the two Democratic groups. Liberals, then as now, demanded a purity of performance that is virtually beyond human capability. If you deviated on any one vote, someone would look upon you as unreliable. Over a given session, there were enough opportunities for a deviation or two that soon every liberal seemed to be pointing an accusing finger at every other.

The Southerners, recognizing human fallibility, insisted only upon the minimum of regularity, the minimum of fidelity, in order to qualify as a reliable associate or ally.* They did not make every issue a major cause. They demanded only that amount of loyalty which was absolutely necessary to maintain control. On the rules of the Senate, they were fundamentalists and unyielding. There could be no flirtation with change or adaptation of the right of unlimited debate or other rules they considered sanctified. The knowledge of the rules and how to use them was the key to southern power.

Unlimited debate—that is, the filibuster—also protected the Southerners from being overwhelmed by the rest of the country, and obviously this was a major, and for years insuperable, barrier to civil rights legislation. (The Southerners could make a persuasive case that the right of unlimited debate had wider and more important ramifications for any minority view. It does give protection against the emotional frenzy of the hour. And while for years the conservatives used it to block race legislation, it can protect liberal minorities too. A few senators willing to face a torrent of public opinion pushing too quickly in a particular direction can say, in effect, "Wait a minute, don't hurry, let's take another look." A brief moment like that can permit some semblance of reason and balance to return to public discussion.)

The seniority system helped Southerners use the rules to their advantage. As a senator achieved seniority, he also achieved power, first as a subcommittee chairman and then as a commit-

---

* Legislation on oil, taxes, and civil rights were the prime measuring sticks. There was not much "wiggle room" allowed there.

tee chairman in some instances.† That brought with it control over the staffs of the committees who serve at the discretion of the chairmen; it brought control over the flow and content of legislation itself. With continuity of service came the additional powerful positions on the steering committee and Democratic policy committee, as well as chairmanships of special and select committees. From the steering committee issued the appointments within the establishment of the Senate: the parliamentarian (a man of incredible influence in the operation of the Senate, influencing the reference of bills and floor proceedings), the secretary of the Senate, the clerks, the sergeant-at-arms, patronage jobs, and even the architect of the Capitol.

The steering committee also makes the assignment of new senators, or the reassignment of old senators, to the various committees. This is obviously a powerful bargaining position. Again, while the Southerners did not represent a majority on the steering committee, they had sufficient numbers, plus the experience and power that come from their service as chairmen of standing committees, to influence decisions.

Even in the election of majority leader, in which a vote should simply be a vote, the Southerners end up with inordinate power. No Democratic majority leader was ever elected without the support of the Southerners; and conversely no one was elected majority leader if he had their opposition.

Having accumulated that much power, it is easy to penetrate the ranks of other Democratic groups. When the crunch came, Southerners with influence could often count on very liberal senators, and even more on moderates, to deliver a vote on some issue. It does not take long to discover that the best way to get along in the Senate is to get along with committee chairmen, subcommittee chairmen, and the power structure.‡

Finally, the Southerners, more than most of the rest of us, operated with good manners, a sense of graciousness, with a sense

† And, in general, this meant power for nominal Democrats. From 1940 to the present, Republicans organized the Senate only twice: 1947–48 and 1953–54.

‡ These recollections are, of course, from a time long past. The Senate has changed a great deal since then—and changed largely for the better—in many respects, as I discovered when I returned to that body in 1971.

of humor and sociability. Graciousness and good manners do not excuse bigotry, stupidity, or simple wrongheadedness. But bad manners and ungraciousness make any resolution of differences far more difficult. And ultimately the resolving and reconciling of opinions and views is what the Senate is all about.

Success in the United States Senate comes most readily to those who are able to get along with people of different philosophies, from different walks of life. The Senate, while it is a political forum and a highly structured parliamentary body, is, after all, a group of men and women who are working together, talking together, thinking together, in a sense almost living together, to reach some conclusion or limited consensus. In all of this, personal relations are very important indeed. At times they are controlling.

Seldom do individuals feel so strongly on an issue that they will refuse to discuss it rationally—at least informally. It is true that there are some major issues that do divide people on party lines. There are major legislative issues that divide people on ideology and philosophy. But, more frequently, the issues are not of that consequence. When they arise, the individual who is able to maintain a close personal relationship with other members of the Senate is often able to get his amendment adopted or his legislation passed—if not in its optimum form, at least in an acceptable form.

If all you can do is rally around you those who see things exactly as you do, then you will always lead a minority, and probably lead it to defeat. What a successful political leader must do is to define some common objectives among people who have different points of view on a host of different issues. This requires very sensitive political antennae, and above all, in a body such as the Senate, it requires good personal relationships.

Compromise is not a dirty word. The Constitution itself represents the first great national compromise. In a democratic, pluralistic society, legislation ought to be a compromise of differing points of view, of different interests. The purveyors of perfection (as they define it at any given moment) are dangerous when they hold a majority so strong that they are unyielding and move self-righteously to dominate. There are those who live by the strict rule that whatever they think right is necessarily right.

They will compromise on nothing. They insist that everyone follow their thinking. They play the music and you march, not in your own cadence, but to their trumpet and to their beat. These rigid minds, which arise on both the left and the right, leave no room for other points of view, for differing human needs.

On the other hand, there are those who believe in little or nothing, have no general ideology, who seem to have arrived at a point of political power without any visible amount of political commitment. Those who live solely by political expediency are also destructive to the proper functioning of a democratic parliamentary body. They function without principle, without program, without consistency.

But between rigidity and vacuous expediency, there is a proper, indeed necessary, area of compromise. If you cannot accept this single point, you cannot understand the democratic process or the United States Senate.

There are times, of course, when it is better to lose than to be partially successful. That is true only if, in the process of winning, you destroy the possibility of ultimate success in securing all you are after. But to make losing a habit in the name of moral principle or liberal convictions is to fail to govern and to demonstrate the incapacity to persuade and convince and to develop a majority.

My experience with legislation—civil rights, aid to education, health care, it doesn't matter—has always been the same: social goals are not often reached quickly or easily.[2]

While one man alone cannot pass anything, one or several senators working the right way can look forward to some success. In any legislation, your goal must be clear, not fuzzy; you must prepare your arguments carefully, lining up the natural advocates as best you can both inside and outside the Senate. And then, after fighting as hard for it as you can—in the subcommittee, committee, on the floor, and in conference—you had better know precisely where you are willing to compromise. You can end up with nothing two ways: by being so rigid that the entire legislation is lost, or so flexible that your opponents gut the bill. But strong and sensible arguments, together with a responsible compromise, prepare the way for a later effort. It is better to gain a foot than to stand still, even when you seek to gain a mile.

As a liberal senator, I preferred to make the full journey, but I learned that it might be necessary to accept less. When a liberal senator adopts this approach, he is bound to engage the wrath and disdain of some of his fellow liberals, particularly in the intellectual community. There are those people who feel that any compromise is a sell-out. They are impractical. If they have had the least experience or have any common sense, they know, or learn quickly, that in a democratic society and in a parliamentary body in which the majorities are constantly fluctuating, it is literally impossible for any one senator or small group of senators to get exactly what they want in exactly the form they want it. But the wrath of the intellectual liberal who can see only utopia now, and is unwilling to create an approximation of utopia by slowly building it brick by brick, is something unbounded. (Such pragmatism permitted Roosevelt to move ahead, pause, and then launch a new effort, which moved closer to the ultimate objective. That was also why the intellectuals began to attack him. It is forgotten now, but by the fall of 1963, the campus and intellectuals had begun to turn on John Kennedy.)[3]

Yet even the purists, aggravating as they have been to me, perform a function that is necessary and vital. We need the self-appointed moralists, the secular theologians who would create the heavenly city on earth by fiat. Without them demanding more than humankind can deliver, those of us who feel that pragmatism is the better method might slide into self-serving rationalizing. The purists are irritating but indispensable, creating the tension and the goals that are necessary for any legislative achievements.

From 1950 to 1952, it appeared that Robert Taft would be the Republican nominee for President, and I think it is fortunate for America that he was not. For whatever his intelligence and reputation for integrity, he was a partisan from head to foot, who once said, "The duty of the opposition is to oppose." And that to him was sufficient; the need to suggest alternatives was irrelevant. He would not use his considerable ability and his immense power of leadership to curb the incredible radicalism and irresponsibility of a man like Joe McCarthy. Proof and truth had little or no place in the political spectrum. "Socialism, soft-on-communism, welfare-statism" became the shibboleths of shallow partisanship.

Against that backdrop Truman proposed needed legislation: a national health insurance program, a comprehensive civil rights program, a massive housing program, and labor legislation to repeal the Taft-Hartley Law and to improve and expand the minimum-wage programs.

Then came the Korean War. At first the conservatives, ideological captives of a missionary militance on the Far East, defended Truman's action. We had a role there, they agreed, but when the tide turned and American men began to lose their lives without apparent success in battle, they turned on Truman, and led by Taft, accused Truman and his administration of everything from disloyalty to simple stupidity to complete incompetence.

The cry soon went up demanding that we get out of Korea, bring our boys home. It was a virulent time of systemic distress. Postwar and new-war angers and problems dominated our national psyche.

Letters from constituents reflected the craze. Do something about housing, do something about education, do something about employment, but cut taxes, slash expenditures, cut the budgets, they said in obvious contradiction. Get out of Korea, but whip the Communist enemy. There was little logic in the air.

It is a testimony to Truman's courage during his time in office that he proposed the forward-looking domestic and international actions he did. It was testimony to his talent that he succeeded as well as he did. His Greek-Turkish aid program of 1947, an enlightened effort to help two nations that desperately needed help, passed Congress only after months of harassment and intense debate.

The North Atlantic Treaty Organization and Alliance were subjected to unnecessarily long, tedious, and strident debate in 1949, with Taft again in the forefront.

Senator Bricker of Ohio, Taft's home-state colleague, just as conservative, not so smart, led the forces who tried to curb the powers of the presidency at a sensitive time.[4] The Bricker Amendment would have severely weakened the initiative and the determination of the American nation in a period of cold war, when the rehabilitation and reconstruction of Europe and Japan were essential in both human and geopolitical terms.

When, in April 1951, Truman fired General Douglas MacArthur, the nation rumbled with anger. MacArthur was a super-hero, acknowledged by himself as well as others as a great military leader. Whatever his skills, his egotism was even greater. He reveled in the role of hero and martyr, wanted to be President of the United States, and willingly lent himself to the forces that found him a useful vehicle to increase the attack on Truman and the Democrats.

He was invited to address a joint session of Congress, an honor rarely given, and did so to the cheers of Robert Taft, Kenneth Wherry, William Knowland, Styles Bridges, Owen Brewster, William Jenner, Homer Capehart, Henry Dworshak, Karl Mundt, Herman Welker, and Richard Nixon, the Republican warriors of the late '40s and early '50s who had committed themselves to unrelenting attack upon the Democratic administration and party, regardless of the national consequences. They were relentless, they were persevering, they were determined, they were reckless.

MacArthur in that atmosphere of adulation and acrimony saw himself as the man on a white horse needed to carry us out of chaos. It was a dangerous time for the country and Truman as he insisted on civilian control over the military.

A few men stood up for him then, and without them it is difficult even now to guess what might have happened in America. Senator Robert Kerr, a Democrat but a very conservative one, respected by other conservatives of both parties, rose to Truman's defense. The Republican governor of Minnesota, Luther Youngdahl, alone among his colleagues, spoke out for Truman. There were few other Republican or conservative voices heard proclaiming the importance of civilian control over the military, which was the ultimate issue.

One of the worse effects of the entire period was the canard that the Democrats, and particularly Truman, had lost China. The China lobby, whatever it was, however you define it, was at work. They peddled the line that we had lost China, somehow implying that we either owned it, deserved it, or were in charge of it.

They attacked the State Department, branding loyal men and women as soft on communism, fuzzy-headed liberals, incompetent and possibly traitorous public servants. McCarthy played his numbers game of "Communists in the State Department," accusatory, demagogic, rarely with anything that approached substance to his charges.

The damage done to individuals and to our State Department and Foreign Service, and indeed to America's reputation during this incredible period of demagoguery and irresponsible attacks has been virtually irreparable.

People who might have saved us from the agony of Vietnam were silenced or driven out, reputations ruined. The nation paid a grave and heavy price. There were perceptive people in government who realized that if they were to tell the truth as they saw it in their overseas posts, their reports might be leaked to the Hill or the press. If in any way they indicated that a Communist movement or party or regime was making economic or social advances or waging a successful political war, they were suspect, potential targets for venomous attacks.

The language of the time, the rhetoric of extremes, had the awful consequence of forcing almost all of us into simplistic positions. When everything we did in relation to the Communists was attacked as evil, bad, wrong, there was little room to respond, "Yes, but. . . ." To be heard, the rhetoric in response required claims just as simplistic: our policies were noble, sound, and perfect. Government is much more complex, and in times of rapid change, when empires are tumbling, social orders disintegrating, and value systems changing, it is very difficult to be precise in what you see and what you know.

It is a time that requires patience and tolerance and understanding. Instead, the disgruntled, angry, discouraged, or rabid wanted, as always, quick and precise answers according to their own dogma or view of what was right and wrong. They had no patience with diplomacy, with the United Nations, with conferences and rational talk.

It was easier to charge that every conference was a sell-out, that the United Nations was useless, that diplomacy was conducted by egg-headed, soft-hearted, weak-brained, pantywaists in the State Department.

All of this came at a time when our nation, and Western democracy, was facing unequivocal, determined policies of the Soviet Union to stretch its influence and power not only over Eastern and Central Europe, but into the neighboring areas of

Asia and North Africa. They were building Communist party strength in Western Europe and extending its apparatus and its ideological thrust, plus its military and economic assistance, into Asia.

The fact is that President Truman stood up to the Russians on the one hand, and to domestic critics on the other, in an extraordinary display of strength. But it is no wonder that America seemed confused or that the average citizen had a difficult time judging just what was going on.

I have talked about the rabid Republican partisans who were, indeed, the main force within their party. Democrats alone, I think, could not have stemmed their irrational tide, and what the consequences might have been for America I cannot surely define. I do not easily talk of fascism, but there is a totalitarian strain in our national character, and where the seeds of hate and discord are sown, weeds of fascism may grow.

Two things certainly helped stem that unpredictable trend in our country. One was the election of Dwight Eisenhower. Eisenhower did not always stand up to the right wing as much as some of us would have liked, but his mere election drained the boil of irascible partisanship. Though the extreme right wing might not be satisfied even by him, most Americans were. They did not see him as an evil man. His career denied that he would "sell out" to the Communists. Despite the fact that his opponent, Adlai Stevenson, was a brilliant man and thoroughly qualified to be President of the United States, a man who would have brought great honor and distinction to the office, it is a simple fact that the election of Dwight Eisenhower permitted substantial defusing of the explosive nature of American politics.

The second fact is that there were men within the Republican party who, though partisan, were fair-minded men who considered their country above their party. Many of them were in the Senate.

Arthur Vandenberg went from isolationist to internationalist and carried other Republicans with him. Charles Tobey of New Hampshire, who talked in a brisk, clipped New England accent, had a mind that worked with precision. He never moved with the Republican mob philosophy away from his firmly held views of democratic progressivism and international responsibility. And there were others: Alexander Smith of New Jersey, while a weaker man, was a good and responsible one, and Alexander Wiley of Wisconsin, while surely not profound or learned, was, again, both kind and reasonable.

Raymond Baldwin of Connecticut was an independent in most matters and one who understood the complexities of the postwar world and the fact that America could not stand alone. Leverett Saltonstall of Massachusetts was a gentle and considerate Brahmin, and his colleague Henry Cabot Lodge had an enlightened view of the world. They were not merely lifelong Republicans; their families had been before them. They were extremely loyal to their party but, like Vandenberg and the others, knew that the predominant rhetoric of the right-wing Republicans was dishonest and dangerous.

But, of all the Republicans, two men for whom I have the greatest affection were two quiet giants from Vermont, George Aiken and Ralph Flanders. They were intelligent and compassionate men, really unsung statesmen, who understood the yearnings of the American people for a better life and accepted as real, not platitude, the idealism of the American nation for a world free of war and want. If I had to choose two men who in their own, unpretentious way represented the very best of what our democratic system can produce, I would have to choose them.

Flanders left the Senate in 1959. He stood up to the vicious, flatulent demagoguery of Joe McCarthy when few others would. It was a heroic act that few of us had the courage to equal. Without flamboyance, he began to let the air out of the overinflated balloon of McCarthy's influence. It was not an act out of keeping with his character, however. He supported civil rights and civil liberties when, I am sure, his constituents were only vaguely interested, and was dedicated to strengthening our relationships with Western Europe in a strong Atlantic alliance.

George Aiken is a man unto himself. He had been a farmer and then governor of his state before coming to Washington and the Senate just before World War II. While he was most keenly interested in agriculture, no problem left him unmoved. The health, education, family life, jobs of people in tiny Vermont or major metropolis outside his state were important to him. In his quiet, reasoned, sensible way, he helped steer this nation. He shone brightly through the miasma of meanness of the forties and early fifties, and his light in the Senate went undiminished until his retirement in 1974.

These men of reason within the Republican party understood that winning peace requires the same kind of dedication, patriotism, and wisdom as is needed in winning war. It requires the same commitment, and possibly even more because there are few dramatics in winning peace, which has to be done in the open, without censorship, with no parades, no martial music.

But no discussion of this period should omit a great Democrat, William Benton of Connecticut. He was my friend and one of the most remarkable men I have ever known.

Senator Benton introduced a resolution calling for the censure of McCarthy and his expulsion from the United States Senate in a truly brilliant speech that fully documented his charges. Following that speech, I told him how much I admired his candor and courage, and hoped that he would go all the way in taking on McCarthy.[5]

He did, and the nation began to recover from its temporary lapse of good sense and reason.

20. TOLERANCE IF NOT AFFECTION

The Senate is a unique political forum, filled with many tensions. It has qualities of both stability and spontaneity. It can be parochial, and it can be, in a sense, universal. It reflects at most times the aspirations and fears of most geographical and ideological sections of the United States. The House of Representatives, much larger, may mirror better the makeup of the country at any given moment, but it is too large to be in focus.

Further, the six-year term permits a senator, if he wishes, to think ahead, to be creative, to design new proposals, to test them, to debate them. He can resist the emotion and frenzy of the moment, the pressures of current political attitudes, the pressures even of constituents and lobbyists, because he has no need of more immediate accomplishments. Since he does not run for re-election in two years, he can start his Senate career with new proposals or refinements of older ones, find out whether they have any appeal, whether he can muster support, or whether he is on an unproductive task. In later years, I would tell a new senator that, of his six-year term, he owed four years to the Lord and our country, and possibly two years to himself and his chance of re-election.

The only restrictions on a senator, protected by the length of the term, are his intelligence and willingness to work, and the nature of his constituency. To some extent, once the citizens of a state develop trust that their senator is honest in his stands and sincere (a word that unfortunately has been cheapened in political rhetoric) in his beliefs, they will permit some deviation from their interests. In my own case, not many people in Minnesota were much concerned with civil rights in 1949 or with nuclear disarmament in the 1950s. But I could work in those areas as long as I took care of more immediate concerns such as agriculture, labor, and health care.

But, for all of that, a senator does represent a state, its cultural patterns, its social attitudes. He is not merely himself; he is somewhat of a reflection of his voting constituency. So whether you work in the Senate or judge it from the outside, you must judge it not only on the personalities and experience of the senators, but in terms of where they come from. What are the influences at work in his state: is it agricultural, is it urban, is it white, black, or does it have other racial or ethnic strains? Is it arid, or does it have floods? Is it gifted with many natural resources, with minerals or timber? The influences of topography, geography, climate, and social attitudes on politics is no less important today in analyzing the Senate than it was when Alexis de Tocqueville wrote in 1835.

Ultimately, after all consideration of traditions and rules, of power structure and public policy, you come to ask what sort of people serve in the Senate. It is made up of a hundred people, most of them prima donnas, all of whom feel they are separate and just a little bit more equal than the others. Most of the people who are elected to the Senate are reasonably talented, in some cases gifted, and they rarely have gotten to the Senate by accident. They have generally come up through a political process that is selective if not perfect; they've been ordinarily elected by a majority of the citizens of their state. Some of the senators are career politicians, who have essentially devoted all of their time to two things: public service and getting re-elected or elected to the next-higher office. Many have had illustrious careers in law, agriculture, teaching, business, or in a host of professional and semiprofessional activities before seeking office.

Senators are neither saints nor devils; they are rarely geniuses or nitwits. Most are a cut above average in intelligence, character, energy, and learning capacity. There are some, from time to time, who fall into the several age-old traps available to man: arrogance, promiscuous use of power, greed—putting personal gain ahead of public service. Some have yielded to the temptations of money and drink. There have been drunks, philanderers, and crooks in the Senate, but they are relatively few. The Senate is also cursed from time to time with the self-righteous senator who claims a pipeline to God and has all-encompassing wisdom. Fortunately, they also are few.

I began my career in the Senate knowing few of these things. Not granted even the normal courtesies of the Senate, my own errors in judgment compounded my difficulties. The attack on Senator Byrd's committee in 1949 brought me to dark days. It was a difficult time, when I despaired of ever functioning well in the Senate.

I hated to expose my feelings to my staff and friends. I did not want to be a whining complainer. Without Muriel, I might have given up. As busy as she was with our children in a new city, she provided the support and solace I needed. She was never too tired to listen. She was a balance wheel, cheering my spirits, helping me resolve not to indulge in self-pity or escape.[1]

Work became my escape. I set out to know more about more things than other senators. If I couldn't get their affection, I might get their respect. I made another decision then which affected my role in the Senate. I accepted the chairmanship of the Americans for Democratic Action. I would be something more than a freshman senator from a relatively small, midwestern state governed by constricting rules of the Senate.

I would become a national leader, if I could, with a national base, with a national constituency. The Senate would be my forum for expounding a point of view, for attracting and persuading people beyond my senatorial audience. There would be time enough to "work" the Senate after I had gathered some additional, external power.

By a strange twist, being ADA chairman in 1949 brought me a kind of immediate recognition. I became a target of the Republican conservatives, having to defend our programs from a constant harangue. To all of them, ADA was an evil, socialist society. They loved to invoke the British Fabian Society as the ADA's natural father. One day, Senator Capehart was raging, charging that the ADA wanted to do to America what the British Labour Party was doing to Britain, when suddenly he shouted at me furiously, "Just name me one thing that Great Britain has that we don't have!" I said quickly, "Westminster Abbey."

It turned out to be a gloriously deflating non sequitur. Senators and galleries burst out in laughter, Capehart sputtered, and the argument died for that day. Strangely, none of my substantive arguments had done anything to turn off the attacks, but a quip punctured bombast. Both Senator Tobey and Senator Vandenberg, who themselves suffered the Republican right wing, came over to me gleefully. Vandenberg said, "They'll respect you from here on out." And that was somewhat true. No one likes to be laughed at, and the political right, more stuffy and serious about themselves, like it less than others; so they treated me more carefully from then on.

Herman Welker, for example, subsequently told me that I was the only liberal he liked, which was high praise coming from one of the few genuinely mean men I had ever known. I discovered that his meanness came, in part, when he had severe migraine headaches and high blood pressure. When he was feeling bad I showed my concern, and he apparently appreciated that. Homer Capehart, after he had been defeated, would often call on me when he came to Washington, and even Bill Jenner and I, who disagreed about as much as two men could, began to get along.

It was not until the debate on the tax bill in 1950, however, that I did anything substantial in developing my role in the Senate. I had not known much about taxation on a federal level, and I had decided that I should.[2]

Too often, liberals are judged by other liberals simply on votes on appropriations. If you are for big appropriations for housing, education, or health, you are a liberal. (One of the ways some senators make themselves the constant darling of liberal groups is to be for impossibly high appropriations. Their more responsible colleagues compromise for what is possible and end up looking like sell-outs or pale carbon copies of the "real" liberal.)

It seemed to me that as important as social legislation and appropriations were, where the money came from and who was paying it were just as important. Were those tax policies fair?

Did they fall unjustly upon those least able to pay? Did they reach properly to those best able to pay? Were there special privileges being granted to some that were not available to others? Could these special privileges be justified as in the national interest? I wanted to know what built-in privileges were available to businessmen but not to workingmen, what was available to the doctor but not the schoolteacher.[3]

And that meant that I had to do my homework. The Senate Finance Committee, where the decisions would be made, had not a single liberal member. (Robert Kerr of Oklahoma sat on the committee and he was a Populist, but he was a conservative when it came to oil and gas issues.) We would have to go it alone.

In many ways, the Finance Committee is one of the most important in the Senate. It deals with the fundamental question in government: how tax monies are raised. And that question in turn has profound consequences for the social structure of the country and the quality of life of its citizens.

So I began to study the tax system, often reading all night, or at least until two or three in the morning. For each loophole that we found in the tax system, Paul Douglas and I prepared a full statement analyzing the law, reviewing its history, showing how it worked and why it constituted an inequity. It was an enormous amount of work, much of it in great—and often painful—detail.

In previous years, tax legislation had been passed with debate on no more than one or two major issues. We had decided, however, that we would debate the whole bill, offering a series of amendments and demanding roll-call votes. To do this, and as freshman senators, we had to take on Walter George of Georgia, chairman of the Finance Committee, and Eugene Milliken of Colorado, the ranking Republican member. Both were brilliant, able, and eloquent. Having learned from the Harry Byrd episode, I went to Senator George to tell him precisely what Paul Douglas and I intended to do. He said, "Go right ahead. That's what a senator is supposed to do." That visit convinced him that I was serious about debating tax policy and that I was not playing to the galleries.

We had prepared the roster of amendments, and after one last, crowded week of additional research, I was ready to take them to the floor.*

The debate that followed was extraordinary, and lasted a full week. We asked the right questions, forced responsive answers, and scrutinized every section of the tax bill.

And, basically, we lost. We lost on excess-profits tax, on taxing certain tax-exempt government securities, on increasing the corporate income tax from 42 per cent (the figure in the bill) to 45 per cent, and in our proposal to ban low taxation on spin-offs.

We did win one amendment: a proposal to strike out a provision that cut the holding period on long-term capital gains from six months to three months.

Even though we had lost the individual battles on amendments, we had won the larger war for the liberals. We had challenged two men who were rarely challenged in their field of competence. The fact that they took us seriously, responded in debate with respect for our arguments, treated us as peers and not with scorn and ridicule, told the rest of the Senate that we were to be considered men of ability and moment. When the debate was over, both of them came over and congratulated us on the quality of the debate, on the responsible and constructive way we had worked. That gesture was not lost on the others.

In the single debate, I proved that I wasn't just talkative, just another emotional liberal, but, rather, a student of government, willing to work, state my case, debate, call for a vote, and accept the decision. My position in the Senate improved, particularly among the conservatives, who still opposed my political philosophy and activity, but generally spoke well of me as a senator from that time on. I had largely overcome the anger of some over my civil rights stand and the disappointment and disdain of others over the fact that I was even in the Senate.

I made up my mind then never to enter a debate on any bill without being prepared to debate in detail. I also learned then that as long as you treated other senators as honest men, sincere

---

* As it happened, the regular Senate chamber was being renovated at the time, so the debate took place in the nineteenth-century Senate chamber, which had also been used for a time by the Supreme Court—a much smaller room, but the same one in which Daniel Webster and Henry Clay had spoken their minds.

in their convictions, that you could usually gain the tolerance, if not affection, of even those who disagreed strongly with you.

That code of behavior makes sense. Where widely disparate positions confront one another, where opposing ideologies meet head on, rules that are designed to curb emotions and establish rational discussions are important. You do not question motives or attack the character of another or the state from which he comes. You keep your word. You do not embarrass a man through trickery or double cross. Sometimes, when the issue is important and you feel deeply about what you are doing, it is tough to abide by that code. Your opponent appears stupid or intellectually dishonest, your anger rises, and you want to flail out. Very likely, your opponent is not stupid and believes what he is saying, too. It is imperative to understand that.

21. THREE WISE MEN

Though I was much closer politically, personally and philosophically to such Senators as Herbert Lehman, Paul Douglas, William Benton, Wayne Morse, Lister Hill and Brien McMahon, there were several other men who were special creatures in Congressional life and history.

During my first term in the Senate, I met three men who had been elected to the House of Representatives for the first time when I was about a year old. In the intervening decades, each had attained substantial power in Washington and had influenced Congressional life and national legislation tremendously. They were very different men in style and interests, but each intrigued me, and from each of them—Carl Hayden, Sam Rayburn, and Alben Barkley—I was to gain important insights into politics and government.

Shortly after I got to Washington, I asked President Truman for advice on how to conduct myself in the Senate. He said, "The man to watch and the man to pattern your Senate career after is Carl Hayden. He's a worker, he takes care of the duties of a senator, fulfills his committee assignments, he doesn't say too much, but he gets a lot done."

Hayden had been a sheriff in the territory of Arizona and later its delegate to the House. When Arizona became a state, he was elected to the U. S. Senate. His entire political career was, of course, closely involved with Arizona's growth and development.

Because of longevity and talent, however, his power was far greater than one might expect of a senator from a small state.

When Kenneth McKellar of Tennessee died, during my first term, Hayden succeeded him as chairman of the Appropriations Committee, and with the purse strings came increased power. Now Hayden, more than any other man, could determine the funding not only for the various agencies of government and for our national programs, but for the local and regional projects that every senator and his constituents seek.

To some this is simply opprobrious pork barrel, the federal funding of projects of little national significance. Some of that is true, but not all. In our federal system, local projects that help a state or region may not satisfy a limited accounting view of cost-benefit ratios, but they do ultimately serve the national interest.

The Central Arizona Project, for which Hayden carefully and methodically sought support, was such a project.* It was attacked as a wasteful use of money with costs out of proportion to the benefits it would bring even to the limited area it was intended to serve.

But flood control, dams, and irrigation helped remake a part of our nation. The contribution of the western states now and in the future to our country's economic health will be substantial because of what men like Hayden did. It is a national responsibility to make our deserts bloom, to make the land habitable for a growing and shifting population.

Clearly, there are dangers in public works projects—dangers of wasted money, of desecrated land, of people moved unnecessarily in the name of progress, of lives upset. I learned from Hayden that, with care, this need not be the case.

Hayden also taught me that regionalism in our federal system can never be submerged totally to what is deemed "national interest." I have not always believed this, but some understanding and tolerance of regional differences are necessary even when there is a clear and overriding national interest.

I learned, too, from Carl Hayden how the Senate operated. He was in a position to permit funding of other senators' projects

---

* The issue sharply divided the Senate. Paul Douglas and I split on the issue, for example, one of the few areas of serious disagreement between us in our early years. He thought it an awful boondoggle.

and to tacitly receive their support for votes he wanted. There was no crass quid pro quo, but a gentlemen's agreement.

It was clear to me that the maxim "You have to go along to get along" was generally accurate. The sense of the "Club," which offended me in principle and whose rules I violated when I felt it necessary, nevertheless demanded forms of behavior that permitted the Senate to be a legislating body and not simply a debating society. The Senate was, after all, a body of people, not philosopher-kings, and it had certain rules and traditions.

Hayden's interests were not limited to domestic concerns. He used his power while I was in the Senate to support international policies of Truman, Eisenhower, and Kennedy without regard to party. Those who knew Hayden only in his final years in the Senate, as a shuffling old man with cane and hearing aid who probably stayed a term too long, were sadly deprived, never knowing the virile, wise, and gentle spirit of his earlier years. He had a fine mind and was an exceptional student of the legislative process. He was one of the people who influenced my life in the Senate, often indirectly, but very positively. I went to him on many occasions for advice on legislation, particularly as it related to some of the needs of my home state.†

The "go along to get along" line is attributed to Sam Rayburn, who like Hayden had been first elected in 1912. I did not get to watch Rayburn as frequently as I did Hayden, but his influence on Congress was more visible. As speaker for eighteen years, he not only grew to power in the House but helped shape it. He governed the House of Representatives through compromise generally, through sheer power when he had to. He led it when possible, he followed it when necessary; he was rarely overruled by it.[1]

He was an interesting mixture of personality traits. He could be folksy and humorous, spinning out yarns about the people of his district or his experiences of government, regaling his rapt listeners with wit and humor. Or he could be stern and taciturn, glowering, eyes intense underneath his bald pate, rejecting what he considered foolish or impossible.

He and young Lyndon Johnson were the closest friends, par-

† One bit of Hayden's advice that I did not take too seriously was, "Don't talk; vote."

tially, I suppose, because they both came from Texas, but far more importantly because they were both creatures of the Hill and Washington. I'm sure that it was a rare day when they did not speak about legislative strategy and other matters of mutual interest.

Every afternoon, Rayburn was the host in his office for what he called "board of education" meetings, an informal gathering of his intimates and a few Congressional outsiders. "It's time to strike a blow for liberty," he would declare, and break out the liquor bottles. With a smile, Rayburn would say, "Why be stupid and weak when with one drink you can feel smart and strong."

Then, over the drink or two in a relaxed atmosphere, serious talk of national import took place. Many debates on the floor had less relevance than most of those afternoon sessions. It was there that strategy was planned, compromises worked out, decisions made.

One might expect from such an atmosphere a certain narrowness of vision, of partisanship. Yet Rayburn never fell into that pattern. During the Eisenhower years, he and Johnson both tried to co-operate with the President on international affairs and even to work with the Administration on domestic issues where that was possible. While he was an intensely loyal party man and believed in the party system, he was a national leader who gained and retained the respect of his Republican colleagues in the House.

Much later, during my service as majority whip, I attended breakfasts of Congressional leaders every Wednesday morning at the White House. Rayburn, of course, was one of them. He never said much, but when he did, everyone, including the President, listened. He knew Washington and what could be done so well that his every comment seemed on target, without superfluous or irrelevant padding. The sound of his own voice was of little interest to him.

From that class of 1912, Alben Barkley was the man I knew best and enjoyed most. He had been majority leader during the Roosevelt years. After serving in the House, the Senate, and as Vice President, from 1912 to 1952, he was out of office for two years. Then, in 1954, he was elected again to the Senate, and he and I sat next to each other in the back row of the Senate. When he spoke of his experiences or what America could be, his eyes shone brightly. To him politics was, as John Adams described it, "the spirit of public happiness." He was an optimist about our country. He was a philosopher about our people, our heritage, and our destiny.

I met Barkley the summer of 1948 at the Philadelphia convention and liked him immediately. When he spoke to the convention, I became an admirer. The party, as I've said earlier, was divided by internal tensions and almost punch-drunk from the steady hammering of the Republicans in the postwar period. Barkley, with wisdom and with charm and content, was able to lift the spirits of the delegates.

Later that year, he came to Minnesota to campaign for the Truman-Barkley ticket and with and for me. We traveled around the state in a chartered DC-3, often landing at tiny airports that were more suitable for crop-spraying planes. Barkley seemed oblivious to the short runways and my tension, as he chatted on about issues and people.

To say we had small crowds at the airport rallies would be an overstatement, yet, again, Barkley seemed oblivious. No matter how small the gathering, he was the perfect showman; he entertained and educated, at one moment a gentle philosopher, the next a thundering partisan.

In Rochester, where we did have an adequate crowd, Barkley gave a classic political speech. He talked about American foreign policy in the postwar period, calling on America to take the leadership role in binding up the wounds, sharing our abundance and wealth to help the victims of war. Then he shifted beautifully into local issues—farm and rural problems—and finally to my campaign for the Senate.

After the speech, as he spoke to a cluster of newsmen, one asked how he could be supporting me when he had years earlier said such kind things about my opponent, Joe Ball.

Barkley had told me that he never spoke in a derogatory fashion about any member of the United States Senate, regardless of party, and I did not expect him to take on Ball. I knew he would simply express his support for me.

Ball was a particular problem. In 1944, Ball was an internationalist who left his party to support Roosevelt. Further, he had been one of the main sponsors of the B2-H2 (Burton, Ball, Hill and Hatch) resolution, calling for the establishment of an international organization to insure world peace. That support, which was important and probably not too easy for Ball, came while Barkley was majority leader, and he felt a debt of gratitude to Ball.

Barkley said, "It is true that I have said many good things in the past about Joe Ball, all of which he richly deserved." Then he said that the situation reminded him of a Scandinavian family in Minnesota whose old, immigrant father had died. Barkley continued, "When the old man had been laid to rest, the family discovered they had no photograph to remember him by. So they called in a local artist to paint his picture. They described their deceased father and husband, his habits, his physical makeup, how he walked, how he stood tall, how much he weighed, color of his hair and eyes.

"Months later, the artist returned and the family gathered for the unveiling. Ole, the eldest son, said, 'Now we are going to have the painting of the old man.' When the artist hung it on the wall, Ole looked at it from one side, then walked to the other and peered at it silently. Then he stood on a chair and looked down at it. Then he knelt and looked up at it. The artist got nervous and asked, 'Well, Ole, what do you think? Isn't that a good likeness of your father?' Ole replied, 'Yah, sure, I guess that's the old man all right but, my, how he has changed.'"

There was laughter, Barkley avoided any direct attack on Ball, and the facts that the press already knew let them fill in the story. Ball had indeed changed. Having suffered from the antagonism of his colleagues for supporting Roosevelt, he became more conservative, more a party man, associating himself most particularly with Senator Robert Taft. He had become much less of an internationalist, and a hostile critic of the Roosevelt and Truman administrations.

When Barkley was Vice President, he violated Senate protocol and made me a member of a Senate group traveling to conferences in Germany and Austria. Ordinarily, the list of senators is made up by the majority leader, and the Vice President simply concurs. Scott Lucas was majority leader and still had not forgiven me for Philadelphia, when I had opposed him on the civil rights plank. The extra perks of office that he could deny, he did deny. Bill Benton, senator from Connecticut, suggested that Barkley add me to the list, and he did.

I had never before been outside the United States. The trip provided a variety of experiences. I saw the devastation of war—the bombed-out cities along the Rhine: Cologne, Stuttgart, and Düsseldorf. It was so bleak to see the rubble, so sad to imagine the human suffering.

When we flew by DC-3 through the safe air corridor from Bonn to Vienna, we landed in a mixture of uniforms. I saw Soviet soldiers for the first time. But I also saw our own soldiers there as the Star-Spangled Banner was played over the loud speaker. I was gripped by a flow of patriotic emotion and fervor. The juxta-position of hammer and sickle, stars and stripes, Russian uni-forms, American uniforms, was jangling.

It was later on that trip that Benton took me to a restaurant that he airily described as the "second best in the world and the best in Paris." I don't recall whether he ever told me the name of the first best, but you had the feeling that he had been to all the good restaurants everywhere. Since he considered me such an unpolished Midwesterner, he insisted on ordering dinner for me, selecting the wines, tasting, commenting, directing the dinner in a grand manner.

When we came to dessert, he was either relaxed or tired, and let me order my own. I suppose he thought I had learned enough in the preceding several hours and expected I would order some exquisite French pastry. When the waiter asked what I would have, I said, "A chocolate sundae." Benton was struck dumb, just shook his head in disbelief, realizing we were many miles from Huron but not far enough.

Though I have traveled often since, to various parts of the world, that first trip, when I was a kind of innocent abroad, has really never been equaled. It gave substance and meaning to my philosophic attitudes on international relations.

Barkley helped me once more against the wishes of the leader-ship. I wanted very much to serve on the Senate Select Commit-tee on Small Business, partially out of my interest, which began in our drugstore, but also because I felt I needed some lines into the business community in Minnesota before my re-election campaign of 1954. The leadership said no, but Barkley pleaded my case and got me appointed.

Barkley, strangely, was able to violate, or at least push, the traditions of the Senate in a way that no other man I have known could. Conference committees,[2] for example, are invariably drawn from the committees with legislative oversight on the particular subject. Tradition has dictated that the members of the conference committees are the senior members from each of the two committees. Too often, particularly in areas of concern to liberals, senior members (and this was particularly true during the Truman years) had voted against the bill in question or against important amendments that had been added as a result of floor debate. It was not unusual, therefore, for legislation to come back in final form without important parts that had already passed the Senate. It was a take-it-or-leave-it situation then and the ultimate weapon for conservatives who might have been beaten earlier.

For years, Congress and the nation put up with this debilitating tradition. Barkley, presiding over the Senate as Vice President, suggested that it was not necessary for the rule of seniority to be applied. A bill concerning immigration laws had been reported out of committee in one form, and then the Senate as a whole had substantially changed it. Barkley felt that a substantial number of those senators selected for the conference should be supporters of the original committee bill.

He told the Senate, "The Chair has the right to appoint conferees. He desires to have that right in his own name. The Chair would say . . . that at least a majority of the conferees should be among those who supported the action of the Senate committee."

That action did not have the force of a precedent, and a substitute list of conferees was readily accepted. But Barkley had voiced his opinion about one way in which to emancipate the Senate from the slavery of seniority.‡

One day in the Senate, I was asked to sit as chairman of hearings we were holding on the foreign aid bill. I considered it an

‡ During 1971–72, Senators Harris, Talmadge, and I served on an ad hoc committee of the Democratic caucus that was appointed to make recommendations on this very subject. We did, but the caucus watered it down.

honor, since there were senior members present. During the course of the afternoon, one senator after another slipped away. By five o'clock, when the last witness had testified, I was not only chairing the meeting but was the only member left. I didn't think much of being alone and was eager to get home to tell Muriel how pleased I was by the honor my colleagues had given me. I had to hurry, too, because we had been invited to Nelson Rockefeller's home for dinner and I was late.

I drove cheerfully home to Chevy Chase to get cleaned up and dressed and to pick up Muriel. By the time we arrived at Rockefeller's elegant home on Rock Creek Park, we were quite late and indeed the last couple to arrive. When we walked into the garden, there were all the members of the Foreign Relations Committee who had left the hearings early to arrive on time. I had been left holding the hearings and the bag.

When dinner ended, Barkley and his wife started out to call a taxi, and Muriel and I offered them a ride home. Barkley's first wife had died and he had married a really handsome woman in her forties, some thirty years younger than he. Here was the Vice President of the United States, no chauffeured limousine, no Secret Service, just two folks about to hail a cab to their apartment on Connecticut Avenue. The imperial presidency and vice presidency had not yet descended upon us.

Hayden, Rayburn, and Barkley were very different men—in interests, personality, style—but all three understood Washington, and particularly the Hill, as few others did. To watch them, to learn from them, was important to me and my own understanding of how to function.

As elected officials, they had been through the administrations of Woodrow Wilson, Warren Harding, Calvin Coolidge, Herbert Hoover, Franklin Roosevelt, Harry Truman, and into Dwight Eisenhower's. Rayburn and Barkley were to live on into the Kennedy days, and Hayden into the Johnson administration.

They shared some common traits. No hint of personal scandal or abuse of public trust was ever leveled against them. They were men of character to whom public service was a high calling, a vocation. They were intensely partisan men, with great loyalty to their party, but it was a loyalty that was neither blind nor petty. Their partisanship never overcame their sense of citizenship and responsibility to the nation.

22. "QUIT FOOLING AROUND WITH PEOPLE YOU CAN'T DEPEND ON"

My life as a senator, though still difficult, improved a bit as I learned what was productive and what was not. My apprenticeship of isolation drew to a close as I got to know Lyndon Johnson, and that changed my role in the Senate. During my first year, Johnson and I had virtually no contact, reflecting, I suppose, the general attitude of the senators toward me. And we might not have had any then except for a suggestion by Senator Russell Long, whom I had known slightly at Louisiana State University and who was now a neighbor of mine in Maryland. Long suggested that I start having lunch occasionally in a senators' dining room where no outsiders, neither staff nor visitors, were permitted. Democrats and Republicans ate in separate rooms divided by an open door, each group at a large, community table. Since there was seldom talk of issues or legislation, lunch was usually a relaxed social hour of storytelling, chatter about the sports page, whatever was not political or controversial. And because of the physical setup, it was conversation among equals. Fortunately, I work well, even wear well, in such a milieu. A spirit of friendship and camaraderie grew.

On any given day, many of the southern and conservative senators would be there: Richard Russell, John Stennis, James Eastland, John McClellan, Russell Long, Lister Hill, and from time to time Lyndon Johnson.

My friendship with Johnson began in a most perfunctory way. After we had a chance to take each other's measure, Johnson began to invite me to his office for talk and frequently for a drink. Sometimes another senator would be present, more often we talked alone, about the Senate and legislation. The invitations were important because we got to know each other better, but they had a second value: they seemed to have Richard Russell's tacit approval. He was close to Johnson and was frequently the senator present when Johnson invited me to meet with him.*

Johnson had been elected to the Senate just as I had, in 1948, and by far fewer votes. He won by eighty-seven votes out of a total of 988,295 cast. But he began as a formidable figure. He had first come to Washington as a Congressional staff member in 1931, and himself represented Texas' Tenth District for twelve years. He knew Franklin Roosevelt and had served as Texas director of the National Youth Administration as a Roosevelt appointee. Most important, he was the protégé of the speaker of the House, Sam Rayburn. And his close friendship with Richard Russell was carefully strengthened every day Lyndon Johnson served in the Senate.

But it wasn't only friendship that permitted Johnson to start strong. He knew Washington, and he knew Congress as no other man in my experience. He understood the structure and pressure points of the government, and the process and problems of legislation. He understood the men of Congress, both the elected members and the appointed officials. He knew how to appeal to their vanity, to their needs, to their ambitions.

He knew the satellite worlds of Washington: the business lobbyists, the labor movement, the farm and rural-electrification lobbyists, the people interested in health research and social security. (One good friend who remained close to him for almost forty years was David Dubinsky of the International Ladies Garment Workers Union. One a six-foot-four-inch Texan, with a drawl and manner to match; the other a five-foot-two-inch immigrant trade unionist out of the New York garment district, with a Yiddish accent. Both with a determination that the minimum wage be raised.)

---

* None of this could have happened successfully before the debate over the tax bill.

The South was an important base which he never lost in the Senate. Johnson did not consider himself a Southerner and he knew that he could not be its captive. While his confidantes and advisers were Richard Russell, Harry Byrd, and Walter George, he was much more liberal and progressive than they. Yet he never lost their confidence. He was a Democrat and a Texan, enjoying the benefits of southern hospitality, southern power, southern support, but who carefully avoided the liabilities of being clearly labeled a Southerner.

After the defeat of Senator Scott Lucas in 1950, Senator Ernest McFarland of Arizona became the minority leader, and Lyndon Johnson became the assistant minority leader, or minority whip. When McFarland was himself defeated, in 1952, Johnson obviously intended to seek the leader's post, and our ADA liberal group was upset by the prospect. There was no chance of defeating him but, after some discussion, we decided that we ought to nominate our own candidate, at least as symbolic resistance. At that stage in American liberalism, it seemed important to have a symbol, even if you lost with it. Some liberals feel the only way you can be truly liberal is to take a position that cannot possibly succeed, and then go down fighting with flags flying. With that view, you are never so happy as when you are unhappy, and you're never quite so unhappy as when you succeed.

Just after we had decided that Senator James Murray of Montana would be our candidate, Johnson called me at home to talk about the minority leader's job. I said I had already made a commitment and couldn't support him. He said he was sorry, in part because he was considering me for the minority whip job. That was exhilarating, since it indicated that my work and socializing were paying off. But the liberals had other goals, apart from the leadership fight. We wanted better committee assignments, more power for liberals on the steering and policy committees of the Senate Democratic caucus. To secure those goals, we were prepared to trade our support.

I led a delegation of Senators Lester Hunt of Wyoming, Herbert Lehman of New York, and Paul Douglas to present our offer to Johnson. He listened to us briefly, then politely but curtly dismissed us by telling us that he had the votes he needed and that he wasn't in the mood to make concessions.

I had just returned to my office from that awful meeting when Johnson called and said, "Come on down here alone. I want to talk to you." In his office I found him in a take-charge, no-nonsense mood I would see often after that. He said, "Now, look here. Let me tell you something, Hubert. You're depending on votes you don't have. How many votes do you think you have?"

"Well, I think we have anywhere from thirteen to seventeen."

He stared at me for a quiet moment and said, "First of all, you ought to be sure of your count. That's too much of a spread. But you don't have them anyway. *Who* do you think you have?" I went down the list of senators and checked some off. He shook his head on most of them. "You don't have those senators. I have personal commitments that they're going to vote for me. As a matter of fact, Senator Hunt, who was just in here with you, is going to vote for me. You ought to quit fooling around with people you can't depend on."

His stern tone changed to a friendlier one. "Now, look, I think you're honest about these matters. You turned me down when I called you and that was a foolish mistake, because I took Mike Mansfield instead of you. You could have been minority whip, and you'll regret your decision, but at least you told me straight. You didn't talk out of both sides of your mouth. When this election's over and I'm leader, I want you to come back to me and we'll talk about what we're going to do. I want to work with you and only you from the bomb throwers."

When the vote was taken, Senator Murray had his own vote and mine, plus three or four others. Everyone else had gone over to Johnson. Murray withdrew from the race, and Johnson was elected unanimously. After the meeting, I went back to his office and he said, "Now, what do you liberals really want?"

The dialogue was brief and to the point. "The first thing we want is some representation on the policy committee."

"All right, you'll have it. Who do you want?"

"Well, I think it ought to be Jim Murray."

"I don't think he's the right man, because he's older and he won't be effective, but if that's who you want, that'll be done. What else do you want?"

I listed our other requests (formerly demands), which included representation on the steering committee and the major substantive committees of Finance, Judiciary, Commerce, and Appropriations. Johnson agreed and said, "Now you go back and tell your liberal friends that you're the one to talk to me and that if they'll talk through you as their leader we can get some things done."

I had become his conduit and their spokesman not by their election, but by his appointment. I would be the bridge from Johnson to my liberal colleagues. I was pleased with the accomplishments of the meeting, particularly the prospect that my being spokesman might bring effective participation by liberals in the power structure of the Senate.

Our relationship was essentially one of mutual need, though I needed him more than he needed me. I knew clearly by then that I had no chance of influencing legislation in any major way without the help of the majority leader. With his influence, I might get the necessary votes for legislation I was interested in.

My success made little impression on my liberal colleagues. They looked on it as tokenism, and since it flowed from Johnson, it was suspect. Purist liberals are virtually impossible to discipline or organize. Each goes his separate way, feeling that he is a little more liberal, a little purer than any of the others, and the idea of someone being a spokesman among theoretical equals was repugnant. At the time, we did not talk much about the arrangement. I simply tried to make it work. From a position of weakness, we had accomplished what we had wanted. That was enough for me.

Johnson produced on his promises, and ultimately went beyond our limited objectives. As majority leader, which he became when the Democrats reached a majority in 1954, Johnson changed Democratic policy so that every freshman Democrat was assigned to a major committee his first year. This had happened on occasion but was not a standard practice. Johnson made it the rule and made it possible for liberal senators to serve on such powerful committees as Appropriations, Finance, Foreign Relations, and Judiciary, for example.[1]

23. "FEEL FREE TO ATTACK
ME ANYTIME"

As I look back on those first four years, the Truman years, I see
relatively little that had my design on it. While I worked hard on
committees, tried to perform as a liberal spokesman, a freshman
senator had in those days few levers of power and so little seniority and status, that any senator, including the most innovative,
was restrained.

When the Hoover Commission on Reorganization of the Executive Branch issued its findings, I worked hard to get their reports adopted, and received a citation for my work. Among other
things, I worked with Mike Monroney on getting the merit system applied to Internal Revenue employees. And I authored legislation that ultimately led to the creation of the Department of
Housing and Urban Development.

What success I had was largely dependent on President
Truman. My major success was in passing legislation that permitted us, under liberal credit terms, to sell India wheat to prevent starvation.* During the early fifties, while America accumulated a substantial surplus of wheat, other parts of the world
suffered from inadequate food production. In years of good
crops or bad, India was always short of food for its massive population.

Gandhi's passive resistance to the British had, of course, captured our imagination. We were more aware of India, its problems and potential, than we were of most other distant places.

* This was, of course, the forerunner of our "Food for Peace" programs.

India was half a billion people who had just come out of a colonial system and had rejected the usual route of dictatorship of generals. It had moved into the more difficult trail of free elections, of free speech, free assembly, of the right to petition the government. For humanity's sake and because it aimed to be a free and independent, democratic country, India needed and deserved our encouragement and our generous assistance.

It also required our patience and forbearance. Then and now, I felt that we must lean over backward to be of help regardless of how difficult our relationships might become. And they were often strained and difficult. Indian leaders had to deal with a multiparty system, including a vocal Communist party. Their attitudes, not unlike the attitudes of Third World countries in the sixties and seventies, were a composite of self-righteousness, fierce independence, and some belligerence, as they reached for self-identity.

The post-Gandhi leadership was difficult to work with—combining in personal and sometimes, it seemed, a national personality an insufferable combination of patronizing demeanor and bowing and scraping.

Like watching an adolescent come of age, you combined understanding with patience, even as you grew bored with the effort and wished they would get it together. But disagreeable democrats seemed vastly more worthy than pleasant dictators, and I felt we had to send the food they needed.†

Unfortunately, there was no legislation on the books that permitted our government to give, or even sell on favorable terms, our surplus wheat. When Bishop Clarence Pickett, a Methodist who had spent twenty-five years in India, came home, he called on me to describe the conditions he had just left. They were dire, and I went almost immediately to the State Department to see James Webb, the under secretary. He listened to my sad story, and then explained that there was nothing that could be done, there was no authority to handle the problem, and if there were, there was no allocation in the budget to do so.

I tried to explain to him as I had to others on lower levels in the previous days that I would try to take care of the enabling

† I became such an advocate that Paul Douglas began to call me the senator from India, and I suppose in a sense I was.

legislation. What I wanted from them was an indication that the department would support my efforts. What I got was bureaucratic double talk, deep concern articulated with head-shaking seriousness, but no help.

I went then in desperation to the American Red Cross and convinced them to accept donations for food for India and to start a special and major campaign. I called a meeting of other voluntary agencies and enlisted their support. I badgered CBS for time on the radio to make an appeal for donations to the Red Cross. I tried with others to dramatize the problem by encouraging young people in rural parts of America to send small, token bags of wheat to the Indian Embassy as an expression of concern about conditions in India.

Through the Red Cross, we were able to start the flow of wheat to India, though in extremely inadequate quantities. As people starved, I learned an early lesson on the lethargy of government and the vitality of voluntarism.

Clearly, our efforts were so limited that only a change in government policy would have sufficient impact on our ability to help. I turned to President Truman, asking him to meet with me and Bishop Pickett. He agreed. When the bishop finished his description of the awful conditions that would become catastrophic if we did nothing, I made a pitch for government support. The President asked what I wanted him to do, and I said I had to have State Department support. He said, "Why, of course; I'll see that it comes promptly. I'll just call up Dean Acheson and tell him that we want to do everything we can to get this legislation through Congress."

Within two or three hours I had a call from Acheson saying that he personally and the department would provide whatever help I asked for. It was interesting to see how a department of government that one day could offer no help, no encouragement, no support, suddenly came to life. It was an example of what happens when a President exerts leadership, overcoming the natural reticence and conservatism of the bureaucracy.

I introduced and we passed legislation to authorize an emergency shipment of four million tons of wheat. I had originally intended that it be a gift from the American people, but Prime

Minister Nehru, in addressing the Indian Parliament, said that India would prefer to purchase the wheat, under generous terms, he hoped, which would permit repayment over a long period of time. Though desperate, they did not want charity which in any way demeaned the pride they felt in their new nationhood.

On the domestic scene, while I sponsored and cosponsored many bills across the entire spectrum of my liberal interests, one bill, dubbed fair-trade legislation, was of particular interest to me. Some people thought it an undesirable bill, but I was convinced that it provided stability in our economic life, offering some protection and encouragement to independent small business.

The bill permitted manufacturers to establish a price on a product, particularly "name brand" items, which had to be adhered to or the manufacturer could withdraw it from the distributor. In effect, it put a floor price on various items. Many people thought it bad legislation, preferring that price be set by traditional competitive practices. I thought it important to protect the small, independent businessman from mercantile giants who could cut prices and ultimately drive little stores to bankruptcy.‡ With competition gone, I was convinced, the consumer would be the final loser.

The Justice Department and the Federal Trade Commission opposed the bill as violating antitrust law. I had been able to overcome their opposition in the Congress, but I feared that they might get the President to veto it, though Truman as senator had supported a similar bill.

I went to the President, and as I made my arguments for the bill, reminded him of his prior support. As we concluded, he said, "Of course, you know that I must look at this matter from the point of view of the nation, and as President, not as senator." On that equivocal note, I started to leave, and he said, "Go argue it out with Charlie Murphy.¹ See if you can convince him." I stopped in Murphy's office and made my arguments again. Murphy was noncommittal.

‡ I had seen that in the drugstore business—how the big chain druggists would drive the independent stores out of business. Once the competition was gone, they could charge whatever they wanted.

It was the end of the session in 1952, and Muriel and I and our children piled into our car to drive to Minnesota via Niagara Falls.*

We stayed in a motel there that had no phones in the rooms, and one evening the motel keeper came running down the walk, shaking with excitement and shouting as she approached our room, "Senator Humphrey, the White House is calling, the White House is calling. The President wants to talk to you."

We raced back up the walk and I picked up the phone, showing only a little less excitement than she. Soon the President was on the line saying, "Hubert, I just wanted you to know that I've signed that damned bill. I hope it will do all the good things that you said it would. If not, you've got me into a heap of trouble."[2]

While the bill itself was important to me, it really represented only a part of a more comprehensive view I had of what the American economy and society ought to be. I believe, and I hope it is not just nostalgia for my South Dakota origins, that smaller cities and towns, small merchants everywhere, provide a kind of balance in our society.

It may require certain short-run uneconomical actions on the part of both business and government, but I think it is crucial, even more today than when I began in the Senate, to create countervailing forces to the bigness of so much of what is American.

Thus, if small towns are to exist and are to attract families, they are going to have to have the schools, the medical services, the recreation areas, the merchants, the air service, the roads, the economic vitality which, if they don't match big cities, at least come close.

The problems of metropolis grow ever larger and the quality of life diminishes. The cities become a magnet for people they can't handle.† Railroads stop serving a rural America that withers as agriculture becomes a topic of indifference to most Americans. The commerce of the small towns slowly dies as the big chains

---

* This trip was an annual condition. Generally, however, Muriel would have to do it without me, with four little kids, pulling at one another, crying, sleeping, wanting to go to the bathroom.

† This may be changing in the 1970s. Smaller towns are growing and there is an out-migration from big cities. In 1972, I successfully sponsored the National Rural Development Act to address that situation. It became Public Law 92-419 in August of that year.

and huge discount stores replace the local shopkeeper. The struggle to maintain adequate education equivalent to the suburbs and city is a constant, if not losing, one.

It is not nostalgia, nor is it even that Minnesota was a rural state, that prompted my votes and legislative priorities. It was a vision of an urban, industrial America with attractive and varied alternatives, with people living near the land, in towns; of small businesses healthy and profitable and immediate, as a slight antidote to the massive concentration of business wealth.

It is, however, a vision that is impossible and irrelevant without government acting positively.

On another occasion, I urged President Truman to veto a different kind of pricing legislation, an intricate bill that would have set the price of steel for a particular area or base point. In a sense, the "basing point" concept was not significantly different from "fair trade," but steel is not home appliances, not toasters or TV sets. It was competition between little giants and bigger giants, and I felt the bill's results would simply be to keep prices up, with ill effects on the economy.

High steel costs are reflected in a wave effect throughout industry, on the price of cars, on the price of agricultural equipment, on construction costs.

Uncertain what the President intended to do, I marshaled the arguments against the bill. When I finished my pitch, the President said, "Hubert, I'm like the Missouri judge who said of a defendant, 'I'm going to give him a fair trial and then hang the S.O.B.' We're going to give this basing-point legislation a good fair hearing and then I'm going to veto it." His eyes twinkled brightly through his glasses, and I was charmed once again by his directness.

That charm was there when I went to him on another, more embarrassing occasion. While I had been treated well by the Minneapolis papers as mayor, their goodwill did not extend so favorably to the Senate. I became the big spender, the defender of President Truman and his budgets.‡ The weekly newspaper editors and out-state dailies, never much taken with me anyway, had a field day with every bill I introduced. They were in tune

‡ I used to save hostile editorials and send them back at Christmastime, saying "In the spirit of the holidays, all is forgiven."

with the Republican party line and soon attached a price tag to each Humphrey bill, keeping a running total.

One day, aggravated by the steady stream of abuse, I announced to my staff that I knew how to get a favorable story. I said, "All I have to do is demonstrate some doubt about President Truman, some little act of less than total loyalty, and I will be a hero in headlines."

When Richard Wilson, the bureau chief of the Minneapolis *Tribune,* came to interview me about the President's budget, I said, "It's too much, too extravagant. There's waste in it and we could cut several billion dollars and still not jeopardize essential government services." Wilson asked for specifics.

I had not even studied the budget carefully at that point and simply picked two or three places almost at random. That was enough. I was, indeed, a headlined hero the next day. Then editorials of surprised praise followed. What I had said and done seriously in trying to be a good legislator was as nothing compared to this gimmick.

The Trumans were living in Blair House, across Pennsylvania Avenue, while the White House was being repaired and refurbished. President Truman, trying to break out of the jail of the White House and to keep in touch with the Hill, would often have a small group of senators and congressmen in for an informal dinner.

Invited soon after my newspaper ploy, I carried a copy of the editorial that praised me most excessively. When the dinner broke up, I said to the President privately, "Mr. President, I want you to read this editorial. I really feel ashamed that I've done this, but I just wanted to prove to my staff what it takes to get a good story if you're a Truman Democrat."

He read it and reacted much as Herbert Hoover had done in a similar situation.[3] He asked if it helped me politically. I said I guessed that it did. He said, and meant it: "Feel free to attack me anytime if you think it's going to help you back home in Minnesota. I know you're with me and we need you here. If it helps to kick me in the shins, go ahead and do it. It may hurt, but at least I know it's from a friend."

If I was a friend then, I was much more so after the spring of 1952.[4]

During the campaign of 1950, I had asked President Truman to campaign with us in Minnesota, and he agreed to do so. Our DFL was not terribly strong yet, and we thought the President would add excitement and stir our troops into enough activity to win some additional offices.

The United States was fighting in Korea, and even by then the war was not going well, yet the President drew a standing-room-only crowd at the St. Paul Auditorium. I had written an introduction and was eager to deliver it.

Unexpectedly, in a wildly successful political move, the Republican governor of Minnesota, Luther Youngdahl, showed up. We had both been elected in 1948 and he was immensely popular with the people, though some of his fellow Republicans found him too liberal for their tastes. His legislature, predominantly Republican and conservative, fought him with the viciousness of a family quarrel. His appearance was courageous as well as smart. He praised Truman and welcomed him to Minnesota in a speech that went on for about ten minutes, the time allotted for my introduction. By the time he finished, there was about forty seconds left for me, since the President was to broadcast on a state-wide radio network. The speech I worked so carefully on was condensed on the spot. I said, "Ladies and gentlemen, my fellow Minnesotans, I have the high honor and privilege of introducing to you the President of the United States, Harry S Truman." I retired to my seat looking darkly at Governor Youngdahl, who had usurped my time and my glory.

Despite that moment, I liked Youngdahl. We had met shortly after the 1948 election at the home of Ray Ewald, an independent Republican businessman of substantial means who had worked with me while I was mayor. During the party, Ewald said, "Hubert, if there is ever a chance for you to recommend Luther to the federal bench, I want you to promise that you will do it." While it was part jest, it was mostly serious. I talked with Youngdahl himself later that evening, and he said that he was not feeling well, was tired of the hassle with his own party, and had always dreamed of being a federal judge.

I watched Youngdahl with special care, because he had become the logical person to oppose me in my 1954 re-election campaign. He would be coming off three terms as governor, im-

mensely popular, a commanding presence on the political platform. In a state that was still basically Republican, he would be
a formidable opponent and might very well beat me.

But, one morning in 1952, while having breakfast and reading
the Washington *Post,* I noted on the obituary page the death notice of a federal judge in the District of Columbia. Muriel
thought I had taken leave of my senses as I jumped up and almost shouted, "That's it."

I hardly stopped to explain to her what I was up to as I seized
the phone and called the White House. I told Matt Connolly that
I had to see the President on a private matter of urgency.[5] He
agreed to set up an appointment and I proceeded to my office to
wait. Matt called and said the President would see me before
noon. Suddenly, after many months, I was immensely pleased
that Youngdahl had upstaged me by introducing President
Truman.

When I got into the Oval Office, I blurted out that I wanted to
talk about a federal judgeship.

The President looked at me quizzically. "Is there an opening
in your state?"

"No, but there is one in the District of Columbia."

"Well, those judgeships are generally claimed by senators either from Virginia or Maryland, but they don't deserve them. I
don't see any reason at all why Harry Byrd ought to get another
judgeship, do you?"

I tried to seem thoughtful and fair and not excessively self-
serving, but it was hard. The mere possibility that Youngdahl
might be considered delighted me. I replied, "Well, Byrd doesn't
deserve it, considering the help he's given you, Mr. President."

I then mentioned Luther Youngdahl. I told the President what
a liberal, progressive man Youngdahl was despite his party
affiliation. I recalled for Truman the gesture of Youngdahl's introduction of him in 1950, and more importantly, the fact that
Youngdahl had been the only Republican governor to stand up
for Truman when he had fired MacArthur.

Then I talked about how he and Youngdahl shared great interest in the Shriners and Masons. And finally, I got to the politics
of it. I told him of my fear that Youngdahl would take me on in

the 1954 election and, while I thought I could defeat him, it would be a tough fight with a man I liked and respected. "If there is any way to avoid that fight, I'd like to."

The President nodded and said, "I understand very well what you're talking about." Again his eyes twinkled. "I see no damned reason at all why this judgeship should go to some senator who hasn't done a damn thing for me or this administration."

Then he asked, "Have you talked to the governor about it?" I had to admit I hadn't. The President asked that I do it immediately, not wanting to offer something that would be refused. I told him of my previous talks with Youngdahl and my feeling that he would accept it. He asked that I talk to no one else about what I was doing, reporting directly back to him.

I decided that I couldn't call the governor's office directly, knowing that someone would leak the fact, if not the substance, of my call. I tried, therefore, to reach his brother, Reuben,[6] who was my close friend, but it took me a day to do so. Reuben was in northern Minnesota, at some remote lake, on a fishing trip. When we finally made contact, I asked him to have his brother call me as quickly as possible from a secure phone.

That night, Luther did and we talked in a kind of shorthand. I said, "Are you interested in the matter that we discussed with Ray Ewald? If you are, I think there is something available."

"Well, where is it?"

"The District of Columbia."

"I'm interested."

I then asked him to fly immediately to Washington, told him that I would have Bill Simms pick him up at the airport, that I would make a reservation for him at the Statler under an assumed name. He arrived one night, and the next morning we went to a 9:00 A.M. appointment made after our phone conversation.

We had waited a few minutes outside the Oval Office when the door opened and the President himself stuck his head out and said, "Gentlemen, come in." He shook hands with Youngdahl and immediately said, "Governor, do you want to be a federal judge? If you do, I've got a position for you." Youngdahl was almost as speechless as my mother had been a couple of years before in Truman's presence, but managed to say, "I'm interested."

President Truman continued, "Hubert has been here to talk about an opening on the bench in the District of Columbia. If you want it, you can have it." Youngdahl said, "I want it."

The business of the visit was done in about a minute, but for a half hour more the President and Youngdahl chatted about Minnesota lakes, about the MacArthur flap, and about their common interest in the Masons. I didn't say much, but beamed with pleasure at what I had pulled off. Youngdahl was pleased to get out of the governor's office onto the bench. President Truman seemed to take unspoken satisfaction in knowing that even then Harry Byrd must have been preparing his own recommendation on the assumption that the job was his to fill.

Youngdahl and I stepped outside the office and talked about how to make the announcement. He wanted to announce it himself, leaving the impression, in part, that the President had instigated the offer, minimizing my role as much as possible. We decided we would walk into the White House press area and I would introduce him, saying he had an announcement.

The previous day, I had tried to alert the Minnesota press, telling them that I would be at the White House in the morning and it might be worthwhile for them to be there, too. One reporter said he would, but the reporter for the Minneapolis *Tribune* insisted on knowing what was going to happen. He told me that Congressman Harold Hagen of the Seventh District of Minnesota was holding a meeting of his House Committee on the Post Office and Civil Service on postage rates. He wanted to be assured it was more important that he be at the White House. I decided not to give him any assurances, insulted that my suggestion was not sufficient. "Write about postage stamps while the Republican governor resigns and is appointed to the bench by a Democratic President," I thought.

When Youngdahl made his announcement, I watched the face of the St. Paul *Pioneer Press* reporter. The cliché about a jaw going slack would have been invented at that moment if it had never been used before. His brain went a little slack, too. He asked, "Does this mean you are going to resign your governorship?" Youngdahl said, "That's exactly what I intend to do." When the reporter asked, "When?" Youngdahl said, "As soon as possible."

When I got back to my office, the Minneapolis *Tribune* reporter was calling, agitated, aggravated, and scooped. He whined, "You didn't tell me the governor was going to be there." If he could have seen my smile, his aggravation might have become apoplexy.

Back home, the reaction was a mixture of shock and pleasure. Harold Stassen, though no longer a resident of Minnesota, was visiting, and he attacked the appointment as a dirty political trick on my part.[7]

Youngdahl was succeeded by the lieutenant governor, C. Elmer Anderson, a decent enough man but clearly incapable of providing leadership to his political party or the state. At most, he could be expected to perform honestly as a caretaker governor.

Then I learned another lesson of American life. When I was home, shortly after the Youngdahl appointment, Gideon Seymour, the editor of the Minneapolis *Tribune,* said to me, "You know, Hubert, you think you've pulled off a pretty big political coup, and indeed you have. The Republicans are in a state of shock, but I think you ought to know what is going to happen. When the Republicans get through building up C. Elmer and we get through reporting it, his every weakness will be built into an asset.

"Those times when it looks like he is listening but doesn't know what is going on, we're going to make him look like he is pondering and meditating. We are going to make the fact that he can't make a speech an asset. He's going to be interpreted as a man who doesn't talk, but quietly gets things done."

In 1952, between the puffery of the papers and General Eisenhower's landslide victory, Anderson was elected to a full term as governor, defeating Orville Freeman, who was not only bright and articulate but who had run a very good campaign. Two years later, reality overcame the image and Freeman was elected in a rerun.

24. THE LOYAL OPPOSITION

As the presidential primaries of 1952 drew near, I found myself in an awkward position. I was devoted to President Truman and had been prepared to support him again, but he had not publicly stated whether he would run or not. Senator Kefauver had already said he would challenge Truman in the primaries, and his friends in Minnesota said he would enter our primary.

What happened in Minnesota was of great political concern to me, and I asked Truman's political advisers what they wanted done. They urged me to become a favorite-son candidate as a holding operation until Truman made up his mind. At a minimum, they thought it would keep Kefauver out.

It was risky. Truman was not particularly popular, his rating in public opinion polls very low. To be the surrogate for a popular President is not easy. For an unpopular one, it is worse. Voters, and particularly in an independent-minded state like Minnesota, are not comfortable, for the most part, with the gimmickry of stand-ins. They prefer to vote for bona-fide candidates, which I clearly was not.

If I entered as a favorite son and Kefauver came in, there was at least the chance that I would be beaten, embarrassing me at home and probably in Washington, too. If I were to lose, it would encourage the Republicans to consider me vulnerable in 1954.

But Truman had been a good President and good to me. My loyalty overcame my caution and I let my name be entered in the primary. Kefauver stayed out, saying he did not want to cause me any political trouble or embarrassment. I easily won the primary.

When President Truman announced that he would not run for re-election, it was not unexpected. He had been through exceedingly abrasive years, though I think that alone would not have prompted his decision. It was, I suspect, more a personal decision than a political one. He and Bess Truman had had enough of Washington. Power, even of the presidency, was not that attractive or compelling for either of them. He had done as well as he could, made the decisions he thought were right for the country, and the time had come to move aside.

He had urged Adlai Stevenson, who was not well known to many politicians and clearly not to the American public, to run for the presidency. Stevenson hesitated, his detractors calling him indecisive, his friends calling him humble. In the vacuum, Kefauver seemed to be running away with the nomination.

By convention time, however, despite Kefauver's victories in primaries, the momentum was toward Stevenson, who had finally agreed to run. As cochairmen of the Minnesota delegation, Orville Freeman and I were able to deliver the delegation to Stevenson, though he didn't make it easy for us. Our people, mostly Truman loyalists, were irritated by Stevenson's arm's-length treatment of the President.

The Republicans had their own struggles in the primaries and at the convention, but General Eisenhower, as their nominee, was, of course, finally victorious. In retrospect, there was probably no chance for Stevenson to overcome the hero image of Eisenhower at that particularly frenzied period of American history. America needed a rest, it needed calm, it needed consensus; and the general provided those.

The Eisenhower years were not filled with fun and laughter, as serious businessman types wandered into and out of powerful positions in Washington. Democrats seem to love government, while, I suspect, high-level Republicans too often really do not. For too many of them, service in Washington is often nothing more than a break between two jobs in private industry, or banking or law, and the art of government is itself less appealing, less exciting than it is to Democrats.

While Democratic enthusiasm may lead us into too much government, too much activity (sometimes, it seems, for the sake of activity itself), the Republican mood is of quiescence, which under some conditions turns into an indifference to problems, an inability to experiment—to try something that is not proven. Politically safe replaces politically creative.

The addition of Secretary of the Treasury George Humphrey, however, brought me some light moments and some political gain. Our views on the economy were about as far apart as two men can get and still stay within the same economic system.[1]

Frequently when I would return to Minnesota someone would stop me and say, "I just read about you in the paper; keep up the good work." I'd smile and thank the person, not knowing what they were talking about. When I'd pick up the local paper, a story would be there about George Humphrey.

People do not pay as much attention to political commentary as the politicians themselves do. Particularly in Washington we read, analyze, and read again every story. Every nuance contains implications of cosmic importance, or so we think. Though national problems are of interest and concern, the average citizen is busy with other things. He has his mind on his job, his family, maybe his plans for a vacation, his favorite athletic teams and their success. His personal problems invariably take precedence over what seems so important to us. Mostly, he reads the headlines and possibly a few lead paragraphs.

What is always remembered is the name, so George Humphrey helped me in spite of himself. While the Republican Senate Campaign Committee made me a prime target for defeat in 1954, I let George do it for me in gaining further public exposure.

The period just after President Eisenhower took office was uneasy for many top-echelon people in agencies of government. The Republicans had been out of office for twenty years, and when they came in, they fired everyone they could and replaced them with Republicans in a classic "to the victor belong the spoils" mood.

One day, my secretary buzzed me and said the White House was on the line. I took the call, wondering why they would be calling me. When I said, "Hello," a voice said, "Mr. Humphrey, we have Mr. ——— [I don't remember the name] from Akron, Ohio, here and he says that you promised him a job. What do you want me to do with him?"

As seriously as I could, I said, "Why, get him a job. The promise was made and the promise must be kept." The voice on the other end of the line said, "Thanks, that's all we wanted to know. We'll take care of it." I hoped the mistake would be made often, but that was the last bit of Republican patronage I was to control.

My favorite target among the Republican Cabinet was Ezra Taft Benson, the Secretary of Agriculture. Though George Humphrey and I were far apart on economic policy, my differences with Benson on agricultural policy made George Humphrey and me look like Siamese twins.

Benson was self-sure, an unbending exponent of policies of another age, preferring to leave the farmer at the mercy of the elements and the market place. From South Dakota on, I had concluded the elements were unreliable and the market place a jungle as far as the farmer was concerned. Since we couldn't do anything about the weather, I chose to advocate policies that might bring parity and equity into the market place.

I had supported an agricultural policy that provided for effective, fixed price supports for crop loans to the farmers so that they could hold crops and market them at the most favorable time. I also supported a program to cut back on production so that the market place would not be burdened with price-depressing surpluses.

Benson opposed all of this, advocating what the Republicans euphemistically called flexible supports, which in fact simply "flexed" farm income down. He preferred no crop loans, wanted the government out of the normal-granary food-reserve effort. I considered all of this contrary to good public policy and strange, indeed, from a man who, as Secretary of Agriculture, was ostensibly the spokesman and advocate for farmers.

After all, the American farmer was the feeder of the nation. And yet agriculture generally remained one of the most consistently depressed sectors of the American economy. One need not yearn for an impossible dream of Jeffersonian yeomen tilling the fields to feel that agriculture was still basic to a healthy economic system in modern America.

Farmers were leaving the farms by the millions for a number of reasons, some inexorable and impossible to change, but others amenable to change by government policies. The city became the only possible haven, a mirage of the good life, of jobs and success. Our urban crises of the sixties were in part the reverse side of the coin of prior rural poverty and economic distress and displacement.

For virtually every day that Ezra Benson served in the Cabinet, I rose in the Senate to condemn his policies, to suggest alternatives, and to make him a political issue. I drew vivid word pictures of people driven off the farm into a slum of city misery. I attacked the Eisenhower-Benson policies not only to change them, but to make clear the political issue for the 1956 and 1958 elections.

By 1958, Benson and his policies were a decisive issue in many Congressional and Senatorial races in the Midwest, the South, and some of the Rocky Mountain states where agriculture was a basic industry.

While I was the most aggressive spokesman on agriculture, I involved a number of other senators, and it was during this time that I made a special effort with Senator John Kennedy, who readily admitted that he knew virtually nothing about agricultural policy. I tried to explain parity, and crop management, the virtues of on-the-farm storage, and endless other esoterica of agricultural America. Kennedy would smile and say, "Don't confuse me with the facts, Hubert. Just tell me the right thing to do and what your farmers need and I'll help you out if I can."

Despite his protestations, he learned much about agriculture and rural America. He did not always vote as I urged, often feeling that things I advocated did not serve the interests of Massachusetts very well. When he thought he could, he followed our lead.

Though Ezra Benson and George Humphrey were powerful, the real strongman of the Eisenhower Cabinet was John Foster

Dulles. He was a bright, articulate conservative, evangelical and often rigid, dividing the world into static categories of friends and enemies.

He traveled constantly, almost compulsively, developing his own hip-pocket diplomacy as he went. As a result of conditions in the world and his energy, foreign policy was at the heart of almost everything transpiring in the early fifties. Republican conservatives waged continuous political war on the policies of Roosevelt and Truman, screaming about the Yalta agreements. Joe McCarthy, though drinking heavily and already preparing his own doom, still rode high and roughshod.

In face of this, Lyndon Johnson and Sam Rayburn were determined to strengthen the Senate Foreign Relations Committee so that it could help slow this onslaught of reaction.[2]

Their concern was as much for Eisenhower and his basically international instincts, which were in fact closer to the Democratic middle than to the Republicans in power. They feared that Dulles, with support from Knowland, Bricker, Homer Capehart, William Jenner, and Styles Bridges, would turn us into a tory island of isolation and simplistic anti-communism.

Johnson asked Mike Mansfield and me to serve on Foreign Relations. Both Johnson and Rayburn thought well of Mansfield, who had served in the House and before that had been a professor of history at the University of Montana with special interest in Far Eastern politics and history.

Johnson appealed to my vanity, saying I owed it to the country to sit on Foreign Relations at such a crucial time. He knew I shared his concern about the Republican attacks on the United Nations and our participation in it. He said that I couldn't express anxiety about our national direction, make speeches about foreign aid and mutual security programs, urge support of NATO, and still refuse his request.

He was right, but I was reluctant to give up the seniority that had brought me several subcommittee chairmanships. I had to give up Agriculture and the Committee on Labor and Public Welfare, which served my own and Minnesota's interests. (Johnson promised to get me back on Agriculture at the first opportunity.)

Going on Foreign Relations was an important move for me. It

lent authority to my speeches and points of view, it forced
deeper study on issues, it required travel overseas and contacts
with people such as Harold Wilson and Willy Brandt, who
would rise to power in their countries later.*

In 1953, Herbert Waters, a California newspaperman who had
worked for Charles Brannan, Truman's last Secretary of Agriculture, joined my staff. Herb had written speeches on agriculture
for President Truman[3] and had been recommended to me as a
man who had better comprehension of agricultural economics
and the politics of agriculture than anyone else in Washington. I
found that an accurate description.

Herb was also a shrewd politician[4] and sensed immediately the
classic danger for senators—that as they gain seniority and
power, and grow more nationally oriented, they become separated from their political base and prospects for defeat. In my
case, he saw that I had left committees of interest to my constit-
uencies in both labor and agriculture. Herb tried to fuse my new
foreign-policy responsibilities with agriculture. In part stimulated by a political need, he refined an altruistic concept of a
food-for-peace program. I was able to attach the concept in a
general statement, but without a full-fledged program, as an
amendment to the foreign-aid bill in 1953.

Herb was a friend of the liberal Farmers Union, but he also
understood the needs of agriculturally related business. He
educated me in detail on foreign agricultural trade and the importance of exports. Working virtually day and night, he kept up
a constant, and informative, flow of position papers, policy statements, and arguments on what should be done legislatively.

At one point, he provided me a two-hundred-page critique of
Eisenhower-Benson farm policies. It was the most comprehensive analysis of the limitations and fallacies of those policies I
had seen. I shared it with my colleagues, and he soon became an
informal adviser to many of them. Later he briefed their staff
people, holding seminars for them. During most of the fifties, no
debate on agricultural policy in which I was involved took place
without his input. At my side on the Senate floor, he was like an

* Ultimately, it also led to my appointment by President Eisenhower as
a Congressional delegate to the United Nations in 1956–57.

encyclopedia of facts and strategy. If I was never at a loss for words, it was because he was never at a loss for facts.

In 1954, having returned to the Agriculture Committee on the death of Senator Clyde Hoey of North Carolina, I asked Senator Andrew Schoeppel, a conservative Kansas Republican, to join in sponsoring a food-for-peace bill that filled in the outlines of my 1953 amendment.

The bill had four objectives: to dispose of surplus agricultural commodities, to develop new markets, to serve our foreign-policy objectives, and to meet humanitarian needs in other countries.

The legislation benefited the hungry, helped American farmers, and aided the economic and foreign policy of our country. Further, countries paid for what they received, and those payments were retained by us in those countries for use in other economic-assistance programs.

In the twenty years of Public Law 480, over 240 million tons of grain, millions of pounds of American dairy products, hundreds of thousands of bales of American cotton have fed and clothed people in developing nations.[5]

In recent years, the Food for Peace program lost sight of those early objectives. Humanitarian needs in most of the world were ignored, and the political value of foodstuffs dominated, being used to support the war effort in Vietnam and to help bring about a diplomatic settlement in the Middle East.[6]

As legitimate as those uses might be, it meant that we were less able to respond to disasters and famine elsewhere. In 1975, I finally introduced legislation to clarify the purposes and priorities of the program, reaffirming its humanitarian goals and requiring at least a 70 per cent share guaranteed for purely humanitarian needs, an ironic necessity for such a program.

Agriculture brought me closer to a flamboyant but wise character, M. W. Thatcher, who was different from any other man I have known. Bill Thatcher ran the Farmers Union Grain Terminal Association, one of the largest grain co-operatives in the world. An accountant by training, he had been a kind of prairie radical, part of the Non-Partisan League in North Dakota. Bill had an uncanny business sense, which he turned not to personal profit, but to helping farmers. He would have been an incredibly charismatic political leader, but chose to lead through the co-operative movement, in which his constituency was family farmers across the Midwest.

He was a demanding, irascible, occasionally petulant friend. But he was devoted and generous, too, to farmers and politicians alike. In the thirties, he had advised Franklin Roosevelt on farm policy, helping develop the Federal Bank for Co-operatives and other forms of farm financing, emancipating farmers from the captivity of private banks. He was a close friend of Henry Wallace, then Roosevelt's Secretary of Agriculture.

In Washington, with evangelical fervor, Thatcher banged on any door to convert people to his views. He was a political maverick whose only ideology was helping farmers market their products profitably. He supported anyone who could help—Eugene McCarthy, George McGovern, Quentin Burdick, me—at the same time as he aided such very different political characters as Milton Young and Karl Mundt. He was even a close friend of Robert Taft and supported him in the 1952 presidential primaries against Eisenhower simply because Taft was more friendly toward co-operatives.

Thatcher never felt he had to wear bib overalls or faded denim to prove his identification with his farm members. And he didn't believe in ashes and sackcloth. To the contrary, he felt a certain elegance pleased his members. He drove a big car, dressed like a banker (he, in fact, became a bank director), socialized with the Establishment, and held a seat on the Grain Exchange, the normal domain of conservative Yankee busi-nessmen whose interest was profits not parity.

The first time I entered the board room in his headquarters, I commented on its fine wood, the soft, big chairs. Thatcher ex-plained, "When a farmer comes in here, he is a director of a busi-ness and ought to feel like it. Comfort doesn't belong just to the rich."[7]

The board room was for more than farmers' visits. Politicians came there to pay their respects to a living force. Harry Truman, Robert Taft, Henry Wallace, Lyndon Johnson, and John Ken-nedy, among many others, arrived in that room.

When John Kennedy was to visit the Twin Cities in 1962, his staff agreed to a meeting with Thatcher and suggested the Presi-dent's suite at the hotel. I tried to explain that Thatcher didn't visit Presidents, they visited him. The reaction was a mixture of laughter and outrage. "Who the hell does Thatcher think he is?" I tried to explain that Presidents come and go, Thatcher remained. The President's audience with *Mr.* Thatcher was in the GTA board room (to many of us, the "Throne Room"). Though retired today at ninety-four, Bill Thatcher is still a commanding personality to be reckoned with.

In the fall of 1955, party leaders in Minnesota urged Adlai Stevenson to announce that he would enter our presidential primary in 1956. We were convinced that we could "deliver" the state for him. The entire power structure of the DFL was for him: Freeman, who was governor; Karl Rolvaag, lieutenant governor; Eugene McCarthy and John Blatnik, our two leading congressmen; our state party chairman, Ray Hemenway; Dorothy Jacobson, state chairwoman; Eugenie Anderson, national committeewoman; and Gerry Heaney, national committeeman. We had labor and most of the farm leadership for him, too.

It seemed impossible for him to lose. But three men, good party members but mavericks all, took us on by supporting and organizing for Kefauver. Robert Short, a businessman who had run unsuccessfully for office, and two state legislators from St. Paul, Donald Wozniak and Peter Popovich, joined by Congresswoman Coya Knutson made the issue "bossism." In a state where Republicans can vote in the Democratic primary, they beat us.

Kefauver liked campaigning, moving around the state, waving his coonskin cap. In his fatigue, he would sometimes mispronounce the names of his closest supporters, tell the audience how pleased he was to be in Wisconsin, get the town name wrong. It didn't make any difference; the people liked him.

Stevenson, who really hated that kind of campaigning, nevertheless did it, going from small town to small town, smiling bravely, being cheerful. But it was not his milieu. I remember his face when a town father pinned a phony beard on him as part of a local civic celebration. I remember the faces in his audience when in the basement of a veterans hall in Little Falls he spoke of "the disingenous dissembling of the Eisenhower administration." At the end of one of our trips, he looked at me, shaking his head in disbelief, and said, "Hubert, you really *like* this!"

After that disastrous March primary, we kept in touch, and in early summer, when we were both in Washington, we met after a fund-raising dinner.[8] Max Kampelman and I joined Stevenson and James Finnegan, secretary of state of Pennsylvania and Stevenson's campaign manager, in a room at the Mayflower Hotel. William McCormick Blair, Stevenson's friend and aide, who was dealing with other people, was in and out of the room.

Adlai wanted to talk about the vice-presidential nominee. He was blunt: he did not want Kefauver, and he talked then of others he was considering, among them Mayor Robert Wagner of New York, Senator Stuart Symington, Senator Albert Gore. We discussed political and personal strengths and weaknesses.

When we had gone over every possible candidate, Stevenson said, "Well, Hubert, why don't you think about it yourself?" He said that I was the most qualified. That was pleasing, of course, but we raised one slight problem: southern opposition.

Stevenson asked Finnegan to overcome that obstacle by finding Southerners who would urge him to "accept" me. If that happened, as I understood the conversation, Adlai would choose me as his vice-presidential running mate. Max and I left the meeting convinced there was a commitment, and when Finnegan and Max and I got the prominent southern legislators John Sparkman, Lister Hill, Richard Russell, Walter George, Lyndon Johnson, and Sam Rayburn to recommend my selection to Stevenson, the condition seemed to be satisfied.

Bill Blair continued to call Herb Waters with periodic reports of additional support. As we settled in at the Chicago convention, I had to start writing an acceptance speech and planning a campaign.

We were all gathered in my hotel suite talking and watching television when we heard that Adlai had announced that the vice-presidential nomination was to be thrown open to the delegates, that he would not avail himself of the normal prerogative of choosing his own running mate.

In that room, shock was followed by fury and then frenzy. But it was too late. I had gone around to various delegations to make an appearance, but had not really worked hard at getting commitments from delegates because I didn't think I needed them. I thought, for example, that George Smathers was for me and could deliver the Florida delegation. He was really for Jack Kennedy. More importantly, the New England states were for Kennedy, organized well by John Bailey and Abe Ribicoff. And he had other votes as well.

Kefauver had about three hundred delegates for President and they were easily convertible to a vice-presidential nomination. Then Albert Gore was nominated by a bloc of border states. I ended up with about one hundred thirty votes on the first ballot, behind all three of them. The choice was Kefauver.

I would have preferred to deliver the Minnesota delegation to Kennedy, particularly knowing how Stevenson felt about Kefauver, but I couldn't. Kefauver was strong with our farm people and, except for a couple of us, no one really knew Kennedy.

The following day, Adlai called to apologize for the change in his plans and for not having informed me ahead of time. I was civil, but cold, listening to but not accepting his apology.

But I was not up for re-election and set aside any leftover anger quickly to campaign for Adlai, whose immense distinction overcame my personal hurt. Though his defeat seemed almost inevitable from the start, it made me sad that the American people once again rejected him.

In retrospect, his defeats in 1952 and 1956 helped me grow as a senator. At that stage of my career, it was probably helpful not to be aligned with the party in power. As loyal opposition, I could look at government, and my own role, from a little distance.

Early in the Eisenhower period, I took the lead on a piece of legislation that went to the heart of something that had been troubling since my days as mayor. The federal system just didn't work as smoothly as it should (or our founding fathers thought it might). Simply, my experience as mayor was in jarring conflict with the political-science theory I had learned and taught to many students. The traditional description came, of course, from the Tenth Amendment to the Constitution: *The powers not delegated to the United States belong to the states or the people thereof.* Clearly, the power of government was to rest with the people and the states, except where specifically delineated otherwise.

But, to the people's disadvantage, the power struggle between the national and state governments often paralyzed both. The argument between those who venerated states' rights and the advocates of big federal government made for good theoretical discussion and good newspaper copy, while too many times the people's needs were ignored.

The doctrine of states' rights, narrowly construed, frequently prevented any expression of national will or adequate solutions for problems on a national basis. What was reasonable in a small nation, largely rural and agricultural, hog-tied an increasingly urban, expanding population whose commerce and industry and problems swept across geographic boundaries of the states.

Conflict between state and federal governments was only one dimension of the inadequate working of our federal system. State governments and local governments were even less co-operative, less able to function in any way close to equal relationship. (Most state legislatures in America, until the Supreme Court "One man, one vote" decision in 1964, were disproportionately rural despite vast population changes.[9])

Survival required turning directly to the federal government, something that had begun during the Roosevelt days, when it was clearly necessary to provide financial assistance directly to local governments. Work programs and housing programs were among many examples of federal efforts negotiated directly with cities or counties. Yet federalism was not so much a partnership, but a series of confrontations.

What haunted me was the specter of government increasingly immobilized by conflicting interests, a structure incapable of dealing with postwar society. I introduced legislation authorizing a presidential commission to study the relationships among the various levels of government.

Commissions don't always solve problems—studies often go directly from the print shop to the archives—but in this instance I could see no other way to force attention to the problem.

My cosponsor, Senator Homer Ferguson of Michigan, was a man with whom I agreed rarely, but who, in this instance, shared my concern. We were not strong enough to get the resolution passed, and I sought another unlikely ally, Senator Robert Taft of Ohio. The concept of government functioning more efficiently appealed to him.

As "Mr. Republican," he was able to gain support from the Republican administration as well as Congressional Republicans. When the first commission was about to be named, Taft discovered that I was not on it.

In a decent and uncharacteristically bipartisan act, he urged the White House to put me on the commission. I served for four years.

Eisenhower's presence in the White House also forced me to think about the traditional liberal reaction to military men in civilian positions of power. I shared most of the feelings—fear, distrust, and a kind of knee-jerk opposition—when I came to Washington, but was soon faced with evidence that didn't fit the neat categories of prejudice.

Here, as elsewhere, stereotyping didn't work. Some military men—MacArthur, Curtis LeMay—are indeed the captives of their experience and think in rigid "friends-and-enemies," confrontation terms. But others do not, and they really represent a civilian spirit despite lifelong careers in the military. Indeed, to exclude all military men from civilian government would be to cheat the nation of a valuable resource.

Without George Marshall, for example, our postwar policies might have been less impressive. He had the greatest respect for the office of the President, he understood that the armed forces were only a single, albeit powerful, institution in our republic, and never questioned the overriding importance of civilian control of the military.

In his various roles as Secretary of State, Secretary of Defense, or the President's personal representative to China, he performed marvelously—and as a civilian. That he became the prime target of Joe McCarthy's wild charges was ironic, as well as grossly undeserved.

Walter Bedell Smith was another distinguished general with an enviable reputation as a World War II leader. He served in the State Department and as our Ambassador to the Soviet Union, in every sense as much a civilian as those who had never been in the service. He also served at the Central Intelligence Agency, and without evidence to the contrary, one must assume he brought no more than a mixture of his civilian-military background to that job.

The one military man with whom I had worked closely in my first term was Omar Bradley. As head of the Veterans Administration, his military background was relevant, but it never hindered his civilian role or judgments. We worked to reorganize and improve the medical program of the VA in an effort to make it a first-class agency of deep concern and real help to our veterans.

Finally, of course, one must judge Eisenhower himself. He brought certain views of staff organization to the White House that may have derived from his life in the Army, and I am not sure that they always worked well. But he was not a militarist as President. He was the man who called the nation's attention to the dangers of the military-industrial complex, of its real and potential power in government and industry.

(Malcolm Moos, a Minnesotan whose father had also been a pharmacist, ghosted the speech, and later, while he was president of the University of Minnesota, he told me that he had anticipated that President Eisenhower would delete that phrase or section. But Eisenhower agreed, and delivered the speech virtually without change. It may well be the one lasting phrase from all of Eisenhower's speeches to become part of the American idiom.)

The insidious nature of the military-industrial power comes not from the men who leave the military for high government civilian posts, but from those who leave for defense-industry jobs. Their vision is largely unchanged, and though their pay comes in civilian clothes from a civilian source, their head and heart remain in uniform. And while some suspicion remains healthy whenever a military man moves into a position of civilian power, the most able of them shift from uniform to civilian garb serving our country with distinction, honor, and a sense of democratic duty.

It was also during the Eisenhower administration that I focused on the central document of the entire federal government: the annual budget of the President. It lays out the expenditures of public funds. More significantly, it shows the priorities of an administration and the goals it hopes to achieve. Yet, whether there has been a Democrat or a Republican in the White House, the budget has remained more secret than the plans for an atomic bomb.

The federal budget—though its impact reaches to the lowest level of government, though it involves the governmental life-blood of states, cities, counties—is entirely the product of a small bureaucracy within the executive branch. It is the embodiment of the bureaucracy, when it really ought to be a creation of partners, in a truly federal spirit.

Budgeting is a process of economic analysis and proposals by people within the federal government structure, and that is its central weakness. As the proposals move from the various departments and agencies through the Bureau of the Budget (the name changes, the function remains the same) to the President, it is a subliminal process.

The press in Washington, which can expose almost everything that happens in our country, from the private life of a belly dancer to the secrets of the Central Intelligence Agency, seems deaf, blind, and dumb when it comes to the preparation of the budget.

As a result, when the budget comes down to Congress, it is as though it were Holy Writ newly discovered. It is wrapped in the gold paper of the Executive Office of the President; it is tied and bound and finally crowned with the sealing wax of the presidential seal. It is opened and revealed to the waiting publicans with an almost religious mystique.

From then on, the Congress is on the defensive, able merely to attack, adjust, minimize, expand, or contract what has been presented by the President.[10] But the *initiative* for planning, for determining the amount and timing of expenditures, is in the hands of the President. Congress, no matter how well run, how wisely populated, seems to haggle, delay, argue, debate while the country and the President wait.

Yet, if the Congress is left out of the first part of the process, the most distant representatives of the people—the mayors, state legislators, governors—are treated as passive recipients of whatever largess comes their way.

What the budget says may very well have more impact on

what happens in a city or state or county than almost anything done in the city council or state legislature or county commission.

Conservatives are correct that all too often the federal budget overrides state and local judgment by making available large sums of matching money. It entices state and local governments into programs that may not really be priority items in a particular area.

Simply, the bureaucracy can be the enemy of what is proper and necessary in a federal system. This is not to malign the motives and public interest of civil servants so much as it is to question the nature of the institution that has developed.

25. "IT IS A BONE IN MY THROAT"

For twelve years, as a liberal spokesman, I had been on the front page of the New York *Times* and the Washington *Post* frequently. I had spoken in every region of the United States. I had appeared before hundreds of national conventions of every conceivable sort. I had been on "Meet the Press" and other public-issues programs more than any of my colleagues.

Yet, when a poll was taken in 1959 on simple name recognition, very few people polled could identify me. That was difficult to believe and accept. Surrounded by people who tell you that you are important, fed by your own sense of accomplishment, nurtured by the Washington atmosphere, you begin to believe that everyone knows you.

The 1960 presidential campaign, in the normal pattern of American politics, began several years ahead of time. For John Kennedy, it started immediately after his unsuccessful attempt to secure the vice-presidential nomination in 1956. For most candidates, however, the campaign begins when the media want it to start. Long before an individual may have decided whether he is going to seek the nomination, his name may appear as a potential candidate.

Shortly after the 1958 Congressional elections, *Time* ran a cover with pictures of presidential possibilities: Stuart Symington, G. Mennen Williams, Adlai Stevenson, Lyndon Johnson,

Jack Kennedy, and me. At that point, it was like being a little bit pregnant. Ready or not, you are in the race.

Once mentioned, though doubts remain, you are almost immediately convinced. And, insidiously, you begin to see your strengths as great, the weaknesses of others as even greater. The logic of becoming an active candidate is soon overwhelming, at least to yourself.

Once, in 1956, A. B. "Happy" Chandler, governor, then senator, from Kentucky before an equally unillustrious career as baseball commissioner, was asked how he presumed to seek the Democratic nomination for President. He replied, "Have you looked at the other fellows?" It is a question that will be and has been asked by virtually all senators, most governors, and a few congressmen in the period preceding every presidential election.

While I was eager to run, I was not sure I was a viable presidential candidate, and ultimately let myself get into the race without adequate financing or planning. There was no honorable way I could get adequate funds, but my planning should have been better.

Yet, for a time, I hesitated and wavered. Could I win? Would I be a good President? Could I raise the necessary money? Who would support me? The answers were less clear than the questions, and they changed from week to week.

Then, in December of 1958, something happened that gave me additional confidence. I visited eight countries in Europe to encourage international co-operation in science and medical research.[1] I had been conducting Senate hearings and studies on ways and means of improving our systems of co-ordination of scientific and medical information.

My European inquiry took me to scientific and medical laboratories in England, France, Germany, Holland, Norway, Sweden, Finland, and the Soviet Union. In Moscow I spent several days talking to specialists and scientists in information retrieval, cancer research, agriculture, and education.

While I was in Geneva for a brief visit to the World Health Organization and the United Nations Disarmament Committee, I had the opportunity to see Mr. Kusnetzov of the Soviet Union. I had gotten to know him while we both were delegates to the UN General Assembly, in 1956–57. At our Geneva meeting, I made a request to meet with Nikita Khrushchev when my itinerary brought me to Russia—with little hope that my request would be granted. Later, after I had arrived in Moscow, I repeated the same request, again with little hope. But, at 2:30 P.M. on December 1, I was suddenly told that "the First Minister" would see me at three. I was surprised and excited and had little time to organize my thoughts.

I said, "I'm going to call my wife." My Russian escort said, "There isn't time," and began to ease me toward the door.

I replied, "Then we will make time." Khrushchev, after all, was his dictator, not mine, and I pulled away, insistent on using the phone. It took a while, but I finally reached Muriel at the National Hotel and told her that I was off to see Khrushchev, but added that I expected to be back by suppertime. In a matter of minutes, I was at the Kremlin.

We walked at least one hundred feet down a tremendous carpeted corridor on the second floor, then another fifty feet or so along a similar corridor to our right, before we entered the outer office of the Premier's suite.

At three minutes to three o'clock I was ushered into Khrushchev's office. It was big, about fifty feet by thirty-five feet, but not ornate. On the wall was a picture of Lenin, and some maps. Nothing else. Khrushchev was seated at a very plain desk of dark wood. He got up and walked around the desk with his hand outstretched.

He wore a neat dark blue suit with two small decorations in the form of red stars on his lapel, a white shirt with simple cuff links, and a light tie.

After we had greeted each other, through the interpreter, Khrushchev asked if I would mind having a few photographs taken.

The Soviet photographers ordered Khrushchev and me around, and I said that photographers are the same everywhere —always asking for "just one more." We had already found one common denominator between our two political systems.

Picture-taking over, Khrushchev motioned me to a long conference table that sat at right angles to his desk. We sat opposite each other with the interpreter at the end between us.

During the early part of our talk, Khrushchev sat well back in his chair, relaxed, not uninterested but detached. When we got to subjects of special interest to him, he sat up, leaned forward and occasionally emphasized his remarks by pointing his forefinger at me or tapping on the felt cover of the table.

In an emotional moment, his voice, normally a conversational monotone, took on fuller resonance. In moments of greater intensity, his brows would furrow and his hazel-brown eyes would narrow, often disclosing his attitudes better than his words.

His eyes were damp when he spoke of a son who had been killed during World War II. They gleamed in sentimental remembrance when he recalled the poverty of his boyhood, his Christian upbringing, and his turn to atheism. They narrowed, sharpened, and seemed to burn when he shook his finger in anger and said, "Don't threaten me," when I spoke of American military might.

Through it all, Nikita Khrushchev remained a determined man, never permitting himself to be taken lightly. But he laughed, made small jokes, and veered suddenly from the gravest topics with a quick jest or some soothing banality.*

Like Russia itself, he had risen from poverty and weakness to wealth and power but was never wholly confident of himself and his new status. Khrushchev was a little *too* assertive, a little *too* confident.[2] Here, I thought, was a man who might be capable of attempting just about anything in order to prove to himself, as well as to others, that he and his country were as strong and invincible as he wanted to believe they were.

I had no idea how long Khrushchev intended for me to stay, and I soon got nervous about staying too long. On three occasions early in our conversation, I asked the interpreter whether I was overstaying my welcome. He said to leave that decision to Khrushchev, counseling quietly, "If he wants you to go, he will let you know."

At one point, to ease my obvious tension, the interpreter men-

---

* Once, he literally jumped from his chair, walked over to a map case, pulled down the map of North America, and said to me, "Senator, where is your home?"

I said, "Minneapolis, Minnesota." He beckoned me to show him on the map.

I did so, and then he looked at me and said, "I promise you, we shall never bomb it."

tioned my concern to Khrushchev, who waved his hands, dismissing the question, and said, "*Nyet, nyet,* stay. We have much to talk about."

During the first hour and a half, Khrushchev seemed to encourage me to do most of the talking, as if to take my measure. It was clear, however, that he knew something about me. At one point, he said, "I know you do not decide these affairs, but you will play a part. You are a member of the Democratic majority and a member of the Senate Foreign Relations Committee."

I said that there were many areas for non-political co-operation open to our governments and people, emphasizing my interest in scientific and cultural co-operation. I urged Khrushchev to take a personal interest in these subjects. My chief emphasis was on the worldwide need for international co-operation in medical research—a kind of "health for peace" program.

As I spoke he frequently interjected, "*Da, da, da.*" While his interest seemed genuine, it was the restrained reaction of a man discussing things normally left to others. It was only when our conversation shifted to Berlin, nuclear armaments, and trade that he really warmed up.

Khrushchev said with obvious irritation, "Your troops in Berlin are of no importance unless you want to make war. Why do you maintain this thorn?" And then, changing his metaphor, "It is a bone in my throat."

Clearly, the Germans were a matter of importance and worry to Khrushchev. Trying to lighten the situation somewhat, I said, "Our Germans are wine drinkers, lovers, and farmers. Your Germans are Prussians—and you'd better keep an eye on them." Khrushchev's eyes twinkled and his mouth began a smile, but he remained stern.

Yet he said shortly after, "I have the deepest respect for President Eisenhower. I like President Eisenhower. We want no evil to the United States or a free Berlin. You must assure the President of this."

When I spoke of Eisenhower as a man of integrity, Khrushchev agreed. "He is a very honest man who wants peace." But he was disdainful of John Foster Dulles. "I am very sorry that the policies of the United States are made by Dulles. He is a man of very special character. This is your own internal matter, but that is not only my view. Throughout the whole world he is regarded in the same way. It is not just I who do not like Mr. Dulles. If you don't think so, read the British press and the French press and the press of other countries. However, the Soviet Union will survive. We have survived many Secretaries of State."

He characterized Dulles as "imperialist" and "war-like" with such intensity that I felt called upon to defend Dulles. When I did so sharply, we dropped the subject and talked of him no more.†

He praised a speech of Vice President Richard Nixon and said of former President Truman, in an oddly familiar but mixed way, "I did not like Truman. I did not like Truman's policies, but Truman did make decisions."

Khrushchev covered the whole spectrum of issues between our two countries and systems. He was full of himself and obviously anxious to impress me so that I would report back to our government his views. On nuclear weaponry and trade, on military confrontation and economic competition, he left no major topic untouched.

He suggested the United States should be discussing questions of outer space directly with the Soviet Union instead of raising them within the United Nations. "So now," Khrushchev said sarcastically, "The United States discusses outer space with Guatemala—but Guatemala does not seem to be too advanced in space science."

† At one point, Khrushchev talked of his political difficulties. He spoke of Bulganin and Voroshilov—both prominent and powerful figures in the Soviet political hierarchy. He held them in disdain, calling them "fools," and then he turned to me like a professional actor and said, "Now I've told you about my fools; you tell me about yours." He would constantly try to keep me off balance—jabbing and poking like a boxer, then quickly changing the subject. He was filled with his plans for Soviet economic development and repeatedly reminded me of the rich natural resources of the U.S.S.R. and their huge undertakings in agriculture, steel, and electrical power.

Always competitive and always determined to compare the U.S.S.R. with the United States, he said, "We shall beat you in production of steel." To Khrushchev, all other countries were second-rate. Whenever he spoke of China he would compare it to Great Britain and then conclude his comparison by saying, "Britain is a second-rate power." It was a clever but subtle reminder that, in his mind, China was second-rate as well.

One of the few subjects that Khrushchev was reluctant to discuss was Communist China and his government's relations with it. When I edged up to the subject, he said, "*Nyet, nyet*. You are a subtle man, you are trying to trap me into talking about China. They are our allies, our good relations."

"Without getting into the ally business," I said, "I'd like to ask one question about the new communes."

Khrushchev's response was possibly the most interesting part of the whole interview. He said, "They are old-fashioned, they are reactionary. We tried that right after the Revolution. It just doesn't work. That system is not nearly so good as the state farms and the collective farms. You know, Senator, what those communes are based on? They are based on that principle 'From each according to his abilities, to each according to his needs.' You know that won't work. You can't get production without incentive."

I could hardly believe that the leader of world communism was rejecting the core of Marxist theory. I said simply, "That is rather capitalistic." Khrushchev replied, "Call it what you will. It works."‡

We had been talking without pause for four hours when, at about seven o'clock, Khrushchev stood up and said, "Let's go to the toilet."* While he was in the private dressing quarters that adjoined his office, I said to the interpreter, "I have been here much too long," but the interpreter said I should not leave until Khrushchev suggested it.

When Khrushchev came back, instead of bidding me good-by he proposed that we have a snack in the office and continue our talk.

When he and I were seated once again, I told him an old, and probably apocryphal, story about Winston Churchill and Clement Attlee. Churchill and Attlee, as opposing party leaders, had an intense partisan debate in Parliament. When the debate was

‡ Shortly after that, China did slow down the commune system, but when I reported that dialogue subsequently, Khrushchev denounced me and denied saying it.

* I recall seeing in Khrushchev's toilet room a number of medications on the shelf. I had known that he was under doctors' care. Had I been able to read Russian, I could have learned what medicine he was taking. As a pharmacist, I was intrigued.

over, the two of them walked from the floor of Commons toward a men's room nearby.

Their conversation was animated, and Attlee continued to talk with intensity as he approached the urinal, thinking that Churchill was still at his side. When Attlee looked up at a pause in his discourse, he found that he had been talking to himself, that Churchill was at the very end of the row, out of earshot.

Attlee, angered that he had been left talking to himself, berated Churchill when he returned. "Look, Winston," he said, "your behaviour is atrocious! We can be partisans in the House, but once we leave it we are gentlemen and friends. To leave me talking to myself is outrageous."

Churchill removed his cigar and said, "Look, Clem, you socialists are all alike. Whenever you see something that is big and functioning smoothly, you always want to nationalize it!"

Khrushchev roared and insisted that I tell it again slowly to make sure that the interpreter got it right.

As I told the story, it was obvious from the scurrying of office aides and waiters that no meal had been planned. Nevertheless, food soon appeared. We started with small sandwiches of pork, cheese, and crab meat. Then we had caviar and fresh fruit, followed by broiled slices of beef and a fowl I never did identify.

At about nine o'clock I remarked that I had met Anastas Mikoyan at a diplomatic reception, and Khrushchev said a talk with Mikoyan about trade and economic competition would be good for me. He told an aide to find Mikoyan, and in about fifteen minutes, Mikoyan appeared. When the pleasantries were over and we sat down again, Khrushchev said, "Tell Mikoyan your story about Churchill and Attlee."

I did, and Khrushchev laughed heartily once again and told us that he was going to have the story sent out to all the Russian ambassadors around the world. I smiled to myself at the thought of the diplomatic cables filled with serious matters and my silly story. Would they scramble it into code? Would the CIA break the code?

We talked more seriously for another two hours, when, at about eleven twenty-five, Mikoyan stood up and said, "I am tired. It is time to go home." I also left then, but I had the feel-

13. "I needed to reach beyond the normal . . . government . . . to do anything useful. I needed the consent . . . of the people, and got it."

14. The Humphrey family. Standing left to right, brother Ralph, sister Mrs. Fern Baynes, the author. Seated are the author's father and mother. One other sister, Mrs. Frances Howard, is missing from the photograph.

15. Muriel and the author with their children Nancy and "Skip," around 1943.

16. "I arrived in Washington [in 1948] with all the excitement of a kid in a new neighborhood . . . all was yet to be discovered."

ing that had it not been for Mikoyan's fatigue, Khrushchev and I might have gone on for another eight and a half hours.

The unexpected visit was enlightening, and the resulting publicity helped give me more national prominence. But the prominence was less important than how I saw myself. I knew now that I was able to deal effectively with heads of state.

26. A COLD WINTER IN WISCONSIN

Sometime in mid-1959, I started to give really serious thought to entering the presidential primaries. I talked to many friends, but possibly the most important was James Rowe, a Washington attorney and good friend who had been around politics since he worked as a young man in the Roosevelt White House.[1] He seemed to have contacts with every important politician in the country and was much wiser than most. Rowe felt that I had to enter some primaries to give my candidacy credibility. He insisted that there was no way I could be successful by going to Democratic state conventions and working in the non-primary states for delegates. He said, "You are just not that well known, and if you are going to have any chance at all, you are going to have to challenge Kennedy in the primaries."

We agreed that I was about a ten-to-one long shot at best and that the primary way, though difficult, was the only way. He said I must make a full-time commitment, leaving my Senate duties in limbo, being away even when there were key votes.

He was to the point. "You can't be a good Senator and a good presidential candidate at the same time. If you try to split your time, you'll make neither a good senator nor a good presidential candidate." I listened to Jim, pondered his advice, but did not take it seriously enough. Surely, I thought, it is possible to carry on most of my Senate duties and at the same time campaign. He was right and I was wrong.

Being a presidential candidate requires a tremendous amount of effort and almost undivided attention. Jack Kennedy made up his mind to be a full-time candidate and he didn't worry about the Senate. He wanted the nomination and he set out to get it with everything at his command. And he had plenty: a good organization, trained professionals, personal popularity, money. And he had them all at the same time, which is the compound that makes political success possible. The other candidates, such as I, simply never focused as Kennedy did.

I continued to discuss my possible candidacy with friends, most of them long-time associates in Minnesota, and with a small group in Washington.[2]

Our strengths were also our weaknesses. These people knew me well, and we had worked together for many years. They were the best there was in honest, straightforward, issues-oriented politicians. Most of them had helped create Minnesota's deserved reputation for superior politics. With few exceptions, we were all Minnesotans, with limited knowledge and ability to deal with the new dimension of national politics and fund-raising. The heroes of local success, we would be, ultimately, the victims of national ineptitude.

Our announcement was a good example of how not to begin. In contrast to Kennedy's, it seemed childish and clearly unsophisticated.

Kennedy launched his campaign in the Senate Caucus Room surrounded by the aura of that handsome chamber, his every word and gesture chronicled by reporters and cameras, even then overwhelming his theoretically objective listeners. With dignity and presence, he performed as a President might. He involved the national reporters, columnists, and commentators, making them feel important. Without stooping, he in a sense curried their favor intelligently and legitimately.

My announcement leaked prematurely out of the governor's office in St. Paul one day in the fall of 1959. Devoid of drama or impact, the casual word was that I would be a candidate and would enter the Wisconsin and West Virginia primaries. To say the least, I was furious, but once the news was out there was no chance for replay in a more favorable setting.

By announcing in Minnesota, we seemed to be ignoring the

national press, neither involving them nor exciting them, and indeed, almost insulting their self-view as arbiters of who shall be considered a serious candidate. Had we done it on purpose, it would have been stupid. Doing it by accident was worse. It was simply a lousy way to become a candidate.

But worse was to come. The Wisconsin primary seemed a good place to start. It came early, following closely after the first primary, in New Hampshire. It was close to Minnesota geographically, and in other ways too.

We thought of it as we would a campaign in Minnesota: a separate, local campaign. That was a mistake. We gave little thought to what would come after. We worried about the voters, and not enough about how the national press would describe our activities. And we spent all of our money there.

Money for a campaign is as basic as gasoline for a motor. If you run out, the vehicle stops.

We opened an office in Milwaukee in the summer of 1959, and several months later, out of money, closed it. Later still, we opened it again, as well as several smaller offices in other parts of the state, but money problems continued to haunt us: our phones were cut off, we weren't able to pay our advertising bills; we had minuscule radio and television budgets.[3]

I tried to overcome the lack of money and political organization by hard work. For years, I worked a good deal with Wisconsin Democrats.[4] Both Senate seats and the statehouse had been controlled by the Republicans for much of the recent past. I had often been introduced as the third senator from Wisconsin, representing, as it were, the liberal voices there. It was repeated so often that I began to believe it.

My base was with the leadership of the Wisconsin labor movement, the Wisconsin Farmers Union, and among teachers and other public employees. I was well known in the western part of the state, where Minnesota newspapers circulated, but as we moved eastward across the state toward the more populous areas, recognition diminished rapidly.

The illusion of widespread recognition and approval was doubly damaging. First, it affected our planning; second, the Kennedy campaign was able to use the illusion, making him seem the underdog; the urbane Easterner taking on the friendly rustic neighbor, the third senator.

In fact, Kennedy was as well, if not better, known in major areas of the state. Particularly in southern Wisconsin, which was served by the Chicago press, radio, and television, and in the Fox River Valley, northeast of Milwaukee. His well-financed campaign was filled with beautiful people. Muriel and I and our "plain folks" entourage were no match for the glamour of Jackie Kennedy and the other Kennedy women, for Peter Lawford and Sargent Shriver, for Frank Sinatra singing their commercial, "High Hopes." Jack Kennedy brought family and Hollywood to Wisconsin. The people loved it and the press ate it up.

While we worked to get a couple of dozen folks to coffee parties in a farm home or in a worker's home in Sheboygan or Wausau or Eau Claire, the Kennedys, with engraved invitations, were packing ballrooms in Milwaukee or Superior or Green Bay. Mink never wore so well, cloth coats so poorly.*

Nothing so well symbolizes the difference in the two campaigns as modes of transportation—a difference that is less important in sunny, southern states than in the frozen winters of Wisconsin.

The Kennedys flew in their private Convair, the *Caroline*. We chugged about in an old, slow, and cold rented bus. It had no place for anyone to rest except for the traditional narrow reclining seats. Finally, one of the more compassionate members of my staff bought an army cot and put it at the back of the bus with a blanket and pillow.

I would frequently stretch out on that cot, reporters interviewing me as we rolled from town to town, all of us half freezing and uncomfortable.

Once, as we started into the darkness of the rural countryside, I heard a plane overhead. On my cot, bundled in layers of uncomfortable clothes, both chilled and sweaty, I yelled, "Come down here, Jack, and play fair."

There were times when the bus slid off the icy road or broke down completely. When it did get us to our destination, we were zombies, almost always late, rumpled, bleary-eyed. It was depressing to pick up a paper in the morning, knowing how hard all of us were working, and to see the cheerful reports from all

* Ironically, in the presidential election, Kennedy lost Wisconsin by about sixty-five thousand votes.

over the state of the Kennedy tentacles, like a friendly Irish octo-
pus, ensnaring voters.

There were Jack and Bobby and Teddy moving in alternating
waves of grace and toughness and charm. Rose Kennedy, maternal, dignified, moving with delicacy and immense effectiveness.
Or Jackie, whose fragile beauty beguiled and entranced men and
women and children in an almost mystical way. They were
queen and queen mother among the commoners, extracting
obeisance, awe, and respect. They lacked only tiaras, and you
knew that if crowns were needed, Joe Kennedy would buy them.
I felt like an independent merchant competing against a chain
store: the Kennedys were everywhere.

In counterpoint, my campaign had trouble, both literally and
figuratively, in getting off the ground. At one point, Joseph
Alsop, a respected Washington columnist (more likely to be
mistaken for a nineteenth-century British civil servant in India
than a pollster), went door to door in Wausau and soon announced as a result of his private poll that I would be lucky to
come out of that town with a hundred votes.[5] Other reporters
followed his "lead."

Paradoxically, while Americans love an underdog for a time,
they ultimately prefer a winner. Kennedy was no longer an underdog, but a miracle worker. He would, the press predicted,
carry eight of the ten Congressional districts, and possibly sweep
them all. This forecasting added momentum to the Kennedy
campaign. The Kennedys had orchestrated a symphony of victory, and everyone seemed to want a chair in the orchestra.

Toward the end of the campaign, we attacked the Kennedy
record in the Senate and in particular his voting record on agricultural issues. It was tough and made points for us, but it was
honest and fair.[6]

As a professional politician, I was able to accept and indeed
respect the efficacy of the Kennedy campaign. But underneath
the beautiful exterior, there was an element of ruthlessness and
toughness that I had trouble either accepting or forgetting.

Possibly the best single example was Bob Kennedy's peddling the story that my campaign was being financed by
Teamster president Jimmy Hoffa. Hoffa, later sent to jail, was
virtually no one's hero, and for most the symbol of abusive labor

power. The story had it that this was Hoffa's way of getting even with the Kennedys and particularly with Bob because of his investigative work on the Teamsters. Both he and Jack knew the story was untrue and could have stopped it, but the rumor-mongering persisted despite our direct entreaties that it be stopped.

Another act of duplicity, which I cannot attribute to the Kennedys with the same absolute assurance, was the anonymous mailing of anti-Catholic, Protestant fundamentalist tracts to Catholic households. Understandably, it angered the Catholics who received the tracts and solidified any latent identification they had with Kennedy. This was immensely important in Wisconsin, because voters did not register by party. Thus, Catholic Republicans who would in the fall vote for Richard Nixon could vote in the Democratic primary for Kennedy—which they did in large numbers.[7]

Despite the superior Kennedy campaign, its money, relative smoothness, and élan, the momentum did return to me in the final weeks of the campaign. Somehow Muriel and I, Jane and Orville Freeman, Eugene and Abigail McCarthy, Gene Foley, and our associates, in our own disorganized, underfinanced way, fought back to carry four of ten Congressional districts, and came close in a fifth. Our friends in the labor movement and the young people on the college campuses worked tirelessly for me, and they produced the votes.

A good share of the credit must go to Muriel, who came into her own as a political person in the Wisconsin primary. Apart from Eleanor Roosevelt, who was a presence all the time if not particularly during campaigns, it was rare for a candidate's wife to move out on her own, not content to play the smiling, silent helpmate at the head table or sitting, smiling demurely, on the platform.

Muriel could not compete with the Hollywood celebrity glamour that some of the Kennedy women brought to Wisconsin, the polished and practiced charm of others. Instead, she projected not an "image" but what she was: a warm and loving woman, sensitive and concerned. I never feared that she would embarrass herself or me. She knew me, herself, and the issues. She simply got into her own car, our Pontiac station wagon, and drove around the state with a couple of local women for companions, from town to town, from farmhouse to farmhouse, campaigning for me.

It was not a role that came easily to her. Muriel is basically a shy person, not given to public posing, and she had carried an inordinate burden in bringing up our children while I dashed across the political landscape. Yet now, without being pushed, she recognized what had to be done and did it without complaint.

My children, too, went to work. They had suffered from my absences and the claims of others on my time and attention. I could have fairly demanded little from them, since they at best had been ambivalent about my life, and often understandably hostile to it.

But they, too, pitched in without complaint to do the grubby, unglamorous work of the campaign. Our youngest son, Douglas, then just twelve years old, often stood alongside me on frigid mornings at plant gates, passing out pamphlets to workers brushing by on their way to work. I will always remember that little fellow (not five feet tall, about ninety pounds), shivering in the cold, peddling pamphlets, asking the workers to vote for his dad.

The plant-gate tradition is both the idiocy and the glory of politicking in a democratic society. Every voter is made important by the one-to-one contact, though clearly nothing of substance takes place. But the tradition is there and, morning after morning, I would get up at five, grumpy after a few hours of sleep, the grayness of the dawn matched by the color of my skin, stomp through twenty-below weather, the compacted snow crunching with a sound like chalk scraping across a blackboard, a smile almost literally frozen on my face, gloveless hands soon numb, shifting from one icy stump to the other, slurping coffee from a paper cup.

We learned again that workers going in to work will pause to smile, but those leaving a shift will run right over you in the haste to get away. A plant gate in summer is only slightly absurd; but in a Wisconsin winter, it is cruel and inhuman punishment.

While campaigning in Madison during the week before the election, a Republican state legislator I knew stopped me to say that a concerted effort had begun to have Republicans cross over into the Democratic primary to vote for Kennedy.

I'd seen this happen in Minnesota in 1956, when Estes Kefauver beat Adlai Stevenson, and knew there was no way to stop it.

If candidate selection is to be done by the primary system, then it is only fair that registered Democrats vote in the Democratic primary and registered Republicans in their party primary. To allow a situation in which anyone, Republican or Democrat or independent, may vote in any primary without regard to party affiliation, would make a mockery of the political-party nominee-selection process.

Election night, I sat in Milwaukee with family and friends surveying the mixed results. I considered the election a victory, if not in delegate strength and total votes, at least in projecting myself onto the national scene as a genuine contender. I had escaped with my dignity; I had avoided humiliation. On the other hand, I had no money left, and I might end up looking anti-Catholic—neither of which would help my 1960 election chances. I had made a major step forward toward national recognition. Kennedy and I both appeared on the cover of *Life*, and the rest of the press, even when they weren't kind, carried my face, name, and message to a more attentive audience than ever before. In short, I became, as I had not been before, a national figure.

Also, we learned a good deal about national politics: the need for organization and financing, and the attitudes and workings of the national press on the campaign trail. The campaign in Wisconsin was the "cover story" of our early presidential-campaign effort, but it was not the only focus of my attention. Our travels included Alaska, Washington, Oregon, Montana, Colorado, Idaho, Utah, North and South Dakota, Iowa, Michigan, and other western and north-central states. The reception was good and encouraging. We were tying down delegate votes which stayed with me to the day of the convention in Los Angeles, in July 1960. The Wisconsin results—carrying four of the districts and coming hairline close in a fifth—gave impetus to my campaign in the non-primary states. While I had lost in Wisconsin in terms of election arithmetic, I had won national attention and demonstrated that I could wage a sustained, hard-hitting campaign. I was a contender, not to be pushed aside.

That night, virtually all my advisers felt that I should stop the primary fight then. We had spent all our money, and they were concerned that in West Virginia we would once again face a well-financed and well-organized Kennedy campaign.[8]

27. IN THE HILLS AND HOLLOWS OF WEST VIRGINIA

I needed time to think. I had much to consider and couldn't do it in the pressure chamber of Washington. So Muriel and I went to the Greenbrier Hotel in West Virginia for a couple of days of rest and contemplation. The Greenbrier is an expensive resort, dripping Old South gentility, an oasis of affluence in a desert of poverty. Nevertheless, it seemed useful politically to be there rather than in some Florida hotel, our only warm alternative.

We had already paid the one-thousand-dollar fee to enter the West Virginia primary, but my closest advisers continued to be virtually unanimous in warning against taking on the Kennedys so soon. "Where," they asked, "would we get the money?" Broke, and in most peoples' eyes beaten, we began to listen to offers of help from other candidates. They knew they could succeed only if Kennedy and I blocked each other, but when the chips should have been down, Johnson's people refused money absolutely and Symington's were to come up with only a little later. For the moment, however, we were totally on our own.

But, I thought, West Virginia has no major metropolitan areas which require huge outlays for radio and television. I felt, therefore, that the kind of personal campaigning I did well, moving from town to town, from hand to hand, could be a substitute for more expensive campaigning.

Further, the state was made for my politics and not for Jack Kennedy's. It was a low-income state with a strong labor movement. It was almost purely Protestant, and very fundamentalist, too. There were only 3 per cent Catholics, and so the state was not susceptible to bloc appeals to Catholic voters. I assumed I would benefit from that fact.

Indeed, the conventional wisdom in the press and among politicians was that bigotry was a way of life in West Virginia,[1] that the heavy Protestant fundamentalism was so ingrained that no Catholic could be expected to do well, that Kennedy would have insuperable problems there.

Ironically, once the Kennedys determined to go into the state, they were able to exploit those conditions to their own purposes. No one likes to admit bigotry, and the spotlight turned on them by the media left the West Virginians with a sense of guilt. They were shamed into rising above prejudice to prove their fairness. Or all of us may have misread the core of basic decency that underlay the more obvious patterns of life.

But the Kennedys understood something that neither the press nor I fully grasped. The Democratic politics of West Virginia was tightly controlled by a political machine, often run in each county by the sheriff. And more importantly, that machine could be "bought," county by county, through a locally accepted and legal process called slating.

The Democratic party of West Virginia "slated" candidates. That is, a sample ballot of approved names went out from the state central committee. In most cases, unless there was a fight within the state, the county machines worked hand in hand with the state organization. But no one could stop a county machine from making its own slate. Each candidate on the primary ballot was asked to contribute to the party in return for being included. Slating was in itself not related to direct vote buying, but quite often the qualifying factor became: "Who is the highest bidder?"

When I returned from the Greenbrier, I had decided to make the race. Herb Waters and I talked. It is a conversation indelibly recorded in my mind.

Herb explained the slating process and I asked, "Well, what does this entail? What do we have to do?"

"Frankly, it means money."

I asked how much and Herb replied, "I don't know, but I've

told the appropriate people we're prepared to put up twenty-five thousand dollars."

I was shocked, first at the idea, but also at the amount.

Herb said, "I felt we had to make the offer."

"What was the response?"

"I was laughed out of the office."

We left the question unresolved, but soon after, the message of money power came through even clearer.

Before speaking at a banquet in Franklin County, I stopped in the men's room. Before I could wash my hands, I was approached by a local judge, who explained that he was personally for me but as a party organization man he was going to support Jack Kennedy.*

The judge said, "Senator Humphrey, I have to tell you that you don't have a chance in the primary." I argued, "Why do you make that kind of statement? We're making steady progress, the reception of the public has not only been good, it has been enthusiastic."

The judge delivered his decision. "Senator, that doesn't mean a thing. What counts in this state is slating, and Kennedy is going to be slated *and* he is going to carry the state, because the party sees to it that it delivers what it contracts for. We have contracted with Senator Kennedy's people and he will win."

The baldness, the primitive truth shook me. I could hardly accept the obvious. Our campaign had, in fact, already given in to the system by then. Hoping to get some consideration from the party, it had raised money and given it to the party for slating in various counties.

I was later told a campaign worker went to an office with a second payment of twenty-five hundred dollars. When he entered the outer office, the secretary said, "Just a moment, Mr. O'Brien." Taken aback, he said he was not Larry O'Brien. The embarrassed secretary disappeared for a moment, reappeared, and led our man to the inner office.

---

* The whispered conversation in a men's room is commonplace in politics. Somehow, a person who will not speak honestly to you in a more public place for fear of being overheard will sneak in a few words in the relative privacy of a washroom.

There he was told that our arrangement was off. The county was now for Jack Kennedy, not Hubert Humphrey. When he asked for the chance to meet the Kennedy pledge, he was told we were not even close and, in a rare display of honor, was offered the first twenty-five hundred dollars back.

Obviously, our highest possible contribution was peanuts compared to what they had received from the Kennedy organization. Much later, I heard several stories that made the situation even more clear in retrospect.

Larry O'Brien, who understandably remembers the Kennedy effort differently from us, did recall in his book *No Final Victories,*

> I negotiated our payments for campaign expenses. Neither Jack nor Bob Kennedy knew what agreements I made—that was my responsibility. I had to have cash at hand and I usually left it with my secretary, Phyllis Maddock, for safekeeping. On one occasion, in the lobby of Charleston's Kanawha Hotel, I completed agreements with the leaders of slates in two extremely important counties, representing the largest single expenditure of the campaign. I called Phyllis on the house phone and whispered, "Bring me five." Phyllis kept the money in her suitcase under her bed, and in a moment she appeared in the lobby and slipped me five hundred dollars. . . .
>
> "Not five *hundred*, Phyllis," I told her. "Five *thousand*."

I have some trouble believing that agreement really involved the largest commitment of the Kennedy campaign but, in any case, I had been told another story about West Virginia financing.

During the 1966 Congressional campaign, in Boston for a series of speeches, I arranged to call on Richard Cardinal Cushing, whom I had come to know and like, an affection which, I think, he returned.

There is a kind of quiet awe that is created in places of power —the White House, the Kremlin, the Vatican—and the cardinal's big old home had some of that. He greeted us at the door, tall, already gaunt from illness and heavy-featured in his old age, but bantering in a cheerful mood with nearby students and seminarians about some minor controversy at Boston College.

He combined, in his priestly robes, a kind of dignity and jolly good humor of an Irish barkeep. I've heard a story that on occasion he would move into a room of strangers saying, "Hi, Dick Cushing," as he extended his cardinal's ring, which Catholics kissed as they knelt before him.

He led us—Governor Endicott Peabody, Eddie McCormack, and me—into his library, and as we sat there he turned to Peabody, who was running for the Senate, and asked, "Do you think Teddy is going to support you in your campaign?"

Peabody said he thought so and the Cardinal responded without pause, "I don't think you're right. You crossed Teddy. When you do that once to a Kennedy, they never forget. I don't believe you are going to have his help."

I was amazed at what he said, how he said it, and that he said it at all. He loved the Kennedy family and they loved and respected him, yet he had no hesitation in speaking the political truth as he saw it.

My shock had not disappeared when he launched into discourse on the 1960 campaign. There had been a spate of books by various people on their own roles in the Kennedy campaigns and administration. The cardinal was irritated by what he considered the self-aggrandizement and self-importance of each author. He had just finished reading Ted Sorensen's book and said, "I keep reading these books by the young men around Jack Kennedy and how they claim credit for electing him. I'll tell you who elected Jack Kennedy. It was his father, Joe, and me, *right here in this room*."

We sat in rather stunned silence while he continued in his Boston Irish accent, "You-bert, I believe you should know that the decisions on West Virginia were made here, in this library. Joe Kennedy and I sat and discussed the strategy of that campaign in this room. We decided which of the Protestant ministers would receive a contribution for their church."

The cardinal said he and the elder Kennedy determined that one of the ways to overcome the feeling about Kennedy and Catholicism was to contribute to the Protestant churches, particularly to the smaller churches in black communities.

He said, "We decided which church and preacher would get two hundred dollars or one hundred dollars or five hundred dollars." He ended with a whimsical, if not beatific, smile, asking rhetorically, "What better way is there to spend campaign money than to help a preacher and his flock? It's good for the Lord. It's good for the church. It's good for the preacher, and it's good for the candidate."

Despite all this, the truth is that I was whipped not only by money and organization but, more particularly, by an extraordinary man. Jack Kennedy was at his best in West Virginia, and his best was without equal. He understood the importance of the spectacular, of the unusual, and he understood that the conventional political wisdom—that his background was wrong, his religion wrong—was itself wrong.

Here was the rich son of a richer man, Harvard-educated with a Boston accent, Catholic and Irish, campaigning in one of the most poverty-stricken states of the union, through the hills and valleys and hollows, from little town to smaller village, among coal miners and poor illiterates of Appalachia. It should have been a disaster for him.

Yet he brought at least a ray of sunshine and glory and glamour into that gloomy, gray atmosphere. He brought hope to people who had none. The chemistry worked in an almost palpable way, and I think that Jack himself got something crucial back, possibly his first real understanding and empathy for the "other America," so distant from his own life.[2]

In any case, we struggled on without the professional or fiscal competence of the Kennedy campaign. On one occasion, I went into a radio station and discovered that they would broadcast only if I gave them a personal check. I did. Small as it was, I had to call my father and brother for money to cover it and other expenses, and they sent enough for that and a little more.

Muriel, with the strength of the Wisconsin experience behind her, performed exceptionally. She drove that station wagon along those narrow mountain roads in a lonely effort to help. While we were not much more at home in the environment than the Kennedys (no friends and few hangers-on, paid or otherwise), the people of West Virginia were warm and friendly. Possibly it was because they had so little and political people usually seemed to pay so little attention to their elemental needs. Wherever we stopped, people gathered and listened attentively. We thoroughly enjoyed our travels and meetings, the obvious friendship of the people was a rich reward in itself. Against the backdrops of ugly poverty, we found a rich strength of character, a real pride in self and country.

Muriel had loaded our station wagon with campaign literature and carried a five-gallon coffee urn in the back so that she could go to a plant gate or mine-shaft entrance or street corner and set up shop with one of our sons or a campaign worker. She'd offer a cup of coffee to people coming by, giving them campaign literature or buttons.

She spoke at rallies and coffee parties. It was frequently frustrating work, but she never stopped, never gave less than all her energy. Had she been a political creature like me, such effort would have been expected, more natural.

We had a sort of family contract, unwritten, almost unspoken, but understood, in our younger days as our family was growing up. I was the public man, restless, busy, traveling, speaking, working long hours at my job. "Muriel, in a very real and almost total sense, held the family together," giving doubly of herself to the children. She also knew without saying that my kind of restlessness required a place and time for withdrawal, for peace and rest. She took on extra burdens, sparing me from my share of the home chores as best she could. Our home was my haven and our children my joy and my pride.

Fortunately, in 1960, our children were coming of age and Muriel was freer to move about and participate, and they to help. Rather than leave them behind, she would often take them with her on weekends, and it was a mutually beneficial arrangement. Muriel enjoyed having them along and they, possibly for the first time, were able to feel a part of my political life.

For Muriel, the Wisconsin campaign had been her first real test in national politics. When I had needed her in a public role, she was somehow remarkably able to find the strength to be there and to succeed there, too.

She and Jane Freeman had developed the coffee-party routine very well in the 1950s in Minnesota, but it is one thing to do it in a friendly, home state, where you are well known, and quite another in strange surroundings without friends at hand.

Muriel really didn't like to speak, and when she did, she did it quietly. Her speeches were short, thoughtful, and filled with good common sense and humility. This sincerity and integrity, coupled with a large measure of personal charm, brought her affection from those who met her. There have been many people who have not liked me, but few who have had anything less than kind words and real warmth for Muriel.

That warmth was present in West Virginia from the people if not always from political bosses, and we both felt it. We quickly fell in love with the state and the people, many of whom lived in a strange and touching atmosphere of both deprivation and hope. And because of that affection, the result in the May primary was very hard to take.

Fortunately, I had seen it coming and was prepared to some extent for defeat. I had forewarned Muriel. I debated Jack Kennedy in Charleston and he won. I pride myself on my debating ability, and I knew that I had the issues and record on my side. I was unquestionably the New Dealer if there was one in that campaign. I had been in the forefront of the fight for Medicare programs and had fought many battles for legislation aimed to help working people. I had the civil rights record, which I thought would carry the black voters. And I made all those points in the debate.

Jack weakened my case right away with an artful presentation. He reached beneath the table at which he sat, pulling out cans of beans, powdered milk, and the limited variety of surplus foods available to the poor. Then he decried the inadequate efforts of the Eisenhower administration in dealing with problems of the poor.

He said if he were elected President of the United States all of that would be changed. He claimed, as it truly had, that the campaign had opened his eyes to the unbelievable poverty and misery of many people surrounded by the affluence of others. It was dramatic and effective.

When the votes were counted, Kennedy had 61 per cent of the vote and I had carried only seven of fifty-five counties. I lost heavily where there were large concentrations of black voters. I carried Cabell County, the area around Huntington, where the party organization did not have complete control, where the voters themselves made their own decisions in a really free and open ballot. The judge in the men's room had been right. So had Jim Rowe.

It was clearly the end, and in our headquarters there was a pall of sadness wetted by free-flowing tears. I conceded the election to Jack Kennedy, because it was soon clear that he had won an overwhelming victory. When asked what I was going to do next, I said I was going back to tend to my business in the Senate.[3]

About midnight, a call came to our headquarters from Bob Kennedy saying he wanted to stop over, and I invited him to do so. For the first time in my political career, I saw Muriel angry about an election, weeping with the honest emotions of a woman in love with her husband and deeply committed to his public work, upset with what she thought was a petty and unfair campaign.

She did not want to see any Kennedy, much less be touched by one. When Bob arrived in our room, he moved quickly to her and kissed her on the cheek. Muriel stiffened, stared, and turned in silent hostility, walking away from him, fighting back tears and angry words.

There wasn't much to say, but I said I would like to visit the Kennedy headquarters to extend my personal congratulations to his supporters. I did it as graciously as I could, facing people who had fought me and the press who had reported my failures.[4] I returned to our room to comfort Muriel (and myself) and to console my small and dispirited staff, my sister Frances, and the few close friends who had gathered.

About three o'clock in the morning, I crawled into bed, having psychologically closed out my campaign for the presidential nomination. I was sure I would never do it again.

At eight the next morning, I was airborne for Washington.† Defeated and dejected, I went directly to my Senate office and then to the Senate floor, the pain less as long as I kept moving.

I was tired, but Lyndon Johnson thought it would be therapeutic to call up a bill I had sponsored and successfully reported out of committee. It was not a particularly crucial or contro-

† Muriel went on to Minnesota to help Nancy prepare for her wedding, which was just three weeks off.

versial bill. Apparently Johnson felt that its passage would ease my distress from the previous day.

The bill provided for federal payments to state and local governments in lieu of taxes on federal property. It seemed a simple matter of equity. The Supreme Court had long before ruled that a state could not tax federal property, yet the federal installations created substantial costs to various governmental subdivisions. Defense plants, for example, often required special sewage and water systems; military reservations and other public buildings required streets and fire and police services.

My bill provided a formula for reimbursing state and local governments for these expenses, and we expected that it would take about an hour to move it through the Senate. Senator Karl Mundt of South Dakota decided, for some inexplicable reason, to debate the bill. He was joined by a group of his Republican colleagues, and an exhausting eight-hour debate followed.

The opposition seemed gratuitous, and that day remains one of my few really unpleasant Senate memories. On several occasions throughout the day, Johnson suggested that we withdraw the bill and bring it up at a later time, when I would have been more at ease and better rested. In bullheaded stubbornness I refused, and ultimately we passed the bill with a vote that was obviously there when we began.

That day was followed by other anguished ones as I came down off the high of the campaign. I had to work to focus on Senate duties, and now on a re-election campaign for the Senate.

In early June, several weeks after the West Virginia debacle, the Minnesota DFL party held its annual Jefferson-Jackson Day dinner, and various candidates for the presidential nomination, or their representatives, were invited to speak. It was to be an emotional night for me, since it was the first time that my friends and supporters, many of whom had helped in my abortive presidential primary campaign, had gathered together.

I flew to Minneapolis with Jack Kennedy after a long day in the Senate and it was, at last, my chance to see the *Caroline* from the inside. To say the least, it was somewhat more comfortable than our bus in Wisconsin and West Virginia. There was a bedroom for Senator Kennedy, and a stewardess to look after our needs. When she served us a bowl of chicken noodle soup and a variety of sandwiches, I could not resist commenting.

Jack said, with a smile he intended to be ingratiating, "Well, Hubert, now you know why I never offered you a ride during the Wisconsin primary. I suppose the smartest thing that I did during the primary was to deny you a ride on the plane the day both of us had to get back to Washington to vote. You would have painted me as a man enjoying the luxuries of life while the people down below were struggling. You would have torn me apart."

I, of course, had used the theme some anyway. "You're right, Jack. Had I been able to see the inside of this plane, I would have described you even better than I did as one of the rich, above the masses, who enjoyed the super luxuries of life while the rest of us were traveling around in buses."

It took us four and a half hours to get to Minneapolis. We arrived after ten-thirty and went to the Nicollet Hotel, outside of which my political odyssey had begun about seventeen years before.

Speeches had been going on for hours, but the crowd was excited to meet Kennedy. I was excited too, for I wanted to heal the wounds of the primary and to show that I harbored no lasting grudges.

Kennedy's appearance was a mixed success. He spoke brilliantly for about fifteen minutes to an audience that was, at best, ambivalent toward him. Many, of course, were already transfixed by him, but more were hostile—some because of their loyalty to me, some because they were rural people and farm leaders who disagreed with his agricultural views and some of his votes, some because they were labor leaders or working people who had grave doubts that this particular rich man could understand their needs, and some, finally, who distrusted his religion.

It amused me, since I am so frequently criticized for talking too long, to have a number of people say afterward, "Why did he talk so briefly? Doesn't he think we are worth more of his time?" I asked, "Didn't you think it was a good speech?"

"Yes," they'd respond, "but it wasn't long enough. He didn't say enough."

In the Midwest of the Chautauqua tradition, people travel a long distance from rural towns and farms expecting to be overwhelmed by speeches and political entertainment. Summer picnics of their co-operatives or various other kinds of political and social gatherings, or religious tent meetings, take up a whole afternoon or evening.

Brief speeches that are perfect for an eastern audience, for the journalists and columnists who set their own standards for political etiquette, just don't make it with large sections of the population in the Midwest.[5]

The Kennedy speech had its real success with our party leaders. The governor, Orville Freeman, and our lieutenant governor, Karl Rolvaag—who commanded strong allegiance—were particularly impressed and taken with Kennedy.

The night was propitious for at least one other reason. It gave me the opportunity to introduce Jack Kennedy to Walter Heller, an outstanding economist well known to his academic colleagues but not well enough to politicians who might affect economic policy.

Heller had worked with the Freeman administration and was well regarded by both business and labor communities in Minnesota. I had learned a great deal from him. During the rest of the year, he provided a number of economic papers which I passed on to Kennedy.

By that night, the primary campaign was largely over and we all looked forward to the national convention in Los Angeles. While I had to concern myself with senatorial re-election, Kennedy's visit to Minnesota made me think more about the primaries that had wiped me out.

A campaign ought to be more than exhortation, rhetoric, and Madison Avenue. There is a lot of silliness about our campaigns, a great deal of waste and posturing, an unrealistic demand on time and energy of the participants. The press and some candidates leave the impression that campaign talk is buncombe and fluff, devoid of substance or sincerity.

But that is not always so, and it should not be so. A campaign should have a twofold objective: to educate the candidate and to educate the electorate.

No candidate, however well he articulates a national point of view, has, at the start, the experience on a national scale that he needs. He may have viewed the body politic through a telescope or a microscope. What he needs to do is view it through a kaleidoscope filled with the changing patterns and subtleties of America.

Every candidate for national office, when he begins, is really the product of a narrow base and constituency. In short, the candidate is a provincial, no matter how sophisticated.

The momentum of a campaign compels a candidate to get away from the high-intensity politics of Washington and into the countryside, visiting places he has never seen, meeting people where they live. A mayor, for example, who comes to Washington is a supplicant; a mayor on his home turf is, if not exactly a potentate, at least a power to be listened to. If nothing else, he or she may be a delegate to the next convention.

There is simply no substitute for firsthand contact, no matter how brief or superficial, no substitute for meeting people and hearing them describe the issues that concern them. The candidate is the supplicant. No public opinion poll, no history book can describe the many-splendored, multi-textured fabric of America. For a politician, America is, indeed, hard to see if you stand still. It is only by coming in contact with the real life of the nation and the real lives of people that you begin to realize what America is, what it has to offer, and what it needs.

A campaign is special training and higher education. It is like a training camp for the athlete, a graduate seminar for the scholar, the workshop for the social scientist. Its tensions are an invaluable reflection of America. It is absolutely essential that we understand each other, that we understand the interlocking relationships between rural and urban America, between labor and capital, and indeed, among all the ethnic and cultural groups.

Doctrines of separatism may temporarily gain you political strength or muscle in specific areas, but if you are to become the leader of a nation, you must be able to reconcile differences, to co-ordinate the many and sometimes contrary talents and needs of our people, to promote a sense of common purpose.

If your vision is limited by sectionalism or regionalism or racism, you are ill-prepared to give the country the kind of leadership and direction it needs.

A candidate must keep in mind the ultimate purpose of his

efforts: it is not only to win nomination or the election but, having won, to be able to define again, in contemporary terms, America's purpose and calling.

This is why, as a candidate for President, you must speak on the great issues of the day, not lend yourself exclusively to the temporary, to the immediate, to parochial and sectional interests.

The purpose of a campaign is not to get above the battle, but to change the course of the battle so that national interest becomes paramount and other interests are viewed as part of the total struggle for justice.

Clearly, there is a danger that a candidate seeking to determine the national interest will sink instead to the lowest common denominator, spewing forth pap and bromides.

It is the campaign that uniquely separates those who can enunciate what is real and elevating, from those who cannot. Because you are under tremendous pressure, a campaign brings your skills, ideas, and limitations into high relief.

Presidential primaries, for all their flaws, can still provide one of the most rewarding experiences for the person in public life. To survive, you have to study more, you have to learn to communicate better. If you campaign in all parts of the nation, you become acquainted with the customs, the habits, the practices, the prejudices and casual attitudes of the people. If *you* don't hear them, your message in turn falls on deaf ears and you end up talking only to yourself, your friends, and the convinced.

In 1960, particularly, the primaries had a heightened function. In a sense, the quiescence of the Eisenhower years had cast a spell that had to be broken. Problems requiring national attention grew but remained virtually unrecognized, because no national leader was out front trying to educate the electorate—a preliminary, but imperative, step toward successfully passing necessary legislation.

I had hoped to make the problems of our cities a main theme. Few people were ready to face the fact that the quality of life for many urban citizens was deteriorating fast and that the main urban centers of America were ready to explode. Almost no one was willing to ask why our large metropolitan areas were in such deplorable condition.

Sociological, technological, and economic developments as well as World War II had brought about the great migration from rural to urban America. Did we understand that the urban crisis was the painful voice of rural decay? As conditions changed in the rural countryside, with low farm prices and important changes in the technology of agriculture, millions of country people left their villages and farms to come to the cities, thinking that there they could find work.

Yet those migrants and the cities were ill-prepared for each other. Many of the new city dwellers, indeed almost all of them, were black or Chicano or American Indian or poor white. Virtually all had suffered from inadequate educational opportunities; many had never lived in a congested area or been employed in a factory. They were strangers in a strange land, Americans thrust into the relatively dehumanized, indifferent sector of urban industrialism.

To speak to urban America wasn't enough. You had to speak to and of rural America, hoping to foster an interchange of understanding, information, and ideas. Without cities burning, however, neither city nor country listened much.

The campaign of 1960 also dealt with arms control and disarmament. The nation was more ready for that discussion, filled as we were with fear of nuclear holocaust, building bomb shelters in a national frenzy. I had spent several years as the chairman of a special Senate subcommittee on disarmament, and since I was knowledgeable I made it a primary matter in my campaign.

Back in 1956, Adlai Stevenson had spoken up for a nuclear test ban treaty. He was viciously attacked by his Republican opposition, accused of trying to weaken our defenses, of playing into the hands of the Communists.

When the idea came up at a Stevenson campaign strategy meeting, it was thought to be so politically dangerous that Arthur Schlesinger, Jr., said, "Let Hubert try it. He's expendable." When that was reported to me, I resented Schlesinger's attitude, but in a sense he was right: someone had to get out front with it.

Stevenson had more courage than Schlesinger and did, indeed, go forth with the proposal. It was not a popular issue with the people, finding at the time support only within limited intellectual, journalistic, and political communities. Popular feelings were essentially hostile to the idea, opening advocates of a treaty to attack not only from the right wing, but also occasionally from moderate voices fearful of jeopardizing national security. While he was berated for his statements, Stevenson made it easier for me to later hold serious senatorial hearings and gain attention for the entire subject.

Those hearings, Stevenson's political godchild, gathered considerable testimony that showed not only that a test ban treaty was feasible but that it would not endanger American security.

Those hearings, in turn, provided a base for favorable actions by President Eisenhower and later by President Kennedy in their efforts to reach agreement with the Soviets.

Without them, the 1963 limited test ban, prohibiting further tests in the air, on the surface, or beneath the sea, would not have been possible. Neither would there have been an Arms Control and Disarmament Agency, a specific proposal of mine at which I pounded away in every part of the country.

Federal aid to education was another issue to which both John Kennedy and I drew attention in the 1960 campaigns. It had become increasingly obvious that local and state governments, with their limited tax base, could not properly or adequately finance a modern educational program. The American public itself, therefore, had to be educated. We had to demonstrate that this aid could be granted without the federal government's prescribing the curriculum or having excessive control over administration or teachers.

There had been, to be sure, discussion of federal aid in other campaigns and bills introduced in Congress. Some had even passed one body or the other. But no major, general aid-to-education bill had passed both houses, with the single exception of the National Defense Education Act, in the mid-1950s.

Federal aid was always shot down either on the basis of states' rights or religion. Conservatives objected that the federal government would take over the direction of education if it gave assistance. Southerners were certain that federal financing would bring desegregation, even though desegregation had been clearly on its way since the 1954 Supreme Court decision.

Some liberals were doctrinaire on church-state separation and were worried that federal aid to education would assist parochial schools. And then there were the Catholics who wanted no increased federal expenditures for public education unless there were the strongest assurances that private and parochial schools would also get significant additional aid.

It was in the Wisconsin and West Virginia primaries that I outlined my proposal for the Peace Corps. I had been speaking about the possibility of enlisting talented young men and women in an overseas operation for education, health care, vocational training, and community development. I envisioned a program of national service in an international endeavor. This was not to be a substitute for Selective Service, for the military. It was to be another dimension of American aid to the less fortunate—not in the form of massive economic aid but, rather, personal aid in the form of training and education. The primary campaign gave me a national audience, and soon the media began to carry my message. The Peace Corps, as I called it, was to become a reality in 1961. It was an idea in 1959, a proposal in 1960, and a program in 1961.

Amid the campaign hyperbole and hoopla, there was a core of serious discussion. Thus, if there must be sad losers in presidential primaries, as I was in 1960, there is the solace that some constructive purposes are served.

In any case, that June night in Minnesota permitted me to look not only backward, but forward to a closer association with Kennedy. Our relationship did develop rapidly in the coming months. Since I was not to get the presidential nomination, I was determined that Kennedy adopt as many of my proposals as possible. I set out to influence his decisions, particularly in the areas in which I could make my greatest contributions: agricultural policies, civil rights, economic development, arms control, and the Peace Corps.

Among opinion leaders and voters who cared about these things, I had strong support and experience, but Jack Kennedy was relatively weak. He needed me if he wanted their support. I needed him if my views were to become national policy.

For a Massachusetts congressman and then senator, agricul-

tural policy was of little interest and no political appeal. That is
not surprising. Congress has an understandable tendency to be
parochial. Representatives from the Far West are strong advocates of irrigation and land reclamation, those from the Mississippi Valley of flood control projects.

All these things seemed costly and wasteful to eastern congressmen and senators. In short, one man's pork barrel was
another's justice and equity and good sense.

Sound agricultural policy as seen by those of us from the
Midwest was boring to most Easterners and a constant target for
criticism by eastern journalists. Price supports, soil banks, and
farm subsidies were concerns of magnificent indifference to
Democrats and Republicans alike along much of the eastern
seaboard.

I began to try after 1956 to capture Kennedy's interest in these
matters. I told him that any man with presidential ambitions,
and his were clear and unambiguous, must think more seriously
about agricultural America.

Even in those days, Kennedy would jokingly call me his "farm
adviser," and more seriously would say, "Hubert, you are causing
me nothing but trouble. We don't have many farmers in Boston
and they don't understand all this price-support stuff that you
are trying to get me to vote for."

While he joked, he made an effort to learn more about agriculture. The main vehicle of his education came through members
of the National Farmers Union, an organization made up of
family farmers, unlike the Farm Bureau, whose membership included many small-town businessmen and whose legislative
priorities were hardly distinguishable from the United States
Chamber of Commerce.

The Farmers Union has a broadly progressive point of view,
on matters relating not only to the agricultural economy but to
the entire spectrum of American life. To its leadership, the
phrase "feeding the hungry" has the force of a moral imperative,
and they have struggled to maintain a system of small, family
farms, the traditional American dream, in face of contrary, contemporary pressures for larger, corporate farms.[6]

As I watched Kennedy absorb information, ideas, and views
about which he had been most casual in his earlier years, I grew
ever more comfortable with him as a presidential nominee.

By the time we all went to Los Angeles for the Democratic National Convention, I was convinced that he would be the nominee, but I was left in a quandary.

Many of my supporters, particularly in Minnesota, who were not yet convinced that he was capable of the growth and change I saw, were adamant in wanting to continue to support me. That pleased me but made the politics of the convention difficult. Their support would have no political value, yet I could not simply ignore their continuing loyalty without being rude, indifferent to their feelings.

On the other hand, Orville Freeman and others were now solidly for Kennedy. Orville, like a number of other governors, had been left with the impression, primarily given by Bob Kennedy, that he might be the vice-presidential nominee. He was eager that I support Kennedy, if not for that reason at least because the inevitability of his nomination seemed clear.

Others in Minnesota were still emotionally committed to Adlai Stevenson, Eugene McCarthy among them. I shared their emotion and Freeman's pragmatism and spent several tormented days trying to define a role and public posture.

I could have nominated either one, and it was particularly difficult to resist the request to nominate Stevenson. I admired him so much as a person and political leader and felt he had done so much to raise the quality of American political debate in the fifties that I wanted to be for him despite the indecisive and belated effort he was making to get the nomination a third time.

When Eleanor Roosevelt and Herbert Lehman, two people I loved and respected at least as much as Stevenson, urged me to nominate him or at least support him, I wanted desperately to agree. But I held them off, suggesting that Gene McCarthy be asked to nominate Stevenson. He was asked and agreed to do it.

When Bob Kennedy called me to make a similar request to second the nomination of Jack Kennedy, the answer was easier personally but politically more difficult. I thought Jack Kennedy would be the nominee, I thought he could be elected President, and I knew that my power would be enhanced if he were.

I urged Bob to ask Orville Freeman, a vigorous Kennedy man, to make the nominating speech and deferred making any personal commitment. That commitment could not be delayed much further, and the night before the nominations, Freeman and other Kennedy advocates in our Minnesota delegation joined me in my suite to push for my endorsement. When they left, well after midnight, I felt that I should join with Orville and back Kennedy.

I was left, however, with my doubts. Muriel and Herb Waters and I talked quietly then without the pressure of others, and my resentment of the West Virginia and Wisconsin campaigns, which both of them felt intensely too, surged to the surface. My lingering doubts about Kennedy's commitment to certain liberal principles returned, possibly as a rationalization for what I really wanted to do, endorse Adlai Stevenson, out of respect and without regard to the political consequences.

I knew that the import of our postmidnight conversation with Freeman would have been reported to the Kennedys and that my turnaround to Stevenson would now be doubly offensive to them. Nevertheless, I had to risk their displeasure and unforgiving instincts to do what I thought was right.

I was almost equally concerned that my close relationship with Orv, a precious one and politically productive, would be irreparably strained if not destroyed. He was understandably upset. He felt, I am sure, that his vice-presidential hopes were shattered, and he knew that I had broken my commitment to him.

The agitation in our delegation was great, McCarthy and his followers on one side, Freeman and his on another, and a third group still for me, oblivious, it seemed, to anything beyond their loyalty.

When Kennedy's nomination became clear, I told my people that I wanted to move to make his nomination unanimous, indicating the unity of our party. Since he had beaten me in the primaries and our delegation had been so divided, I thought it would be an impressive Minnesota gesture.

I was shocked to find that I couldn't move several of our delegates, who threatened to take the microphone and indicate their opposition to Kennedy if I were to make the motion. (One farmer said, "That man couldn't tell a corn cob from a ukulele.")

I was irritated, but that simple act of defiance was indicative of the strength of real grassroots democracy in Minnesota. I was at the height of my power then and still could not command, as a political boss might, the actions of those independent-minded delegates.

Their strength, if not their obedience, made the DFL strong and made my 1960 re-election campaign relatively easy, permitting me to travel extensively for the Kennedy-Johnson ticket. They used me largely in California and New York, where my civil rights and liberal credentials were helpful, and in the Midwest, where my standing with the farmers was high.

I was determined that we carry Minnesota for Kennedy if for no other reason than to prove my support for him. Above all, I wanted a Democrat in the White House. Both Orv Freeman and I campaigned all over the state urging our people to vote for Kennedy.

I recall an experience in northern Minnesota, at Thief River Falls. The area is primarily Scandinavian, Protestant, and rural. I was having an early-morning coffee party for the farmers and townspeople. It was well attended and the discussion flowed to Kennedy. What kind of man was he? Would he understand the problems of the farmer? Was he strong enough to stand up against special interests (the subtle way of asking whether he would be under the control of the Catholic Church)?

I decided to meet this issue of religion by assuring the audience that Kennedy was his own man, free of any control by church or any other group, that he was committed to the Democratic platform, which had a strong agricultural plank. Then I said, "Take a look at this man Kennedy. Remember he is Irish, and remember that the Vikings occupied Ireland for one hundred years. Those Vikings found those lovely Irish maidens and soon there were Irish Vikings—the best of two races.

"Look at Kennedy. See that rusty reddish hair, those blue eyes, that ruddy complexion? Why, he is one of us!" To those Minnesotans of Scandinavian ancestry, that was proof enough that Kennedy was O.K. The men laughed, the women chuckled, and Jack Kennedy became a member of the family. My argument for Kennedy was not exactly an intellectual tour-de-force, but it was effective. Kennedy carried western and northern Minnesota.

To the surprise of most pundits, we carried Minnesota for Kennedy, but Orville, running for his fourth term as governor, lost, having expended much of his political credit and energy for the national ticket. Kennedy won by twenty-two thousand votes, Freeman lost by about the same margin, and I had a plurality of 240,000 votes.

Election night was memorable. Not only had I been re-elected by a large majority, but Muriel and I became grandparents for the first time. The baby was born just after midnight, and Nancy and her husband, Bruce Solomonson, named the child Victoria to celebrate in the child's name our political victory.

The next day, tired as always at the end of a campaign but exuberant with Kennedy's victory and my own, we were told that Vicky was retarded, a victim of Down's syndrome, or mongolism as it is more generally described.

Muriel and I wept with Nancy and Bruce, shocked by the baby's unexpected condition, frightened in our lack of knowledge about retardation, totally unsure what Vicky would be like, how long she might live, what effect her condition would have on our family.

We could not tell then what a source of joy and love she would be, how her handicap would lead us, and more particularly Muriel, into some of the most satisfying and productive work of our lives, working with the families, teachers, and medical specialists for whom retardation is a special concern.

I was fortunately not permitted much time for self-pity. Shortly after the election, President-elect Kennedy called me and involved me in his preinauguration planning and activities. During that first call, he asked, "Is that economist you introduced me to, the same man who sent me papers and discussions on economic matters? Is it Walter Heller?"

I said, "Yes, it is," and he replied, "Well, I'd like you to feel him out to see if he'd like to be on the President's Council of Economic Advisers." I told him that I'd do what he wanted, but that Heller had recently been appointed chairman of the Department of Economics at the University of Minnesota and I wasn't sure he would want to leave.

Heller confirmed that while he was interested, simply being a member was probably not enough to entice him to Washington. I conveyed that message to the President-elect, who said directly, "I'm ready to make him chairman."

Subsequently, Kennedy made the offer directly, and Heller, as he told me he would, accepted. I think his appointment was one of the best Kennedy made. Walter was not only a brilliant, highly regarded economist, but he had special talent for translating economic terms and conditions into understandable language. He served both Kennedy and, later, Lyndon Johnson, two very different men who valued his counsel.

By the time I got back to Washington, Kennedy had already set up offices in the Capitol so that he could be close to the members of Congress, consulting with them as he prepared to assume the presidency. I saw him frequently then and watched the almost immediate change in his relationships—not something he insisted on, but something implicit in the nature of the presidency.

While only days before, he had been "John" or "Jack" or "Senator" to all of us, he was now the President-elect, and the whole atmosphere changed. This is part of every new presidency. Men who were Franklin or Harry or Ike suddenly become Mr. President. It is not groveling; it is a healthy respect for the institution and office.‡

There is a story attributed to Sam Rayburn that rings true. Vice President Harry Truman had been in Rayburn's office, probably having a drink, when he was informed of Franklin Roosevelt's death.

He and Rayburn were close friends, but the next day when Rayburn called, he said, "Harry, this will be the last time that I will address you in such an informal manner, calling you by your first name. From here on out, I will address you as 'Mr. President,' because that's the way I think our relationship ought to be. But I have just one other thing I want to say to you. While you are President of the United States, you are going to have a staff around you that is going to tell you day in and day out that you are the smartest man in the world, and that's going to have a real effect on you. But the truth is, Mr. President, you and I both know it's a damn lie."

Every President is, indeed, surrounded quickly by staff members who feel it is almost a religious duty to tell the Presi-

‡ There are dangers in this custom, of course, but the alternative is, I think, worse. The lack of that respectful quality in the Watergate tape transcripts told me something about all the participants.

dent how right his judgments are. Rare is the staff man or friend who will say without mitigating clauses or gestures, "Mr. President, you are wrong."

Even though Presidents may ask for this kind of candor, may indeed plead for and desperately need it, it is hard to come by. The fact, unfortunately, is that staff people who have been willing to tell a President he is wrong tend to be eliminated from the inner circle. Survival and self-protection, the desire to stay as a member of the intimate presidential family circle, overwhelms the need for candor and openness. The rationalization (and it has much substance) that, by staying, at least *some* changes can be made is the flame to which staff moths fly.

Neither Harry Truman nor John Kennedy was taken in by sycophancy, but the more formal relationships have inevitable effects. When first names disappear and "Mr. President" is the replacement, every discussion and proffered observation is colored by the restricted give-and-take. In most instances, at least, once a man becomes President of the United States, there is a hesitancy on the part of those who come into that Oval Office or even to the President's living quarters to be as frank as in earlier days.

Even before the Heller conversation, I was called on to suggest a Secretary of Agriculture. I first thought of Orville Freeman,* but Orv, dejected after his defeat, was put off by several things. First, it apparently seemed to him that I was making up to him after our convention problem and trying to find jobs for my friends in the new administration. Second, and I really should have been sensitive to this, he felt that if Kennedy really wanted him, he should ask directly.

Orv simply deferred any decision by taking off to Latin America with a group of other governors. Because of his basically negative reaction, I next suggested my old friend and neighbor George McGovern, who had been defeated in his first Senate race. Bob Kennedy was strongly for him; Jack was not.

I then proposed Fred Henkel, the head of the Missouri Farmers' Association, for the agriculture post. He was highly regarded by members of Congress and respected by most, if not all, agricultural groups.

Though he had been a Kennedy supporter and knew agricul-

---

* Orville had been offered the position as administrator of the Veterans Administration, but it had no attraction for him.

ture well, his interview with President-elect Kennedy did not go well, and Bob, who was involved in appointments, found his age, almost sixty, too advanced and his style too dull.

I didn't care much about his style, and his age seemed a likely asset, if anything, since the average age of farmers is not young either. But Bob sensibly kept coming back to Orv, and I, of course, agreed that he would be superb if he would consider it.

When Orv returned from Latin America rested and less unhappy, I simply told him that the President-elect would be calling him and that they were still hopeful that he would accept the Cabinet job. When it was offered, he accepted and did an excellent job in a very tough position.

Primarily because respect for Minnesota politicians and politics was deservedly high, there were many other appointments that we were able to effect. Though the Kennedys and Gene McCarthy had a mutual disdain, even his suggestions coupled with Freeman's or mine received special consideration, since the Kennedys knew we would recommend people of integrity and merit.

More than almost any other, I was pleased by the appointment of Lud Andolsek as civil service commissioner. Lud was a rather roughhewn son of Yugoslav immigrants who had grown up on Minnesota's Iron Range, hardly a finishing school for sophisticated bureaucrats.

Early in his career, he had worked for the Veterans Administration and later, for almost fifteen years, as the administrative assistant to Congressman John Blatnik, who, like Lud, was a second-generation Yugoslav from the Range. Like an attorney who dreams of the Supreme Court, a journalist who yearns for a job on the New York *Times*, or a ballplayer who dreams of the major leagues, Lud wanted to be a civil service commissioner.

One morning after breakfast, when the other Congressional leaders had gone, I made a pitch to the President. I told him that Lud came from a poor mining family, not unlike those we had met in West Virginia, that he had come up the hard way, working his way through college, and had spent his entire adult life in government service. I felt that it was time that someone with special empathy for low- and moderate-income employees served at the top of the civil service commission.

John Blatnik had first recommended Lud, and I joined with

my normal enthusiasm in seconding his recommendation. Kennedy did appoint Lud; and on the day he was sworn in, I watched this tough man weep with joy as he spoke of what this meant to his immigrant family.

The satisfaction was not only in sharing Lud's pleasure, but in seeing the Kennedys reach beyond the normal profile of appointees.

One of the outstanding features of the Kennedy administration was the quality of men and women brought into the Administration. Each President stamps his own personality on the office, and Kennedy's Cabinet was filled with men who, like him, were willing to try new things and who gave wholeheartedly of themselves in the public interest.

Sargent Shriver was in charge of the general talent hunt, and Bob screened Cabinet-level and other top appointments. Together they did, in fact, attract many of "the best and the brightest," in David Halberstam's words.

Critics of the Kennedy administration, including Halberstam, will point out that less was done than was promised and that some of these able men helped propel and keep us in the Vietnam War through both the Kennedy and Johnson administrations. That is a troubling fact, but Kennedy and his men brought to Washington style and élan, competence and talent.

In some ways, however, it was the intimate associates of Kennedy who enlarged this sense of excitement. Like every President, he had a few insiders who shared his personal and social life as well as his political life. The rest of us were outsiders in a series of concentric circles of decreasing intimacy; but, unlike more recent White Houses, access remained possible even through the palace guard.

Among the guard, Bob Kennedy was, of course, a special case and the President's closest adviser. The two were very different in many ways, but they complemented each other and it was obvious that Jack Kennedy depended a great deal on Bob for advice and counsel on policy and people, and to do the difficult, tough political things that had to be done.

Kenny O'Donnell, a sometimes taciturn, long-time friend of the Kennedys from Massachusetts, held the crucial post of appointment secretary. There is simply no more sensitive job. He determined who should see the President and who should not. It is a job that can be easily abused, substituting personal whimsy or animosity for good judgment, and in which most decisions are beyond appeal.

Kenny, who seemed totally in tune with what the President needed and wanted, screened the contacts fairly and sensibly. He also was Kennedy's eyes and ears within the Democratic party and within the Kennedy organization subculture.

Larry O'Brien was another of the stalwarts, whose Massachusetts career had begun as a red-haired teen-ager warming up the crowds for James Michael Curley. His genius for organization made the 1960 campaign a classic one, and that same ability served him well in his legislative liaison work with Congress. He was a conciliator and co-ordinator who had a natural talent for working with various and often contrary members of Congress.

Their combined special strength derived from the confidence an outsider had that they were extensions of the President, that when you talked to one of them you were in effect talking to the President. They were antennae and transmitters of high fidelity.

David Powers was a third member of the inner group, and a very special one. He did not pretend to political or policy roles, but served more human needs of the President. He provided a kind of emotional massage, relaxing the tension with irrelevancies and earthy good humor. It was to him that the President would turn to share his most intimate thoughts, and it was an invaluable role.

Beyond those three, but still among the insiders, were Ralph Dungan, Fred Dutton, Myer Feldman, Ted Sorensen, Arthur Schlesinger, Richard Goodwin, and Pierre Salinger. Dungan, Sorensen, Feldman, and Salinger stayed at the White House for the entire Kennedy period. Schlesinger and Goodwin, particularly, had diminishing roles and access to the President. Goodwin, a brilliant writer, was the least anonymous ghost writer around, and that, in part, led to his ultimate exclusion.

All of these men reflected a mood set by Kennedy himself. He was an open man. You never felt with him that he was withholding something that was relevant to your discussion. And while there was that respect and distance that comes from calling a man "Mr. President," there was never a ponderous self-importance and stuffiness, at least not from him or the Irish Mafia.

Even during times of serious discussion of a legislative crisis, the President and his immediate aides could talk without being pompous or pontifical, without talking down or with sufferance. There would always be a moment of banter that broke the strain, a moment of levity that did not destroy the importance of the conversation.

A presidency without that is grim. Without that, too easily can the man, a voice of the people in a democracy, become emperor, king, prince, or despot.

Public life and politics are not all serious business, because life is not. Occasionally, the social life of the Kennedy administration broke into print in ways startling to the hidebound, stuffy conservatives, but it was a necessary relief from the expenditure of energy and vitality and commitment during those thousand days of the Kennedy administration.

There was simply a new step, a new cadence, to American life from the minute Kennedy gave his inaugural address. The whole country seemed to have awakened from the dormancy of the Eisenhower years, and the White House and the presidency served as a foundation of inspiration and a source of national revival.

What marked the Kennedy administration more than anything else was this spirit, its morale, its sense of purpose. Possibly more than any legislative or executive accomplishment, this may be the legacy of John Kennedy's presidency.

I think there is a lesson to be learned from the openness of those years, particularly when juxtaposed with the experience of subsequent administrations. One of the well-known problems of the presidency is that the man in the office frequently gets closed off from the outside world. The responsibilities of the Oval Office are not only confining psychologically; they are almost totally confining physically.

The President tends to lose touch with the political party he heads, with members of Congress on whom he depends for legislative action, and with the many friends who may have given time and devotion to elect him.

It isn't simply the frequency of personal contact, but the quality of the contact, the nature of the relationship, the consuming pressure of decision-making with worldwide consequences.

After all my years watching the White House carefully, I still don't know what personality or psychological traits guarantee a good President, but I am convinced that a "loner," be he Democrat or Republican, is a dangerous man. In a sense, isolation is the natural consequence of election. The President is one of the few Americans who doesn't commute to work. It takes a determined effort to reach beyond the White House gate to the real world.

Ideologues, too, even when they are not complete loners, can be troublesome to the country. The presidency is complexity itself, and men with blinders, surrounded by other men with similar blinders, can only lead the country down a narrow path of conflict, if not disaster.

There is a clear and present danger to American democracy when the people rush to a banner, when they seize on the slogans of a campaign as reality. Life, and surely the life of a President, never falls into the tidy categories suggested by a campaign slogan.

Even worse, when a candidate, once elected President, begins to talk of a "mandate," the country should be suspicious. Our electoral process, even in one-sided elections—in a landslide—is more a choice between two men and the imprecise differences of two parties. It mandates no specific program, but rather a direction and some sense of relative priorities in governmental activity.

Shortly after the election, I had lunch with my good friends former Senator William Benton and Adlai Stevenson in Benton's apartment on the forty-second floor of the Waldorf Astoria Hotel in New York. The apartment was a massive one, filled with original art and sculpture, one man's million-dollar private museum. He had a huge collection of Reginald Marsh paintings he had purchased during the depression, when Marsh was poor and unknown. Benton still lectured me about his interests, determined to make a civilized man out of a midwestern country boy. He insisted that I read more about art and music, and attend the opera and concerts and legitimate theater.

Benton was a man of great self-assurance not only in his aesthetic tastes, but on political matters, too. That day, with Adlai in the room, he was less professorial and our conversation was easy, filled with light banter and gossip about the campaign. In good humor, we talked of Kennedy and his coming administration. Adlai turned serious and said he wanted to be Secretary of State and felt he deserved it if for no other reason than his significant efforts for Kennedy during the campaign.

He told us in disappointment that he had instead been offered the ambassadorship to the United Nations, a post that held little attraction for him. He intended to reject it.

Benton agreed and counseled Stevenson to hold out for the Secretary of State job. I had to tell them both that I had talked to the President-elect and Bob Kennedy and there was no chance that he would get what he wanted. Neither Kennedy was comfortable with him, and no pressure was going to make them change their views.

I therefore lobbied hard with Stevenson to accept the job as Ambassador to the UN. His special combination of intelligence, talent, and sophistication and the high regard in which he was held around the world made his presence important.

I spoke with passion. "Look, Adlai, you and I and Bill traveled this country urging people to vote for Jack Kennedy because his judgment was good and his leadership important. He's asked you to be UN Ambassador and you'll be a good one. You have an obligation to take it. You can't just stay a private citizen pouting."

Despite Benton's continued opposition, Stevenson ultimately agreed that he would, and I urged him to call Kennedy immediately and indicate his acceptance. Just then, I got a call from the new Vice President, Lyndon Johnson, who said he was going to recommend me as majority whip of the Senate. He indicated that the President wanted me to accept the job and that he had cleared it with Senator Mansfield, Senator Richard Russell, and other Senate leaders. I told him I was honored by the suggestion, but wanted to talk it over with my friends before accepting.

When I told Benton and Stevenson of the offer, Adlai adamantly opposed my accepting the job. He said, "Your future rests in being an independent person with no ties to anyone. You ought not to be locked into a leadership position."

The argument went on, a virtual replica of our earlier conversation. I felt the job would provide additional power to pass programs I had been able only to talk about in previous years.

After about an hour, I called Johnson back and indicated that I would accept the whip position. There was really never any doubt in either of our minds that I would. I began then one of the most productive periods of my senatorial life. The period from 1961 to 1965 was a legislative dream come true.

Shortly after I became majority whip, Lyndon Johnson called a meeting at the Sheraton-Carlton Hotel, probably hoping to keep it a secret. Besides the two of us, there were Bob Kerr, Dick Russell, Bobby Baker, and George Smathers. Johnson wanted to remain chairman of the Senate Democratic caucus, maintaining the powerful position from which he had often controlled, constantly influenced, the course of legislation.

I felt, and said, that I could see no way such an arrangement could succeed. It inevitably would offend Mike Mansfield and other leaders, but Johnson insisted, and as a matter of fact presided at the first meeting of the caucus. It was an awkward and untenable situation. Once a man leaves the Senate and becomes Vice President, he is no longer a member of the Club, no matter how loved, respected, feared, or honored.

It was tough for Lyndon to accept that, and it fell to Richard Russell, his old friend, to bring him the obvious news that he could not hang onto power he once had. It was a shock and great disappointment to Johnson that he could not be Vice President and de facto majority leader.

Interestingly, while Johnson lost power, he insisted on keeping all the rooms he had accumulated for himself and his staff, one of the emoluments of seniority and power. He was possibly the best-housed public official that Washington had known for a long time, occupying real estate as a vestige of lost glory.

28. CRACKING THE WHIP

John Kennedy, as everyone says, brought to the office of President excitement and glamour that have not been present in Washington since and rarely before in this century. He also brought it a kind of distinction. It has almost nothing to do with competence and accomplishment. He had a spark that reignited American hopes, and particularly the hopes of the dispossessed. There is debate now about "the politics of expectation," but it is important as well as ironic that this wealthy, educated, sophisticated man established an almost instant bond with those who were none of those things.

Even his inauguration had a special quality. It had snowed heavily (more appropriate for a Minnesotan, I thought) and the city was virtually at a standstill (the way Jack had been claiming it was, anyhow), filled with the special quiet that follows an immobilizing storm.

In the cold and wind, there was still something enchanting about the frosty, breathy, interminable invocation of Cardinal Cushing, the fumbling of Robert Frost as he tried to read a poem and finally just "said" one, the lectern breaking out in its own small fire, and finally the inaugural address: brief, eloquent, challenging, and quotable.

In that moment when the new President said, "Ask not what your country can do for you, but what you can do for your country," there suddenly seemed a kind of unity of purpose, or at least unity of determination, in the air. When John Kennedy stood and took the oath of office, I must admit to a moment of envy. A year before, I had thought I could do the job better than he. In a reverse of the cliché about misfortune, I thought, "There but for the grace of God go I." But envy fled before the inescapable impression that President Kennedy would, indeed, get America moving again. And with my help.

As majority whip of the Senate, I would help move it and help people define its direction. No longer the new boy, my role as whip made me a member of the inner circle, part of the leadership. I was already a member of the Senate steering committee, which made assignments to other committees, and now I would serve on the policy committee, too. It is there that the flow of legislation is determined, a process sometimes as important as content in passing legislation.

With twelve years of seniority, I had begun to hold power. I served on Foreign Relations, Agriculture, and was a subcommittee chairman in Government Operations. Additionally, I became a member of Appropriations, possibly the most powerful committee in the Senate. It decided where and how much money was spent.

The whip is more unifier than overseer. The whole is greater than the sum of the parts, because of the unique relationship the role affords with all senators, but particularly with the majority members. You are, bluntly, in a position to do favors, scheduling a vote or delaying one for the convenience or needs of a member, looking after a bill of particular interest to someone. Whether a senator likes you or not, he has to deal with you, and that is power.

How I would handle that responsibility was important, and I had to define my own style. I thought a good deal about Lyndon Johnson and Mike Mansfield, who had been leader and whip, respectively, for much of my career in the Senate. Leadership obviously relates to character and personality, and there are some things that can't be easily changed. But there are areas where technique can be rationally determined.

I have described Lyndon Johnson's methods, his interest in facts salacious as well as salutary, nothing escaping his observation and judgment, attending to every little detail, using virtually all he knew to bargain, persuade, pressure, punish, or reward.

Mansfield is very different. He tried to be effective without being oppressive. He succeeded because he is a man of absolute honor and integrity. He is a quiet, contemplative leader, never forcing his own deeply held convictions on others. Wheeling and dealing are not his style. Mike never seeks to bully, punish, or even reward senators for their votes. If home-state politics or constituent pressure means a senator couldn't follow his lead, he was understanding or forgiving.

He did not use me as an assistant, letting me operate pretty much by my own standards. I was much more aggressive than he, soliciting votes for administration bills even when there was resistance, pushing senators to the limit.

I saw the whip's role not entirely as a creature of the Senate, but as a sometime extension of the Administration. With an activist President surrounded by eager, not passive, staff, it seemed necessary to push, cajole, and plead at least some of the time.

To do that well, according to Lyndon, it was necessary first to know the rules and then to know the players. For most of us, rules and parliamentary procedure are dull. I studied the rules more carefully than ever before. Even when you think you have the votes to pass a bill, it is possible to be outmaneuvered quickly in a thoroughly honest and honorable way.

As important as the rules were, the people were what interested me more, and it was with them that I functioned easily. I learned better than before that legislation is often a matter of timing and that timing demands that you know what to expect from each senator. As in all human endeavor, there are times when a senator is simply not as co-operative as he might be. He may be having trouble with the issue—with principles or politics; he may be having problems at home—an unhappy wife, a troublesome child, sickness. A senator may be just hung over, or exhausted from a long trip. He may be having political problems back home, worried about re-election. So I listened more than ever and chose carefully when I asked for a vote.

As whip, it became important, too, to establish closer relations with the Republicans. That was more difficult, but my counterpart, Senator Thomas Kuchel of California, was a bright, witty, charming, liberal Republican who was easy to work with.[1]

Our friendship guaranteed that I would not violate a cardinal principle of the Senate: that you work as openly and honestly with your opponents as you do with your own political colleagues, particularly when you have the votes to win. Everyone must know what the rules are, what the game plan is.

You don't lie, cheat, embarrass, or cut corners. You don't shout "Surprise," and run off with a legislative victory. Power in any democratic institution must be used with restraint, and by following that precept my life as whip was a happy one.

I enjoyed, too, the physical surroundings. My office, not large, was narrow and long, tucked into a corner of the Capitol, but it had a certain character and historical quality about it. When I was weary, I would look out on the East Front of the Capitol watching the tourists, parents with small children, holding hands, skipping up the broad stairs. Buses would disgorge troops of girl scouts and boy scouts in neat uniforms. There was a freedom and joy in their movements as they came to gawk and talk to their elected representatives.

Some days, as I looked past them, past the grass and trees to the Supreme Court building and the Library of Congress, I felt myself, in a sense, a tourist like them. Maybe all senators, all politicians, are.

At night, working late, the sound of music would drift up from the bandstand in front of the steps, on which hundreds of citizens sat. On those same steps, on a temporary platform, John Kennedy had taken the oath of office.

International relations capture the imaginations of modern Presidents, and John Kennedy, in that respect, was no different from others. The reasons are several. Some foreign relations are important. But there are less logical reasons: A sense of time; unlike domestic problems which can seemingly wait for solution, international events frequently appear to demand more immediate attention. Or a sense of escape; in both democratic and totalitarian societies, leaders may use the dramatic and highly visible event or crisis involving other nations to escape from day-to-day work at home.

This is not always diversion, of course, since, in a nuclear age, factions and frictions between the major powers can lead to catastrophe. The Kennedy years were not uniformly successful ones for American foreign relations.

The "multilateral force" concept of combining our allies in Western Europe in a more common arsenal died a deserved death. The Alliance for Progress, an effort to export democracy to Latin America, which I supported and for which I held out great hope, never lived up to its promise.

But it was with the Soviet Union that President Kennedy had the greatest difficulty. In June 1961, Kennedy scheduled a summit meeting with Nikita Khrushchev that ended up miserably. It could have contributed to Khrushchev's 1962 attempt to place missiles in Cuba. There was a tinge of arrogance in the people surrounding Kennedy at that time. They were still high from their victory, and in light of our criticisms of President Eisenhower, seemed determined to do things and do them fast. As the presidential party left for Vienna, I wondered why some of us—Eleanor Roosevelt, Adlai Stevenson, or I, for example—had not been asked for our views of Khrushchev and how he operated, since all of us had spent time with him.

Khrushchev's style alternated bluster and threat with a placating tone. He would attack and back off, take a hard line and then a conciliatory one. I think that in Vienna Khrushchev caught the President inadequately briefed, off guard, and thought he sensed psychological advantage that would permit him to dominate the man then and in the future.

It is possible, of course, that the President, with the best of briefings, might have been unable to deal productively with Khrushchev, whose interests at the moment may have required a contentious, unco-operative pose inevitably leading to a failed meeting.

In any case, a little more than a year later, in the fall of 1962, the Russians began to set up missile sites in Cuba and to ship the missiles in. They clearly knew, or had reason to believe, that such provocative action would bring a confrontation, but, I think, felt they might get away with it. Kennedy could be pushed around as he seemed to have been in Vienna.

The weekend that the crisis came to a head, the President was in Minnesota campaigning for Don Fraser for Congress and Karl Rolvaag for governor. On Saturday night, he spoke to an overflow crowd at our state fairgrounds. The next morning, after church and another meeting in St. Paul, he suddenly canceled the rest of the trip, ostensibly because he had a cold and was returning to Washington on doctor's orders.

The "cold" he caught was the news that despite his warning to the Soviets, aerial reconnaissance photographs had just been read showing missiles on decks of ships approaching Cuba. The next day, Ken O'Donnell called to say the President needed the Congressional leadership in Washington to discuss a critical situation. A military plane picked me up, and we stopped in Iowa for Senator Bourke Hickenlooper, a ranking Republican member of the Foreign Relations Committee, and were soon gathered in the Cabinet Room with the President and his advisers, including the director of the CIA, the Secretaries of State and Defense, and the chairman of the Joint Chiefs of Staff. Meetings continued periodically all week, and it appeared that military action, if not likely, was a real possibility.

After one of the meetings, the President asked me to come into the Oval Office, and he talked *at* me for a while, reviewing his thoughts and the facts, discussing his options. Then, in the midst of this preoccupation and tension, he smiled and said: "Hubert, if I'd known it was going to be like this, I would have let you win."

I smiled back. "Well, Mr. President, I knew it might be like this and that's why I *let* you win."

It was clear when I left that this was no replay of Vienna. Khrushchev & Co. got the same message, and withdrew the missiles.

Domestic matters went more smoothly, for a time. On Wednesday mornings, President Kennedy met with the Congressional leadership. He, Vice President Johnson, Speaker Sam Rayburn, Majority Leader of the House John McCormack, House Majority Whip Carl Albert, Senate Majority Leader Mike Mansfield, I, often members of the Cabinet, and when appropriate, people working in national security areas met. Those breakfasts were a combination of information and lobbying, insiders' gossip, and formulation of legislation and strategy. General needs for legislation were translated into action.

There was never a dull breakfast. The early sixties were years of the civil rights revolution, and the beginnings of modern militancy in American politics. We began to face up to the problems of an urbanized America and of rural poverty. We talked of economic assistance to Appalachia, a program that evolved into the Economic Development Administration. We talked of a war on poverty that later became the Office of Economic Opportunity, including the Job Corps for disadvantaged young people, which I had been pushing for several years. We argued about federal aid to education and how it could be advanced, about the Civil Rights bill, how far we could go with which provisions, what the President would say, and do, and what the consequences of certain actions of the Congress would be.

To be involved at the highest level of government in fashioning these programs, to be there at their creation, made my juices flow. Objectives I had talked about for so long, I could, as part of that breakfast group, help to make real.

There were three bills of particular emotional importance to me: the Peace Corps, a disarmament agency, and the Nuclear Test Ban Treaty. The President, knowing how I felt, asked me to introduce legislation for all three, though, more traditionally, he should have asked the appropriate committee chairmen to do so.

Just as I had felt we had to do something for disadvantaged youth through the Job Corps bill, I felt that our "advantaged" youth had a role to play in the outreach of American democracy.

I introduced the first Peace Corps bill in 1957. It did not meet with much enthusiasm. Some traditional diplomats quaked at the thought of thousands of young Americans scattered across their world. Many senators, including liberal ones, thought it a silly and unworkable idea. Now, with a young President urging its passage, it became possible and we pushed it rapidly through the Senate. It is fashionable now to suggest that Peace Corps volunteers gained as much, or more, from their experience as the countries where they worked. That may be true, but it ought not to demean their work. They touched many lives and made them better. Critics ask what visible, lasting effects there are, as if care, concern, love, help can be measured in concrete and steel or dollars or ergs. Education, whether in mathematics, language, health, nutrition, farm techniques, or peaceful coexistence may not always be visible, but the effects endure.[2]

The hideous, vast destructive power of nuclear arms was obvious to anyone who cared. The lunacy of limitless arms race should have been equally so. Yet there seemed to be no way to slow it down. When candidate Adlai Stevenson had talked of a test ban in 1956, his proposal was received generally with apathy or derision. It was "political suicide."

I had urged a subcommittee to deal with disarmament, and finally, in July 1955, the Subcommittee on Disarmament was set up over the objection of Senator Fulbright, Chairman of the Foreign Relations Committee. Until John Kennedy became President, however, little additional headway was made.

One day, the President asked me to lunch. We talked about legislation for a while, and then he suggested we swim in the White House pool. His idea of swimming was skinny-dipping, and he used the pool as a conference room. It certainly encouraged the naked truth. Seriously, because of his back trouble, he needed the soothing exercise, and as we swam in that 90-degree water, I talked about the need for a disarmament agency.

After we dressed and lunched in the Rose Garden, I told him that I wanted to introduce legislation, but that it had not a prayer of success without his all-out support.

We agreed that the moment was not a propitious time, since the Russians were bearing down heavily on Berlin. The President felt it necessary to call up the reserves to strengthen our forces in Berlin and Western Europe. International tensions were running high, but I felt the right moment might never come.

The President said to go ahead, that State and Defense would undoubtedly offer modifications but would support me. Even with support, it was a hotly contested, emotional subject. But after long hearings, close votes, and a lot of rhetoric, the Arms Control and Disarmament Agency was established.

The name itself was one of three angrily contested concerns. The others were: Should it be an independent agency or part of an existing department? Could it conduct its own research?

Many people, in and outside of government, objected to the idea of disarming. We had a tough time convincing them that I was not urging unilateral disarmament, but sought some balance, some workable arms-control arrangement with the Soviet Union. They said if that was what I meant, why didn't I make it clear in the title? Since Arms Control and Disarmament Agency was, indeed, a more accurate title than simply "Disarmament Agency," I accepted the suggestion, and senators who would not have considered the bill otherwise were now prepared to vote for it.

A more basic compromise had to be worked out. Would the agency be independent, as I thought it should, or a part of either State or Defense? Without independence, I feared, it would become a tool of bureaucracy—emasculated or a parrot of policy it had not developed.

It was finally set up in a unique way, part of the State Department for budget control, but as a separate unit, reporting to the President directly as well as to the Secretary of State. Congress also had easier access to it under that definition.

On the most critical question, research, would it have the authority to study the need for a particular weapons system, could it stand as a separate analyst of weapons technology, or must it shuffle papers provided it by others?

Some senators were willing to vote for the agency only if it had no authority, permitting themselves a cosmetic interest in arms control. I was not willing to compromise here and fought for that authority. Without it, the agency would have been a body without blood, heart, or brain. We won the battle by a single vote, and the Arms Control and Disarmament Agency became a reality.

Even more intensely I was convinced that the United States had to take the lead in controlling the testing of nuclear weapons. For a period, President Eisenhower had a gentlemen's agreement with the Soviet Union, both sides limiting nuclear tests. Later, despite the Kennedy campaign charge of a U.S. missile "gap," the Soviets were actually behind the United States in missile technology and deployment. They needed to test their new missiles, and did so.

I did not believe that a written agreement would prevent the Soviets, in a crisis, from violating an agreement, but I thought it would help. Would it be perfect? Would it be a panacea? No. Yet, certainly it was a chance worth taking, with the survival of the world at stake. As a matter of fact, the technology of surveillance and detection of nuclear explosions had become very sophisticated, and the chance of a violation escaping our attention seemed small.

I talked to the President as often as possible about it, at the leadership breakfasts, on the phone, virtually whenever we met. I talked to his staff and sought allies outside government, too. In June 1961, at American University, President Kennedy said that the United States was prepared to stop all nuclear tests unilaterally in the hope that the Soviet Union would agree to stop theirs.

It was a courageous speech, evoking both praise and criticism, and I moved quickly to support it with a Senate resolution urging the President to try to develop a treaty with the Soviets for the halting of nuclear testing in the atmosphere, on the ground, and under water.

I could not carry the resolution alone and, to be successful, desperately needed a more conservative colleague. For some time, I had been working on Senator Tom Dodd of Connecticut, a domestic liberal but hard-line advocate on international affairs, almost professionally anti-Communist. I finally convinced him that our proposal was limited and not deeply dangerous to the nation's military supremacy.

With Dodd persuading his friends, I was certain we could pass the resolution, and we did. The negotiations the President then began culminated in the signing of a nuclear test ban treaty. When the President signed the bill, he said, "Hubert, this one is for you. It had better work." It has.

The treaty signing was in the Kremlin on August 5, 1963, and Muriel and I went to Russia with a senatorial delegation including Senators Fulbright, Sparkman, Saltonstall, and Aiken. Dean Rusk signed it for the United States. Adlai Stevenson, as our UN Ambassador, was there, too, and for the two of us it had special meaning. We had advocated such action for some years before action and success. Now, with Senate approval, we were able to toast the treaty with Khrushchev in the Kremlin.

Afterward, official duties over, I asked Adlai to take a walk. We strolled along to the train station and talked with Russians who were not part of the government. He said that I was always campaigning. Accompanied by an interpreter, we chatted with people, most of them careful about what they said, but neverthe-less friendly. It had been less than five years since I had last been in Moscow, but both the people and the city looked better. The people were dressed better and more colorfully. The shops had more merchandise in them. Clearly, Khrushchev had lightened the oppression, and life was to some degree improving. Adlai en-joyed the excursion, and later, when there was another break, we visited Gorky Park with an NBC television crew who decided to come along. It was a more relaxed scene, probably because peo-ple were not about to board a train but were just taking the sun. They gathered around us and talked in a way that would have been virtually impossible a decade before.

A veteran of World War II spoke of his American "comrades in arms" and expressed the hope that he might one day visit the United States. One man was brave enough to say that the Soviet Union paid no attention to the views of its citizens. Another said a Soviet government leader could not talk as Adlai and I were doing without being hauled off to jail.

There were also the ideologues, hard-core Communists who talked of America as an imperialist, capitalist country. They mostly wanted to harangue on U.S. race relations and discrim-ination. As I admitted there was prejudice and discrimination in our country, I said that at least blacks and others were able to demonstrate their discontent and that their demonstrations were reported in the papers and on television. I asked what they were doing about civil liberties in the Soviet Union, to the silent approval of others in the crowd. They denied that was a prob-lem, unconvincingly.

One man, standing close by, was staring at my suit. It was an off-the-rack Botany 500, which sold then for about sixty dollars. I asked him if he would like to try the jacket on and he did, caressing the sleeves. So I stood there in shirt sleeves, the Rus-sian in a suit that didn't fit him, while others gathered around touching the cloth. It was a literally touching but slightly silly scene, which broke up Adlai, who was trying to look serious.

More seriously, I explained in answer to a question that it was a suit within the means of average, working Americans, the cost equivalent to about two days' work. The Russians figured it would take a month's salary to buy such a suit if it were available in Moscow. The mute suit said more than my other arguments.

Things became still more serious. The NBC crew ran through a canister of film and put it down next to their equipment, replacing it with a new roll. Someone, probably the omnipresent but anonymous Soviet agent, picked up the film while all of us were otherwise occupied, and disappeared. Adlai and I wondered afterward what might have happened to the people whose faces and words were recorded on film, some too friendly, and some too critical of their government.

As we had seen before, saw then, and have seen since, clearly the desire for freedom is a powerful one, incapable of total suppression even in a tightly run police state.

It is squelched at immense human cost. In a world in which real liberty is rare, the United States remains, for millions of people, the clear symbol not of perfection, but of what liberty can be.

After the Second World War, things were relatively simple (or seem so now). We could export material goods; help reconstruct battered nations; provide arms to our friends; stand as an obstacle, implicitly threatening, to our enemies.

For a while, our government talked hollowly of "massive retaliation," of freeing captive nations. Later still, we talked about a multilateral force with our European allies, an Alliance for Progress with Latin America. We tried the Peace Corps as a more subtle form of diplomacy. We faced down the Russians in Berlin and Cuba, and moved into, almost wandered into, involvement in Indochina.

Today, in a much more complicated world, beset with our own economic and social problems, our proper role is much harder to define. There is, in the post-Vietnam War period, a kind of neoisolationism beneath the surface. The Middle East is troublesome and threatens to remain so for a long time. Portugal, Latin America, Africa, other situations flare up.

We cannot be the world's policeman, and the anguished cry of "No more Vietnams" is one that must be heeded. We cannot be the world's apathetic great nation either. The dreams of liberty, the muffled but anguished cries for justice must not be ignored. The United States is *more* than symbol; it is the dynamic arena of the most precious human values, of liberty, of justice, where we try every year new experiments in their infinite possibilities. That we cannot export those qualities or our system like Coca-Cola or wheat is true; that we cannot or do not want to force them on the world in military adventurism is also true. We have no manifest destiny to make the world over in our image.

But we must find ways to continue to encourage freedom, justice, and—yes—democracy wherever we responsibly can. To do so in peace is really the central challenge for the people, the President, the Congress, and other institutions of the United States through the remaining years of this century.

Particularly as an aftereffect of Vietnam, but even for decades before, we have too often tended to accept criticism of the United States as the total reality of attitudes toward the United States. We tend equally to ignore the vast goodwill toward us that remains among the people in many, perhaps most, countries of the world. In greater or lesser degree, that goodwill is as real, and substantial, in the Peoples Republic of China or Egypt or Cuba as it is in Western Europe or Israel or Scandinavia, even where government leaders find it convenient steadily to attack us, where relatively small groups find it useful loudly to condemn us. The ideals of the U.S.A. and, indeed, our accomplishments remain a beacon in darkness. In the life of humanity, it is still the dawn's early light.

If nothing else has demonstrated that identification with America, reactions to the death of John F. Kennedy should have. Jack and those of us in his party, those in his administration, those of us in the Congress, had displayed many faces to the rest of the world: we had done things wise and decent, thoughtful or rash, statesmanlike or stupid. Yet people wept in villages of Africa and Asia, in *barrios* of Latin America, in cities everywhere. The legacy of our President and my friend has been a mixed one, and historians will go on sorting it out eternally. But the life of the man, what he meant to us, was a beacon. If the hopes of the world were diminished by his death, America remains, and must remain, the hope of mankind.

29. "LET US CONTINUE"

John Kennedy had been dead in Dallas less than an hour when I walked the corridors of the White House talking with White House staff and Cabinet officers—none of us with words to describe our feelings. We moved compulsively, because we could not stand still for very long or talk at length to anyone. Strong men wept.

As I moved past the President's office, I saw on the corridor wall two Texas Ranger pistols buckled to a piece of Texas ranch fence. Above them was a little sign that said THE TEXAS PEACEMAKERS.

"How in God's name," I thought, "could this country permit the hate, the insanity out of which this assassination rose?"

That day had begun like many other days: breakfast at home with Muriel, orange juice, two fried eggs, crisp bacon, toast and coffee, the Washington *Post*, the New York *Times*. Then to my Capitol office and the morning hour in the Senate, kidding, chatting with my colleagues, and a luncheon.

The luncheon that day was given by Ambassador Radomiro Tomic of Chile in honor of Sir Howard Veale, the Ambassador of Australia. Muriel and I arrived at the Chilean Embassy about 1:10 P.M., joining about forty other guests, including Ralph Dungan of the White House staff and his wife, Mary; an old friend, Edward P. Morgan of the American Broadcasting Company; and Ambassador and Mrs. Nehru of India.

Mrs. Nehru teased about how difficult it was to get me to their embassy, and about how angry she had been, months before, when I had come to lunch but spent most of my time talking to their honored guest, President Kennedy. I apologized, and she laughingly said, "It was not your fault, Senator, but the President's. He kept saying, 'Hubert, come here. Hubert, I want to talk to you.'" I was pleased with Mrs. Nehru's diplomatic recognition of how close President Kennedy and I had become. In a light and pleasant mood, we moved cheerfully into lunch about 1:30 P.M.

Presently, Ed Morgan was called to the phone, came back quickly, obviously upset. He whispered in my ear that the President had been shot in Dallas but was still alive. I could hear the words, but shock made them difficult to believe.

I mumbled to Ed that we ought to excuse ourselves and call Ralph Dungan into the hall. Since none of the guests was aware of anything untoward, they paid little attention to us. In the hall, I heard myself tell Ralph what we had learned, and he called the White House immediately, confirming from the Secret Service, after a delay that seemed forever but took just a few minutes, that the report was true.

We discussed what to do. Ralph decided to return to the White House, Ed went to ABC, and I went out to my car in front of the embassy to listen to the radio for a moment. I heard that two priests had gone into the hospital and the thought pounded into my consciousness that the President was dying or already dead.

John Kennedy was my colleague, my opponent, my President, and my friend. As a colleague in the Senate, I had sometimes resented him and been angry with him for doing less than I thought he could and should in the tough work of getting legislation passed. As an opponent in the presidential primaries, I had envied him—his charm, his grace, his money, his success. As President of the United States, I grew to respect his intelligence and how he put it to work, his commitment and how he stuck by it, his vision and how he communicated it to our people. As a friend, I grew to love him for his warmth and wit and compassion, and for what he gave to me personally by sharing those qualities.

And now he was dying or dead and I had to go back into that luncheon and tell the happy people what I knew. I spoke first to the ambassador and Muriel and then reported to the other guests. As I did, Ralph Dungan, already back at the White House, called to say the President had died. I could hardly believe it. Thinking it might be so was one thing, knowing it for sure was yet another. A bewildering sense of loss shook me as I stood alone and silent in the library, where I had taken the call. I forced myself to move into the hall, trying desperately to control myself, but I couldn't. I broke down. Fighting to regain my composure, I moved again, almost mechanically, back into the dining room, where I announced that the President was dead. Then I broke down again. Ambassador Tomic rose and briefly eulogized President Kennedy. He spoke, his voice quivering with grief and emotion, of the love and admiration that the people of Chile had for both President and Mrs. Kennedy.

And then Muriel and I were in our car. Tom Graham, my driver, himself stunned, drove us to the northwest gate of the White House, as Ralph Dungan had suggested. The faces of the people on the street and those gathered at the White House gate were like a sad pantomime—unreal but true, mirroring disbelief and anxiety, incredulity and sorrow, fear and tragedy.

Looking at Muriel—silent, struggling unsuccessfully to keep back the tears—I realized how close we felt to the President, how much he really meant to us. For the longest time, to make myself believe it, I silently repeated, "John Kennedy is dead. John Kennedy is gone."

And then I thought of his family, particularly of Jacqueline, and what they must be going through. And for the first time, as I entered the West Wing, I thought of Lyndon Johnson.

He was President now, elevated to office by an assassination. I worried about his health—he'd had a serious heart attack in 1955—and his emotional well-being. Strong man that he was, I feared he might be shaken by the trauma of the day, a day designed to smooth over local Texas political problems, a day that had exploded into a national disaster.

But concern about Lyndon was lost immediately in the White House, which was still, at that moment, John Kennedy's. For most of us who gathered there, there was nothing, really, to do.

The fact of his death was so overwhelming; yet in this house where he worked, ate, slept, played with his kids, it was impossible to think of him in the past tense. The reality was so horrendous that the whole atmosphere, paradoxically, took on an almost unreal quality.

About two hours later, I left the White House and went to my Senate office. Muriel and I rode together from there to Andrews Air Force Base to join others waiting for Air Force One. We shared in person what millions of Americans saw on television: Jackie Kennedy, blood-splattered still, moving in shocked grace; the three loyal friends dedicated to John Kennedy even in death: Kenny O'Donnell, Larry O'Brien, and Dave Powers, tenderly watching over and handling the casket as it was lowered from the plane and moved into the ambulance.

Lady Bird Johnson came down the ramp and walked to where we stood, kissed us both, and said quietly, "We need you both so much."

When John Kennedy's body, accompanied by Jackie and Robert Kennedy left the field, the Congressional delegation—Everett Dirksen, Mike Mansfield, Tommy Kuchel, Carl Albert, Hale Boggs, George Smathers, Charlie Halleck, Les Arends, and I—flew by helicopter to the White House and went directly to the old Executive Office Building, next door. Lyndon Johnson, as Vice President, had his office there.

About 7:30 P.M. we finally met with the new President, who simply asked for our help.

I stayed back after the meeting broke up to assure President Johnson privately of my desire to be of all possible assistance. He put his arm around me and said that he needed me desperately. He had leaned on me before, but this was no longer Lyndon asking for help. It was the President. The difference was great. It was nothing either of us said. It was something the institution of the presidency evokes.

Oddly, during the day when I thought of Jack's death, I thought in personal terms. Now, with a man I'd known better, our relationship was already less personal. No more "Lyndons." Now it was more structured, though neither of us had had the time to think of it. The man dies, the institution continues. With the obvious difference of democracy, it was the enactment of monarchy's age-old cry, "The King is dead! Long live the King!"

About 8:30 P.M., I went back to my office, where Senator George Smathers and I talked about President Johnson's leadership qualities, his needs, his nature, and what we might do to help him. Smathers spoke of the many times that President Johnson, as majority leader, talked about my support. Smathers, too, left me with the thought that Johnson as President was going to need me more than ever. Once again, however, my thoughts did not stay long on the new President.

For the next couple of hours, our office was deluged by phone calls, mostly from Minnesota but also from all over the country, calls from people who merely wanted to tell how saddened they were by the death of President Kennedy. People would call, weeping, simply wanting someone who knew John Kennedy to share their grief.

One call, from a Twin City cab driver, was typical. He had just finished work and called to say that his whole family was praying for Mrs. Kennedy and her children, and how sorry they were that they had lost their great friend, President Kennedy.

Every call was filled with sorrow and sympathy and understanding, because so many Americans had identified with Jack and Jackie Kennedy almost as friends and equals. In life, that identification had transcended logic and fact; now, in death and martyrdom, it quickly assumed enormous proportions.

Jack Kennedy—like any man—had shortcomings, to be sure, but he did enunciate and articulate a beautiful dream and vision for this nation. He gave young people inspiration and strength. It was not so important at the time what his administration had or had not accomplished. It was irrelevant that, given a full term, history might have judged him more severely.

What Adlai Stevenson gave in depth to limited parts of our society, John Kennedy gave to a broader audience: a belief that politics and government could be an honorable calling, worthy of the best of us, producing light and hope and joy and compassionate concern for the least of us. Not many men in our history have been able to do that, and particularly not when times are relatively good. Some called it charisma, but that is an inadequate description. Possibly, like love or jazz, it is something felt, which to the unfeeling cannot be explained.

About 10:30 P.M., I went home to Muriel. We watched TV and listened to the radio. I shared with that cab driver, as we looked at the day's ghostly events replayed, the urge to call someone and to say I had lost a friend, too.

On Saturday, the Congressional leadership, along with the Cabinet, the Supreme Court, some officials in the executive branch, members of the family, and personal friends were invited to the White House to pay their respects. The coffin, robed in an American flag, lay in the East Room. The scene is hard to describe. It was a tragedy of international import; yet, in that room, as elsewhere, people thought first of their own, personal loss.

I went back up to the Capitol after the ceremony to face endless requests for interviews. I did three, something for the "Today" show, a bit for CBS, and a brief interview with Ray Scherer of NBC, who was a friend as well as a good newsman.

I thought it crucial that someone close to both Kennedy and Johnson go on the air to emphasize, first of all, that our constitutional system provides for the orderly transfer of power, even in times of tearing tragedy and sudden crisis. And secondly, to underscore the good qualities of President Johnson.

I thought it important to dwell on the positive aspects of the Kennedy-Johnson relationship, and more importantly to point out that President Johnson, beyond personal loyalty to the late President (something both earlier and later pundits questioned —falsely I feel), had a deep commitment to programs and policies that were labeled as Kennedy's but indeed bore the imprint of many, including Lyndon Johnson.

That weekend, I wrote for my files: "I have watched President Johnson grow, not only in the field of domestic matters—where his commitment to the tax program, to full employment, the Medicare program, is well known, and his commitment to civil rights a matter of national attention—but I have also seen him become better acquainted with the world in which we live. . . . President Johnson, during his service as a United States senator and majority leader, did not travel much abroad. His knowledge of the world is rather limited and somewhat conditioned by his experience as chairman of the Preparedness Subcommittee of the Armed Forces Committee of the Senate, his activity on the Space Committee, and his chairmanship of the Appropriations Subcommittee on the State Department and Foreign Aid."

Then I wrote something which has special force today:

". . . No one can predict what a President will do in foreign affairs. Even those men who have been equipped by education and training for the responsibilities of foreign policy sometimes do not live up to the requirements of great leadership in this area. The only way that one can judge a President on matters of foreign policy and international relations is to wait and see how he handles the critical situations that develop.

"It is difficult, if not impossible, to judge one in terms of his experience in the Senate. I say this because as senator, while you have responsibility, you do not have authority. You can be much more free with your words and much more at ease with your responsibilities. When you become President, you are the nation's chief spokesman in foreign affairs. You are genuinely responsible for matters of foreign policy. You have to deal day by day with the difficult practical situations that arise in country after country in different regions of the world."

Vice Presidents, whatever their temporary notice or notoriety, do not remain well defined for most Americans, and certainly not for people in other lands. I hammered the theme of Johnson as part of the Kennedy team, with deep commitment to the Kennedy program, to reassure anyone who was concerned, at home or abroad. Neither our domestic nor our foreign policy could afford to have serious doubts raised as to our purposes, our objectives, and our will to carry out our commitments.

The entire weekend was a counterpoint of trying to focus on problems that we faced immediately and then having that focus dissolve into sorrow. Just before noon on Sunday, Muriel and I went to our church, Chevy Chase Methodist Church, and there, amid the hymns and sermon and familiar ritual, another wave of grief overtook us.

After church, I went to the offices of the speaker of the House of Representatives, joining again with the Congressional leadership group. At 1:30 P.M. we walked to the rotunda, where the presidential coffin was placed for public viewing. The Kennedy family arrived, as did members of the Cabinet, the Supreme Court, the armed services, and members of the diplomatic community. Senator Mansfield, Chief Justice Warren, and Speaker McCormack spoke briefly.

Mrs. Kennedy and Caroline displayed incredible poise, courage, calm—to a degree almost beyond belief. But those qualities seemed to rise from almost everyone, in superhuman quantities, that weekend.

People poured into Washington, driving for many hours over long distances to stand in line for many more hours in the streets near the Capitol. It was a cold, dreary weekend, and the chilled and weary people shuffled in a line twenty blocks long—some waiting for five or six hours—for a fleeting moment beside the coffin.

On Sunday night, Muriel and I had a few friends join us for dinner. Adlai Stevenson, Jane and Orville Freeman, and Maggie and Max Kampelman[1] were there, when President Johnson called to ask about legislation that was coming up that week. His main concern at that moment was Senator Karl Mundt's bill to prevent any guarantee of credits for the sale of American products behind the Iron Curtain.

The President spoke sternly: "Why are you bringing the bill up? This is a poor time to do it." I reminded him that there was a unanimous consent agreement, arrived at about two weeks earlier, that we couldn't alter. Mansfield had agreed to it and the vote was set.

The President asked, "How many votes do you have?"

I admitted, "I'm not sure." To which the President predictably replied, "That's the trouble with that place up there. You fellows don't count votes."

I promised a clean count before the bill was called up for final passage. On Monday morning, before the funeral, I set several people to work counting votes.

At that point, I shifted back from the problems ahead, joining many of the same people I had been with at various times over the weekend. We gathered in the front of the White House for the funeral procession to St. Matthew's Cathedral.

I suppose that a man who has been in public life and in Washington for so many years should not have been awe-struck by the simple presence of so many heads of state, by so many major participants in history. I was. De Gaulle, Haile Selassie, Eisenhower, Truman lent a quality of majesty to a sad day.

Together with the Kennedy family and American leaders, they walked the five and a half blocks to St. Matthew's. At the church, Cardinal Cushing said a simple funeral mass, touchingly beautiful, coming as it did after the emotional drain of the previous couple of days. Across the church aisle sat Jacqueline, Caroline, and John John. Caroline was so composed, a diminutive mirror image of her mother, and John John restless and squirming as any uncomfortable small boy might.

Following the mass, we must have passed a million people standing along the route of the funeral procession to Arlington Cemetery. I had never seen so many people in one place, a panorama of grief-stricken faces stretching for miles.

In the emotion of the event, everything seemed appropriate and poignant: the blowing of taps, the flight of fast fighter planes and bombers overhead, and then Air Force One, the President's personal jet, flying at low level, paying its last respects to the Commander-in-Chief.

On Tuesday morning, I tallied the votes on the Mundt bill and called President Johnson to say that we would carry the vote about 56 to 37.

When the final vote, taken about nine-fifteen that night, was 57 to 35, I was pleased—first, of course, because we had won, but secondly because I had a good count on a tough bill.

I called President Johnson again, dripping self-satisfaction. "Mr. President, I want to report to you your first Congressional victory. We have defeated the Mundt bill by a vote of 57 to 35. I'm sorry I misinformed you earlier."

He asked what I was doing for dinner. I told him I had had a snack, but he said, "Well, come on over anyway and have something more to eat. I want to talk to you."

When I arrived at the President's home,* we talked about the day in the Senate. In addition to the President and myself, there were Abe Fortas, Jack Valenti, Mrs. Johnson, Lynda Johnson, and Cliff Carter.

After a drink, we sat down at the dinner table, and the President asked for copies of the speech that he was going to deliver on Wednesday to the joint session of Congress. Several people had produced drafts and we went over the ones he liked.[2]

---

* He was not yet in the White House, but in his private home, the Elms. He had a portrait of Diem in the hallway, and as we passed it he said, "We had a hand in killing him. Now it's happening here."

The President read them aloud and we commented on them. My view of the speech was that it ought to be short and emphasize President Johnson's determination to follow through on the policies and programs of the late President.

Finally, after considerable discussion, the President said, "Hubert, you and Abe go ahead and redraft these speeches and get me one that will be suitable for tomorrow." Fortas and I worked until two in the morning. I added references to Roosevelt and the Youth Employment Program, and strengthened the sections on the United Nations and the Alliance for Progress.

I also developed the line "Let us continue" and that portion of the speech that reiterated the commitment of the United States to its allies.

During the weekend, other people close to President Johnson urged him to speak to the American people directly on television. I was determined that his first speech be given where he was at home and before the live audience. He would be credible if he could forget about cameras and just deliver his address to the joint session. It was a fine beginning.

30. "OUT OF THE SHADOWS"

By the early 1960s, civil rights, equality under the law for black Americans, had become a central issue for all America, growing slowly but steadily from the Supreme Court decision in 1954 that "separate, but equal" education facilities were not constitutionally valid.

Until then, civil rights legislation was doomed not because the Congress opposed it (which it did), but because there was little pressure from outside. Most churches had been essentially indifferent, a few liberal church leaders providing limited support and demand.

The American labor movement, again with a few important exceptions, had been concerned with other questions: housing, education, economics, medical care.

The business community continued its old, simplistic rhetoric about the sanctity of "property rights" as opposed to human rights. The press, from whom one could have expected more, was not much interested either. Most papers and reporters ignored the question almost entirely.

From my mayor days on, I was so convinced that what I was advocating was right that, in a simple-minded way, I assumed that I could constantly convince more people. I did not fully appreciate the enormity of the task.

But it didn't take long to learn that any success would come only with perseverance and the willingness to absorb a good deal of humiliation and rejection. Clearly and unmistakably, I was not going to make it into the Senate "Club" on the strength of civil rights.[1]

Civil rights was thwarted there by the charge of southern Democrats and Taft Republicans that the federal government was trying to control the lives of the people, that "statism" was interference in people's private lives.

They argued against any compulsory or enforceable fair employment practices act, and "voluntary" became the catch phrase. What they wanted, in effect, was a law that enunciated some general principle relating to equal opportunity, but no machinery to enforce it. Pious pronouncements, preachments, declarations of good intent instead of legislation.

Finally, there was talk of administrative machinery to permit conciliation and mediation, again without any real power. A federal civil rights commission was proposed to monitor what was going on and to report yearly on progress or lack of it.

In 1953, several groups organized the Leadership Conference on Civil Rights. Its minuscule budget[2] provided not much more than an office and a phone, but it grew in strength during the next decade and was crucial in our victories in 1963 and 1964.

Lyndon Johnson, as Senate majority leader, began to prepare the way for civil rights legislation. By assigning liberals to major committees, he overcame the previous southern veto power on those committees. He put liberals on the steering committee and on the policy committee, giving them power and prestige within the Senate establishment, and he modified, if only slightly, the cloture rule.

In 1957, Johnson guided into law the first civil rights bill since Reconstruction, and in 1960 followed up with a second act. The focus of both was on the protection of voting rights and the creation of administrative agencies such as the U. S. Commission on Civil Rights and the Civil Rights Division of the Justice Department.

While many of the pro-civil rights forces were highly critical of these early laws, the logjam had been broken. Something was better than nothing, and we could concentrate on expanding our limited successes.

That fall when John Kennedy was elected President, the concern over civil rights was no longer limited to a few liberal senators, a few churchmen and labor leaders, and black leaders of the old school. Nevertheless, President Kennedy concluded that general civil rights legislation could not pass in 1961 and 1962, and he did not want, in any case, to endanger other aspects of his legislative program by what would unquestionably have been the traditionally divisive battle. It was obvious to the President and to those who would lead the Senate fight that the content of civil rights legislation was almost irrelevant to the chance of passing it.

The major obstacle was, of course, Senate Rule XXII, which protected the "right" of unlimited debate, or filibustering. Until 1959, it required two thirds of all senators to vote to curtail debate. It was modified then to two thirds of senators *present and voting*. Some people, particularly Lyndon Johnson, considered that a major achievement. I didn't. I believed majority rule was sufficient, that a constitutional majority, that is half of all senators plus one (in the current Senate of one hundred senators, fifty-one votes) should be enough, once a suitable period of debate had passed.

The fact is that the Constitution makes no provisions for a cloture rule requiring a two-thirds vote and states quite clearly that a majority shall constitute a quorum for the purpose of doing business.

In theory, at least, twenty-six senators* can pass major legislation or even declare war. Clearly, when the framers of the Constitution felt a two-thirds vote was needed, they expressly said so, as in the case of impeachment of a President or adoption of a treaty or overriding a veto.

Further, no state legislature in the United States and no parliamentary body in any democratic country in the world permits unlimited debate. The rationale for Rule XXII was that it could, in our federal system, protect the interests of small states from being overrun by the rest of the country and prevent majority rule from wiping out the legitimate protestations of a minority, possibly preventing, in the excesses of an emotional moment in our history, the trampling of minority views.

---

* If just a quorum of fifty-one is present for the purpose of doing business, then twenty-six votes carries the motion.

So our procedural problem remained what it had always been: how to break the inevitable filibuster if a comprehensive and enforceable civil rights bill ever reached the floor. The coalition of southern Democrats and the Republican leadership in the Senate was still immensely strong, and during the fifties, for example, our pro-civil rights forces could rarely gather even thirty votes for cloture (that is, to limit debate to one hour for each senator), far short of the two-thirds vote we needed to break a filibuster.

Without the votes for cloture, in theory, it was possible to hold the Senate in session around the clock, exhausting the filibustering senators and thus breaking the filibuster. But this tactic in fact didn't work. Filibustering senators would divide into teams of three, scheduling eight-hour shifts for each team. That left proponents up all night to answer quorum calls, having to produce fifty-one bodies whenever, in Senate jargon, someone said, "I suggest the absence of a quorum." Unless a quorum could be produced, the Senate would be forced to adjourn.

Inevitably, non-filibustering senators always wore out first. While many were ready to vote right on final passage, they were not prepared to sit all night in the Senate cloakroom waiting for quorum calls. Further, the pressure grows on non-filibustering senators to give up so that other legislative business can go forward. Most senators were not ready to see pet projects or other important legislation blocked. No other matters could come up so long as the filibuster was in progress.

With most legislation, it was usually possible, in a spirit of compromise, to accede to certain substantive demands of the filibustering senators. But civil rights was something else. In the instance of fair employment, for example, until the sixties it simply meant abandoning the legislation.

But the times, indeed, were changing. The use of state and local laws to enforce discrimination and inequality had become more and more a national disgrace. The sit-in movement, the freedom rides, the widespread new commitment of blacks, young people, and churchmen had made the nation aware, as never before, of the still unfulfilled promise of equality for many Americans. All this activity indicated that civil rights was a widespread concern, and John Kennedy's determination to "get this country moving again" gave hope to the activists.

Again and again, the ugliness of the resistance to change appeared on television screens and in newspapers. There was violence in Oxford, Mississippi, when James Meredith tried to enroll at the university, in September 1962. As Dr. Martin Luther King, Jr., and his supporters confronted fire hoses and police dogs in Birmingham, as the police beat both blacks and whites peacefully demonstrating, the basic decency of Americans was outraged, and President Kennedy finally sent a new civil rights bill to Congress, in June 1963.

His address to the nation put the full prestige of the presidency behind the moral necessity of desegregation and civil rights. It was a magnificent moment in American life, which illumined the best that is in us, giving hope to those who had been denied it, isolating most of those who had denied it, and joining the rest of us in an almost prayerful proclamation that the bright sunshine of human rights might yet warm us all.

In late August 1963, two hundred thousand Americans, mostly black, but with tens of thousands of whites, were to join together at the Lincoln Memorial to petition for a redress of grievances, to seek "jobs and freedom." If I had to pick one day in my public life when I was most encouraged that democracy could work, when my spirit soared on the wings of the American dream of social justice for everyone, it was that day.

The March on Washington had been superbly organized by Bayard Rustin and the Leadership Conference on Civil Rights, which in one decade had become a tremendously powerful focal point for civil rights advocates. During the weeks preceding the March, establishment Washington was clouded by increasing fears of possible disorder and violence. President Kennedy himself had asked to be informed of whatever I learned about the March. Others were reporting to him, too.

The day before the March, I said in the Senate:

"There is no sense of threat or intimidation among these people. They are not traveling to Washington to disrupt the established legislative procedures followed by the Congress in considering the civil rights legislation. But they are coming to express their deep convictions that the President's legislation should be enacted promptly."[3]

The morning of the march, I had breakfast with a group of

United Church of Christ ministers and laymen who had come to Washington and whose church, more liberal than most others, worked then and later so effectively for the civil rights legislation. About noon, our Minnesota delegation, Gene McCarthy and I leading, marched the several miles to the Memorial grounds. There were incredibly touching scenes. It truly was America the beautiful, with a sea of shining faces parting at one moment to let a smiling group of bib-overalled Mississippi farmers, marching proudly and with immense dignity, move closer to the platform. There was a spirit of love and kindness everywhere. In all that crush of people, there was no pushing or shoving. If two people bumped into each other, if a toe got stepped on, there would be a gentle "Excuse me" and a warm smile.

By the time Dr. King stood before that crowd and proclaimed, "I have a dream," it finally seemed possible that the Congress of the United States might pass comprehensive, far-reaching civil rights legislation. This was America on its feet, America on the move, America marching under the open sky and in the nation's capital. Americans were there to speak their minds and not to shake their fists. They were there in peaceful assembly, in the highest tradition of free speech.

That day and that event did more to bring the truth of human rights and civil rights to the attention of the entire nation than anything that had happened in all of our history.

Despite the fears of some (and unlike the mood in Washington during later demonstrations), the city was not barricaded, it was not a darkened fortress under siege, and the White House was not turned into an island separated and "protected" from the American community. Washington, the White House, the Congress, and the executive branch were all part of a great human movement that day.

In a shining example of democracy at work, John Kennedy invited Martin Luther King, Roy Wilkins of the NAACP, and other leaders of the rally to *their* house, the White House, to sit together and talk together about what was happening in America.

While the President voiced his support for fair employment practices legislation that I had labored over so long, it was not originally part of his omnibus bill. Quite apart from its merits, he thought and Bob Kennedy concurred, fair employment could not pass and would doom the entire bill.

But civil rights forces in the House, most particularly William McCullough of Ohio, the ranking Republican on the Judiciary Committee, worked out a compromise bill that included an Equal Employment Opportunity Commission with court, rather than administrative, enforcement of its decisions. With the support of both House Democratic and Republican leadership, just two days before the assassination in Dallas, the Judiciary Committee reported out that bill, substantially stronger than the Administration's original version.

When the new President, Lyndon Johnson, addressed a somber Congress and nation on the Wednesday after the assassination, he appealed for the passage of the civil rights bill in the memory of the late President: "No memorial or eulogy could more eloquently honor President Kennedy than the earliest possible passage of the civil rights bill for which he fought so long."

It was an appeal heard across the country, building on the glow of goodwill that the August March had created. The memory of the young President who had proposed the bill and the shock of his death were important parts of the favorable political climate that permitted work on this historic legislation to go forward.

Later, during the Senate debate, in a moving moment, Senator Edward Kennedy closed his maiden speech in the Senate by saying, "My brother was the first President of the United States to state publicly that segregation was morally wrong. His heart and soul are in this bill. . . ."

In February 1964 the House of Representatives passed the bill and the stage was set for a remarkable drama in the Senate, the graveyard of so many civil rights proposals.

We had learned our lessons from the civil rights compromises of 1957 and 1960, the defeat of 1962, and our lack of success in changing the filibuster rule. Much had happened in America while the legislation was moving toward the Senate: outrages in Birmingham, a moving presidential speech by Kennedy, a tremendous march in Washington, the assassination of a young President, and more. This time the country was watching and ready. This time we had the people with us. This time, in the Senate, we were carefully organized.

Early in the year, Mike Mansfield, at President Johnson's suggestion, asked me to be floor leader when the bill came over. Usually, the chairman of the relevant committee acts as floor leader, but Mississippi Senator James Eastland, chairman of the Judiciary Committee, was clearly not appropriate. On other occasions, the majority leader himself becomes the floor leader on a major piece of legislation like this one, but Senator Mansfield, knowing of my long commitment to civil rights legislation and preferring to stay free himself for other Senate duties, gave me the opportunity and responsibility for managing the floor debate on the civil rights bill.

I met with Johnson immediately, and he told me, as he had others, that his objective during the remaining months of the term to which Kennedy had been elected was to see that every program Kennedy had laid before Congress became law. He desperately wanted this law passed not only as a memorial to Kennedy, but because of his feeling that it was right.

But Johnson began by saying he didn't think we (the Senate liberals) would succeed. He expressed faith in me, but launched into one of his traditional speeches about liberals: "You bomb-throwers make good speeches, you have big hearts, you believe in what you say you stand for, but you're never on the job when you need to be there. You spread yourselves too thin making speeches to the faithful."

He pointed out that Richard Russell, who would be leading the opposition, knew *all* the rules of the Senate and how to use them. He said liberals had never really worked to understand the rules and how to use them, that we never organized effectively and would therefore go down to defeat.

He was relentless, goading me, challenging me, belittling liberals in general as inept in dealing with parliamentary situations. He shook his head in apparent despair, predicting that we would fall apart in dissension, be absent when quorum calls were made and when critical votes were being taken.

I would have been outraged if he hadn't been basically right and historically accurate. As it was, I suffered his attack mostly in silence, with an occasional protest that things had changed. Having made his point, he shifted the conversation and more quietly and equally firmly he promised he would back me to the hilt. As I left, he stood and moved toward me with his towering intensity: "Call me whenever there's trouble or anything you want me to do."

The assignment as floor leader would be tough, but I was glad to have it. I canceled everything else to work full time on this one bill. Any diversion could be dangerous, since I had to walk across very thin legislative ice. A parliamentary situation can change very suddenly and go wrong in a host of different ways—especially in as complicated a job as building the conditions for invoking cloture on a civil rights bill.

And a filibuster was, of course, guaranteed. Our bipartisan civil rights bloc, stronger than ever before, still lacked the two-thirds majority (about 65–67 votes) to close off debate. Somewhere we would have to pick up about nine additional votes, almost all from traditionally conservative midwestern Republicans, an unlikely source on such controversial legislation.

These senators, led by Minority Leader Everett McKinley Dirksen, were most troubled by Title II, the public accommodations section, and Title VII, the fair employment section. The problem was as difficult as it was clear: how do you get their support for cloture without any critical weakening of those two titles?

As debate neared, Mansfield announced that there would be no round-the-clock sessions, even though many civil rights organizations thought this was the only way to break the filibuster. Many southern opponents were old men, but any attempt to break the anti-civil rights filibuster through physical exhaustion would have backfired. Mansfield's decision was a wise one. We decided early in the struggle to let the filibuster run as long as the southern senators wanted to talk.

Senate liberals had in the past been disorganized. This time, I assured myself, it would be different. While they talked, we would organize.

The New York *Times* soon reported, "Civil rights forces, not to be outdone by southern opponents, have thrown up their own well-manned command post in the Senate. . . . As militarily precise as the southerners' three-platoon system, the Humphrey forces are organized down to the last man."

Organization, morale, and momentum are very important in a legislative battle for their effect both on your own forces and on the opposition. We were moving.

We knew, of course, that our effort had to be bipartisan. Senator Thomas Kuchel of California was the Republican floor leader for the bill, and he and I worked as partners with no significant disagreements. Indeed, on occasion, the two of us would stand together against the Senate leaders of both parties, who, under other pressures, were slightly less committed to cloture and a strong bill than we were. More than once, we jointly stopped premature attempts to compromise.

But the key to cloture remained Everett Dirksen. I was determined to work closely with him, though that would not always be easy. He was conservative, closely allied to business interests who could be expected to oppose the bill, opposed at first to the compulsory enforcement powers in the public accommodations section. He was opposed to an Equal Employment Opportunity Commission and had serious doubts about Title VI, the old Adam Clayton Powell amendment, which cut off federal funds where there was discrimination in the application of a program.

But Dirksen had several other qualities that probably saved us. He had a magnificent sense of drama, loved the center stage, enjoyed the sound of his mellifluous, some said unctuous, voice filling the Senate chamber. He loved the legislative game, manipulating language, cadging a vote for an amendment. Laws to him were organic, growing, flowering like the marigolds on which he lavished such care and affection in his yard.

But mostly, when you scraped away everything else, he had a sense of history and his place in it. When, early on, I made an appearance on "Meet the Press," I ignored what he had been saying and implying: that he wanted a totally voluntary approach to enforcing a public accommodations law and equal employment opportunity (something we could not accept) and that he might vote against a bill stronger than that.

Instead, I began a public massage of his ego and appealed to his vanity. I said that he would look upon this issue as "a moral, not a partisan, one." The gentle pressure left room for *him* to be the historically important figure in our struggle, the statesman above partisanship, the thoughtful architect, the master builder of a legislative edifice that would last forever. He liked it.

As much as Dirksen liked the stroking, however, if he thought we had no chance, that we were going through the effort simply for exercise, he would have kept his distance. Had he thought we had just a chance, he would have insisted on major compromises as the price for his support. But Dirksen this time was clearly impressed with the organization of the pro-civil rights forces and with our determination to fight for a strong bill even if the filibuster ran all year. As the opponents talked on and on, public pressure for passage continued to build, and of the greatest importance was President Johnson's public and private pronouncements that no compromises were possible this time. It was going to be a strong bill or nothing.

After about two months of debate, Senator Dirksen, in an encouraging sign, came forward with a number of amendments he wished to discuss with pro-civil rights senators and staff from the Justice Department. It was evident that Dirksen was looking for ways to support the bill, and our job was to find alternative language that satisfied him but left the bill essentially intact.

It was a time-consuming and complex negotiation. More than seventy amendments, which touched almost all sections of the omnibus bill, had been developed by Dirksen's staff. I was terribly dependent then, as I was later, on a young man on my staff, John Stewart. While he was not a senator, of course, his role was absolutely crucial, and without him I could not have done the things I needed to do to persuade, conciliate, and advocate.

Whenever I think of how dependent we are on others for our success, I am compelled to think of John during those difficult months. For endless hours through endless days, whenever I needed him, he was there with ideas, strategy, new language. He co-ordinated staff assistants of other pro-civil rights senators at daily strategy sessions and worked closely with outside civil rights lobbyists. While many people are important to the passage of major legislation and few are really so basic that the legislation would fail without them, the civil rights bill of 1964 would not have been the same without him. I know certainly that I would not have been able to work as well, and had I performed as floor leader significantly less well, the bill could have failed.

Since Dirksen remained the key, I continued to make every effort to involve him. I was his Jiminy Cricket, visiting with him on the floor, in the cloakroom, in the corridors and on the elevators. I constantly encouraged him to take a more prominent role, asked him what changes he wanted to propose, urged him to call meetings to discuss his changes.

A number of Democrats complained that Dirksen was stealing the show. Some insisted that the meetings should have been held in my office rather than in his. I said, "Listen, I don't care *where* we meet. Everett can have the meetings in his office or on a street corner and I'll come. If this thing fails, none of you guys will want to be around me. I'll be a very lonely fellow in defeat. The monkey will be on my back. If it passes, there will be glory enough for everybody."

So hardly a day passed without my refrain, "Everett, we can't pass this bill without you." But working Dirksen was only one part of our strategy. Keeping well organized was another.

We put out a daily newssheet, an innovation that summarized the proceedings and gave the civil rights forces' answers to the arguments of the opposition.

One day, on the floor, Senator John Stennis of Mississippi inquired about this newsletter. "I should like to ask," he said, "who writes these mysterious messages which come to senators before the Congressional Record reaches them, and . . . attempts to refute arguments made on the floor of the Senate. . . ."

I was glad he asked. It gave me a chance to publicize our organization efforts.

"There is no doubt about it," I said. "The newsletter is a bipartisan civil rights newsletter. . . . For the first time, we are putting up a battle. Everything will be done to make us succeed. . . . I wish also to announce that if anyone wishes to have equal time, there is space on the back of it for the opposition. . . ."

Republicans and Democrats had to co-operate. Liberals, moderates, and conservatives had to work together. We had to maintain relations with the House of Representatives lest their rejection of our changes in the bill force a conference, and thus another vote, and thus another filibuster.

We developed a duty system, with a daily list of senators from both parties on duty for quorum calls. We divided into small groups, with a captain for each group. We had people on the floor all day, every man assigned certain hours. From the middle of February to the middle of June, we failed to produce a quorum only once, and when that happened we publicized the names of those who had been absent. That was the end of that. In 1960, the Southerners had hurt us badly with repeated quorum calls, but in 1964 we had the problem licked.

The unwavering support of the President kept senators in line and convinced our opponents that we were, and would continue to be, serious. We had to work closely with others in the executive branch, especially with Attorney General Robert Kennedy and his colleagues in the Justice Department, to check the technicalities of the complicated titles and amendments. I asked Kennedy to assign two outstanding men—Nicholas Katzenbach and Burke Marshall—to the civil rights struggle, and they worked with us every day in developing strategy, counting votes, and writing the new language that would eventually win Dirksen's support. Their help was vital to our ultimate victory.[4]

We had to keep the debate on a high level, with no personal attacks or invective, to maintain good relations with our opponents. Uncommitted senators could be offended if we did not. We dealt with Senator Richard Russell of Georgia, the southern leader, and his colleagues with fairness and careful courtesy. We assured them that we would not try to win by parliamentary tricks. I went out of my way to maintain good personal relations with the southern senators, even while we were arguing with each other constantly on the floor.[5]

We divided responsibility for defending sections of the bill among many senators, to broaden the involvement and the credit.

We had regular meetings, set up a research center and a command center. We carefully presented our case as though the arguments were new, answering every question, developing every point.

We had taken the offensive early—really before we had

planned to—in order to keep the Southerners from dominating the news. We wanted to get our case to the press; and when we did, on the whole we were treated well.

I opened debate on the bill with a statement that took three hours; Senator Kuchel followed. For more than twelve days, proponents held the floor, providing detailed information to let the public know what was in the bill and why it should pass.[6]

We encouraged the senators on our side to go on radio and television and to send newsletters to the folks back home. Sample copies of other senators' newsletters were available. We encouraged reprints of key materials, so that people would know the answers to the attacks. We answered the propaganda of the anti-civil rights groups.

Republican captains led by Senator Kuchel matched our Democratic set. Two or three Republicans who were not deeply committed, and even opposed certain sections of the bill, asked to be relieved of their duties.[7] But most stayed on. Senators Scott, Keating, Javits, Allott, and Cooper, along with Tom Kuchel, were especially important among the Republicans.

When senators got a chance to be team captains for the various titles, they attracted press for themselves and became known as fighters for civil rights. They became more committed.

We met at the Capitol every morning, half an hour before the session. Without round-the-clock sessions, we made the days just long enough so that senators (and eventually the public) would recognize that their time was being frittered away.

Other Senate business, of course, was stalled while the filibuster continued. Pressure to end it grew. The heavy barrage of newsletters going out from our senators pointed out that all this talking was wasting time. The refusal of the southern senators to allow any voting—except in one or two instances on minor amendments—contributed to the mounting exasperation with the filibuster.

I was rather surprised at the Southerners' tactics. I never could quite understand why they didn't let us vote more often. If they had done so, they could have insisted that the legislative process, after all, was working, because amendments were being voted upon. But they didn't do that. Instead they just kept talking and talking. It seemed that they had lost their sense of direction and had little or no real plan.

Our plan was to try to make the growing annoyance with the filibuster work to our advantage—toward votes for cloture instead of toward compromise on the content of the bill.

We kept a good spirit throughout, even on the most difficult days. There was little acrimony and few signs of temper. That may sound like a minor matter, but in a delicate parliamentary situation, that counts. When I became floor manager of the bill, I was determined to keep my patience. I told myself not to lose my temper, no matter how outrageous the arguments might be. I tried to preserve a reasonable degree of good nature and fair play, and I think I succeeded.

For years, the filibuster barrier allowed an intransigent minority to block laws against racial discrimination. To change that, we had to have the votes of more than the committed civil rights liberals in the Senate, and more than the moderates. We needed the votes of conservatives who had grave reservations about extending federal power, and of Senate traditionalists very reluctant ever to vote for limiting debate. Our coalition had to transcend ideological lines, reaching out in an extraordinary way beyond Capitol Hill and beyond Washington pressure groups.

We worked closely with the Leadership Conference on Civil Rights, which mobilized a broad range of civil rights groups, labor groups, liberals, church groups, religious and business leaders, and others. The civil rights groups that before this and again after this would often be at odds co-operated fully during those important months. So did diverse liberal and labor groups. And a wide spectrum of religious groups provided the single most important area of support.

The support of religious leaders was strategically necessary to emphasize the moral dimension of the issue, transcending the ordinary arguments of party and political philosophy. Religious communities could reach places that were difficult for liberal-labor-black groups to reach. To sway senators, sensitive to coercion, it was imperative that our efforts be a dignified, serious appeal to conscience, rather than anything that looked like intimidation.

Early in March we met with Protestant, Catholic, and Jewish representatives and designed plans for civil rights meetings across the country, with the clergy taking the lead. Delegation after delegation of clergymen and church people quietly visited senators. Without the clergy, we could never have passed the bill.†

In a kind of reverse compliment that is impressive because it comes from the opposition, Senator Russell said in his closing speech:

"I have observed with profound sorrow the role that many religious leaders have played in urging the passage of the bill. . . . During the course of the debate, we have seen cardinals, bishops, elders, stated clerks, common preachers, priests, and rabbis come to Washington to press for the passage of the bill; . . . day after day, men of the cloth have been standing on the Mall and urging a favorable vote on the bill. They have encouraged and prompted thousands of good citizens to sign petitions in support of the bill. . . ."

In short, we developed one of the most extraordinary coalitions in the history of American politics.[8] Yet, for all our efforts, there were times when it looked as though we could not line up the necessary votes, even with Dirksen's support. When that fear intruded, hope refused to flee. We just kept working with undecided senators, listening to their concerns, making sure that pro-civil rights forces in their states kept in touch. On the seventy-fifth day of debate, June 10, 1964, the Senate scheduled the historic vote.[9]

The tension that morning was palpable. Confidence and enthusiasm were muted by a fear that, somehow, something had come unraveled. We were uneasy actors in a historical drama. And there gloriously was Dirksen, the sung hero, who intoned, "Stronger than all the armies is an idea whose time has come. The time has come for equality of opportunity in sharing in government, in education, and in employment. . . ."

Before the voting began, I would look up from time to time to the packed gallery filled with citizens of the United States, black and white, watching our democratic process in one of its finer hours. Among those faces were many with whom I had worked closely in recent days, for months, or years. Our eyes, when they met, flashed an unmistakable message: "We are together and we are going to win." We were aglow with the electricity that

† Seminarians, in an ecumenical spirit, maintained a silent vigil, day and night, on the Capitol grounds throughout the long Senate debate.

charged the air in a chamber filled with a dramatic, historic tension beyond anything even the most senior senators had experienced.

Just an hour before the voting began, I wrote a note to Phil Hart[10] predicting sixty-nine favorable votes, two more than needed. But you can never be absolutely certain, and I listened very carefully as each vote was cast, checking my list.

Every single senator was there that day, even Senator Clair Engle of California, dying of a brain tumor and unable to speak. He was wheeled into the chamber and voted "Aye" by pointing to his eye. Carl Hayden, the oldest member of the Senate, both in his own age and years of service, waited in the cloakroom to see whether his vote would be needed. On principle, he had never voted to limit debate; that day, had his vote been needed, he would have risen above principle in search of justice.

We got every vote we counted on and one or two besides. When I heard the sixty-seventh "Aye," I involuntarily raised my arms over my head, in a gesture of deep satisfaction. When the roll was finished, there were seventy-one yeas, twenty-nine nays, four votes to spare.

For me, personally, it was the culmination of the full year's fight for the Civil Rights Act, of fifteen years' battle for civil rights in the United States Senate, and of a lifetime in politics in which equal opportunity had been *the* objective above all others.

For the small band of Senate liberals, it was a full victory at last, after years of frustration, defeat, and compromise. For the civil rights forces, it was the climax of the extraordinary civil rights decade since the Supreme Court's school desegregation decision.

One of the most important, influential, and devoted workers for that decade had been Clarence Mitchell, the director of the Washington bureau of the NAACP. The victory that day was as much his glory as any man's. For years, virtually alone, he, in its finest sense, lobbied graciously, quietly, persistently, keeping pro-civil rights people strong in their resolve, diminishing the antagonism of opponents.[11]

While others drew the headlines and the accolades, Clarence Mitchell did the day-to-day drudge work, making every defeat, every compromise, every minor victory part of a forward movement. He never let us forget the unfinished business that remained. Clarence was a member of an illustrious black Baltimore family, a lawyer and social worker who had been head of the Urban League in St. Paul, Minnesota, when I first met him, around 1940.

He had come to Washington in 1941 to work for Sidney Hillman in the Office of Production Management, and in 1945 went to work for the NAACP. Putting personal feelings aside, knowing little immediate gain was possible, he worked the Southerners over and, strangely, was able to maintain a kind of friendship with them even when they hated what he was doing and when he could never get their votes.

Typically, after the cloture vote, instead of joining the proponents in celebration, he walked Richard Russell back to his Senate office. Russell thanked him for his courtesy both then and during the preceding months and made several points that both pleased and interested me.

He said that if the opponents had not put up the fight they had, the bill would never have been enforceable in the South. He thought it was important to have satisfied the people of the South that everything that could have been done had been done in opposition. He thought now, having been defeated in a proper legislative battle, the South would accept the verdict and that he anticipated little trouble.

Russell also said nice things about me, which I repeat only in part because of vanity but much more because it tells again something about how the Senate operates. He said I personally, and my leadership colleagues, had been eminently fair, permitting the opponents all the time they wanted to have their say, never embarrassing them, never forcing them by parliamentary device. Russell, like many of the old southern senators, loved the institution of the Senate. When it worked its will in a decent fashion, as much as they hated to, they accepted their defeat with as much reciprocal grace as they could.[12]

Now that cloture was accomplished, it was only a matter of time before we would pass the bill. Yet we had to cross some slippery territory of amendments and parliamentary tactics, knowing that our forces would inevitably break up. Further, we had concentrated so much on the cloture fight that we were not as well prepared as we should have been for the following legislative period. But we made it.

I went through the last two days of debate in a daze. My son Bob had not been feeling well and had gone into the hospital to have a swelling in his neck checked. I was called off the Senate floor in midafternoon on June 17 to take a call from Muriel. She told me tearfully that Bob had a malignant, cancerous growth and would have to undergo major surgery in a massive procedure to clean out his lymphatic system. I wanted desperately to be with him and Muriel, but I simply couldn't leave at that crucial moment. The endless conflict between public and private demands wouldn't cease.

I sat in tears and virtually paralyzed in my whip office, near the Senate floor, when Joe Rauh and Clarence Mitchell came in, filled with the joy of our legislative successes. Their joy disappeared as they shared my gloom and fears. Three grown men trying to savor the fullness of our success after decades of failure were instead soon sharing bitter tears.

I had a terrible time pulling myself together to go back to the Senate floor, where I had to be. Arguments and rhetoric that I might have listened to calmly and without emotion were much harder to take when I should have been at Bob's bedside.[13] I stayed, and the next day I would see the final passage of the Civil Rights Act of 1964.

Civil rights proponents, including Everett Dirksen, gathered in Mike Mansfield's office to toast our victory, to pose for pictures, to talk to the press. A couple of hours later, when several of us walked out of the Capitol, there were many hundreds of people waiting to cheer each senator who appeared.

Black and white, young and old, from all parts of the country, people were there to salute an extraordinary event in the history of their Congress and in the expansion of human rights in America. In a striking example of democratic government at its best, the public was involved from start to finish in a unique legislative battle.

The House of Representatives voted to accept the Senate-passed bill, thereby avoiding the need for a conference to resolve differences. President Johnson signed the bill into law on July 2 before a national television audience. Equal employment opportunity, along with a host of other major civil rights provisions, had at least become a legal reality.

Johnson-haters to the contrary notwithstanding, it is appropriate that President Johnson receive both praise and honor for that act. The transcendent legislative achievement of Lyndon Johnson is that he brought the Senate, with minimal acrimony and bitterness, from 1954, the year of *Brown* vs. *Board of Education,* to the Civil Rights Act of 1964. Not in the course of one legislative session, but over the years, he slowly moved the Senate into a new era of equal rights legislation.

During the 1950s, in face of the lackluster leadership of the Eisenhower administration, it was Johnson who prepared the way. By letting the Southerners have face-saving victories while he established the principle of federal intervention, he isolated the most venomous ones, prevented excessive hate from building up, broke down the southern bloc with its own help, which most, if not all, of its members understood. They fought, but fought knowing that they would ultimately lose. That they lost in 1964, long before they expected to, was a shock to them and indeed a joyful surprise to us. The course of racial legislation for those ten years was a monument to Lyndon Johnson's skill and misunderstood liberalism.

As President, and in some instances with the grudging help of Richard Russell, he diluted further the power of the South. It was he who had the power to insist that the Senate break the filibuster and apply cloture, and he used it to keep the bill from being weakened. In 1965, it was Johnson, as President, who by sponsoring voting rights legislation, undermined the old power structure of the South, both in local and in Congressional elections.

It was Johnson, as President, who did more than any predecessor to pass legislation in the fields of education and health and conservation and environment that had a national purpose and national standards. None of those laws paid much homage to states' rights but, rather, called on the states to be partners in the achievement of national goals and national commitments.

The man from Texas who rose to power with the active support of key leaders in the South used that power to pass the most far-reaching legislation this country has ever known, over the fervent objections of southern leadership in the Congress, the southern governors, and the southern Democratic power structure.

Johnson had become a national leader and a liberal one. Vietnam was a distant black cloud on the horizon. What he was doing domestically was what I would have wanted to do had I been successful in 1960. What I had talked about and believed in, he had the power to accomplish.

31. "LET'S GO OVER TO THE WHITE HOUSE FOR A NIGHTCAP"

The period from President Kennedy's death until Lyndon Johnson was elected in his own right, almost a year later, was a strange one. On the surface, the transition was smooth. Johnson moved slowly in replacing Kennedy people both at the White House and in the executive agencies. But, below the surface, there was constant tension caused by the yearning for an attractive, fallen leader and the reservations and suspicions about his successor.

Johnson, although a man of immense ego, felt threatened both by his unnatural accession and by the spoken and unspoken comparisons to Kennedy. He sought desperately and sincerely to continue the JFK programs, to assuage the Kennedy people who were bereft, to assure the nation that he could lead it well. He was, I suppose, like the second husband of a demanding wife: overly sensitive to every nuance, easily angered by real or imagined slights, trying constantly to erase any memories that might lead to negative comparisons.

Sometimes the fervor with which Johnson operated brought the results he wanted; sometimes it simply heightened the differences between Kennedy and him, between their "people." As he was the heir to the presidency, he wanted, too, to be the heir to the affection of the Kennedy insiders as well as of the nation. When it was not readily forthcoming, he tried more desperately to succeed; and both his virtues and his flaws were larger than life.[1]

That year was a difficult one for me, too, but the difficulties were the kind I invited and in a sense enjoyed. The question of civil rights, which had consumed so much of me since 1945, had become now a central issue for all Americans, even a popular cause for some. Blacks, led primarily by Dr. Martin Luther King, Jr., had dramatized both their miseries and their aspirations in a way that had never been successful before. As a result, I was able to become deeply involved in the major legislative achievement of my Senate career: the passage of the Civil Rights Act of 1964.

At the same time, the possibility of becoming the vice-presidential nominee of the Democratic party became real. Within hours of President Kennedy's death, friends and political leaders around the country were calling about my plans for 1964. My reply was brief: I had no plans; whatever Lyndon Johnson wanted, Johnson would get. Clearly, he would want to be elected to a term of his own and there was no question that he would be the nominee.

But, by January, journalists and politicians were discussing publicly and without embarrassment possible candidates for the second spot, and my name was invariably on the list. I savored each favorable comment, hoped Johnson liked them too, but was ever fearful that they would push him too hard or too constantly —to the point of irritation and rejection.

As a matter of fact, beneath the seriousness of the question, there was a semicomic relief in the game for Johnson. It was the kind of situation he delighted in: floating a trial balloon, deflating it, suggesting different names. He held all the cards and played them as the whim struck.

One of the early names he "leaked" was that of Robert McNamara. Johnson told many people that McNamara was the "smartest man he had ever known" and quietly suggested that McNamara might make a fine Vice President. (That the suggestion was taken at all seriously indicates how little handicap Vietnam was at that time.)

McNamara, of course, had no political base, never having been elected to any public office, and there was some question whether he was a Democrat or a Republican. By the time McNamara disclosed that he was indeed a Democrat, Johnson had eliminated him in a ploy aimed entirely at Robert Kennedy, still the Attorney General.

Kennedy's name was frequently suggested, though not by Johnson, and it seemed clear enough that Bob wanted the nomination. Johnson respected Kennedy, but there was no love lost between them. When the McNamara gambit had about run its course and the Kennedy pressure was mounting, Johnson called Kennedy in and told him directly but privately that he would not be the nominee. Then, with a straight face, Johnson announced publicly that no member of the Cabinet would be considered, implying that their immediate responsibilities for the proper functioning of government were too great to be diminished by a campaign. No one, least of all Kennedy, was taken in.

By then, it was clear that Johnson didn't really need anyone to add much to the ticket. Like Truman following Roosevelt's death, he was the beneficiary of the generous spirit of most Americans. However much they lamented the loss of their previous President, their compassion was great for a man on whom the burdens of that office were thrust.

Those feelings translated into popularity, if only for short duration, and in the spring and summer of 1964, Johnson arrived, wallowing in public esteem, with people rallying to him from virtually every stratum of American life. He had the luxury of tossing names out as potential Vice Presidents and having them taken seriously, since almost any qualification seemed enough.

In my role as majority whip, I saw Johnson frequently during those months as he worked to pass legislation that had bogged down in the last year of the Kennedy administration. His personal persuasiveness, which had worked so well while he was majority leader, still was powerful, and from the presidency, occasionally more so.

I had seen the famous Johnsonian influence many times—but never more characteristically than the evening when he talked tough old Harry Byrd into a tax cut: One night in the spring of 1964, I attended the annual Gridiron Dinner and Johnson was there. We left at about the same time, and as I came through the front door of the hotel, he had just gotten into his limousine.

When he saw me, he shouted through the window, "Hubert, get in the car. Let's go over to the White House for a nightcap."

I got in. Johnson continued to peer out, smiling at the crowd that had gathered. Between waves and grins, he spotted Senator Harry Byrd moving slowly down the walk. He turned and said, "Go get Harry and tell him I'd like to have him drop over to the White House."

When I got to Byrd, he said it was late and he thought he ought to go directly home. I asked him to wait as I carried the message. Johnson frowned and in a whispered growl said, "You go get him. Tell him it's important. I need to talk to him."

I went back to Byrd, who finally agreed, though he insisted on driving his own car, which, despite Byrd's great wealth, was a tired, six-year-old Chevrolet.

As Johnson and I approached the White House, the grounds were dark and there was scarcely a light visible in the building itself, since Johnson, on an economy binge, had recently embarked on his turn-off-the-lights campaign.

When Byrd arrived, shortly after, I led him upstairs to the living room. We chatted for a few minutes before Johnson said, "Hubert, step out there in that Kennedy kitchen* and fix us all a drink. Just bring me a little scotch with some water and just fix Harry up with about two fingers of bourbon." He held up his massive hands, two fingers of which amounted to a sizable jolt. I poured our drinks, smiling as I measured two giant Johnsonian fingers of Old Grand-Dad for Byrd.

After about a half hour of casual talk about Congress and the Finance Committee, Byrd sipped his second drink slowly, his face a little flushed. Johnson got up rather suddenly, saying, "Harry, before you go home I think you ought to visit with your girl friend." He moved to the doorway of a nearby bedroom and shouted, "Lady Bird, your boy friend Harry is out here." Mrs. Johnson had been asleep, but she shortly appeared in her dress-

---

* The Kennedy kitchen was a little alcove off a small dining room that President Kennedy had built to avoid a trip to the main kitchen when he wanted a nighttime snack.

Johnson's reference to it was strange, since Byrd had been no particular admirer of John Kennedy. It apparently had some special meaning, which I did not grasp.

ing robe and sat next to Byrd. She had been there long enough to get Byrd laughing and more relaxed when Johnson said, "Well, Lady Bird, we can't keep Harry up much longer. You better go back to bed now. He's had his chance to see you."

As his wife rose to leave, Johnson turned to Byrd and said, "Harry, every time I can't find Lady Bird, I know she's either with you or Laurance Rockefeller or Hubert. That's why I don't dare leave town too much and leave her here."

The old man, massaged by bourbon, jokes, and affectionate chatter, chuckled.

His laughter had not died or Lady Bird quite disappeared when Johnson moved forward, leaning over, peering intensely into Byrd's eyes, and said, "Harry, I know you're opposed to any tax reduction. But frankly I've just got to have that bill out of committee. You know I'm trying to pass the Kennedy program and I feel I owe it to the late President."

Before Byrd could react negatively, Johnson implied a common position between them: "Now, whether we agree or not, and you and I may not feel too strongly about a tax reduction, I need your commitment that you'll get that bill out.

"Now, I know you can't vote for it and I don't expect you to. In fact, I would expect you to oppose it. But I don't want you to bottle it up. Will you give me your word that you'll just report the bill out as soon as possible?"

Byrd, the captive of an elixir that was part Old Grand-Dad, part Lady Bird, part Lyndon Johnson treatment, said with intensity and even some emotion, "Lyndon [he's the only man I ever heard call Johnson by his first name after he became President], if you want that bill out, I'll do nothing to stop it. If there're votes in the committee to report it out, I'll let it come out. You can be sure of that."

Byrd had hardly time to draw a concluding breath when Johnson stood up and said, "Harry, it's time to go to bed. I've kept you up late. Good night." Johnson asked me to escort Byrd to his car, but signaled that I should come back after he was on his way.

When I returned, Johnson concluded with a final order: "Hubert, you sit right alongside of Harry in the Senate. [Mansfield, Byrd, and I occupied the first three seats on the Democratic side of the Senate.] You ask him every day if he remembers what the President said. You tell him that the President is waiting for action. You just keep at him to make sure that bill comes out."

I did my job. More importantly, Harry Byrd did his. One day, Byrd appeared on the floor with the bill in hand, reported it out, and placed it on the calendar. It was called up for action, and Senator Byrd made a brief speech in such low tones that he was virtually inaudible to me, sitting right next to him.

When he was done speaking, he turned and leaned over to me, saying, "Now, you tell the President that I kept my word—that I've reported out the bill, that I've made my speech, and now I'm leaving."

I called the President, who was exuberant. I am sure that as soon as he hung up on our conversation, he placed a call to Byrd to thank him profusely, the final touch of the Johnson treatment. Shortly, the Senate passed the bill.

I continued to see Johnson frequently and, since he was telephone-compulsive, talk to him often between visits. In May, he told me that if nothing arose that put an obstacle in his way, he would prefer to have me as his running mate. But he immediately said it was not a certainty (a phrase I would hear over and over again that year), since political problems might prevent it.

The best chance I had to overcome these undescribed obstacles was to perform well as whip. But, in addition, I had already begun an intensive effort to woo labor leaders I knew, journalists and commentators who wrote and rewrote the vice-presidential story, and leaders of the business community, an area where I was very weak.

I had no natural ties to big business and turned to my longtime, wealthy friend Dwayne Andreas, asking him to be a bridge to the leaders of corporate America. I needed his help badly and, as always, he delivered.

Politics is a profession in which no one succeeds by himself. You can lose by yourself, but you simply cannot succeed without others. Each of us approaches public life with a vision limited by his experience and training, restricted by his prejudices and background. Unless a person is willing to reach out to people who are not just like himself, he remains forever limited, explicating a narrow text, repeating old ideas.

For liberals, this particularly means reaching into the business or financial community; and inevitably those associations become suspect in many peoples' eyes. When the association brings not only ideas and information but financial support for a campaign, both parties become targets for journalists and political ideologues—one as a "bought" man, the other as a venal, self-seeking manipulator.

Through our history, there have been many instances of such relationships, and the suspicion is a healthy one. Even the most casual student of American history is aware of the nineteenth-century robber barons, utility magnates, railroad and mining officials, who "bought" government officials and policy. And currently, of course, anyone who has read a newspaper or watched public officials resign or be convicted of various crimes knows that the venal art has not died.

Still, while skepticism about politics and politicians is healthy, cynicism, which assumes that every politician is corrupt and every contributor dishonest, is not. There are many men who contribute their time and money to political campaigns who neither ask nor receive anything in return. For some, the proximity to a candidate or officeholder is itself enough. The opportunity to say casually, "I told the senator [or mayor or president] . . ." is payment enough. Others believe that a contribution ensures the chance to have ideas heard and (they hope) considered seriously.

With or without public financing of campaigns (though public financing wonderfully diminishes the probability of corruption), the American political system requires people who are willing to back a candidate, with money, work, and ideas, in good times and bad. Without this kind of loyalty, public and political life for most of the men and women who are in politics today would be, to put it plainly, impossible.

I turned naturally to Andreas because he was the one man of wealth who has been closer to me and more generous than any other in my life. He has provided me with his time and counsel, contributed to campaigns, and been a friend for over a quarter of a century.

Contrary to the inevitable gossip that follows such an association, he never asked me to fix a contract or introduce legislation that would benefit him specifically or manipulate something in his behalf.[2]

To the contrary, I not only have sought and received hundreds of thousands of dollars for my own campaigns but have asked him to contribute to many candidates whom he never met and from whom he received nothing but his canceled checks. Governors I like, congressmen I admire, men and women I thought should be elected to office have received from him contributions to the tune of a quarter of a million dollars or more over the years.

In addition, he has given to many Republicans whom he personally liked, from Tom Dewey to Clark MacGregor (a Minnesota congressman who once ran against me for the Senate) to Dwight Eisenhower and to Richard Nixon.

While mayor of Minneapolis, I met a number of people in the agriculturally related business community. Several of them mentioned Dwayne as a young, bright, internationally minded businessman I should meet, but I was busy and never followed up their suggestion.

Then, during my campaign for the Senate in 1948, I received an unsolicited donation of one thousand dollars from him. That was a spectacularly large amount from someone I hadn't met and hadn't asked for help, so I sought him out to thank him and to take his measure. As we talked that first time, we simply clicked as friends; the chemistry was right.

I learned that Dwayne's father had been in the grain-elevator business in Iowa, that he came from an Amish background, that his interests were not narrow or limited to peddling commodities for profit.

We talked about foreign trade and international relations. He was opposed to protectionism, tariffs, and quotas, and was as close to being a classical free-trade man as I had known. We argued about price supports and subsidies for farmers, which I supported and he opposed. He felt there was a danger that farmers would substitute one tyrant for another, replacing the milling companies and railroads, their traditional enemies, with the more capricious political whimsy of the country.

His view of co-operatives was particularly intriguing to me, since it was so unexpected. Long before it was generally popular among farmers themselves, he felt they must organize to protect themselves from the vagaries of the market place. Later in his career, as a matter of fact, he joined the Farmers Union Grain

Terminal Association as its executive vice president. GTA is the largest grain co-operative in the world, and Andreas devoted his energy and sizable business experience to making it even stronger.

We both believed in expanding agricultural production, and with it international trade. But aside from the financial profit to the country, we both agreed that food can be used as the instrument of humanitarian goals and foreign-policy objectives. Andreas was an enthusiastic supporter of the Food for Peace Program, which I had authored, and shared my views about its potential for worldwide goodwill.

In 1954, before he joined the GTA, Andreas wanted to sell butter to the Soviet Union in a complicated barter arrangement, the result of his strong feeling that every effort ought to be made to reach some form of understanding with the Soviets. He was an original *détente* man, while I myself still hesitated because of my strong anti-Communist feelings. I fought him both publicly and privately on his butter-sale program, yet it never diminished our friendship a bit. The butter deal did not come to pass, but I considered his views so seriously that in some ways my own views changed, helping me in ensuing years to think in terms of not *whether*, but *how* we should try to get along with the Soviets.

I found, too, that we shared other interests in areas where I would put my political energy and he his money. He contributed generously to the Urban League, the National Association for the Advancement of Colored People, and the B'nai B'rith Anti-Defamation League, as well as to colleges and universities and other cultural institutions. His dedication to the protection of civil liberties and civil rights was genuine and persistent.[3]

I learned that Dwayne was a very special kind of businessman, a special kind of citizen. And then I found, through him, that there are others like him.

Particularly in the period when I was looking for broad support for my vice-presidential nomination, he brought me into contact with corporate leaders most of whom harbored more serious reservations about me than I did about them.

While I worked personally through Dwayne to build business support or at least diminish hostility, my staff, friends, and I talked to political leaders around the country trying to convince them that I would be the strongest nominee for Vice President. Ironically, in light of subsequent developments, one of the men most helpful to me late in this mini-campaign was Harold Hughes, then Governor of Iowa.† At the time we called him asking for his support, he was about to visit Washington and spend the weekend at the White House as Johnson's guest. He agreed to lobby hard.

There were many others who lined up for me, while Johnson persisted in a name-dropping game. Knowing full well how much I wanted the nomination, how nervous every trial balloon, serious or not, made me, he leaned over one night at a White House dinner and said, "I think I'm going to drop Mike Mansfield's name into the hopper. He'll like it and it will give a lot of people something to talk about."

Within two or three days, Mansfield's name was all over. Mansfield was too wise to be taken in by the publicity and immediately said he wasn't interested in being Vice President.

While Mansfield and Johnson had a mutual respect, their personalities were not compatible, and the President felt Mike was latently, at least, an isolationist; Johnson, of course, was working vigorously on international relations and beginning greater American participation in Southeast Asia. Johnson said to me, "You'll find in every man from Montana a little bit of Burton K. Wheeler."‡

Whether it was isolationism or prophetic wisdom on Mansfield's part may be unclear, but he alone among the possible vice-presidential candidates understood Johnson's game and would have none of it.

In any case, Johnson persisted: one day, Mayor Robert Wagner of New York; the next day, Governor Edmund Brown of California; the following days and weeks, other governors, other senators, other politicians.

Through all of this, two names persisted: Eugene McCarthy's and mine. Gene and Abigail McCarthy were special friends of

† Hughes grew disenchanted with the Vietnam War and President Johnson not long after. He remains my good friend to this day.

‡ Wheeler was, of course, an isolationist in the Senate before World War II.

both the President and Lady Bird, and Lady Bird probably favored Gene.

In addition, McCarthy had gotten along well with Johnson in the Senate, and possibly more important, was very close to Senator Robert Kerr, a colleague on the Finance Committee and most intimate friend of Johnson's for years.

Early on, Jim Rowe, my close friend but an even closer one of Johnson's, asked me to come to his home. We sat on his porch in Cleveland Park, a fashionable neighborhood of substantial old houses in Washington, and he said, "I'm going to talk to you candidly and I want you to do the same. You're being very seriously considered for the vice presidency. The President hasn't made up his mind and there is no commitment. But there are certain things he must know before he makes up his mind.

"What do you think of Lyndon Johnson? How do you think he has conducted himself as President? Is your relationship as good as when he was majority leader? Will you be loyal to him? Do you have any basic disagreements with his policies?"

Then he turned to more personal questions: "You have got to level with me, because the President needs to know. Are there any skeletons in your closet? Is there anything that could come up in case you were nominated that would be scandalous or cause trouble to the administration or you personally?"

I answered all those questions, and I assume that the other potential candidates, including Gene McCarthy, answered similar ones to Johnson's satisfaction.

Later, as the convention neared, Rowe came to my Senate office and we did a replay of the scene on his porch, but this time when we ended he said, "I am going to call the President and I want you to tell him that you and I have talked. I want you to tell him that you understand completely the concerns I have expressed on behalf of the President."

Rowe picked up the phone, placed the call, and the President was immediately on the line. Rowe handed me the phone and I said, "Mr. President, Jim has been here to visit for the past hour. I understand your concern about relationships between the President and Vice President. You can rely on me. I will be loyal."

The President thanked me but said nothing that could possibly have been construed as a commitment. His options were still

17. Senator Humphrey's campaign bus swings through West Virginia in 1960, during the primary campaign.

18. The vice-presidential nominee embraces Muriel during a campaign tour through South Dakota, 1964.

19. Campaigning in downtown Doland. Humphrey's Drug Store is seen in the background.

20. On thin ice in Waverly, Minnesota (left to right): Douglas, Robert, Hubert, Nancy, Muriel, and the author. Like any family, they don't always follow the leader. But whatever the pressures and conflicts of public life, "Our home is my haven."

21. The author's mother meets Senator Johnson in Washington, D.C., 1959.

open. I was precisely where I was before. Other names continued to float, and the President played the game for all it was worth, since it provided the only apparent drama for the convention.

On the Sunday before the convention met, I made a joint appearance with Gene McCarthy on "Meet the Press" and, soon after, Jim Rowe showed up and said, "I can't predict what Johnson is going to do for certain, but it looks like you're the man."

I had begun to feel as secure as one could in dealing with Lyndon Johnson when a convention credentials fight between two contending Democratic groups from Mississippi, one essentially black, the other essentially old-line southern white, broke into the headlines and threatened to divide the convention, creating public turmoil, which none of us, and particularly Johnson, wanted.

The controversy had been heating up for several months, and a month earlier, shortly after the civil rights bill had passed, I had gone to Johnson to alert him to the potential dangers, but he either didn't focus on it or didn't consider it terribly serious, because nothing was done by the White House to resolve the dispute. It festered and grew more serious.[4]

At the last minute, when my attention was on my own situation, Johnson asked me to try to find a solution, preventing, if I could, any disruption of the convention.

I called on my friend Walter Mondale, who was then attorney general of Minnesota, and Johnson also sent in Walter Reuther. We worked out a compromise of sorts that didn't really please anyone involved but kept the convention from falling apart.* Johnson was testing me one more time.

Was I capable of handling a difficult negotiation? Could I be relied on? Those were questions to which the answers should have been clear. I was happy enough to be called on to do a job that had to be done and in which I enjoyed some personal standing with both sides, but it was nevertheless aggravating. Had I failed, would Johnson have chosen McCarthy or someone else? It is a question I have never been able to answer.

---

* We also made certain that overt racial discrimination and intimidation in choosing convention delegates would not be tolerated anywhere in the future.

With the Mississippi credentials fight resolved, I had dinner with Jim Rowe, who said the President had decided that I would be the nominee.† Yet a shadow of doubt lingered. Jim phoned at 1:00 A.M. to say that the nomination was gone if the import of our dinner conversation leaked out. His call came while I was getting a rubdown, trying at that hour to get rid of the fatigue in my aching body. Jim's call put all the tension back.[5]

The next morning, Rowe told me to stay close to the phone, since a call was imminent from the White House. The call came, and Rowe himself showed up in my suite at the Shelburne Hotel. I was excited and preparing to go to the Atlantic City airport to board a private plane to carry me to what I assumed was the anointing ceremony in Washington. Rowe said, "You are to be accompanied by Tom Dodd." I stopped short. "What? Is Tom Dodd being considered, too?"

Rowe reassured me: "No, this is just a cover. Don't be concerned about it. Dodd's going along will keep the press off balance and continue the speculation. That's what the President wants."

I continued to shave and dress and then dashed from my suite across the hall to the waiting elevator, past the TV cameras and correspondents who had accumulated. In the crush, one correspondent, Jules Bergman of ABC, ended up on the elevator with me, holding his microphone, its cord extending behind him through the closed elevator doors to his blind camera.

We paused, in laughter, long enough to open the doors and reunite a chattering Bergman with his camera, and continued our exuberant journey to the airport.

Dodd and I boarded a twin-engine Beech and flew to Washington, where a presidential limousine picked us up. Jack Valenti was in the car and explained that the President wasn't quite ready to receive us. He didn't explain why, but it later seemed clear that they needed the time to summon the White House press corps to drain the last bit of speculation out of Dodd's presence.

We drove aimlessly around downtown Washington for about fifteen minutes before we parked at the south entrance to the

† Muriel and Max Kampelman were at the dinner, too. Rowe swore them to secrecy, any leak meaning disaster.

White House. Dodd was led away to see the President while I sat there. Troubled again by the bizarre way things were being done, I nevertheless fell asleep in the back seat.

A knock on the car door awakened me, and someone said, "Senator Humphrey, the President wants to see you." I was led to the Fish Room, outside the President's office, and shortly Johnson himself appeared, saying, "Hubert, let's go into the Cabinet Room."

It was late afternoon, about five o'clock, and there were few pleasantries. The President said, "Hubert, do you want to be Vice President?" I said, "Yes," and he asked simply, "Why would you want to have the job? You know it is a thankless one."

I felt at the time that I could overcome its "thanklessness." I thought I could be of help with liberals, blacks, and the labor movement, areas in which Johnson could use help if he needed it at all. My greatest strength lay then in the northern industrial states.

Johnson continued, "Hubert, I have got to talk to you about that office, because you and I are good friends. We have worked together in the Congress and you have been very helpful to me as majority whip, but I guess you know that most Presidents and Vice Presidents just don't hit it off. There is something about the jobs and the responsibilities that seem to get in the way of those friendships and understanding."

We covered the same ground several times. "I know that you are an active man and very gregarious," he said, "but this office is going to require that you not be out front, that you not be in the headlines, that your energies and efforts be used within the administration in order to help the President and the administration accomplish agreed-on goals and objectives.

"We're old friends and we get along well, but you have to understand that this is like a marriage with no chance of divorce. I need complete and unswerving loyalty. I know I don't need to impress this on you, but it's a fact that there are always temptations and there will be times when a Vice President can get out of step, out of line, causing the President difficulty and embarrassment.

"I don't want this to happen. So I want us to have a very good understanding that we're going to work together. I want you to feel free to come to see me anytime. My office will be open to you. I want you to feel that you can confide in me and I want to be able to confide in you. That's what I want in a Vice President, Hubert. Do you think that you're that man?"

I said, "I think I am. You can trust me, Mr. President." I went on to say that I understood what he was saying very well, that I was prepared to be the kind of Vice President he was describing, that I was prepared to be loyal, that I would try to confine my activities to consultation and discussion within the administration, that I surely wasn't going to be leading any kind of effort that might be embarrassing or contradicted administration policy.

I said I could be helpful because I had wide contacts in the country and that my relationships with Congress were good. He said he knew all of that and agreed, but he continued, "I think we make a great team. Yet, I know there will be some difficult days ahead and there may be times when you will wish that you never accepted this assignment."

I told him I was prepared for that possibility, it was a great honor even to be considered for the office, and that if we were elected I would be prepared to do whatever was required to fulfill my obligations and responsibilities.

Johnson, a powerful and confident President, looked at me and said, "If any man can do it, I think you can." Then he said privately what he was to say publicly—that he felt I was "the most capable of all the men [he knew] to take on the duties of the presidency if anything should happen." Such words spoken in that atmosphere must be believed. They do not permit false modesty. You cannot reach that point in public life if you don't believe them about yourself. But I repeat them here not only with obvious pleasure, but because they may well spell out the only really relevant qualification for a Vice President.

The President continued, saying in effect; I don't know whether I ought even to ask you to take on the job, because of my personal friendship for you. You most likely won't like it, after you've gotten into it. Seldom do a President and a Vice President get along. Their friendly relationships last about nine months to a year.

Johnson then reminded me that after the first year as Vice

President, Alben Barkley seldom saw President Truman—that hostility, or at least distance, grew between the two. And that Truman himself, as Vice President, had rarely spoken to President Roosevelt.

He did not have to remind me of President Eisenhower's statement, and its implication, when asked about Richard Nixon's contributions as Vice President: "Give me a week and I'll think of one."

The President paused in our conversation to tell me of his experience as Vice President. He said, "You know, Hubert, that I was totally loyal to John Kennedy. Whatever John Kennedy wanted me to do, I did. I never tried to upstage him. You keep out of the news. The news belongs to the President. I never went around the country making speeches without the President knowing about it. Even when it came to Democratic party functions, we had a working agreement."

He told me that President Kennedy had gone out of his way to treat him with respect and with consideration. But he also said, "You'll find out that all the people associated with the President will look down on you. They're not interested in you and they'll try to stir up difficulties between the President and the Vice President. It's not by any vicious conspiracy; it's just the nature of things." So he made it clear—as he offered the job—that it was a difficult one. I did not know then how accurately he had described the trying circumstances to come.

But I accepted under the conditions he had set. I made a commitment and I performed under the "terms of the contract." Whether my decision was the right one is something I suppose I cannot judge clearly. I think it was. I had come a long way in politics, served my country, my ideals, and my constituents as well as I could. To be elected Vice President of the United States seemed a signal honor. At the time, I expected that Lyndon Johnson would be elected President that November and that he would most likely run for re-election in 1968.

When we finished, Johnson said, "Let's call Muriel and fill her in." He placed the call through the White House operator, and in seconds Muriel was on the line with him. He said, "Muriel, how would you like to have your husband be the vice-presidential nominee?" After a pause, while he listened to her favorable response, he went on in his Texas idiom and style, "We're going to nominate your boy." Muriel and I spoke briefly and I was ushered out to the car, where Senator Dodd waited quietly, and the two of us flew back to Atlantic City. I am sure the trip was as endless for him as it was quick for me.

Since Johnson, in a parting shot, had asked me to say nothing about his decision, asking me in effect to continue the charade of doubt, my words had to deny what was clearly on my face.

At the airport and the hotel, having smiled my way past questioners, I hugged and kissed Muriel, and then we moved into another room in our suite, where staff and a few friends were milling around. Still pretending, but not too well, to be unsure of the nomination, I called WCCO radio in Minneapolis to be interviewed. While our conversation was being broadcast live, they interrupted to carry a news flash from CBS News. I listened on a second phone to the bulletin, which finally disclosed that President Johnson was on his way to Atlantic City with the recommendation that I be nominated.

Johnson had drained every bit of juice out of the nomination, and he had drained a good deal out of me. There was a moment when the voices around me grew still and people seemed to stop moving. Then the noise and activity increased to manic proportions. People jumped, embraced, cheered. As I focused on each face, eyes (some filled with tears) danced with a special kind of pleasure, the mixture of selfless devotion and very personal and unspoken motives—who knows what they really are?—that comes with political success.

When Johnson recommended me to the convention, he lavished praise on me to the response of a cheering audience. It was a moment of glory. My eyes filled with tears of joy. My whole family was there, and with them I savored every word of praise, every cheer of assent. My body tingled with excitement. I wished my father were still alive.

That night and most of the next day, we worked on my acceptance speech. A number of people prepared drafts, and Bill Moyers, particularly, supplied a good deal of what went into the speech, including the refrain "But not Senator Goldwater" after each statement about issues most Americans supported but Goldwater opposed.

The cheers of the crowd, their smiling faces, the waving signs filled me with a delicious spirit of success. It was a long way from the day that Richard Russell called me a "damn fool." With a little luck, I was going to be Vice President of the United States.

If the convention moved me, it transported Lyndon Johnson. It may have been his most pleasant time as President. The convention, for all practical purposes, had been his production. He wrote the music, choreographed the action, chose the stars, and virtually wrote their lines. What Lyndon wanted, Lyndon got. He accepted every cheer as adulation, and when it reached a crescendo, it seemed to erase the ghost of John Kennedy's presidency from his mind.

His exuberance was overwhelming. The order came that Muriel and I were to fly with him to the ranch. We had virtually no notice, our own plans a matter of indifference.

When we arrived at the airport, a number of people were there, some to see the President off, others to board planes of their own. A crowd was standing behind a short fence, and the President spotted Katharine Graham, the millionaire publisher of the Washington *Post*. Mrs. Graham is a distinguished woman as well as a powerful one, not at all the Washington social butterfly swept off her feet by politicians or statesmen.

Neither is she tiny; but the President approached the fence, reached over and literally lifted her off her feet, and said, "On the plane, Katie; we're going to Texas and we want you with us."‡

She protested that she had no luggage, that she was flying back to Washington, and that she simply couldn't go with us. Her protests were muted in the bear hug and, moments later, she, like the rest of us, was on her way to the ranch.

If the plane had run out of fuel in mid-air, President Johnson's frenetic energy and excitement would have kept it flying. As "high" as he was, getting home to Texas raised his spirits even more.

President Johnson found great comfort and strength in the hill country of Texas and his ranch home. It was there that he saw

‡ No one who knew Mrs. Graham well ever called her "Katie." To close friends she was Kay or Katharine. I think Johnson knew that as well as I.

his old friends, where he played dominoes, where he could ride in his car and survey his land and look at his cattle. He knew his cattle like most people know their children. He knew how many calves had been born in the previous month and, even when he was back in the White House, he would pick up the telephone to call the ranch foreman to see whether or not a particular calf had survived, or what the price of feed was, whether there was enough rain (you almost felt he could do something about the weather), whether the hay had been brought in.

If the convention was Johnson's road company, Texas was a permanent repertory theater. To visit the ranch was to be an actor on Lyndon Johnson's stage. You might be an extra, or have just a walk-on part. You were part of the audience as well. He would parade across that stage his friends, his relatives, his old cronies, and he would tell stories he had told a thousand times before of his mother and father, of his youth, of student days and teaching. He would talk of his aunts and uncles and he would talk about the land, his hill country, his Texas. He was like the Greek god Antaeus, gaining new strength from touching the land. The ranch was his private preserve, and there was nothing too big or too small for his attention.

When you added the Secret Service communications system to that compulsion, it became almost absurd. If a fence was falling, he'd call his ranch foreman by phone from the car to report it. If a gate was loose, that word would go out. He would check cattle, looking for an injured or diseased one.

When nothing caught his eye, he worried about dinner, calling the cook at the ranch house, asking, "What's for supper?" If it was early enough, he'd help plan the menu. And all of this at the wheel of his speeding white Lincoln. He drove as if he were a test driver or a Demolition Derby fanatic. Reckless abandon is the only apt description. Rest for him was controlled frenzy.

There was a substantial man-made lake not far from his house and, on water as on land, Johnson was a magnificent wild man, taking off in his power boat as though it were jet-propelled, cutting in fast, sharp turns that seemed to violate the laws of nature.

He would skim the shore, steering the boat while he waved his arms pointing at houses of his friends.[6]

In Texas, as Lyndon Johnson's guest, you did things his way.

Early one morning the previous year, we climbed into his Lincoln, and Johnson, guns at the ready, drove slam bang and lickety split across the countryside until we spotted one of the many deer that grazed on his ranch. He slammed on the brakes, and in his commanding voice said, "Hubert, there's one for you. Get it!"

I am a good shot and have hunted duck and pheasant and quail fairly frequently throughout my life. It was an easy and natural thing on the South Dakota prairies and wetlands. But I never liked to shoot four-legged creatures, deer particularly. Nevertheless, I got slowly from the car, lifted my rifle, set myself for its kick, and brought down the deer. I turned to Johnson with a mixture of satisfaction at having done so well what he wanted and revulsion at having killed the deer.

"Well," he said, "Bobby Kennedy got two of them. You're not going to let Bobby get the best of you, are you?" Before there was time for an answer, the car sped on its way again, until we sighted another deer. As he slammed on the brakes once again, Johnson said, "Now's your chance. Hit that one." I hit it, and the deer fell.

In the car once again, Johnson said, "That's enough. You've shot one more than McCarthy and the same number as Bobby. You're in good shape."

I did not feel in particularly good shape and wondered out loud what would happen to the deer. Johnson said, "Don't you worry. I'll make them into sausage and venison steaks and you and Muriel will get it all. And I'm going to send the antlers, too." All of which he did and none of which we really needed. We had enough meat to feed a family our size for two years.

At another point, after the 1964 convention, he decided that I should go horseback riding with him, and he decided, too, that I must dress up as if I were a Texas rancher. He called me into his bedroom and pulled out an outfit that dwarfed me. The pants were huge, so big that I thought I could put both my legs in one pant leg and still dance a polka. The jacket draped like a tent over a shirt whose neck was several sizes too large. I looked ridiculous and I felt ridiculous as I smiled wanly from under a cowboy hat that was made for his head and clearly not for mine.

Trying to walk was tough enough, but nothing compared to what was to follow. Johnson said, "Hubert, get on that horse.

We're going for a ride." As a child, I had been on a horse at my grandfather's farm, and on two or three excursions with my children, we rode horses tame enough to be safe at a children's picnic. The horse Johnson put me on was big and spirited. There seemed to be an acre of cameramen and reporters grinning and clicking as the horse sort of reared, leaving me filled with fear and clutching that horse like a tiny child on his first merry-go-round ride, hanging on for dear life. The President got a big kick out of it, and I survived.

Johnson kept busy, and he liked the people around him to keep busy, too. The story is told, and I'm sure it is true, that Johnson one day walked into the trailer that the Secret Service used at the ranch. Three or four agents were sitting around, ready to move with Johnson should he leave the area. He said, "Why aren't you busy? Why aren't you doing something?"

The agent in charge said, "Well, Mr. President, there isn't much to do. There is no press out here, no trouble, and you have been in the house." Johnson shook off the explanation and said, "Well, for God's sakes, kill flies or *something*, but don't just sit there."

In calmer moments, we talked about the campaign. He would limit his travel while he took care of the business of the nation. He would be President and not candidate, and I would go constantly from August to November, from state to state, to carry the message of our party and the Johnson administration.

Someone dubbed my four-engine Electra, the first private plane I ever had at my command, the "Happy Warrior," and I was exactly that.[7] I loved the campaign and every exhausting moment of it. The President kept in close touch with me and seemed to enjoy my campaigning, giving me instructions and suggestions, and asking me to keep him informed about every development on the campaign trail. We were full partners—he in the White House performing his duties with skill and confidence, and I out on the road, speaking and campaigning night and day. It was a happy time. The Goldwater campaign was a "bomb," and it was perfectly obvious that the Johnson-Humphrey ticket was a winner, with wide and popular support.

Johnson was on the phone, using that instrument as if it were an extension of his body, lining up favorable editorial comment, raising money for the campaign, gaining support from the most unlikely sources. He attracted business people and Republicans of national stature who would never come close to a Democratic candidate under ordinary circumstances. Ironically, it may well have been the very strength of his victory that made him so sensitive when criticism subsequently grew. He reveled in his success, no longer President by accident, but soon to be overwhelmingly elected in his own right.

On election night, I celebrated with several hundred friends and staff in a ballroom at the Sheraton-Ritz Hotel in Minneapolis. Fred Gates had made the elegant arrangements, and as the polls closed we were already toasting the inevitable victory.

Then, sometime after midnight, there was a thrilling moment when the Secret Service agents appeared suddenly at the doors and around my table. I was Vice President-elect. I was about to share in President Lyndon Johnson's power to do great things for America.

BOOK THREE

NEXT DOOR TO POWER

32. VICE PRESIDENT:
AND ONE VIEWPOINT
ON VIETNAM

In a long public life, there are naturally a number of special days that stand out in memory. But inauguration day 1965, when I was sworn in as Vice President of the United States, was more special than any other. It was a day of immense satisfaction, of success without struggle or other distracting circumstances. It was a moment of pure joy.

There is something expansive about that scene. You stand where others have stood and you repeat an oath that they, too, have taken. You are surrounded by your own family and by your official family, members of Congress, diplomats of other nations, the Cabinet, justices of the Supreme Court.

Behind you, though out of sight, the Capitol dome reaches for the sky, flags fly, and in front of you, thousands of Americans cheer, applaud, look up. Behind them, you can see the clean lines and white façade of the Supreme Court, the green dome and elaborate architecture of the Library of Congress. You want to embrace it all in one giant hug and say, "I love you, America." For a moment, at least, you are the center of that special universe.

The past was indeed prologue, and whatever I had been able to accomplish before in public life had now become a base on which much more would be built—solidly, maybe gloriously, built.

As I stood to be sworn in by Speaker of the House John McCormack, Muriel was standing close by. Thirty years before, I had written to her of my dreams of public life and service. Today they were coming true. My friend Fred Gates held Muriel's family Bible, while I took the oath.

The day continued with the same excitement. We reviewed the inaugural parade in front of the White House, hooting with pleasure as the Doland High School band marched by, as the University of Minnesota band played familiar tunes. That night, I danced at the inaugural balls with a lightness and grace that would have made Fred Astaire look clumsy. I went to bed Vice President of these beloved United States.

Three days later, on Friday night, President Johnson was taken to Bethesda Naval Hospital suffering from chest pains.

At first they were thought to be signs of a heart attack, particularly frightening because Lyndon had suffered a serious one ten years before.

Johnson, for some bizarre reason, refused to let any medical facts be given to me immediately. Instead, the orders came that he wanted me to fulfill my scheduled weekend commitments so that no one would think his illness was serious.

When I started out on Saturday morning, I still did not know for sure whether he had suffered another heart attack. I was barely Vice President, and there was the possibility that I might suddenly become President. I looked at Muriel and saw that she shared my fear. It was an awesome prospect, a terrible shock, compounded by not knowing what, precisely, was happening.

First I went to St. Paul to be the Grand Marshal in the Winter Carnival parade, and then on to Tucson, Arizona, for the opening of a poverty program at an Indian reservation. I could not shake my concern for Johnson and myself. Why was I leading a parade? What was I doing in Tucson? Why wasn't I back in Washington, where the trouble was? I should have known that weekend what being Vice President might be like.

Once again, I think my own role and changing attitudes are important primarily as they might reflect how American foreign policy is made, why it resists change, and what implications there may be for defining our future role in international relations.

Though we involved ourselves in Indochina almost immediately after World War II, we never really had a Vietnam policy. (In fact, President Eisenhower once said, in one of those quiet, understated moments of candor, that much of the time the United States has not had a foreign policy. We adapt to circumstances.)

We edged up to it and finally slid in. Policy was never formalized, except in the most general terms. Our predecessors and we never resolved adequate, realistic short- or long-range objectives. Until early 1968, with the "A to Z" review, there never appeared to be any real measurement of the ultimate costs, what our presence entailed, what actual benefits could be expected.

Having fought the Japanese after their attack during World War II, we felt and claimed that Asia was a necessary area for our involvement. Many of our motives were genuinely disinterested. Others grew out of a nineteenth-century missionary spirit, both religious and secular, in which some hoped to transfer our culture, religions, and values to others, and some hoped to make money. Later, our support of French colonialism in Indochina was a mistake begun by the Truman administration (against the views of his predecessor, FDR) with the support of the American people and Congress.

When I spoke out in the fifties against what we were doing, mine was a relatively lonely voice. We narrowly avoided joining the French in the death throes of their Southeast Asian colonialism. This seemed absurd.

Yet, for many years to follow, Indochina became "ours," not ours to own, which we did not seek, but our problem. We could not kick free. A basic problem: Our focus was Western. We thought in terms of leaders—Bao Dai or Diem—and the formal institutions of government. But the government of Vietnam was not in Hanoi or Saigon, as it turned out. It was in the countryside, in the villages and hamlets. The power and the fate of governments reside ultimately in the people.

The French were wise enough to know that there were limits.

The Communists, once the French were gone, knew even better that, no matter how strong a government they had in Hanoi, the strength lay outside the cities.

Asian communism is not urban. Ho Chi Minh knew that from his own experience, and he had the example of China, too: Mao won the peasants before he was successful in the cities. We "knew" it, but didn't seem to understand. We never escaped from the unreality of the cities into the reality of the countryside. We never stopped our civics-book approach to government, expecting the Asians to pad along nicely into the patterns and procedures of Western democracy.

By 1961, when John Kennedy said, "Let every nation know, whether it wish us well or ill, we shall pay any price, bear any burden, meet any hardships, support any friend, oppose any foe, to assure the survival and the success of liberty," the applause came from all of us: Lyndon Johnson, Hubert Humphrey, Robert Kennedy, Eugene McCarthy, William Fulbright, George McGovern, and from most other Americans as well. There were few doves in such days of decision.

Kennedy did not have Vietnam particularly in mind, but his rhetoric nonetheless contributed to the mood of the country, to the sense of national mission. Though it was not a central issue of his administration, compared with Berlin or Cuba, our involvement in Vietnam did continue to grow. And it was rarely discussed.

As majority whip, I had tried to be a spokesman for the Administration, anticipating problems or programs. I used the Senate as forum, and one measure of what was going on in the White House was the number of speeches I made, the material I put into the Congressional Record. My lead for topics often came from the leadership breakfasts with the President or from private discussions in which he indicated that he wanted some issue aired publicly. As I look back over the record, I almost never mentioned Vietnam during those years, because it never seemed as important as Berlin, or the Congo or Laos.

After Kennedy's death, when I was mentioned as a possible vice-presidential nominee, I tried to educate myself on Vietnam. I turned to Colonel (later General) Edward Lansdale, whose special experience was counterinsurgency and who, from his writing, seemed to understand the political as well as the military nature of warfare.

Lansdale differed from Maxwell Taylor, a close friend of the Kennedys, a retired general and then our ambassador to Vietnam, who considered Vietnam a military problem amenable to military solution. Lansdale urged a political approach, which was much different, and after election I became a conduit for his ideas to President Johnson.[1]

This process was delicate since, in effect, I was challenging Maxwell Taylor, for whom Johnson and I had esteem growing in part from Taylor's close association with President Kennedy.

If Lansdale was right, Taylor should have been recalled and replaced.[2] I did not have the assurance to make that kind of frontal attack. Instinct said Lansdale was right—at least more right than Taylor—but my military knowledge was limited. Johnson listened to what I had to say, but he understandably did not consider me an expert, even bolstered by Lansdale, whose views deserved being on par with Taylor's, Bundy's, Rusk's or McNamara's.[3]

Still I used the Lansdale ideas in speeches and articles. In September 1964 I wrote, "We should not attempt to take over the war from the Vietnamese. The present struggle is between Vietnamese of various political beliefs. No lasting solution can be imposed by foreign armies. We must remember the struggle in Vietnam is as much a political and social struggle as a military one. What has been needed in Vietnam is a government in which the people of Vietnam have a stake."[4]

After the 1964 election but before the inauguration, Tom Hughes, my legislative counsel in the Senate from 1955 to 1958, and then assistant secretary of state for research and intelligence, told me of a conversation he had had with Dean Rusk.[5]

Rusk acknowledged my long interest in foreign affairs, but cautioned that I should not expect to be involved in interagency formulation of policy. He noted that Lyndon Johnson as Vice President had not developed a personal foreign-policy staff, relying instead on information from State, Defense, and the CIA. For constitutional as well as practical reasons, he considered it important that the Vice President, whoever he might be, not intrude himself between the President and the established agencies.

Clearly, my role in Rusk's eyes, and I assumed in Johnson's as well, was to be limited—probably to that of becoming a goodwill ambassador traveling primarily to developing nations. Ultimately, Johnson did not hold consistently to that view, but it prevailed, particularly whenever I pushed too hard or said too much.

During the first week of February 1965, the Viet Cong blew up an American billet near Pleiku. Nine American GI's were killed and one hundred forty wounded. McGeorge Bundy, visiting in Vietnam, went up to the scene and fired back a cable of anger and distress to the President.[6]

Up to that moment, we had not bombed in North Vietnam. Now, in outrage and with an apparent need to retaliate in some fashion, new options—including bombing—were pressed on the President. Mac Bundy, Robert McNamara, John McCone (director of the CIA), and the Joint Chiefs of Staff all then recommended that we respond by initiating air strikes against North Vietnam.

I had generally opposed bombing in Hanoi. It was not a big industrial center, but there were electric-power plants that supplied energy to small factories making ammunition and some steel. Saturation bombing in World War II style was out, since the plants were dispersed, many of them close to embassies of other nations. Any mistake, of however minor a nature, might devastate other nationals, and the question remained in my mind whether there would be much positive effect even if we were able to turn out all the lights and energy sources in Hanoi. Even if we were successful in knocking out just our targets, the war effort would go on virtually unimpaired, and inevitably they would have been back at full production in a short time.

Yet it was decided that, for psychological purposes and (in hope) for some limited military purposes, the bombing should take place.

Before one lunch early in 1965, I talked with several of the President's most intimate advisers, expressing my opposition.

One explicitly said he agreed with me, others implied concur-rence. Yet when Johnson went around the table, starting with Dean Rusk, Rusk said he thought we should bomb. Then he turned to me, "Hubert, what do you think?" I said, "I don't think we should." Then Johnson turned to MacNamara, who agreed with Rusk that we should. I ended up the only dissenting vote. My prelunch allies had disappeared.

Presidential advisers too often simply try to anticipate the President's decision, telling him not what he ought to hear, but what they think he wants to hear. As the war went on, there was a clear tendency on the part of the men around Johnson to do that—all of them weary, frustrated with the duration of the struggle and the obvious lack of success.

Until the "A to Z" review, in 1968, I heard very little counsel from any of those genuinely close to the President that could in the most generous fashion be interpreted as opposition to further commitments of American power.

One ad hoc meeting with the President took place in the Cabinet Room the first weekend of February 1965 and went well into the night. In addition to his regular advisers, George Ball, Adlai Stevenson, and I participated. The three of us strongly opposed the bombing of North Vietnam as a dangerous escala-tion. I was particularly opposed because, for one reason, Alexei Kosygin of the Soviet Union was in Hanoi at that moment. I had also argued against large-scale infusion of American combat troops in the South. But the Ball-Stevenson-Humphrey arguments fell before the weight of the others, and I ended my first sig-nificant meetings on Vietnam as part of a rejected minority.

Although I was not part of the decision-making, and my views frequently not particularly welcome, I tried again in late March. At almost the last minute, I was invited to attend a National Se-curity Council meeting. I asked my staff and several advisers to prepare in haste a comprehensive list of unilateral American ac-tions that might lead toward negotiations and/or de-escalation of the war rather than a wider conflict involving American ground forces.

These options ranged from halting the bombing of the North and offering amnesty for the Viet Cong to an announcement by the President that he was sending the Secretary of State or me to a designated neutral point, at a designated time, with authorization to enter into direct discussions with Hanoi.

The reaction was inevitable. My ideas were well-intentioned, they said, but not applicable. The logic ran like this: If South Vietnam was important to Southeast Asia, and if Southeast Asia was important to our security, then we had no choice except to increase both our bombing and our commitment of ground forces. Without force, we would never be able to negotiate from strength and thus achieve any kind of lasting long-term settlement.

Underlying that rejection was the consensus that the South was close to losing the war, and that any of my ideas would be seen by Hanoi as a final gasp of weakness.

I fully concurred, however, with the assumption that Communist success in South Vietnam would shake and endanger all of Southeast Asia.

Still, bombing the North seemed unwise to me and I had thought it unnecessarily provocative while Kosygin was there. It could only excite the Russians and make their commitment to North Vietnam firmer than ever. Nonetheless, the second day that Kosygin was in Hanoi, American and South Vietnamese aircraft struck North Vietnamese training and staging areas. A month later, thirty-five hundred Marines landed to protect our base at Danang.

It seemed time to get certain thoughts on paper for the President, and I decided to cast them in the context of something Lyndon Johnson knew and cared about. After a weekend of briefings, reading the latest Vietnam cable traffic, and studying up-to-date intelligence estimates, including some farsighted dissents from the State Department's Bureau of Intelligence and Research, I put my thoughts together on paper for use with the President. This memorandum resulted:

February 15, 1965

I have been in Georgia over the weekend, and for the first time since Inauguration, have had time to read and think about the fateful decisions which you have just been required to make, and will continue to be making, on Vietnam. I have been reading the Vietnam cables and intelligence estimates of the last two weeks. Because these may be the most fateful decisions of your Administration, I wanted to give you my personal views. You know that I have nothing but sympathy for you and complete understanding for the burden and the anguish which surrounds such decisions. There is obviously no quick or easy solution, and no clear course of right or wrong. Whatever you decide, we will be taking big historic gambles, and we won't know for sure whether they were right until months or perhaps years afterwards. The moral dilemmas are inescapable.

I want to put my comments in the most useful framework. In asking me to be your Vice President, you made it clear that you expected my loyalty, help, and support. I am determined to give it. I don't intend to second-guess your decisions, or kibbitz after the fact. You do not need me to analyze or interpret our information from Vietnam. You have a whole intelligence community for that purpose. You do not need me for foreign policy advice. You have a wise Secretary of State and whole staffs and departments to do that. I am not a military expert. Plenty of others are.

But because I have been privileged to share with you many years of political life in the Senate, because we have recently come through a successful national election together, because I think your respect for me and my value to you significantly consists of my ability to relate politics and policies, and because I believe strongly that the sustainability of the Vietnam policies now being decided are likely to profoundly affect the success of your Administration, I want to summarize my views on what I call the politics of Vietnam.

1. In the recent campaign, Goldwater and Nixon stressed the Vietnam issue, advocated escalation, and stood for a military "solution." The country was frightened by the trigger-happy bomber image which came through from the Goldwater campaign. By contrast we stressed steadiness, staying the course, not enlarging the war, taking on the longer and more difficult task of finding political-military solutions in the South where the war will be won or lost. Already, because of recent decisions on retaliatory bombing, both Goldwater and the Kremlin are now alleging that we have bought the Goldwater position of "going North."

2. In the public mind the Republicans have traditionally

been associated with extreme accusations against Democratic administrations, whether for "losing China," or for failing to win the Korean War, or for failing to invade Cuba during the missile crisis. By contrast we have had to live with responsibility. Some things are beyond our power to prevent. Always we have sought the best possible settlements short of World War III, combinations of firmness and restraint, leaving opponents some options for credit and face-saving, as in Cuba. We have never stood for military solutions alone, or for victory through air power. We have always stressed the political, economic and social dimensions.

3. This Administration has a heavy investment in policies which can be jeopardized by an escalation in Vietnam: the President's image and the American image, the development of the Sino-Soviet rift, progress on detente and arms control, summit meetings with Kosygin, reordering relations with our European allies, progress at the United Nations, stabilizing defense expenditures, drafting reservists.

4. American wars have to be politically understandable by the American public. There has to be a cogent, convincing case if we are to enjoy sustained public support. In World Wars I and II we had this. In Korea we were moving under United Nations auspices to defend South Korea against dramatic, across-the-border, conventional aggression. Yet even with those advantages, we could not sustain American political support for fighting Chinese in Korea in 1952.

Today in Vietnam we lack the very advantages we had in Korea. The public is worried and confused. Our rationale for action has shifted away now even from the notion that we are there as advisers on request of a free government, to the simple and politically barren argument of our "national interest." We have not succeeded in making this national interest interesting enough at home or abroad to generate support. The arguments in fact are probably too complicated (or too weak) to be politically useful or effective.

5. If we go north, people will find it increasingly hard to understand why we risk World War III by enlarging a war under terms we found unacceptable 12 years ago in Korea. Politically people think of North Vietnam and North Korea as similar. They recall all the "lessons" of 1950–53: the limi-

tations of air power, the Chinese intervention, the "Never Again Club" against GI's fighting a land war against Asians in Asia, the frank recognition of all these factors in the Eisenhower Administration's compromise of 1953.

If a war with China was ruled out by the Truman and Eisenhower administrations alike in 1952–53, at a time when we alone had nuclear weapons, people will find it hard to contemplate such a war with China now. No one really believes that the Soviet Union would allow us to destroy Communist China with nuclear weapons.

6. People can't understand why we would run grave risks to support a country which is totally unable to put its own house in order. The chronic instability in Saigon directly undermines American political support for our policy.

7. It is hard to justify dramatic 150 plane U.S. air bombardments across a border as a response to camouflaged, often non-sensational, elusive, small scale terror which has been going on for ten years in what looks largely like a Civil War in the South.

8. Politically in Washington, beneath the surface, the opposition is more Democratic than Republican. This may be even more true at the grassroots across the country.

9. It is always hard to cut losses. But the Johnson Administration is in a stronger position to do so now than any Administration in this century. 1965 is the year of minimum political risk for the Johnson Administration. Indeed it is the first year when we can face the Vietnam problem without being preoccupied with the political repercussions from the Republican right. As indicated earlier, our political problems are likely to come from new and different sources (Democratic liberals, independents, labor) if we pursue an enlarged military policy very long.

10. We now risk creating the impression that we are the prisoner of events in Vietnam. This blurs the Administration's leadership role and has spillover effects across the board. It also helps erode confidence and credibility in our policies.

11. President Johnson is personally identified with, and greatly admired for, political ingenuity. He will be expected to put all his great political sense to work now for interna-

tional political solutions. People will be counting upon him to use on the world scene his unrivaled talents as a politician. They will be watching to see how he makes this transition from the domestic to the world stage.

The best possible outcome a year from now would be a Vietnam settlement which turns out to be better than was in the cards because LBJ's political talents for the first time came to grips with a fateful world crisis and did so successfully. It goes without saying that the subsequent domestic political benefits of such an outcome, and such a new dimension for the President, would be enormous.

12. If, on the other hand, we find ourselves leading from frustration to escalation and end up short of a war with China but embroiled deeper in fighting in Vietnam over the next few months, political opposition will steadily mount. It will underwrite all the negativism and disillusionment which we already have about foreign involvement generally—with serious and direct effects for all the Democratic internationalist programs to which the Johnson Administration remains committed: AID, United Nations, arms control, and socially humane and constructive policies generally.

For all these reasons, the decisions now being made on Vietnam will affect the future of this Administration fundamentally. I intend to support the Administration whatever the President's decisions. But these are my views.

About that same time, I was to make the main speech at the United Nations for a conference called "Pacem in Terris" after Pope John's encyclical.[7] The State Department suggested that I cancel my participation. I refused, since I was already a compromise speaker. We had tried to get the President to use this platform for a major statement on American foreign policy and he had rejected the idea.[8]

Therefore I went to Johnson, told him I wanted to go ahead with my speech, and he agreed. I showed him the text. He suggested that Mac Bundy and John Rielly review it in detail. There were three sections, each containing several ideas that were new and constructive. Bundy told Rielly they were interesting but not official U.S. foreign policy. He cut out all the innovative, peace-seeking material.

After the speech, Bill Benton and I got on a crowded elevator to go up to U Thant's office for a reception. Benton, speaking as if we were the only two in the elevator, said, "Hubert, that is the worst speech I have ever heard you give. You've only been Vice President for a month or so. Have those State Department people already started dishing up that kind of pablum for you?"

The quality of the speech was less important than the fact that by then my participation in Vietnam discussions had ended for 1965. No one ever said, "You're out, and here are the reasons why." In the brief span of my vice presidency, I had spoken my mind on Vietnam only in the councils of government, yet the President, in addition, apparently thought I had leaked something about the meetings. I had not, but that became irrelevant.

I served on the National Security Council as a matter of law, but Johnson held fewer of those regular meetings and began to discuss Vietnam in the informal sessions he preferred—meetings staffed with his own, selected advisers.

Beyond excluding me from substantive discussions, Johnson's annoyance showed in a variety of other ways.

For example, the State Department had recommended strongly that Eugenie Anderson be made director of the Foreign Service Institute and it seemed certain that she would get the appointment. John Macy, who was in charge of personnel selection on the highest levels, mentioned that I had special interest in Eugenie's appointment. Johnson said, "She's not my choice. Take her name off the list."

As the spring of 1965 moved into summer, the military situation was still deteriorating. Clearly, our choice was either to get out or to shore up the South Vietnamese Government, which was plainly unable to defend itself.

The President again asked for advice, and to the best of my recollection, not one adviser recommended getting out. So the question quickly became simply how much more to put in.

Most of the reports and briefings of 1965, while rarely hopeful, failed to describe how perilous the situation really was. When I was on the scene in Vietnam in 1966, it was possible to confirm the two choices that had been realistically available to Johnson during 1965: direct and immediate U.S. combat involvement, and the probable early and general collapse of the regime and armed forces of the South.

It was also clear that nothing more than a stand-off with the Communists was possible unless the South Vietnamese instituted reforms which were so badly needed. Even those would not guarantee a stand-off.

There was one under-the-counter situation that compounded Johnson's dilemma. With the exceptions of Pakistan's Ayub Khan and Zulficar Bhutto, every Asian leader who was publicly critical of us was privately encouraging us to remain in Vietnam.

They considered us the only credible buffer available between them and a China they considered irrational and intent on causing trouble in their midst.

The President was hesitant about additional American involvement but felt that we were effectively committed by our presence, by treaty, and by our over-all foreign policy of resistance to Communist aggression, of helping those in jeopardy.

Also, intelligence information in 1965 began to show clearly that the North Vietnamese regulars were now joining the Vietcong in the South and that Hanoi's goal was no longer limited, if it had ever been, but now was for full conquest.

The Viet Cong were under Communist leadership but they were also, in essence, continuing the anti-colonial battle. Different as we were from the French, we nevertheless inherited the deeply felt animosities against colonial rule.

A good number of the South Vietnamese generals and other military officers had been pro-French and had not fought to break French colonial rule. We had supported the French more than generously during the Eisenhower administration, at one point bearing more than three fourths of the cost.

Too rarely, however, did any of this historical context enter discussions explicitly. After a while, the larger questions hardly appeared even implicitly, and discussion focused more and more on military conditions and tactics.

Essentially, American policy in Vietnam had been set by July 1965 and remained set, despite all the talk and discussion, both within and outside of the government.*

---

* I was on my way to address a national governors conference when the White House reached me in Detroit with the message that the Presi-

From the bombing of the Pleiku billet in February, until July 1965, there were times when other decisions might have been made. After that, nothing changed.

What is important to understand from all this is that our involvement in Vietnam did not develop out of a thoughtful set of precepts about what we were doing there. It grew slowly at first, a brush fire, and then spread more quickly, in ad hoc responses to events.

I contributed little in those crucial six months. I attended National Security Council meetings. At other times, the President would talk to me privately—more to say what was on his mind than to listen to what was on mine.

I desperately needed a high-ranking ally to bolster my views, and I turned to George Ball. He had continued to send memoranda to the President that expounded his dissenting views, and then met with Johnson to expand on them. Knowing that, I sent John Rielly to see Ball's chief assistant, hoping that some informal liaison could be worked out to continue my education on Vietnam. While his assistant knew I was an ally, he also knew I was a dangerous one. Ball's people clearly wanted to keep a safe distance from me, and they did. I could not blame them. There was the unmistakable possibility that he would have joined me in limbo, his access to the President limited, his counsel less welcome.

On July 14, 1965, when Maxwell Taylor had come home and Henry Cabot Lodge was about to replace him as Ambassador to Vietnam (his second tour), there was a meeting in the White House of the regular advisers plus a number of the not-so-regular ones. I was not asked to the meeting.

The President had a picture taken that appeared the next day in the New York *Times*. The fact that I was missing would have been apparent to anyone who was interested, but the President would not let it go at that. He deliberately called attention to the picture, noting my absence.

In October 1965, when Lyndon Johnson had his gall bladder

---

dent had just seen my speech. The word was clear: I was not to use the language in the released text that said we must prepare for a "long, costly and ugly" war. The release was out and there was no calling it back, but I muted the language in delivery.

out, Souvanna Phouma, the Prime Minister of Laos, was scheduled to visit Washington. Because of the President's illness, I
spent more time alone with Souvanna than I might have otherwise. He had been, and was then, a kind of neutralist and na-
tionalist. But beginning with John Foster Dulles, he had been
harshly treated as a pro-Communist and not friendly to the
United States.

Souvanna knew that I had not accepted the Dulles line and
had spoken in the fifties in his behalf—not so much defending
him as seeking simply a more balanced view of what he was
doing. I asked whether he thought our presence in Vietnam was
necessary or important. "Absolutely," he said. "If you leave, it is
all over. The Communists will take it all."

"Well, we don't seem to be turning the battle around. We're
pouring in men and military materials, but it doesn't appear to
have much effect. What do you think we should do?"

"Bomb the dikes in North Vietnam."

I was shocked. "But that would flood the land and drown
thousands of people." I explained that there were those who had
suggested such, but that Johnson had rejected the idea as inhumane.

Souvanna shrugged and said, "That's the only thing that will
be effective."

As the winter of 1965–66 approached, I was still outside. In
fairness, it must be said that Johnson probably never intended for
me to have any greater role in foreign-policy formulation than he
himself had had during the Kennedy years. And there is good
reason for that. A Vice President, without a supporting staff
equal to the President's or the Secretary of State's, inevitably operates with less information. To build such a supporting structure would be expensive, duplicative, and ultimately wrong.
There can be only one foreign policy for the country. A Vice
President cannot sustain a dissenting position. He can express his
views firmly if discreetly. But on matters of high policy, once his
views have been heard and rejected, he must accommodate to
the limited scope of his role. Thereafter, criticism must come
from the Congress or the public.

There were times during this period when Johnson was at his

warmest and friendliest. At cabinet meetings, he could—with no apparent reason or provocation—praise me as the best Vice President in history, urging cabinet members to call on me for guidance and help. (From time to time, men whose concerns were domestic and legislative did.)

But foreign-policy formulation in general, and Southeast Asia in particular, was beyond my influence. Finally, in December, a break came. Johnson hinted that he might want me to travel to Asia. And he not only told me, but told several other people, including Orville Freeman. When word of my impending trip appeared in a newspaper column, he thought I had leaked it. Johnson blew up and canceled the idea. I had not leaked the story, which in fact came out of a casual conversation between Orville Freeman and columnist Rowland Evans.†

Despite his on-again, off-again attitude, Johnson was treating me a little differently, a little better. The liberal community was deeply unhappy with Johnson and Vietnam policy. And while my own reputation with the liberals was bruised, he needed bridges over those troubled waters.

In January 1966, Johnson met in Honolulu with Thieu and Ky and other Vietnamese chiefs. A few days before he left, he said he might want me to do some traveling after his meeting: "Keep your schedule loose."

Once burned, I told no one, not even Muriel, that a trip might be coming. As a result, I was in Chicago when a call came to Washington from Honolulu to a staff member at eleven-thirty one night.

The message was simple, if cryptic. Humphrey was to be ready to leave for a two-and-a-half-week trip to Asia the following day. I would meet Johnson in Los Angeles on my way out and his way back.

The next morning was chaos. Members of my staff, for example, most of whom had never been out of the country, were suddenly required to get passports and a half-dozen medical shots. They went home to pack summer- and winter-weight clothes, say

† I had become used to a fluctuating relationship with Johnson during our Senate years, particularly the mid and late fifties. Our friendship then had its peaks and valleys but, over all, it grew. It had been easier in those early days to speak up, talk back, and be heard.

good-by to husbands, wives, and children for several weeks, unable to tell them where they were going.

So, after a year, more of isolation than participation, I was about to embark on a major trip in a delicate area, with no time for specific preparation, no briefing papers reviewed ahead of time, no time for study in depth.

We flew off to Los Angeles, where Johnson and his entourage had landed. Our planes parked near one another, people who had been in Honolulu with Johnson and who were now joining me hauled luggage from his plane to mine past Secret Service and uniformed guards. Counterparts on our two staffs found each other for quick informal briefings.

Aboard Air Force One, Johnson explained what had gone on in Honolulu and outlined what he wanted done on my trip. My task would be to encourage reform in Saigon and general economic and social co-operation in other Asian nations—in general, to urge the measures and proposals discussed in Honolulu. Johnson intended that my trip both dramatize and publicize "the other war"—what we were doing in a non-military way. We then flew off again, this time to Hawaii to pick up Ky, Thieu, their wives, and other Vietnamese.

The White House press, who ordinarily never covered me, had been encouraged to wait there and join our traveling party. In addition, Johnson sent along Jack Valenti, Lloyd Hand, Mac Bundy, Henry Cabot Lodge, Jr., Averell Harriman, Chet Cooper, and Ed Lansdale, among others.

The press immediately focused on Valenti's presence as an indication that Johnson didn't trust me to be alone, that Valenti was a Johnson spy in our presence. As a matter of fact, Jack did involve himself in the schedule and sent a cable back each day to Johnson, as the President had told him to—something I was not aware of until one went astray and came to our attention. I liked Jack and found his counsel wise and useful. I was glad that he was aboard and would have welcomed him without reservation.‡

‡ My staff did not entirely agree. Some of them felt understandably resentful that the President's man was there, doing a job that one of my staff members would otherwise have done. This is a common situation in government, and there is no real remedy for staff rivalry or jealousy.

The flight to Saigon was exciting, but uneventful. It gave me a chance to talk to Ky and Thieu and to take their measure to some extent. It seemed plain that Thieu was the strongman, who would ultimately be in charge. Ky was the front man, the more articulate and dramatic of the two, but it appeared certain that the taciturn Thieu would take power. And I reported that to the President.

One alarming episode on the trip involved Ky's fascination with his pistols. He played with the damn things like a sheriff in a grade B Western. At one time, while he and others were talking with Averell Harriman, Ky began to twirl the pistols. Harriman's face became a study in terror and outrage, fearful that the guns would go off, furious that this man in whom we had invested so much would attend so casually to the conversation.

Landing in Saigon gave me my first look at a city at war. Uniforms everywhere, guns, barricades, checkpoints, barbed-wire fences. Tension hung in the air. Thunderous planes taking off on missions of destruction, helicopters thumping rhythmically in the sky. Another world, of civilians, incredibly quiet considering their numbers, on foot, riding bicycles, pulling rickshaws. It was a gray and unsmiling world. It was depressing.

Saigon briefings were set up by General Westmoreland. We listened to American soldiers and civilians, some Vietnamese labor leaders. I visited the countryside, talking to Vietnamese civilians and soldiers and to our American forces. I also talked with journalists who had been in Vietnam a long time.

Philip Habib, who worked in the embassy and who subsequently became our negotiator in Paris and later assistant secretary of state for East Asian affairs, took aside one of my staff and expressed his hope that I would reach out to talk to other people beyond those briefing me. While he was totally loyal to the President and American policy, he left the impression that there was much that I wasn't being told.

That impression was reinforced by Jim Thomson of the National Security Council, who was with us. Thomson, who worked for Mac Bundy, met with some of Ed Lansdale's staff, including a young man named Daniel Ellsberg. Ellsberg strenuously supported much of our effort in Vietnam and briefed the press persuasively. Thomson had also talked at length to some reporters, particularly Ward Just of the Washington *Post,* who were highly critical of what was going on.

Still, I did not feel the glimmers of dissent were strong enough for me to dispute the presentation of Westmoreland and Lodge and their subordinates.

I had to accept the validity of what they were saying and the hopeful view they took of our involvement. What I saw, or was permitted to see, of our fighting men confirmed their spirit and their faith that this was a war that could be won.

Nothing I saw or heard, however, destroyed my conviction that it was still a political war. Indeed, the experience in Saigon seemed to support the view that we were beginning to understand and wage that political war. I was for that approach, and continued to encourage emphasis on it.

When we left Saigon, I was still troubled by our military rather then political emphasis, unsure that it could lead to "victory." But I was, in honesty, impressed and heartened by what I saw and heard.

I had been warned that our next stop, Thailand, would be a difficult one. The Thais wanted military and economic commitments that, only weeks earlier, Rusk had turned down. Jim Thomson, Chet Cooper, and Averell Harriman warned me over and over about it, and Cooper went ahead to review the situation. He returned in time to fly on with us and brief me again.

The year 1965 had taught me that Vice Presidents don't make foreign policy and that I was in Asia now to do what Johnson wanted. Averell Harriman, as the senior adviser on the trip, was to clear all official documents.

The last night we were in Bangkok, Graham Martin, our ambassador, and I rode to a state dinner. He showed me a communiqúe he wanted signed. Martin explained why it was now the right thing to do, and I agreed to it, believing it was official policy that had been cleared with Harriman and the others. It never crossed my mind that Martin was doing an end run.

Martin had the communiqué duplicated and released during the night. Tom Wicker of the New York *Times* was alerted to its existence, rose before anyone else, and filed the story while others slept. The rest of the press were, of course, furious that Wicker had gotten the jump on them. Their fury was little compared to Harriman's. And mine.

When we visited Laos, I had lunch with Souvanna Phouma. During the course of the lunch, he said we ought to bomb Red China, that it was the effective way to stop their aid to North Vietnam. If he was a neutralist, then who was a militarist? It shocked Ambassador William Sullivan, John Rielly, and Jack Valenti, who were with me.

In India I met with Indira Gandhi, someone I admired because she was Nehru's daughter (and he had been an idol of mine for his effective work in creating the Indian democracy without violence). Mrs. Gandhi said in our private discussions that our presence in Vietnam was important to India. She was understandably concerned about Chinese support of North Vietnam. She explained further that I would have to understand that her public statements would necessarily be much more neutral, and indeed critical of U.S. involvement, because of public opinion and political pressure within India.

Later, when I disclosed that conversation, she denied it, using the traditional dodge that I must have misunderstood what she had said. There had been no misunderstanding.

The meetings with Souvanna Phouma, Indira Gandhi and other Asian leaders did more than anything else to confirm—against my earlier doubts—what I suppose I now wanted confirmed: that our excursion into Vietnam, bloody and expensive as it was, was indeed a responsible thing to do in defense of the freedom of millions of people in Asia. The leaders of Indonesia had been equally firm in telling me that the United States presence in Vietnam was essential if they were to survive as an independent nation. There is always the danger of hearing what you want to hear, but the messages I heard were unmistakable.

I was so preoccupied with their comments that I made the mistake of citing Souvanna in a background session with reporters on our flight from India to Australia. I was trying to demonstrate American restraint in not following more extreme advice being given Johnson. It was a mistake to do so. I embarrassed Souvanna Phouma and, of course, he had to deny the remarks he had made.

The President wanted help desperately from Korea and the Philippines, and getting additional commitments from these two countries was a principal concern of my trip.

Korea was of particular interest to Johnson. Korean troops were well-trained and superb fighters. They were accustomed to American weapons, since we had been supplying them for years, and they would therefore fit into American military plans very easily.

If the United States had not been South Korea's main bulwark of defense, they would have been difficult to convince. What they wanted, however, beyond old friendship, was new weapons and support. They wanted additional naval vessels, and aid to modernize and strengthen their military forces. They wanted economic aid to bolster their economy. And they wanted two rations of kimchee per day for their troops in Vietnam.

Kimchee is Korean sauerkraut with a kick and odor unlike any consumable food I have ever known. After I tasted it, I decided it was a self-defense mechanism. No one dared get close to you for a week. (It is made by allowing cabbage to ferment in large concrete vats.)

We negotiated the arrangement, and the Koreans agreed to send fifty thousand troops to Vietnam. Some time later, during a cabinet meeting, Secretary McNamara indicated to the President that he was having difficulty with the Koreans. Johnson turned to me and said, "I thought you took care of all that."

I said I had. Then McNamara indicated that the hangup was kimchee. The Pentagon was perfectly willing to send ships, tanks, guns, and ammunition; but when the question of fermented cabbage arose, the budget cutters worked overtime. They had told the Koreans no.

When we sent the kimchee, the problems were solved.*

---

* A year later, in 1967, I asked the Prime Minister why the Koreans seemed to have a better ability than we or the Vietnamese to control their area of responsibility, why there seemed to be such tight control.

He said, "Anything that moves from dusk through the night is shot. That is the time that Viet Cong move, prepare for the next day's attacks, and carry out their assassination program against village leaders, teachers, and other civilians."

I said, "If we had such a rule of indiscriminate shooting, there would be such a great protest at home over the inhumanity that we would never be able to sustain it."

The Prime Minister said coldly, "I think your bombing is more indifferent to human life than our night curfew. You can't be sure you will hit only military targets and military personnel. Besides that, our curfew works."

Pressure began to prepare a report for the President. There was so little time to put my thoughts together, to make a coherent statement of what I had seen, that I cabled the President asking for a day of respite in Honolulu on our way home so that we would not have to write under pressure, aching with fatigue. The President replied that I was needed at home.

Under those circumstances, every available moment had to be used for the report. We scheduled a meeting for ten o'clock our first night in Australia, after a fourteen-hour flight from India. We had already visited Vietnam, Thailand, Laos, India, Pakistan. We still had visits in New Zealand, Korea, and the Philippines ahead.

I had dinner with Averell Harriman, Ambassador Ed Clark, and Robert Menzies, the former Prime Minister of Australia and an old friend. The meeting started about an hour late, and after five or ten minutes Harriman said that he was tired and that we all ought to go to bed. The rest of us stayed on despite his good advice.

Jack Valenti, who had repeatedly said during the trip that "the President wants optimism," began to talk about the threat of the Chinese, in effect using the line that if we weren't successful in Vietnam, we would have to stop them in Honolulu or San Francisco.

Infected with a new sense of patriotism from visiting our troops who were being shot by Chinese bullets, and recalling the warning of Asian leaders, I expressed my own concern about Chinese actions.

Jim Thomson, who had lived in China as a young man, reacted to our talk with vehemence, suggesting that we were wrong and that our position made no sense. I took his words personally and responded sharply. The staff meeting broke up with nothing accomplished and bruised feelings all around.

The next day, I threw away a speech drafted by Thomson, thinking it soft and inappropriate when I was asking the Australians to commit troops to Vietnam. I also had to consider

---

The Koreans understood guerilla war and were merciless in small units trained for hand-to-hand combat, and they were willing to work at night. The South Vietnamese were daytime fighters, who would not fight at night and preferred to withdraw if possible to their base areas at dark.

that Prime Minister Holt, who felt close to President Johnson personally, would have been embarrassed at home if he seemed more "hawkish" than the Americans.

As we flew on to New Zealand, Jim Thomson sent me a note saying he had long been an admirer of mine and meant nothing personal in his attack on Valenti's and my views. It was a gracious and honest effort to make peace, but I had been stung too hard. I was too easily angered by attacks from old friends, from liberals with whom I had stood through years of struggle at home. I was not about to accept Jim's apology. I felt what I was saying was an intellectually honest reflection of what I had seen and heard and was strategically correct. I made another hard-line speech in New Zealand.

As we pounded through the rest of our stops, the question of the report hung over us like a war cloud. My staff polarized. Bill Connell, agreeing with Valenti, urged that the report support our policy in Vietnam, endorsing the government of Vietnam's civilian and military efforts—particularly their cadre training project for the villages. John Rielly warned against such a report, which he felt was unreal and would do neither the President nor me any good. I let the arguments continue in the hope that a balanced view would emerge.

Soon, many people were involved. Valenti and Lloyd Hand, Chet Cooper and Bill Jordan, Rielly, Connell, and Jim Thomson, among others, all took turns. Consensus was not important, but none of the efforts satisfied me. When we arrived back in Washington, the report was still not done. And the reason for that should have told us something profound about our involvement in Southeast Asia: Different people saw Vietnam differently.

Here were a number of intelligent, capable men, all of whom had traveled the same route and talked to the same people about the same things. Each of us was trying to be fair, to be honest, to report as accurately and objectively as he could.

And yet we could not agree. In our little society on the airplane, we were experiencing the same differences of opinion, the same contesting views, which were polarizing American society at large.

A fifty-page report was finally prepared and sent to the White House, where it did not meet with approval. About ten days after we returned, the White House issued a seven-page pro forma report without much substance.

Understandably, the more pessimistic passages, and recommendations for internal personnel and policy changes in my report were not released.

We had labored hard and brought forth a mouse. But whether that report satisfied the President or not, the trip had in fact made me much more a supporter of our policy on Vietnam, and my public statements reflected my views. I spoke more frequently and more ardently in support of American intervention in Vietnam at the same time that the mood of the country, particularly of the press and political liberals, grew more "dovish."

It was not simply the briefings of prowar military and embassy people that moved me. It was the meetings with heads of government in Asian countries. It was also the experience of meeting our enlisted men and field officers. Their spirits were high, their dedication impressive, though some were just hours away from jungle missions where they had been wounded, where men alongside them had been killed.

To be at a front-line field hospital, watching as men wounded not fifteen minutes before are flown in by helicopter and carried to an emergency room to undergo surgery, is an experience that does not leave you unmoved.

The awful ugliness and waste of war were there. Mutilated bodies, men who might not survive, lay in beds in temporary buildings that would simply disappear from the landscape when we were gone.

You wanted to make the war stop that minute, but when you knew you couldn't, you had to accept it. If the war could not be won, if we should not have been there, then there was nothing you could say to a man who no longer had legs, whose sight was gone, who smiled through tubes and bandages as you spoke but might never smile again.

I became more and more the spokesman for the Administration. I met with reporters and with Congressional people and I supported our presence in Indochina as necessary and right. On a "Meet the Press" interview I said, "I would never want anyone to underestimate the meaning of the conference in Honolulu or the Honolulu declaration. If that is studied carefully, I think it has as much significance for the future of Asia as the Atlantic Charter had for the future of Europe."

I quoted from the declaration, its pledge "to defeat aggression, to defeat social misery, to build viable free institutions and to achieve peace." I continued, "These are great commitments. I think there is a tremendous opening here for realizing the dream of the Great Society in the great area of Asia, not just here at home, and I regret that we have not been able to dramatize it more."

Eric Severeid, a member of the questioning panel, asked me if the Johnson administration was proposing a relationship "as fundamental, as long-standing, intimate, and possibly expensive as our historic association with Europe."

I responded, "I think so."

I had not been directed by the White House to make explicit what was implied in the Honolulu declaration, and I may have gone further than I should have. I heard no complaints from the White House, but I heard plenty from my liberal friends in and out of Congress.[9] Inadvertently, I had helped crystallize the opposition to our Vietnam involvement. If the war was intolerable to critics, then a long-term commitment was inconceivable. A mood had begun to grow in the country, and there were few people who cheered the prospect of our being in Asia for years to come.[10]

Even with the huge build-up of our military effort in the preceding months, Johnson was desperate for peace. He had tried in a number of ways to bring about a peace conference. He appealed to the Pope, and the Holy See did indeed make several serious efforts to bring us together with the North Vietnamese.

Johnson asked the Polish Government, as part of the Socialist bloc, to intercede, and they did. He asked the Canadians again and again to contact the North Vietnamese in behalf of peace talks, and they did. He asked Harold Wilson, the Prime Minister of Great Britain, to bring the matter up with Alexei Kosygin when they met, and he did.[11] None of it worked.

It didn't work, I suppose, in part because the North Vietnamese knew even better than we how badly things were going, took our entreaties as signs of weakness, and simply felt that we would sooner or later withdraw. Nor did we look like very serious peace seekers as we put more and more power into South Vietnam.

What of the Cabinet? Johnson did not use cabinet meetings to discuss Vietnam, except in a general way. Had he done so, other points of view might have crept in. There was no discussion of strategy or details of American commitments. The Secretary of Defense and the Secretary of State might provide a general review, indicating what efforts were being made to bring peace in Vietnam and to get the parties to a conference table

So the cabinet meetings glossed over Vietnam and were primarily devoted to discussion of how to achieve Johnson's domestic goals and consideration of economic problems facing the country. Presidents have too often neglected the potential strength that a good Cabinet can provide. Cabinet members must above all be selected for their wisdom, judgment and broad experience, rather than expertise alone. People of such stature, with close connections to all segments of society, have a great deal to contribute to the formulation of public policy. A Secretary of Agriculture or Interior, for example, will in all likelihood have judgments about questions of international politics that should be considered by the President. With such a Cabinet, a President can learn much on all issues and help overcome the stifling confines of an insular White House and a traditional State Department.

In 1966, Johnson raised the question of whether a tax increase should be proposed, in light of the cost of the war and the pressures of inflation. Apparently, an increase had been recommended by his economic advisers, but Johnson had consulted with Congressional leadership and, to a man, they had advised him not to send up a tax bill. He relied heavily on the views of Congressman Wilbur Mills and Senator Everett Dirksen.

There seemed to be consensus that a tax increase would be rejected and that the rejection would hurt his chances on other bills.

The important fact is that we never really had a clearly defined economic policy, either, on how deeply we were going to get involved in Vietnam. If the President and his chief national security advisers had a clear idea on where we were going, they did not share it with others. I doubt they really knew.

Each year when the budget would go up to the Hill, the amount requested for Vietnam was obviously smaller than the cost would be. Later, the Administration would ask for a supplemental budget, and it was in these supplementals that the appropriation grew larger and larger. What that meant was one of two things: either the President was not leveling with the Congress as to what the cost of Vietnam was going to be, or he just didn't know and really had no plan as to the degree and duration of our involvement and participation. I think it was a little of both.

As the image was painted later in the radical press, Johnson as a warmongering, power-mad President, I would think of the many times Johnson sorrowfully talked to me of the indiscriminate killing, the toll on civilians, on women and children. When bombing raids were going on, he frequently stayed up late to hear whether all the planes returned. He thought of every bomber that went out, every flight crew, as if it were his own personal family or property. Some mornings, looking drawn, he would put an arm around my shoulders, almost for support, and say, "Hubert, I lost five of my boys last night. How am I going to explain to their families why they had to die?"

When you send men into battle, you know some are going to lose their lives. That is an awful part of political power. I don't suppose it is easy for anyone, but military people are at least trained in war. Most politicians are not. Yet the compassion breeds an irony: once an early order causes the first person to die, leaders feel required to justify what has been done. Thus, the compassion helps to create an insidious condition that leads, I fear, not to less killing, but to more.

Johnson did not believe in war, but he believed in what he was doing. He believed, as most of us did after World War II, that aggression unchecked was aggression unleashed. We felt that was the lesson of the nations who had let Hitler move from minor victory to minor victory until there was worldwide confrontation.

We felt that way in Korea. Now we felt that way about Vietnam. We were hooked on a valid lesson of history, but one that had little relevance to what was going on in Vietnam.

We simply did not properly weigh the possibility that much of what was happening in Vietnam was the continuation of a savage civil war, aided and abetted, to be sure, by the military force of North Vietnam, supported by the Russians and the Chinese, but the continuation, nevertheless, of a struggle that had started between the Vietnamese themselves, North and South, and the French.

In the confusion that followed the French withdrawal, Ho Chi Minh, a brilliant political leader, and his military tacticians, had put together a powerful military force in the North—and a highly disciplined, totalitarian political and propaganda machine, infiltrating the South and uniting with the Viet Cong there. There is no doubt that the Viet Cong operation in the South was Communist-led, Communist-inspired, and Communist-dominated. But having said all that, I see that our government never quite understood the nature of the struggle.

Night after night, Johnson would sit in the Cabinet Room with a large map of Vietnam spread out before him with several military advisers, asking, "What are the crucial or strategic targets?" General Wheeler would say that there were eighty targets, or sixty, or whatever they thought was important at the moment.[12]

Johnson would lament, "Any damn fool can get a bigger war. What I want is to end the war. What I want is to stop the shooting and killing and get these people to a conference table so we can settle this thing."

Finally, he and his advisers would select ten or twelve or fourteen targets, feeling he was restraining the military and still proceeding toward his goal. The military were frequently unhappy about the limitations imposed by Johnson, and their friends in Congress and around the country would talk about his inhibiting the effective prosecution of the war. Yet, despite right-wing claims to the contrary, we could have bombed eighty targets and not ten and the results would have been scarcely better: peace would have come no quicker, the devastation would have increased, we might have involved other countries, and the war might have made a qualitative leap into total disaster.

We went into Vietnam with conventional military forces, and found military allies who were poorly trained, poorly equipped, and without much stomach for battle. As we trained and equipped, the battle somehow became ours.[13] It is easy now to criticize those decisions, but another irony intrudes on limited intentions: soon General Westmoreland felt, among other things, that he had to have more forces to protect those who were already there. Our modest presence automatically justified increased numbers; Americans were there, and without additional troops they would come under withering, possibly fatal, attack.

Since the Vietnamese were of limited military value, the only answer seemed more American forces; and as we put in more Americans, the attacks from the North increased. The guerrilla warfare, the infiltration, and the mortar attacks on American bases took their toll on our well-trained but conventional forces. Thus, General Westmoreland and the Administration had to ask for more—more American supplies, more American guns, more American men. And it seemed the logical answer, for, after all, hadn't that been the way other wars had been won?†

No, in fact. But we didn't know how different this was. Johnson stood torn, wanting somehow to pull back, yet inevitably agreeing as his military advisers kept telling him that more was the way to end the war. The refrain was constant: "Let us bomb the Ho Chi Minh Trail, let us stop the flow of material coming across the Chinese border."

Remembering what had happened in Korea, Johnson refused, ordering that no plane get closer than thirty-five miles from the Chinese border. He was determined that we should not invade Chinese airspace either by intention or accident, thus inviting their overt intervention. In that time of trial, late spring and early summer, my relations with President Johnson were good.

Muriel and I were at the White House for dinner and movies several evenings in May, and on May 27, my birthday, Johnson called in press and photographers as he gave me gifts: a watch, an electric razor, and three pictures of the two of us together.

---

† Americans are traditionally good at tactical matters: meeting a particular situation at a particular time, providing a specific solution for a specific problem. But we have also traditionally lacked forward planning and long-range strategic concepts for dealing with such vast sections of the globe as Asia and Africa. Our primary orientation has been to Western Europe, and to some degree to Eastern Europe and Latin America. But we have never made a sufficient effort to understand the reality—the political, cultural, religious, and economic composition—of Asia or Africa or even China and the Soviet Union.

In June 1966 I saw the President frequently. We had a number of long visits, often in the late afternoon, before he retired to his bedroom for a nap. On other occasions we had breakfast or morning coffee. (Johnson would occasionally call at 6:30 A.M.—he assumed the world was awake and working—and invite me over.)

Just as he could be mean when he was irritated or dissatisfied, he could be even more generous when he wanted me involved. I attended a series of meetings—including a cabinet meeting and one for the Congressional leadership—on June 16, 17, 20, and 22.

On the seventeenth, Rusk, McNamara, Arthur Goldberg, Admiral Raborn, Walt Rostow, Bill Moyers, Henry Fowler, General Harold Johnson, and I were with the President. The discussion that day was about military operations against North Vietnam, and particularly the selection of key bombing targets. I believed and said that North Vietnam would not come to the negotiating table unless we applied more pressure and remained resolute.[14] Reluctantly, but definitely, I went along with the extension of bombing targets in North Vietnam, including petroleum depots.

Every senior military adviser had recommended a step-up in our bombing operations in the hope that we could slow down infiltration, cause the North Vietnamese to pay a heavier price for their aggression, and place a heavier burden on the North Vietnamese economy.

I accepted the view that the bombing was a military necessity and I thought we ought to run the risk, provided we did not violate Chinese airspace and did not provoke China by inadvertent attacks on her property or personnel.[15] I urged special care that we not hit any Soviet ships in the harbor at Haiphong. McNamara then reviewed instructions given to the pilots. They attempted to minimize any risk of touching Soviet ships or North Vietnamese civilians. The best instructions, however, may not be adequate when a plane traveling over a thousand miles an hour is dropping the bombs.

Rusk and McNamara believed that China would not intervene and that the Soviets would loudly protest but do nothing more. General Wheeler agreed, yet Johnson pressed them all for justification on military grounds. "Would it really help to bomb?" he asked over and over again. Once again, every senior military adviser recommended bombing key targets in Hanoi and Haiphong. The same recommendation had been made for a long time by the embassy in Saigon.

Only Arthur Goldberg strongly disagreed with the bombing strategy, believing that the repercussions would be bad and the military advantages minimal. His view, however, was overwhelmed by the others, and Johnson finally accepted the recommendation to bomb. To balance his decision, which intensified the war, he stepped up efforts on the political and economic side. He sent Robert Komer of the National Security Council staff to Saigon with instructions to improve conditions on the civilian side. The economy of Vietnam was floundering under the impact of inflation, corruption, and mismanagement. The port of Saigon was clogged with ships unable to unload their goods.[16]

It was hard for Johnson, and for us, to accept the increasing criticism and condemnation of his policies. He was portrayed as an insensitive militarist, using massive military power to bring a small nation to its knees. Yet privately he knew that he was restraining the full use of American power, constantly holding back.

He had refused to call up the National Guard; he had refused to ask Congress for a declaration of war (and he could have gotten it during most of his term); he had refused to ask for economic controls or a tax increase, which would have conveyed the sense of high seriousness to the American people.

Because he would not do these things, we remained a nation with a split personality, a nation with two characters, two lives. At home there had never been more prosperity, more jobs, more income, greater national growth, and in some ways a better distribution of income, even as vast social changes brought turmoil and trouble.

Ten thousand miles away, there was a war going on which involved hundreds of thousands of our men and women and billions of dollars of our resources. There were death, maiming, drug addiction, venereal disease, social disintegration, and corruption. There also was bravery.

It was all far away. We were absentee warlords. Without the

press, radio, and particularly television, the poor souls doing the fighting might have become invisible Americans.‡

Though it was far away in fact and in wishful thinking, the war was in a different way quite close. The press was there and the war was fought every night on television news, parents recognizing their own youngsters wounded and bleeding, seeing other peoples' children, Vietnamese as well as American, dying. We became a nation riven by guilt, anger, and confusion.

Unlike World War II, more like Korea, our real enemy lacked sharp definition for many people. So did our "allies." Positive goals of liberty and freedom in a land that had never had them were not as good as an enemy that could be personalized. Ho Chi Minh was not Hitler.[17]

Confusion about why we were there was compounded as the war lingered on with no resolution apparent or imminent. And understandably, confusion was fertile ground for anger. Vietnamese and Americans were dying, both societies torn by opposing views and forces.

Some young men were taken by Selective Service to fight, while others were deferred to go to college. The country boys, the young men of the black ghetto and white poverty, men who didn't go to college but into the labor market, were snatched up to fight the war. Not all our men were of this description, of course, but the brunt seemed to be borne disproportionately.

Everyone involved carried the burden, suffered the heartache and sorrow. Except by them and their families, there was little visible or palpable inconvenience at home.

Many of those who remained coupled guilt with their anger, and their protests became more extreme, more vehement because of mixed emotions. They didn't want to be out there, but felt some conscious or unconscious guilt because they weren't. Many left the country rather than be involved in the war—even by association. Some were concerned about themselves primarily, but others were idealists risking loss of citizenship. The motives for opposition were as mixed as the emotions.

There was a pattern of inequity and injustice, which was

‡ Vietnam was the first war in United States history in which no censorship was imposed.

bound to have a destructive effect upon the American mind and spirit.

We had developed, as inadvertently as we fell into war, a system that permitted, or demanded, a few to take on heavy burdens and sacrifice while privileged others were protected. So, on questions other than foreign, the war seemed futile and foolish to more and more people. As they perceived leaders who did not seem to be listening to them, their anger grew. Their resentment and demonstrations grew more intense as the war evidently led nowhere. Their cries to stop the bombing and, later, to get out of Vietnam, grew ever louder.

We listened to other voices. One night in September 1966, Ne Win, the neutralist president of Burma, had dinner at the White House. After dinner, Ne Win, President Johnson, and I went up to the family quarters to talk. Johnson said, "Tell me what I am doing wrong. I don't want this war. I'm trying everything for peace. What am I doing wrong?"

Ne Win replied, "What you are doing wrong is asking for peace. The North Vietnamese interpret that as weakness."

Johnson said, "But my God, I am President of the United States. The American people want peace. I've got to ask for peace. I've got to do everything I can for peace."

Ne Win responded, "Well, I am not the President of the United States and you have asked me what you are doing wrong. The North Vietnamese do not hear your peace overtures as an honest, legitimate desire for peace, but as weakness. You must make them believe that there will be no peace until they are defeated. When they understand you are going to destroy them, then there will be peace."

Johnson shook his head. "I can't do that. Our people want this war over. They won't stand still for an effort like that. I've got to pursue peace my way." There was nothing more to say.

At the same time Johnson sought to end the war through negotiations, he yearned, in his terms, for a "show of flags" in Vietnam. He wanted to be able to say to America as well as the world, "We are not there alone."

Whenever a head of state would arrive in Washington, Johnson would cajole if he could, pressure if he had to, for some token of assistance. It did not have to be a military force. It could be a hospital, a medical program for the injured or sick, a food program or some sort of technical assistance in the rural areas. The Japanese came in with hospital personnel, as did the West Germans. There were small, but to Johnson immensely important, contingents from Australia and New Zealand. Johnson was offered troops from Taiwan, but turned down the offer as unnecessarily provocative to the Peoples Republic of China.

But this help was no help, really. Evidence continued to arrive that the war was not going well, the bombing not having its intended effect. My support for it continued, however, though it became more painful and anguished.

By mid-1967, dissenters within the government were beginning to marshal their forces more strongly. Some of this had begun in late 1966, but not enough to be marked.

John MacNaughton, assistant secretary of defense for international security affairs, and Paul Warnke, who succeeded him after his death in a plane crash, began to get to Defense Secretary Robert McNamara to convince him that the bombing strategy was not working. Nick Katzenbach and Tom Hughes joined in that view.

Shortly, the Washington rumor mill carried the message that McNamara had changed his mind. Columnists like Joseph Kraft and Mary McGrory made the rumors explicit and public. By then, I was more involved in discussions at the White House and met regularly with the President, Rusk, McNamara, Walt Rostow, and Richard Helms. I never heard McNamara dissent from the President's views in those private discussions, including the very private Tuesday luncheons.

Since I saw and heard no waver on McNamara's part, I was convinced that the reporters were wrong. Had McNamara begun talking privately to the President against the bombing, I am certain I would have learned of his changed views. I, too, continued to support the President and his policies; but as the days wore on, it became more difficult to dismiss the protests as all noise and violence, harder to rationalize away an inconclusive, bloody war.

In late November 1967 I was the American representative at the inauguration of President Thieu and Vice President Ky. This time my briefings were fuller, and the number of countries to visit fewer. One unscheduled briefing was more important than the others: Aboard Air Force Two before we reached Saigon, Lieutenant Colonel Sam Karrick, an army officer who supported the war and had served in it, described widespread corruption in Vietnam, particularly on the province level but reaching to some very high-ranking Vietnamese officers. It was a distressing picture.

(Though I was not to find it out until years later, my former military aide, marine Colonel Herbert L. Beckington, had tried to schedule events that would have permitted me to see the inaccuracy of information I had been receiving. Those events were taken off the schedule by General Westmoreland before I arrived.)

There were several reporters on the trip who spoke to me or my staff saying that official reports of how the war was going were inaccurate, that our policy, however defined, was failing.[18]

Some of what Karrick and others spoke of, I now saw: Americanization of the war was virtually total. We had taken over the economy, we had taken over the fighting, we had taken over South Vietnam. We had brought jobs and prosperity (at great cost to other facets of society, of course). Even Thieu's inaugural address had been largely written by our embassy. I knew then that the American people would not stand for this kind of involvement much longer.

Before meeting with Thieu, I had a visit with Ky and lectured him on what it was like to be Vice President. I explained how he would have to restrain his impulse for publicity, tame his dramatic flair. It was an unnecessary lecture. Thieu had already left instructions that there should be no photographs of Ky and me.

Then, accompanied by Ambassador Bunker and Ted Van Dyk, I met with Thieu. I tried to explain to him that American public opinion was shifting and that the war was becoming increasingly unpopular, and that that unpopularity was reflected in Congress. I told him that even within the executive branch there was discontent. I tried to warn him that the Vietnamese would have to make significant changes if our support was to continue. I said I wasn't sure our people would accept an indefinite long-term involvement.

Thieu listened, delicately holding a cigarette, its smoke drifting up and away from him. He broke the pose to flick the ash from his cigarette in a manner that suggested that he was also flicking away what I had said.

Then he spoke: "No, you will be here for a long time. We are aware of what you say, but we realize that your support will have to continue, and perhaps even increase for the next five or six years." He seemed ready to go on and I interrupted: "Perhaps I haven't made myself clear." I then repeated with greater detail and even more firmly what I had just said, and concluded, "What we are doing to Vietnamese society is not healthy for either you or us."

Once again, he dismissed my comments, with a casual, "Oh, yes . . . yes." Clearly he intended to keep us in Vietnam and himself in power for as long as he could.[19]

When we left, I asked Ellsworth Bunker if I had been undiplomatically harsh. "No," he said, "I think it was just what he needed to hear. That was fine."

If my first trip to Vietnam, almost two years before, had made me certain that what we were doing there was right, my second trip brought back many uncertainties.

I still believed that Communist aggression ought to be stopped; I did not think the Viet Cong were Boy Scouts on an overnight camping trip. However valid our hopes: that we could stop aggression, create a democratic society, and secure freedom for a people who wanted it—and I believed in them—there was little likelihood we could achieve them.

"The critical task of months ahead," I wrote to the President, "will be to help the Thieu-Ky government build a base of popular support throughout the country and follow through on the establishment of a constructive relationship with the new parliament. Unless this is achieved, there is danger of a fallback into chaos and decomposition."

A few days after my return, in later November 1967, I spoke in New York City. I gave a sober account of the situation in Vietnam. I expressed the doubts of the responsible critics. Yet, I said, the risks of withdrawal seemed greater at the moment than the risks of perseverance. I concluded with a call for national patience and will.[20]

After the mission to Vietnam, I urged the President to stop the "search and destroy" missions and switch to a "clear and hold" strategy. Even Thieu had said that we were destroying the countryside, that innocent Vietnamese refugees with no place to go were being killed.

I suggested that our combat presence should be phased down and changes made in our economic support, including cutting our AID mission in half.

When Johnson asked Clark Clifford to undertake a reappraisal (called the "A to Z" review) of our policy, I lobbied for a policy of gradual disengagement.

I hoped still for a negotiated settlement that would leave a government, supported by a majority of the South Vietnamese, to survive the eventual American withdrawal.

But it was clear by this time that the people of the United States, for a variety of reasons, were beginning to waver in support of the war. Clearly, too, a majority would eventually be convinced that the war could not be won.

Would I have behaved differently had I remained in the Senate instead of becoming Vice President?° The answer is yes, and the explanation, I think, is simple. Where you stand often depends on where you sit.

My sources of information would have been different, and a man's judgment is, after all, based not only on his instincts but also on what he is told and what he learns.

° I resigned from the Senate early in December 1964, so that Walter Mondale would get seniority on senators elected in November, who would not be sworn in until January. I went to visit my friends Helen and Connie Valanos, who run the Monacle Restaurant on Capitol Hill, a kind of bipartisan oasis just a block from the Senate Office Building.

As we ate dinner, I said sadly, "This is the first time in many years that I have been out of a job. No paycheck until inauguration day." Connie said he might need a new maitre d', if I had any experience. I launched into a description of work behind Humphrey's soda fountain and Connie disappeared for a moment. He returned with a white towel, which he draped over my arm, and the two of us moved to the entryway of the restaurant.

When the next patrons arrived, I asked with a straight face whether I might show them to their table. I did it well, I thought, but Connie never offered me a job. Nevertheless, Connie and Helen remain very close friends and never complain about my cooking when they visit Muriel and me in Waverly.

As Vice President or President, you listen day after day to certain people for whom you have great respect and whom you basically trust. They are knowledgeable and they are competent. They are dedicated to ideals that you share.

When Lyndon Johnson or I listened to Dean Rusk, Robert McNamara, Averell Harriman, McGeorge Bundy, Walt Rostow, Richard Helms, General Wheeler, and George Ball, they seemed to be struggling with their consciences, with the complexities of life, with the facts of American involvement, just as ardently as we ourselves struggled.

The distance may be only a mile or so from the Hill, but when you sit in the White House or the Executive Office Building, you are not just at the other end of Pennsylvania Avenue, you are literally and psychologically behind a fence, where access is by invitation only.

There, a small group of trusted insiders who become closely identified with the President, see him morning, noon, and night. They are the ones who telephone him and they are the people he calls. The executive branch becomes a kind of closed society and, in war, becomes more closed as time goes on.

It must be remembered that when the increase in our Vietnam involvement began, most of the members of Congress and most of the press in the United States supported it. Public opinion polls showed a large majority of the American people also agreed.

There is an irresistible impulse, once you are settled on a position, to become locked in. Like poured cement, policy remains soft and pliable only briefly. Once it sets, that's it.

To change the metaphor, once a wartime decision has been made and men's lives have been lost, once resources are committed—and most dangerously, once a nation's honor has been committed—what you are doing becomes almost Holy Writ. Any division, dissension, or diversion is suspect.

Your future judgments become tied to what has been done. In my own case, I came to feel, strongly and not indifferently, that what we were doing had to be done.

There were other unsettling aspects. When the critics (many of them my long-term friends) attacked the war policy, they rarely seemed to see anything wrong with the Viet Cong or the North Vietnamese, never expressed sympathy for the South Vietnamese or the peoples of Cambodia or Laos who did not want to live in a Communist society. I looked for some balancing judgment in their criticism about the brutal, cruel, and treacherous attacks of the Viet Cong and the North Vietnamese.

Critics began to sound meddlesome, and nasty, biting at our heels. In retrospect, it may seem that the anti-war factions had always been against the war, that doves everywhere were confounded by a small, swift group of predatory hawks who flew between the Pentagon and the White House. The facts are different.

When I was still in the Senate, the Gulf of Tonkin Resolution passed with only two opposing votes. It had been introduced by Senators Fulbright, Hickenlooper, and Saltonstall, and provided a general authorization to the President "to take all necessary steps, including the use of armed force, to help any SEATO member or protocol state requesting 'help in defense of its freedom.'" It passed in the House by a vote of 416–0, and in the Senate by 98–2.

Some senators said later that they had been taken in, didn't understand. I asked at the time whether the resolution meant that we could end up with American men on the field of battle, whether it committed us to American armed intervention. Senator Fulbright, who handled the resolution on the floor, said, "Yes." There was no ambiguity, no question about what we were voting on.

Retrospection can be blurred, including mine. But most of the criticism early in the Johnson administration had to do with the bombing, not the fact of our presence in Indochina. The call was "Stop the bombing," not "Get out." Those early cries were that we were bombing innocent civilians and bombing hospitals— hardly insignificant mistakes, but different from objection to why we were in the war itself.

Another question that arises in restrospect is why "we" could not hear the voices in Congress who ultimately opposed the war. The reason is that they were hard to hear. For a long time, Johnson conferred with not just a few, but many congressmen and senators. And they, for the most part, supported him or muted their criticism in his presence.

Further, Johnson had been on the Hill long enough to know

that virtually every member of the Congress is a headline seeker. It is part of the trade, part of the business. So conferences with Johnson that might have been productive, ended up in the newspapers or on TV—to the publicity benefit of the members of Congress. Consequently, Johnson became paranoid on the subject. If he thought you were going to visit with him and then go out to the press, overtly or by leaking the story, his mind was closed before the visit began.

I think this is true of most Presidents but undoubtedly more so of Johnson. When you are frustrated with a policy that isn't working, and yet you don't know what other policy to pursue, *and* the Congress continues to give you the funds that they could withhold,[21] then you finally came to believe that the Congressional opposition is not as serious as its pronouncements.

But for all the psychological, idealistic, or pragmatic barriers that screened out some of the protest and criticism, the facts could not be denied any longer. Lyndon Johnson set his mind on getting out of Vietnam.

33. ONE PLACE, ONE MAN

In the chaos of 1968, one place and one person dominated my life that election year. The place: Vietnam. The person: Lyndon Johnson. One was a disaster; the other, a distinctly mixed blessing.

To open the year:

In January 1968 there were 492,900 American men and women at war in Vietnam. Nearly seventeen thousand of their compatriots had already died there. President Johnson had only 48 per cent approval in the Gallup Poll, Gene McCarthy had announced for the presidency, and Bob Kennedy, waiting in the wings, had not.

By late that month, the war had taken a terrible turn for the worse. All our hopes of getting movement toward a cease-fire, a peace conference, had been frustrated. The President had tried again and again, by himself and through others, to get any response from the North Vietnamese. Only history can judge whether he made the right moves. I think he made many.

Those who have badgered, belittled, and second-guessed Lyndon Johnson must know that he wanted peace in Vietnam *desperately*. Those who deny him that bit of humanity are wrong. Johnson knew that getting out of Vietnam, stopping the waste of lives and resources that the war brought, and getting on with his domestic agenda at home, creating his "Great Society," was the only way to assure the place in history he hoped for. And once you are President, your concern about the votes of history becomes one that starts to overpower your wish for the votes of your contemporaries.

As badly as it was going, I still expected that a way would be found to resolve the war, that Johnson, overcoming any challenges from within the Democratic party, would run for re-election and would defeat the likely Republican nominee, Richard Nixon. And I looked forward to re-election as Vice President.

Instead, the major events of 1968 were awful—assassinations, untimely deaths, riots, unnecessary destruction, increasing dissension. It was not the set of conditions a person would choose to live in and certainly not as the environment for the candidacy of incumbents.

In time, that year, I was to fall heir to virtually all the animosity directed toward the Johnson administration and be beneficiary of practically none of the goodwill due an administration whose domestic accomplishments were historic. I found myself boxed in by a number of things: There was the conditioning of my first three years as Vice President, including my concept of loyalty and commitment to the President. There was my desire to develop, and the obvious need for, new approaches to our continuing problems. I wanted to speak out on what had gone wrong, to raise my hopes as national hopes, yet I was still part of the Administration. Finally, there were the frequent moments of near disintegration in our society, the tense thrusts of new and old forces trying to work in and around our political system.

In that complex world, where simple truths were appropriate for prophets or the self-righteous, I had no simple answer for Vietnam. Declare "victory" and bring our "boys" home, as some cynics suggested? Give the military a free hand to bomb where they wanted with whatever weapons they wanted? Vietnamize the war, letting only Vietnamese die instead of Americans?

As I had no single, simple response on Vietnam, I had no single attitude toward Lyndon Johnson. He is not my "fall guy," to be blamed for my mistakes or failures. I owe far too much to him. He made possible my being Senate majority whip and Vice President of the United States. No one played a more important role in my receiving the nomination for the presidency.

Part of our problems came from the institutions of President and Vice President, part from the uneasy juxtaposition of our two personalities. What I have tried to describe is how our relationships—intimate, friendly and respectful, sometimes strained and suspicious—affected, from my point of view, the campaign of 1968.

When I am critical of Lyndon Johnson, it is in the context that I consider him an outstanding President whose domestic achievements were formidable. He signed into law more legislation to improve the lot of more Americans than any President before him. History will give him more credit than pollsters or politicians.

When he could not get out of Vietnam, he got out of the presidency. His military problems became my political problems, and we, long-time friends and political allies, struggled in our attempts to deal with Vietnam and each other.

Tet, or the new year, in Vietnam is a time of celebration and holiday. Tet of 1968 was different. The North Vietnamese and the Viet Cong launched a massive attack on January 30 against South Vietnamese and American forces there.

The Tet Offensive had as its military aim the utter destruction of those forces. Politically, its purpose was to take over the provinces and villages. Over one hundred district capitals were attacked and hundreds of villages shelled. In a dramatic move, the American Embassy in Saigon became a specific target, the Viet Cong gaining entry to the grounds.

The American and South Vietnamese forces fought back well, the South Vietnamese surprisingly well. As a result, the North Vietnamese and Viet Cong suffered tremendous losses. While they proved they could strike at will, they also demonstrated that they could not hold a village, or a district or provincial capital. Their acts of brutality, their terrorism toward the population were merciless. They took fantastic chances, and they were turned back.

Finally they were entrenched only in the old capital of Hue, where we were reluctant to bomb because of its ancient temples and religious monuments. When the enemy was driven from Hue, the Tet Offensive was over.

What had been, in objective terms, a major military defeat for the Viet Cong and the North Vietnamese was also an unlimited disaster for the Johnson administration. The war was at that point, if not before, a political catastrophe for President Johnson. Why?

The American public had been reassured often that the enemy was losing strength and wouldn't be able to continue the war much longer. The mere fact of the offensive shocked people into realizing that what they'd been hearing could not be true. That fact irrevocably destroyed administration credibility. It shattered political resolve and will in the United States.

It caused us, then, to re-evaluate totally what we were doing. The military made their regular response: more troops, more supplies, a bigger effort. Leaked to the press, these requests got huge play.

The important, and essentially new, response was from the President's non-military advisers, who, with one or two exceptions, said that the time had come for him to change strategy and tactics, that he should cease the bombing of the North, that he should not send additional troops, that there should be a policy of de-escalation. These meetings with advisers took place during February and March of 1968. I thought we should halt the bombing of the North and said so.

One night, the President and I sat alone in his bedroom talking about the war. He had decided not to send the large number of new troops the military wanted. He had also determined to stop the bombing above the nineteenth parallel, thus excluding Haiphong and Hanoi, 90 per cent of the population, and 70 per cent of the territory of North Vietnam from the bombing area.

I agreed that more troops was not the answer, but I also thought he would be stopping the bombing at the wrong place. "Mr. President, stopping at the nineteenth parallel is not going to do much good. What you should do is stop it all. Stop north of the seventeenth parallel, north of the demilitarized zone."

I suppose that he felt, having rejected the military appeal for more troops, he had to give in on the other count. Though I did not agree, anyone without sympathy for the military, who thought them unrealistic, was missing the raw reality: military men were the ones who were fighting and dying, who were bearing the burden and suffering of the battlefield. It was inevitable that their high command would bring pressure on the President to continue pressure on the North.

On the morning of March 31, Muriel and I were packing our bags for a trip to Mexico City, where, as the U.S. representative, I would sign a nuclear non-proliferation treaty for the Western Hemisphere. There was an unexpected knock at the door. When we opened it, there stood the President, his daughter Luci, and her husband, Pat Nugent, on their way home from church. The President quickly indicated that he wanted to talk with me alone. Muriel, anxious to finish packing, tried to entertain the Nugents while the President and I disappeared into my den.

There he told me of the speech he had scheduled for that night. He urged me to interrupt whatever I was doing in Mexico City to listen. Then he showed me two endings drafted for it, saying he had not yet decided which one to use. I could barely believe what I was reading. One of them had Lyndon Johnson withdrawing from the 1968 election. I urged him not to do it. He shrugged and asked me not to tell Muriel the content of our discussion, and we moved out to where the others were.

The President had told me that unless he removed himself from the politics of 1968, his efforts to achieve peace, to enter into negotiations with the North Vietnamese and the Viet Cong, would be attacked as being no more than election politics. Furthermore, he needed to ask Congress for an increase in taxes. He insisted that these two objectives could not be pursued if he was a candidate.

Then he added a more personal note: he reminded me that all the men in his family had died in their early sixties or before. "Even if I should run and be re-elected, I most likely would not live out my term," he said.

As they left, he hugged Muriel and leaned over and kissed her cheek, as he often did. But when the door closed behind him, Muriel asked, "What's wrong?"

I was as casual as I could be. "Not much. The President is going to give a serious speech tonight and wanted to talk about it." When we got into the car to leave for Andrews Air Force Base, she asked again, and I fuzzily answered that he had some statements about the war and would be discussing them over the air that night. Muriel did not pursue me, but sensed my distress. I was, inwardly, thunderstruck. If Lyndon Johnson withdrew, what would it mean for the country? Would it really end the war? Would it be a healing act of statesmanship—or merely considered as proof that he had been driven from office?

And what would it mean for me? I believed that the President could not only be renominated but re-elected, despite Vietnam, polls, predictions, and antagonists. This is what I had urged him to do. If he were to renounce renomination, should I become a candidate? Gene McCarthy and more recently Bob Kennedy were in the primaries. They had staff, had raised money. What was I to do, what were the possible "endings" for the silent speech I was making within?

That night at the time of the President's speech, I was to host a dinner at Ambassador Fulton Freeman's residence for the President of Mexico, Gustavo Díaz Ordaz.* First, with our wives, we sat in the library while the guests waited in other rooms. Just before the speech began, Marvin Watson called me from Washington to say the President would use the second ending, the one announcing his withdrawal. Until that instant, I had hoped he would run for re-election. That hope gone, I sat on the leather couch with Muriel and listened, wondering how we would handle the press who had traveled with us and were just outside.

As the speech drew to a close and the President stated his intention to withdraw, Muriel and I stared at one another for a silent moment before the frenzied excitement hit, leaving the next few moments a blur.

Muriel, in a nervous gesture, reached to touch her leg, and a ring snagged her hose. She excused herself and went upstairs to change them. Once out of sight, she wept. Part of the reason for Muriel's tears was concern for me, for us. Part was resentment that there had been no warning for us that permitted rational planning.

When Muriel returned, having put on a brave face, we stood

* It was the first time a Mexican President set foot in the American Embassy since the Mexican Revolution.

in line, responding noncommittally to comments about our future. Comments to the press were equally guarded.

Back in Washington, Bill Connell, who had been my main political operative since 1961, called Marvin Watson to make sure that what he had heard on television was, in fact, true. Assured that it was, he tried to call me but couldn't get through. He then began a series of calls to party leaders, labor officials, and governors and senators, urging them to stay free of commitments until I returned. He made almost a hundred calls, talking till well past midnight. In many instances, he found his call had been preceded by one from either Bob or Ted Kennedy.

Al Barkan of the AFL-CIO Committee on Political Education also made many calls to labor leaders around the country, asking them much the same thing: to hold on and make no immediate commitments.[1]

Being in Mexico City, which had seemed so awful the night before, now seemed fortuitous. I would have an extra day to think through what had to be done if I was to run.

When our plane landed at Andrews Air Force Base on Monday evening, I was greeted by a crowd of friends and well-wishers. Dean Rusk, Willard Wirtz, and Orville Freeman were there from the Cabinet, and others who had been in my earlier campaigns waved signs and cheered. It was like coming home to Minnesota.

From the airport, we went to our apartment, and a group gathered there—Connell, Max Kampelman, Bill Welsh, Norman Sherman, Gus Tyler, Dick Maguire—and we talked about what I might do. Muriel and I had already decided that I would not commit myself then.

The next day, of course, our office was in an uproar, a fury of activity, of calls going out and calls coming in. The staff was beautifully frantic. That afternoon, after George Meany had called on me, urging me to announce at once, I thought I might have to tranquilize Connell and at least half my staff. It was an exciting day, when every call was someone asking me to run. I loved it, but it was also a time when mistakes can be made, so I became, strangely, the calming influence, urging everyone to ease off.

Meany did not. He went to the White House to urge the President to call me and suggest that I immediately declare my candidacy. The President didn't and in fact never urged me to run explicitly.† Many feared that the labor movement would be torn apart by contesting Kennedy and McCarthy forces. He felt my immediate declaration was necessary to prevent splintering and possible irreparable confusion within the ranks of labor for that election.

If I did intend to declare, his point was well taken and almost persuasive. But I thought that a declaration of candidacy so soon after Johnson's withdrawal would be too eager, too self-seeking, overly ambitious. I had been through abortive efforts at the nomination before, and I was simply not about to make the effort again unless the odds were at least a little in my favor, through delegate and financial support.

That week, I talked with Democratic officeholders—mayors, particularly—but governors and senators and congressmen, and party leaders, and labor leaders. It was clear quickly that Bob Kennedy was not going to run away with the nomination. In fact, he had far less organizational support than one would have imagined. Gene McCarthy had even less. I stood then with the odds sufficiently favorable, and for the first time in my national political life with what seemed firm financial pledges.

Tuesday night of that week, there was a fund-raising dinner set for the Democratic Congressional campaign committees. I was at the head table, smiling and talking, when I was handed a note from a staff member saying the Secret Service had just learned that Dr. Martin Luther King, Jr., had been shot in Memphis. The dinner went on, but when I received a second note saying he had died, I wrote a brief eulogy, delivered it, and suggested to the chairman of the dinner that we stop. He hesitated, and I resolved the question by taking the microphone and announcing that the dinner was over.

As Muriel and I stood behind the dais, Max Kampelman came

† While the President never urged me to run, he clearly assumed I would. When we talked around the issue after his withdrawal, he suggested that I had not been very perceptive if I hadn't picked up the possibility that he might not run. This was a lack of perception that I shared with much of America. It is true, however, that Dean Rusk, in January or February of 1968, took me aside one day at the White House to say that he thought it quite possible that the President would not run for re-election. The President himself, the day after the election in 1964, told me at his ranch that he would not run for re-election. I did not believe it.

up to talk about Dr. King's death, and we invited him to come home with us so that we could talk. Just then, Ed and Jane Muskie walked by, and I said to Max, "If I run, that's my Vice President." Max said if that was the case, I'd be better off visiting with them instead of him. We did invite Ed and Jane to join us, though we talked little presidential or vice-presidential politics. For Martin Luther King's death was an immense loss, and not just to black America. My contacts with him had been few, but I felt strongly that I shared his dream.

Lyndon Johnson became in his own eyes a non-partisan President, and ceased at that moment to take any overt national leadership in the Democratic party. And yet he gave up the reins reluctantly. (On the one hand, he instructed cabinet members to keep away from politics, not to involve themselves in the Democratic primary and preconvention battles. On the other hand, he kept a firm grip on the nominating convention and our platform plank on Vietnam.)

Sadly, Johnson's credibility, in the overused term, was so suspect by the time of his speech that his efforts to de-escalate and his order to stop the bombing did little to diminish the bitterness toward him by the dissenters and protesters. Had he stopped the bombing north of the DMZ, it would have been a major tactical and strategic move that could not have been distorted by his critics. He left them the opportunity to condemn and harpoon him because he didn't go all the way down to the seventeenth parallel. They ignored him for what he had done, attacked him for what he had not done, leaving the political atmosphere largely unchanged.

Even if he had halted all bombing, it probably would not have satisfied his critics. As it was, they shifted from the cry of "Stop the bombing" to "Get out entirely."

Years later, one may wonder what had happened to this man, who was elected by a huge majority and who was everywhere known as a skillful politician.

The power of an incumbent President is great. He can dominate the news. He can, within reasonable and responsible limits, create the news and time its release. He can use the power of patronage already delivered and of patronage anticipated to elicit support. He can invoke the aura of the office. He can wrap himself in the flag, rallying the "people" to his cause.

Generally, any President who is willing to use that power can get his party's nomination. I believe this would have been the case for Lyndon Johnson, even under the difficult and contrary circumstances of 1968.

But the President had said that he could not be credible as long as he was a candidate. The only way, he thought, that people would believe he really wanted to get out of Vietnam was for him, this most political of men, to take vows of political celibacy. He was determined to complete his term by reaching two goals: end the war and slow down inflation.

I doubted that his withdrawal would help and had told him so. Those who did not like him, did not believe him—and they were not about to change their views. Further, announcing his decision in March made him a lame-duck President, with powers diminished.

Before he pulled out, the New Hampshire primary was over. Eugene McCarthy, the only one on the ballot, drew 42 per cent of the vote. Lyndon Johnson, not on the ballot, received 49 per cent of the vote as a write-in candidate. The press, however, played the results as a major victory for McCarthy.‡

History will judge Gene McCarthy's efforts, the content of his challenge, the conduct of his campaign and its validity. But his importance and symbolic effect are clear now and cannot be gainsaid. With a press corps that was viscerally and intellectually anti-Johnson, McCarthy's every sentence became a proclamation, every twist a movement, every vote for him a landslide.

When Robert Kennedy entered the primaries, the McCarthy advantage was cut down.

Bob Kennedy had earlier offered a "deal" to the President that, had the President accepted, would have kept Kennedy out of the primaries. But it would have required, for all practical purposes, Johnson's political abdication. He would have been President-in-hostage, virtually unable to govern in foreign affairs without Kennedy's approval.

‡ Senator McCarthy entered seven contested primaries and won one, in Oregon. He ran second or third in New Hampshire, Nebraska, Indiana, South Dakota, Florida, and California.

The proposal essentially involved a Kennedy commission to examine the war, making its report available to the President, the Secretary of State, and the Congress. Clark Clifford, Secretary of Defense and a personal friend of Senator Robert Kennedy, met with him, at the President's request, to hear his proposal in greater detail, and ultimately to tell him that the demands could not be met. I felt very strongly that the proposal was an impossible one and that it could not be granted—indeed, never should have been suggested.

That was the price that Kennedy wanted to stay out of the presidential primaries, and when the price would not be met, Washington rumor mills again made Johnson look like he was in a personal vendetta and indifferent to seeking ways to end the war.

When Johnson withdrew, the Wisconsin primary was just two days away. The Democratic party there was chopped badly among McCarthy, Kennedy, and Johnson forces, and the President realized the likelihood of a defeat. I knew from personal experience how devastating the Republican cross-over could be.* The local disorganization would have mattered less if the Democratic National Committee had been strong and significantly able to direct a campaign. It was not. It was weak and basically incapable of mobilizing what Johnson support there was. Its decrepit condition was, ironically, the direct result of Lyndon Johnson's attitude toward it.

In the best of times, in the most favorable conditions, the Democratic National Committee is a frail political child. When there is a Republican President, it has relatively little power, often lacks the focus of a strong national leader, and is suspect by much of the Democratic Congressional leadership. When there is a Democratic President, the committee's activities are circumscribed by him. It becomes entirely dependent on what the President wants. And President Johnson wanted it weak. He kept politics close to himself, run directly out of the White

---

* When there is no real primary on the Republican side, large numbers cross over into the Democratic column, often voting for the person least likely to succeed, or at least voting in a way to embarrass the Democratic front-runner. Some studies have indicated that as many as 50 per cent of the Republicans voting in some primaries vote on the Democratic side.

House, first with Walter Jenkins, later with Marvin Watson and his successor, young Jim Jones.†

This was in part true because of his experience with the national committee. It had become a haven, in too many instances, for people that political leaders did not want at the White House, in government agencies, or in their own offices. Political retainers and sycophants accumulated there, smothering able people in an atmosphere of flabby incompetence.

Outraged at the waste, the President trimmed the fat quickly. Unfortunately, he cut off some of the muscle. He had, it seemed to me, disdain for the national committee not only as it was, but even for what it might ideally be.

Johnson's problem in dealing with politicians was not limited to the Democratic National Committee. It was reflected in his high-level government appointments, too. He knew that some people thought that he was unprincipled, and yearned to shake that reputation. For example, he took great pleasure in talking about how many civil servants he had promoted, as though that would make him non-political.

There is nothing to be said for appointing political incompetents. There is much to be said for appointing competent people with political backgrounds. They bring a different kind of dedication to the execution of programs, and their enthusiasm and commitment to an administration is socially useful and politically productive.

To reject patronage and exclude working political people from important levels of service is to deny a part of our political sys-

† Johnson's White House political operatives worked early through John Bailey and Richard Maguire at the committee, and later through Cliff Carter and John Criswell. The functionaries at the committee, with the exception of Maguire, who was the money-raiser, were on a short lead, clearing even the smallest details with Jenkins or Watson, who appeared almost always to check them with the President.

The result was unfortunate, with decisions made too slowly, overcautiously, and without benefit of the personal relationships that would have cemented state leaders to the Administration. Ironically, Johnson, dealing too frequently with every little detail, lost touch with the real political players. He continued to think that he had the same kind of control he had held in the Senate, sensing the mood, knowing what he needed to know. He simply did not.

tem. Patronage and legitimate rewards can be synonymous, not at odds. A President must be both a national leader and, in the best sense of the word, a political leader.

Johnson's reputation as "political operator" was true only in the sense of getting things done in a legislative body. His world was the specific one of Capitol Hill. It was not the amorphous world of state chairmen and -women, of national committeemen and -women. He wanted no satellite political force.

Johnson had many of the qualities of a true political leader: drive, confidence, great ability, toughness, persistence. But, legend to the contrary notwithstanding, when it came to party politics, he was not good. Even in Texas, his political battles were hard ones, won but barely. They were, in any case, parochial, and left him with little appreciation for the need of a national political structure to do the necessary day-to-day work.

As a result, he never did develop such a structure as President. From time to time, he invited political leaders to talk, but they were essentially people who supported him, and many were not Democratic political leaders.

The Democratic National Committee itself had been left more or less in a state of slumber during the Johnson presidency. The major activity was a fund-raising effort run by Arthur Krim and Richard Maguire.‡ The President's Club, as it was called, was used primarily to raise money to pay off Democratic committee debts not only from the campaign of 1964, but also those inherited from the Kennedy regime. In addition, it did raise substantial sums for the 1966 Congressional campaigns.

Since the party organization was neglected, party workers, from state chairmen on down, felt it, resented it, and had minimal interest when called on for the primaries. Johnson's treatment of National Chairman John Bailey, an able and loyal man who often hid his Harvard law degree behind a "party boss"

‡ Arthur Krim is a lawyer and the chairman of the board of United Artists. He was a prominent fund-raiser for both Presidents Kennedy and Johnson.

Dick Maguire was part of the Irish triumvirate of O'Donnell, O'Brien, and Maguire who came to Washington as part of the Kennedy group. He became treasurer of the Democratic National Committee during the Kennedy administration.

cigar, was symptomatic. Bailey, who had been made national chairman by John Kennedy, was kept on as chairman not because he was Lyndon Johnson's political man, but because, I think, Johnson didn't care enough to make a change. Johnson knew that political power comes to people in Washington according to their proximity to the "throne." If a governor or a state party chairman knew John Bailey had little power, he would ignore him in crucial moments; if another was known to be closer to the President, that's where he would turn.

When personal popularity waned, when counterforces built up across the nation, Lyndon Johnson had virtually nowhere to turn, no strong political arm or institution to lean on for support.

I always thought, of course, that a Vice President might very well have assisted with, even fulfilled that role of political leader. It was not to be so. While the President listened to my political ideas and analysis, and seemed to give them credence, he had conflicting emotions when it came to my political initiative or possible prominence. After all, by the very nature of things, the President was the political leader. There couldn't be two.

He would say, "Hubert, now you get out and talk to party leaders. Move around now, get acquainted." But he never put out the word that I was speaking for him. Unless the President tells party leaders the Vice President speaks for him, all the smiles and small friendships count for little.

I am convinced that a Vice President, regardless of talent and the President's personality, has a choice between two relationships: acquiescence and hostility. The Vice President simply cannot move without the President's seal of approval.

Had I, for example, tried to move in on the national committee, I would have been rebuffed, since it had no mandate from the President to accept my leadership. It may have been weak, but it had strength enough to repel a Vice President operating on his own. Had I begun working with the state committees, spending my time on the politics of the Democratic party, someone—a reporter or a politician—would have interpreted this as political self-aggrandizement, probably at the President's expense. The publication of such a story would have caused President Johnson or his aides to take a dim view and to end it.

And as he had himself pointed out, in August 1964, when he

offered me the nomination, his staff could be expected to be more sensitive than he. Even moving as delicately as we did, some of his people stirred up counterpressures whenever we showed any substantial interest in the activities of the Democratic National Committee.

Just as I could not work as Johnson's representative, I would not have been able to develop an overt political base of my own. First, of course, it didn't seem that I would need one. I had obviously had no plans to run for the presidency in 1968, and 1972 was a long way off. Neither did I expect any effort to dump me as the vice-presidential candidate in 1968.

Enjoying people as I do, I naturally seek new friends and keep old friendships going. As a matter of course, some of these friendships do have political value, and every politician is human enough to develop some friendships primarily for their potential political value. So I suppose it is honest to say that, within the limitations of my position and the strictures placed on me, I did instinctively try to develop a political base while I was Vice President, building primarily on the base I already had from my senatorial career—my long, happy relationships with the labor movement, the Jewish and black communities, liberal farm organizations. I had also been expanding my contacts in the business world.[2]

34. THE POLITICS OF JOY

Within days after Johnson's withdrawal, I had decided to run.

The question then became how and when to declare. We went through a period searching for the right way. You don't just come down to the street after breakfast some morning and say, "Good morning, world. I am seeking the Democratic nomination for President." Many people counseled us: some wanted me to go on national television; others thought a simple press conference would do; there was even the suggestion that I get away from the Washington environment, picking a middle American city for the announcement.

Finally, after endless debate on the theatrics of the announcement, I decided the statement would be made in Washington at a time when it would dominate the Sunday papers and provide news for the TV commentators both Saturday and Sunday.

Further, I would invite people from all over the country who were supporting me, trying to demonstrate the breadth of my support. I knew that, surrounded by friends, in a festive atmosphere, I would do a good job.

Then came the more substantial problem of deciding the nature and content of the speech. Once more, there were endless suggestions, some drafts, and then, the only way I could be comfortable, rewriting it in large part myself, giving it at least the personal touches I thought it needed.

In the course of delivering the speech, I added the expression "politics of joy"—a phrase I did not invent but that was to haunt me. I simply meant that the right to participate in democratic processes was, in part, "the pursuit of happiness" of which our founding fathers spoke.

No matter what I meant, I failed to get my message across. The press grabbed onto it. It was an unfortunate statement.

The McCarthy and Kennedy forces, and particularly some of the press who agreed with them, pummeled me verbally as a fatuous man, ignorant and blind to the miseries of the world. "How could we be happy in these trying times after the death of Martin Luther King? How could there be a 'politics of joy' when there were riots in the cities and when there was war in Vietnam?" One has only himself to blame for a mistake like that, but I believed then, as I do even now, that it was wrenched without conscience from both the context of my life and the context of the speech. I constantly had to explain that I was not unaware of the misery in our land and world. It is ironic to have subsequently seen Gene McCarthy talk of the pursuit of the public happiness (as he had before) and be hailed a political philosopher.

With that exception, the day went magnificently. Muriel was radiant. My family was there, my friends were there.[1] I was surrounded by love and hope. It seemed an auspicious beginning.

I also announced that two brilliant, young, active United States senators would be my co-chairmen. One, Fred Harris of Oklahoma, a gut liberal, principled, tough, and an outstanding member of the Kerner Commission, was a member of the "Kennedy clan." The other was Walter "Fritz" Mondale of Minnesota, who in 1948, when he was eighteen years old, was my campaign manager in the Second Congressional District of Minnesota. In 1968, he was my successor in the U. S. Senate, appointed by Governor Karl Rolvaag. He, like Harris, was an exceptional and attractive person.

Since I was so closely, and justifiably, identified with the Johnson administration, I wanted to get men out front who were loyal both to the President and to me, and who were at the same time young and vigorous and intelligent and articulate. That is what I had in Mondale and Harris.

22. Vice-President Humphrey exchanges greetings with an Indian farmer during his visit to Ludhaina, India, in 1966.

23. In Birmingham for the Red Cross annual awards luncheon in 1967, the Vice President compares casts with a local student.

24. Touring the District of Columbia's youth summer employment projects in 1967. Rufus Mayfield, director of PRIDE, Inc., is on the author's right.

25. The author sings along with Christmas carolers in a Head Start school in St. Louis, 1967.

26. Humphrey wins presidential nomination on the first ballot as banners wave in the convention hall, 1968.

27. The author, surrounded by policemen and aides, during a campaign speech in New York City, October 1968.

I knew I needed a bridge to disaffected youth who found Gene McCarthy and Bob Kennedy immensely appealing. I did not realize how deep the hatred and anger of the young had become, what little effective appeal I could make as a part of the Johnson-Humphrey administration. The young people of the McCarthy and Kennedy campaigns were for the most part beyond my reach. Not realizing that, I tried to reach them, and I still think the selection of Mondale and Harris was sound. It had been a decision opposed by some close advisers. They were understandably upset about outsiders coming in at the top (though Mondale was hardly an outsider).

The two senators, on the other hand, had some disdain for my staff and older advisers who were not their senatorial peers. They were busy in the Senate, needed to travel in my behalf, and I did not think of them as administrators. When they brought in their own staff people, we had a Hydra-headed monster, and inevitably ill feelings arose among the several power centers. As is so often the case in campaigns, we spent far too much time ironing out difficulties that with a little more maturity, we might have avoided.

What I needed was a single boss and we simply didn't have one. Bill Connell is more than able and intelligent, but he had been a Senate staff man too long to be acceptable as the leader by two vigorous, young United States senators. Ideally, Bill should have been my inside man, doing what I needed to have done in the way of non-public contacts and work, leaving the two senators out front.

The campaign probably would have benefited from centralizing the power in one place. But even with our leadership widely diversified and somewhat confused, we still made remarkable success in the preconvention weeks. An enormous amount of work was done by the key staff people and our labor supporters, the kind of work that is crucial to a solid campaign and is not often seen, because it is not in the forefront: lining up delegates; working the states where delegates were selected in caucuses; getting commitments; putting together the coalition.

Campaigns create a kind of fiscal insanity in which many people suddenly take upon themselves the authority to spend money. Often there are tremendous expenditures without regard to what is available. Since I couldn't get the sense of accurate acccounting either on income or outgo, I called in my old friend Freddy Gates. Fred, during the early months, cracked heads and made sure money was spent more carefully and effectively.

During this period—up to mid-June—I was running ahead in all the public opinion polls. It appeared that both the Democratic nomination and the presidency were within my grasp.

And then came the assassination of Robert Kennedy. I was in Colorado Springs preparing to deliver the commencement address the next day at the Air Force Academy. My staff and I were in the Officers Quarters on the base, where we watched the election returns from California for a long while and then went to bed. I had not yet fallen asleep when D. J. Leary, a friend and advance man, still watching television, saw the report of Sirhan's shot. His shouts brought me out of my half-sleep.

Pajama-clad, I watched television. It is hard not to seem melodramatic in describing the shock, the shivers of revulsion that sped through my body at the thought that this could have happened yet again to a Kennedy. As we listened to the first medical reports, Edgar Berman, a doctor friend who traveled with me, said "It doesn't sound like he can survive."

I called the hospital and spoke to Pierre Salinger, who gave me no hope, and I offered to do whatever I could. He called back shortly and said that they would like to have a neurosurgeon flown from Massachusetts to Los Angeles and asked me to secure a military plane to get him there.

I called the operations officer at the academy and explained to him what I wanted. He asked, legitimately I suppose, under what authority I was ordering the plane. I shouted into the phone, "I am Vice-Commander-in-Chief," making up a position that did not exist. My intensity overcame his reluctance and the doctor was flown to Los Angeles.

The question immediately arose whether I would deliver the commencement address as planned. I couldn't imagine speaking to any group, no matter how non-political the appearance was. I sent word to the air force officials of my decision.

The next morning, Air Force Secretary Harold Brown, General John McConnell, and several other generals came to my quarters to urge me to reconsider. I had just taken a shower, was only partially clothed, and stood before the bathroom mirror shaving. They stood in the doorway and made a kind of *macho* appeal: "It is the manly thing to do. Stand up at a moment of adversity. These are our future officers preparing to go off to battle. They deserve to have a commitment honored."

Sleepless, depressed, overwhelmed by the continuing tragedy that followed the Kennedys, knowing that Bob might not survive, I barely remained civil as I repeated that I would not speak. I urged them to leave me as quickly as possible.

It seems insensitive even now to talk about the political implications of a family's tragedy. Still, in a sense, Bob Kennedy's death was a national tragedy, a major political earthquake that shook our entire political world. Once more, the poison and hate demonstrated in the new act of assassination traumatized the survivors and permeated the nation.

To campaign in such a situation was unthinkable, even if one were not affected by the act, as I deeply was. This was particularly so for a man connected, as I was, with Lyndon Johnson. So I immediately put a stop to our campaign efforts. We withdrew from the New York campaign entirely, even though we'd already spent considerably more there than any sensible organization should have. We lost a month of campaign activity, since it wasn't until July that we really geared up once again. Momentum was lost, and now we reeled under the strain.

Then came the Republican convention, dominating the news. After that, we moved strenuously to tie down delegates. In a year of unpredictable events, we appeared to have the strength to secure the nomination if nothing else unpredictable took place.

When historians write about 1968, they will write about three very different men: Robert Kennedy, Eugene McCarthy, and George Wallace. One a rich man's son, brother of a President, heir to fortune and glamour. The second, the son of a Minnesota farmer, handsome, witty, teacher, poet, Irish mystic, and a clever politician, cleverer for denying it. The third, the "know-nothing" candidate of our period, a canny and shrewd politician who captured the votes of those whose fears and hates and alienation he articulated. Each in his own way, one tragically, became obstacles for me in my quest for the presidency.

I did not know Robert Kennedy during his early years in Washington. I was first really aware of him in 1960 in West Virginia and Wisconsin, when he played a prominent part in John Kennedy's primary campaigns. I did not like him then. He seemed tough and hostile beyond the needs of political opposition.

I suppose I never quite forgave him for that period, but I had started to respect him—indeed, to like him. After his brother's death, I think Robert Kennedy became a man. Out of that tragedy, he developed concern and compassion and understanding that he had seemed to lack previously. I campaigned for him in his New York senatorial race in 1966, and I did so out of respect for him, and not grudgingly.

By 1968, when he finally became a candidate for the nomination, he excited the spirit of many people, often those who shared least in our society. He was a folk hero, as tough and competitive as ever but with a quality he had lacked a decade before: deep and sincere concern for those left out or forgotten.

I saw Bob in the Senate from time to time. We did not talk about supporting one another, but I think we each knew what would be done after the convention.

During the summer, I met with his political people, primarily Ken O'Donnell and Larry O'Brien. We had not been friends before John Kennedy's election, and viewed one another with some suspicion during and immediately following our political battles. But during the early sixties, we worked together for President Kennedy's programs and developed a mutual respect and some affection.

In May, O'Donnell came to my Washington apartment for breakfast and to talk about the campaign. He told me that he had come at Bob Kennedy's direction, with the explicit message that Kennedy had no animosity toward me and that his problem was solely with Lyndon Johnson. Ken said he hoped I would withdraw from the race, and I said, of course, that I couldn't. I also said that I understood that Bob couldn't either, but I assured Ken that he would have my total support if he were to get the nomination.

Kenny indicated that if Bob did not do well in California, he would pull out and support me. Whether this was still the case in June, less than a month later, I did not know, but I have no reason to doubt it, particularly in light of their views of Gene McCarthy. We agreed, in any case, that we ought to reassess the situation after the California primary.

Could Bob have gotten the nomination had he lived? Many journalists and some politicians have indicated that they think so. I think they are wrong. When we met head on in state convention fights (in Pennsylvania, Vermont, Idaho, and Iowa, among others), I won.[2] I have written elsewhere that his death had many effects on me and my campaign. But in the harsh terms of political fact, it had three practical consequences. First, his death had a demoralizing and depressing effect. Second, it caused a month's hiatus in my campaign; momentum lost was barely regained and only toward the end of the campaign. Third, a large share of the money pledged to me came from New York business leaders who feared and distrusted Bob. With his death, their interest in me waned.

Robert Kennedy had a great stake in the Democratic party, one he was not about to cast aside. He was a young man, and had he lived and not gotten the nomination, I believe, he would have been a willing and effective supporter. Had he lived and I won the nomination, I would have seemed still stronger, less the candidate of bosses, more my own man. With his support, I think I would have been elected President of the United States. Had he won the nomination, I would have supported him.

In 1948, when I was elected to the Senate from Minnesota, Eugene McCarthy had been elected to the House of Representatives. From 1958 to 1964, we both served in the Senate. Through all those years we often saw each other in Washington or in Minnesota, voted the same way on most issues, had mutual friends. We campaigned for each other. In 1956, he nominated me for Vice President at the Democratic National Convention in Chicago. In 1960, he was cochairman of my campaign committee for the Democratic nomination for President.

Still, we are very different in style, temperament, and interests. We like different kinds of people. Nevertheless, I always considered Gene a friend. I still do, knowing that he often ridiculed some of the things I did. But he does that to most people.

Basically, Gene disdains whatever peer group he is in. If he was teaching college students, he found most of his colleagues dull. When he was in the House, he grew tired of congressmen. In the Senate, he found few senators or senatorial duties that interested him.

So I was not surprised at a conversation late in 1967 in the Vice President's office in the Executive Office Building. He told me he intended to enter the primaries, challenging President Johnson. He spoke so casually, as he usually does, that I felt it was just sort of a lark on his part. I asked whether he had thought it through carefully, including the difficulties of unseating an incumbent President. He said, in essence, "Well, I don't have any feeling that I can win, but I don't like the Senate. I've lost interest in it, and I feel very strongly about the war. I guess the best way to show my feelings about it is to go on out and enter the primaries."

Up to that time, Gene had not been one of the Senate's leading doves. He'd voted for the Gulf of Tonkin resolution and for appropriations for Vietnam. His antagonism toward our Vietnam policy, so clearly stated later, in the fall of 1967 and 1968, had been vague and periodic.

But this change of mind and mood on the war was quite real. There are those who ascribe his efforts of 1968 in terms of pique and vindictiveness toward Lyndon Johnson. Gene is more vain and arrogant than his admirers wanted to admit, but I do not believe that the personal animosity he had for Johnson was a primary impetus in 1967 or 1968.

During the first half of 1968, Gene and I met from time to time, sometimes in my office, on occasion at my home. I tried to maintain cordial relations with him, all the while realizing that our relationship couldn't be as it once had been. I am not sure that Gene responded in kind, but he could have been much more difficult than he was.

In early August, two weeks before the convention, Gene said he didn't expect to get the nomination and that he would be able to come out for me sometime around the middle of September. I urged him to do it the night I got the nomination, if I did. Such a statement was a traditional thing to do, would have demonstrated unity and solidarity, and is what I would have done for him.

This tradition, like others, did not appeal to Gene, and he told me that he wouldn't be able to do that. He was afraid, he said, that his supporters would revolt, that they would turn on him. What he was saying in his own, indirect way—and he almost always worked indirectly—was that it would take a little time to bring his people around.

That didn't happen. After my nomination, some of his supporters came around on their own. If Gene tried to influence anyone to support me, I am not aware of it. First he wandered off to the Riviera. When he came back, he covered the World Series for *Life* magazine. Then there were his shifting "conditions" on what I should say about Vietnam. Finally Gene made a less-than-enthusiastic endorsement.

Would a more hearty and earlier endorsement have helped? I think it would have. He did have substantial support in several states—New Jersey, Ohio, Illinois, and surely California—where a united party working in my behalf might have changed the electoral outcome. Those states could have been won; all were lost. Particularly in California, had McCarthy campaigned early and hard for me and the Democratic party, he might have turned it.[3]

While Gene contended that the nature of his supporters prevented him from moving to support me quickly, I have found that real leaders can move many of their followers. As it was, I carried most of the heavy McCarthy areas, but this was a last-minute conversion, and partly an anti-Nixon vote. Had they been encouraged to early support or at least silence, I might have been able to function better and more effectively. Besides, early support can be contagious, and that's like compound interest for a banker.

There is no question that the movement surrounding McCarthy in 1968 was something special. In an atmosphere of bitterness toward Lyndon Johnson, of dismay at a continuing war, many young people, including some young professional and well-educated people of all ages, found the McCarthy banner an exciting one to follow. A sense of mission attracts good people into politics. McCarthy himself had come into elective office in such an atmosphere twenty years before.

Political parties are a kind of living organism. They need regular infusions of new blood and spirit. They try to slough off the old and worn out, but some of the old lingers, and some of the new is absorbed, some rejected. This has been the case throughout American history, but in my political lifetime it has surely been so: the young New Dealers around Franklin Roosevelt, many of the people attracted to the Henry Wallace campaign in 1948, clearly the excited people of the Stevenson campaign of 1952, and in 1960, Jack Kennedy stirred a whole generation of young people. On the Republican side, both Wendell Willkie in 1944 and Dwight Eisenhower in 1952 attracted new people.

Gene McCarthy and 1968 were made for each other. The students, almost two and a half times more in colleges and universities than in 1948, radicalized by years of sit-ins and demonstrations, affluent and mobile, rose in a great crusade.[4] But the McCarthy movement was not just the exuberance of youth. It moved across many age groups in many places. Tired of the war, bored with political rhetoric, they found in the new face, quiet voice, and subtle, enigmatic phrasing of Eugene McCarthy a leader worth following.

If the prime purpose of the McCarthy movement was to drive Lyndon Johnson from office and change the United States policy in Vietnam, it succeeded by half.

Domestically, there never was a main thrust to the McCarthy movement as it affected public policy. But McCarthy himself put up the stop, look, and listen sign on executive power—a signal Nixon failed to heed.[5] Politically, the movement did have some major consequences, primarily in accelerating changes within the Democratic party.

By 1968, there had been a generation of marked social change, if not real revolution, in the United States. Mark the beginnings where you will: 1948, when Strom Thurmond led the Dixiecrats out of the Democratic party, which then committed itself, in principle at least, to changes in race relations; 1947, when Jackie Robinson broke the color line in baseball. Or 1954, when the U. S. Supreme Court ruled in *Brown* vs. *Board of Education* that "separate, but equal" was not equal enough. There had been a decade of militancy and advocacy, of resistance and reaction, of marches and demonstrations, of pressure for jobs and equal accommodations, of hopes for better housing and better education.

Black anger, conservative hostility, liberal guilt and support stewed in a new melting pot amid mutterings from one side or the other: too little, too late—too much, too soon. And finally, 1968 had been a year, like no other, of death and riot and destruction.

And in that year a southern governor, George Wallace, demagogued his way into the hearts and minds of those who wanted simplistic answers to difficult problems, justifiably concerned about violence and crime in the streets and with less reason about job and neighborhood exclusivity.

When George Wallace spoke, he spoke especially to some lower- and middle-income Americans, factory workers, and rural citizens, to first- and second-generation Americans who felt resentful and threatened in virtually every aspect of their lives. In their view, their sons fought in Vietnam while "hippie, long-haired kids" of the seemingly well-to-do demonstrated and cursed and smoked marijuana; they worked hard for years, in the factories and mills, and now their seniority and jobs were in jeopardy because of favored treatment of blacks; and their homes, paid for over the years out of limited income, would be worthless because of blacks moving onto their block. And finally "crime" and "black" got tied together, so that every threat to their property or their persons appeared to be a black threat.

And so in precinct after precinct, in Pittsburgh, in Cincinnati, in Cleveland, in Toledo, in Akron, in Jersey City and Los Angeles, Wallace gained support that belonged, by habit and tradition if not ideology, to the Democrats.

Polls taken in September and early October by the labor movement in some northern industrial and border states had as much as 35 and 40 per cent of the union members intending to vote for Wallace. I remember going through a Ford plant in Flint, Michigan, where man after man on the assembly line wore a paper Wallace hat modeled after the American Legion cap. Some were friendly enough under the circumstances, but more than a few exuded the hate I found on right and left that year.

There are those who look back at the 1968 election and announce that the old liberal-labor alliance is dead, that labor can no longer produce its bloc vote.[6] Like others, that death has been announced inaccurately, or at least prematurely. Intensive and expensive effort by the AFL-CIO Committee on Political Education, the United Auto Workers, and the Machinists Union brought back a large share of their membership.

One stumbling block in this effort, for both the international union leadership and me, was understandable. Local union leaders, whose livelihood depended on being elected, could see that a large number of their members were for Wallace. Then they looked to the public opinion polls, which said the Humphrey-Muskie ticket was going to be whipped badly. They assumed that they, too, would lose in their next union election if they got aggressive in our behalf.

What I did, therefore, was to call in union leaders in each community I visited, giving them a heart-to-heart pep talk. "The difference between defeat and victory is quite possibly in your hands. With your help, Ed Muskie and I can win. Without it, we can't."

I meant what I said, and most of my listeners believed me. Those who did were then willing to stand up and fight for us, often, as I have said, at great risk to their personal careers. Their courage was matched by that of their international union leadership. If there had been a string of locals where the leadership was overturned, the tide might well have struck also at the international presidents and staffs. My trade union friends stood firm when a lot of my liberal, former ADA colleagues and some Democratic politicians ran for cover.

While Wallace got slightly more votes than predicted in the early months of 1968, his total was considerably less than his high point, which had come in September.[7] Had we, in conjunction with the labor movement, been as successful in Ohio and New Jersey as the labor movement had been elsewhere, we might have carried those states and thrown the election into the House of Representatives.

But the tragedy for our campaign resulting from the Wallace incursion was not simply the loss of votes; it was the atmosphere of heightened hostility and anger in the country, the irritability and the grating antagonisms.

35. "I GATHER YOU ARE NOT ASKING MY ADVICE"

The Republican convention looked like a tranquil interlude in the chaos, riots, killings, fighting, crime, and war—all identified with Democrats—that filled the year 1968.

Their convention was held in the attractive surroundings of Miami Beach—a resort city with clean, gleaming buildings, with waterways and ships and boats, expensive hotels and swimming pools, and palm trees and beautiful girls.

Well covered by television, the convention had just enough activity to make it interesting, with Reagan forces showing some life and with the Rockefeller forces coming down with all the fanfare that good public relations can stir up, but differences muted and insignificant, draped in party unity and political pleasantness.

Enter Richard Nixon, looking cool, confident, everything under control. It was a convention proceeding according to script, a little mechanical, a little dull, but the people looked good, the place looked good, and the politics seemed decent. For the larger American public, it was life as they thought it should be—a public function in which there were no protesters or demonstrators or hippies or angry blacks, in which argument was conducted politely and politics seemed rational.[1] As that convention soporifically dominated the news and television for a week, it tended to mollify and tranquilize the American people.

The only surprises were the nomination of Spiro Agnew, governor of Maryland, and the role of Strom Thurmond. Agnew, with a brief and uninspired career in public office, was a bewildering choice except in the narrowest of political terms.

Politics is full of ironies, and I suppose I, better than most, should understand how they come to be, but the moment when Mayor John Lindsay of New York, the Republican liberal soon to be Democrat, nominated Governor Spiro Agnew of Maryland, the Republican unknown, deserves, without question, a special place in political history.

Strom Thurmond, once Democrat, then Dixiecrat, now Republican, and one of the physically strong men of his age in the Senate, became Nixon's emissary to the South. His apparent veto power led to the exclusion of more liberal and logical vice-presidential candidates and to the selection of Agnew. It was a price of some dimension for Nixon to pay, but from his point of view probably worthwhile, since it prevented the conservative bloc in the South from moving to anyone else. The Reagan excursion into the South was futile. Thurmond led the southern bloc quietly into the Nixon camp.

The Rockefeller forces had no place to go either. Nixon had taken liberal enough public positions to make it comfortable for the eastern liberal Republican wing, and Rockefeller did not dare stand aside doing nothing, as he had done in the 1964, Goldwater, election. He had invested too much of himself and his status as political leader and public servant to turn his back on the Republican party. Had he done so, he would have been finished as a Republican leader.[2]

So you had the Republican right and left converging predictably, naturally, on the Nixon center. His nomination, the convention climax, was excellently managed.

Nixon looked presidential. His acceptance speech was superbly done. The substance of the speech made me think he had been reading carefully some of the stuff we'd been saying. His technique was good and the camera work as good as I have ever seen in an event like that. With Agnew and Thurmond tying down the conservative vote, the speech incorporated what was moderately liberal and progressive in much of the Democratic rhetoric of 1968. It was good political workmanship and deserved the respect it has received from the architects and engineers of political campaigns.

Particularly in light of what followed at the Democratic convention and the early part of our campaign, the first days following the Republican convention were also smoothly programmed. Nixon exuded a new sense of confidence, husbanding his energy and resources, not moving until every detail was worked out.

But here is where the timing of a convention means so much. The Republican Convention was in July, the Democratic Convention in the last week of August. Those precious five weeks are invaluable to any candidate, particularly when there is money available for TV and radio to keep up the tempo of the convention build-up. After all, a candidate under normal circumstances ought to come out of a convention with increased strength. Indeed, Nixon did.

He was able to use his time as he wished: organizing, planning, raising money, and healing whatever wounds there were in the Republican party by calling in party leaders. He was able to spend time wooing, or at least talking to, Nelson Rockefeller, John Lindsay, George Romney, and Ronald Reagan, among others. He was able to visit with a number of governors. He was able to do all of this without rushing.

Nixon's use of television following the convention was effective, too. By using excerpts from his acceptance speech, well edited, striking a telling theme of uniting the country, a theme of working together, he made an impression that was helpful: considered, thoughtful, not contentious, at the same time buying himself time to do the things he had to do.

Coming after the Johnson period, in which the President's nature and particularly the way the press had unmercifully depicted him provided a stark comparison, Nixon looked good. What followed at the Democratic convention and in the early weeks of my hectic campaign made him look even better.

The Democratic convention in 1968 would have been a difficult one anywhere. Chicago was just the worst possible place for it. The site was picked by President Johnson when he thought he would be the candidate again. The site-selection committee of the Democratic National Committee simply ratified the decision, confirming what had already been worked out between Richard Daley and the President.

Later, when other people, including me, urged the President

to help move the convention from Chicago to Miami, he refused. He had given his word to Daley and he wasn't going to back down.

There were good reasons to change. (And there were people prepared to pay off all the Chicago costs and to move us to Miami.) There were a number of strikes—electricians, telephone workers, and, the week before the convention, taxi drivers. Easy and rapid communication is terribly important in a convention situation, in which rumors, problems, decisions have to be dealt with quickly. Four years earlier in Atlantic City, working jointly with Gene McCarthy, we had a switchboard with dozens of lines. In 1968, battling for the presidential nomination, we had three or four lines and no way to connect easily with our people working in other locations.

And then there were the problems of the media—particularly radio and TV. Strikes made their lives, professionally and personally, much more difficult and prevented some live coverage. Further, had they been able to stay in Miami Beach with their equipment, it would have saved the three networks and the smaller groups hundreds of thousands of dollars. If some of us felt that they overreacted to the developing situation, it must be admitted that they had a number of unnecessary impediments.

If the general impression of what was coming was bad, my specific view was made even worse by detailed reports of meetings of such SDS radical factions as the Weathermen. As reported by people at those meetings, the plans were so specific that I had to consider them real, particularly since they involved not only me, but my family.

I was prepared to take a certain amount of verbal abuse, but the idea of embarrassment or physical harm to Muriel and my children enraged me. The plans began with talk of dousing Muriel with red paint to symbolize the blood of the war. Then there was talk of throwing human excrement on her and the kids, and finally serious discussion of kidnaping one of the children.* When you're involved in the most democratic process in the world leading to the selection of a head of state, it is unsettling, at the least, to contemplate injury or mayhem to your family as a result of your involvement.

* We found this out through Secret Service reports.

The reports kept coming. More meetings in Chicago led by professional radicals, not just American youngsters who deplored the war but others, who hated the whole system. Their intention was to organize local blacks in protest, stirring racial strife, and then to organize the students for a confrontation with the police. Expect violence not just in the streets, but directed at the convention hall.

Tensions increased, positions hardened. All of us in a maddening circle of action, and inaction, reaction. Pictures and words—revolution, barbed wire, threats, armed camp, fortress, prison—all of this created an atmosphere of fear, frustration, anxiety, and hatred. It played into the hands of the organizers of violence, it served no one else well, neither the Democrats nor the truly peaceful demonstrators for peace.†

Thousands of young people came to Chicago with no intention of violence, no intent to cause bloody disruption, no intention except to show their deep feelings about the war. But there were revolutionaries and anarchists among them, not many, but a few, enough, who were capable and determined to play with aroused emotions, to escalate their own war, and manipulate a situation in which a sharp confrontation with the police was inevitable.

(The irony is that saying so made a political person a fascist in many young people's eyes. To be sufficiently liberal, you had to deny the facts.)

That there was police brutality is also a fact that cannot be denied. Some police were new recruits and not well trained for riot duty or how to handle militant political demonstrations. Most had been on duty many hours that day and on extended shifts in the preceding days. All were up-tight—tired or tense. Most of the police, like most of the demonstrators, were doing their "thing"—theirs being to keep order. Some of the police came to those lines filled with anger and disgust, wearing Wallace for

† Jerry Rubin, one of the Chicago Seven, said in March 1976, "I was secretly rooting for the prosecution . . . because the prosecution was right all along." He said further, we were "guilty as hell." Rubin said, we "made our demands so outrageous because we wanted the city to deny us what we were asking.

"We did all of this with one purpose in mind—to make the city react as if it was a police state and to focus the attention of the whole world on us."

President pins and sharing the view that they were dealing with spoiled kids with advantages neither they nor their own children had. The clash was a microcosm of the whole year in our whole society.

The members of that society who weren't in Chicago saw those events amplified and magnified by an outraged and angry press.[3]

At such a point, the press, and particularly a television crew, become more than reporters of an event. They become a *part* of the event, inadvertently helping to increase the passions, causing even the docile to smile and wave, the fact of their presence encouraging the agitated to jump and scream. TV has its own built-in activator, and when the hot coals of protest and dissent are already present and mobilized, bringing in a TV camera is like adding gasoline.

When the police, lumping together all targets of their distemper, roughed up some members of the press, things got even worse. The reporting lost, at least temporarily, whatever objectivity it should have had. A viewer could only assume that either revolution or fascism had come to the heartland of America.

And one man, Chicago's Mayor Richard Daley, was pictured as the prime culprit. Whatever he did looked wrong on television. No villain in soap opera or Western was so type-cast. As a result, it was easy to use Richard Daley as the scapegoat for all the troubles of Chicago. It was particularly desirable if you wanted to parade your "liberalism," as some convention speakers did.

Daley was only grudgingly for me for President, but I cannot even now picture him as a petty tyrant, as people did then and have since.

Richard Daley may be a number of things, but he does not seem to me an evil man. He has been an effective mayor of the dynamic city he loves. Most people find it hard to think of him as sentimental, but he is about his city. Daley loves Chicago in a way most of us simply cannot comprehend. The threats, the chaos, the ugliness, the destruction moved him, I am sure, to a kind of primitive hostility toward those who, in his eyes, defiled his city.

It is true, and sad, that decent young people expressing their democratic right to dissent were beaten and injured needlessly and sometimes brutally. The event left one more hideous stain on American politics. It is also true that the police were provoked in an environment created in large part by a few people whose threats, plotting, and determination to wreck the Democratic convention were almost as central to the havoc in Grant Park as the billy clubs.

I repeat this simply because so much of my post-Chicago time was spent talking to people who saw only one side or the other. Passion blinds. This is not an insight I invented. But it blinds the television eye as it does the human eye, and few people were able to see the many important changes taking place in the convention hall itself.

While chaos reigned, we hoped still to be able to write a platform that would satisfy not only my supporters, but also the responsible elements who had opposed me and supported either Bob Kennedy or Gene McCarthy. We tried to work out a plank on Vietnam that would not betray the nation's commitments or the Administration's and yet would offer a genuine olive branch to its rational critics. There were certain people who could not be placated, and we had no intention of trying. There were some positions we could not and would not take. But there seemed sufficient middle ground, and we set to work with some of the Kennedy people. I had asked David Ginsberg, a Washington attorney and friend, to work as my man in Chicago on platform matters.[4]

On Saturday, Ginsberg had met with Charlie Murphy, my old friend from the Truman days and now an adviser to Lyndon Johnson. Charlie took sharp issue with some of the language on bombing, troop withdrawal, and future policies. But they worked out an acceptable language. Then Ted Sorensen met with the McCarthy people and asked, "What is it that Gene McCarthy wants?" David felt that they found language that substantially met the spirit and mood of McCarthy's demands without abandoning my own views.

I spent the day in my office in Washington, and Ginsberg reached me there, dictating the contents of the resolution to me. I took it down in longhand, checking the language carefully. We made a few changes, and I then told him I intended to call Dean

Rusk, Walt Rostow, and several others to read them the text. I had previously talked to President Johnson about the platform, and he had said that on matters relating to Vietnam I should "just keep in touch with Dean Rusk." I reached Secretary of State Rusk on the phone and we went over it together. He made one or two suggestions I readily accepted and he said, in effect, "It isn't all we'd like, but under the circumstances, it will do. It's a constructive, sensible plank. We can live with this, Hubert."

I then called Walt Rostow. In order not to prejudice him, I did not say that I had talked to Rusk. Rostow accepted the plank without a change. He said he thought it sounded fine.

Then I talked to several other people, including George Meany, indicating only that this was language being talked about. I said that I wanted to talk to a few close friends to get their points of view. Not one of the people I talked to objected to the plank. I called Ginsberg back, said, "Go ahead. It meets with everybody's approval. Let's go with it."

I was pleased with such consensus. Ken O'Donnell had worked on it. Ted Sorensen and Fred Dutton had worked on it. Hale Boggs had seen it. In short, at least some Johnson, Kennedy, and Humphrey people had come to a common understanding.

About 80 per cent of the McCarthy demands were directly met; the text had been cleared with State and Defense; Ginsberg had talked to virtually every member of the platform committee and had checked it with Larry O'Brien.

It appeared that we had been able to work together with disparate groups in the convention on the most complex, delicate question and come to an agreement, probably leaving only a small group of hard-line McCarthy people in opposition.

By the time I got to Chicago on Sunday night, there were the first audible rumbles from the ranch in Texas. The President didn't like the platform.

Ginsberg called the ranch and talked to Jim Jones about two or three minor points that Charlie Murphy found difficult to accept. The President's voice could be heard clearly in the background and it grew louder and more angry, although the discussion was really more on nuances than substance.

On Monday morning, we proceeded to clear the plank with

half a dozen southern governors, including John Connally and John McKeithen of Louisiana. No changes were proposed.

The next morning, I got a phone call from presidential aide Marvin Watson, who had come to Chicago. Because my suite was so well covered by press, I went to see him. He told me that the President didn't like the plank. "Well, Marvin," I said, "I cleared this with the Secretary of State, and I've cleared it with Walt Rostow." Marvin said, "That doesn't make any difference. It's been looked over again and it just doesn't meet with the President's approval."

This was an outrageous turn of events, and I returned to my hotel upset and angry. Since I did not know even then what the President wanted, I called him. His first admonition was simple: "I don't want you to tell anybody that you're clearing any of these things with me." There was not much danger of that. I said, "I understand that you or some of your people are not pleased with this plank." He said, "We're not." I said, "Dean Rusk approved it." The President: "That's not the way I hear it." I said, "Well, he did, and so did Walt Rostow." The President made his position clear: "Well, this plank just undercuts our whole policy and, by God, the Democratic party ought not to be doing that to me and you ought not to be doing it; you've been a part of this policy."

In the gentlest words I could muster, I told the President that I thought the plank was acceptable and not offensive. I said again that I had read it and discussed it with both Rusk and Rostow and that I was sorry he now felt as he did. But he was immovable. He would have no part of it. When I said, "Well, Mr. President, we'll have to do the best we can. Possibly we can get something that is acceptable, but I'm afraid we're going to have serious troubles here," we concluded the conversation.

I met then with my people and told them I thought we ought to stick with the plank as it had been written and worked out with O'Donnell, Sorensen, Dutton, and others. If I had had any objection to it, I had had the opportunity to say so. Having talked to Rusk and Rostow and having given my blessing, I felt an obligation to stick with it.

Then Hale Boggs arrived. The congressman's position was clear and also immovable. If the President would not accept the plank, then he, as chairman of the Platform Committee, would resist it, sending out the word that the plank was unacceptable.

Our choice was to stand and fight the President's emissaries or to give in to the inevitable. Now I know, in retrospect, that I should have stood my ground. I told our people I was still for the plank, but I didn't put up a real fight. That was a mistake. I am not sure it would have made any difference in the election, but once we had arrived at that point, at some consensus with the Kennedy people, I should not have yielded.

Having said that, I feel it is highly questionable whether I could have succeeded. President Johnson, enraged, would have become a formidable foe, causing troubles that I could probably not have overcome.

Some of my unfailing crop of critics failed to understand, as I have said earlier, that the Vice President has very few guns in a battle with the presidential artillery. He can be shot down before he takes off. During those summer and fall months right up to the election, I always had the problem of how much I could say that varied from administration policy even if only in tone and detail and not in basic principle or substance without having the President turn on me angrily, and publicly, as he did on several occasions privately.

Thursday morning, I had to make the final decision on a vice-presidential running mate. As early as April I had thought that Ed Muskie would be my choice, but that morning I was still considering Governor Richard Hughes of New Jersey, Terry Sanford of North Carolina, and Fred Harris of Oklahoma.[5] It was not any easy decision. Each man had some excellent qualifications—some political, some in terms of potential contribution to the country.

Fred Harris had some special claims. He had been a neighbor and friend of Bobby Kennedy and been wooed ardently by the Kennedy forces. He and his wife, LaDonna, had been flown up to Hyannis Port in the *Caroline* as part of the Kennedy effort to cement support. But Fred and LaDonna had remained staunchly loyal to me.

Richard Hughes was another friend who had been frequently urged on me, more than either Fred or Ed Muskie. He was less glittering than Fred, but a substantial, though frequently underestimated, governor of a state I would need to carry if I would become President. I seriously considered him not simply for his state and for other political values, but for personal qualities I found attractive: political courage, a liberal and humane view of government. Once again, as with the Harrises, he and his wife, Betty, had been kind and close to Muriel and me.

Terry Sanford had served as the chairman of my citizens committees. He had a splendid progressive record as a young governor of North Carolina. He, like Harris, had a strong following among young people.

Finally, however, I went back to my earlier inclination to go with Muskie. I had watched him carefully in the Senate. He was thorough as well as bright. He was committed to liberal goals and he worked sensibly toward them. Ed had integrity and good judgment beyond the average. I liked him as a man and as a politician.

Since he had relatively few advocates, coming as he did from a small state, I started early to prepare the way for my ultimate decision if it should be for Muskie. One of the tasks of a political leader is, after all, to set the stage for decisions he wishes to make. I started out, in the best (or worst) Washington tradition, of leaking the idea that he might be the candidate for Vice President. Then, more overtly, I would ask people what they thought of him, tell them that I was thinking seriously of him, listing his important qualities. Most of the evaluations from those I talked to were favorable. There were few negative comments, thus confirming my own views.

Once I had made up my mind, and this was one decision that was mine and mine alone, I called a number of people as a courtesy.[6] Then I called President Johnson. He was not for Muskie. He was for Terry Sanford of North Carolina or, if not Sanford, Carl Sanders of Georgia or Richard Hughes. When I told him I thought it would be Ed Muskie, he said, "Well, that's your decision and I hope you're right. He's a good senator, but I don't know what political good this can do you." He had in mind someone who could help me in the South or the border states.

What I had in mind was radical, perhaps: having a competent, able man who could do a good job as President. Particularly in light of Nixon's selection of Agnew, what I needed was quality, character, ability, not some kind of compromise for geography or ideology.

I have never regretted for a single minute my decision to select Ed Muskie. Before Ed's nomination, he was a good United
States senator, well respected in his own area but without any
significant national following. By the end of the campaign he
was a national figure. Muskie was clearly an asset to the ticket.

Had I selected someone else, one who was the least bit shop-
worn, or tried to balance geography or ideology, the press, anything but friendly just then, would have worked that selection
over unmercifully. As it was, Muskie was not identified with the
Johnson administration or with the Vietnam War. He was relatively new on the national scene and therefore got a great deal of
attention. He did well on the campus, and he quickly became a
hero to columnists and other press.

This pleased me, even though it implicitly measured him more
favorably than me. But I had chosen him, knowing how special
he was, anticipating the favorable public reaction. If I had been
afraid of that kind of competition, I would have found a lesser
man.

I intended to make the Vice President's office what I thought it
should be, giving the Vice President responsibilities befitting his
talent and experience. I would have divided up the work of the
executive branch in a way that hasn't been done in this century.

Ed Muskie and I knew how the federal government acted and
reacted; we understood its pressure points and powers. We
would have been able to make it work. Muskie, as Vice President, would have co-ordinated our domestic programs, particularly those relating to our urban centers, as chairman of a domestic development council. The realities of power get through to
people in the bureaucracy and in the legislative branches. I
would have invested authority in Muskie sufficient to do the job.
I would have made it clear, beyond question, that day-to-day operations as well as long-term domestic policy were to clear first
with the Vice President. He would, of course, have been responsible to me; he would have cleared many basic decisions with me
or been so intimately acquainted with my thinking that he could
have safely acted, himself. There are those, I am sure, who doubt
that this kind of delegation of authority is possible. History is on
their side. My own experience may deny its possibility. But I
think it might succeed if there is complete trust and no concern
on the part of the President that he is going to be upstaged. In

an administration in which nothing much is being tried or done, it doesn't make much difference. But where government is moving ahead in our complicated time, it is crucial for a President to have that kind of prestigious assistance.

The role of the Vice President in international affairs is more complicated and difficult. If he is so deeply and directly involved in domestic policy and administration as I would have him, he is not as free to be involved in international questions. But that is all right. The purpose of his domestic involvement is to free the President from enough pressure at home to do creative things in foreign affairs. Responsibility here ought not to be divided, but a Vice President, smart and tuned to the President's thoughts, can perform important functions as a domestic and occasionally international ambassador at large.

Ed and I were prepared to move as a team to get our priorities straightened out, and most importantly we were agreed on finding a solution to the Vietnam War. We would have gotten out of Indochina.

During the day on Thursday, amid calls and meetings, we worked on my acceptance speech. A number of my staff and friends—Jack Valenti, Ted Van Dyk, John Stewart, Max Kampelman, Gus Tyler—produced a final draft that I didn't like at all.

The street demonstrations, the police, the tumult and dissension in the convention, the protesters—all of this created a situation that required a very special kind of acceptance message. What had been prepared before the convention just wasn't right for what was happening. I had to tell my speech writers that what we had was not good enough.

So I began in the afternoon to dictate to my two personal secretaries, Vi Williams[7] and Marsha Greenwood. I'd dictate to one, and while she'd go type, I'd dictate to the other. We alternated right up to the time we had to leave for the convention hall.

The tension increased as reports kept coming that there might be a walkout, some sort of demonstration, when I arose to accept the nomination. On a day when I might have been able to relax some and savor the moment, the strain continued. Here was a great day in my life, and yet it might be torn by violence, disorder, and repudiation. It was a bleak prospect.

We arrived at the Stockyards, through checkpoints and barbed wire, without incident.

Finally it was time. I moved to the podium, my moment of triumph. Faces looking up, the hall filled, the color, the lights, the thirteen thousand people, mostly cheering, some possibly ready to embarrass me. (Where are they? I thought. New York back there. California.) Signs waving. The noise level building. And the TV cameras going to carry what I have to say to 20 million Americans.

I have never had a more difficult assignment. It tested every nerve in my body, and it tested my will, my courage, and my capacity to overcome crisis and difficulty, to try to sway an audience to my side, to at least calm the fears of some, fortify the hopes of others, and hold a party together that was on the verge of an explosion that would have fractured it for a long, long time.

Had I wavered, the campaign might have disintegrated almost before it began. I tried to move and speak with assurance, dealing as best I could with the battles outside the convention itself: "One cannot help but reflect the deep sadness we've felt over the troubles and violence which have erupted regularly and tragically in the streets of this great city, and for the personal injuries that occurred." I moved quickly on to the prayer of St. Francis of Assisi:

> "Where there is hatred, let me sow love;
> Where there is injury, pardon;
> Where there is doubt, faith;
> Where there is despair, hope;
> Where there is darkness, light."

It is a prayer I have liked for many years, and it seemed to capture the attention of the audience.‡ Within a short time, they were responding. The first time they came to their feet during

‡ One of my staff members thought the prayer inappropriate. Each time I put it in a draft, he would take it out. As I rode to the convention hall, I discovered he had done it again—it was omitted from my final dictation. I finally called the Chicago Public Library on the car phone and had them dictate it to me.

the speech, I knew I was safe. As I talked about a new day for America, I thought I also saw signs of hope for the future of our party and the candidacy of Ed Muskie and myself.

Through most of my life, even when I have spoken on controversial subjects before hostile audiences, listeners have shown their animosity in the conventional ways: withheld applause, critical or disbelieving questions, an occasional boo. All of that, however, was within certain social bounds of decorum.

But discussions during the Vietnam period understandably went far beyond those bounds. Feelings were so intense that their demonstration was loud, personal, and incessant.

I had decided early that I could not run away from the protest. I had to stand up, fight back, and try to control the situation. That was neither pleasant nor easy. At Stanford University, the protest crowd outside the hall where I spoke was belligerent and in an ugly mood. The Secret Service and the local police urged me to change my plans for walking to my car, which was parked some distance away. I refused, and walked with as much dignity as I could through the shouting, pushing crowd. Human excrement was thrown, hitting the Secret Service men but not me.

Quite apart from the question of whether I was right or wrong on the war, the protests distressed me on another level, too. All I had ever been as a liberal spokesman seemed lost, all that I had acomplished in significant programs was ignored. I felt robbed of my personal history.

One day at Kent State, a panel of students questioned me. A young, articulate black man named Robert Pickett challenged my credentials and commitment to civil rights, asking in effect what I had ever done for black people. I was shocked by his attack, and spoke with some feeling about my career. At the end of the meeting, he came over to me and asked if he could join my campaign staff. I was pleased to have him not only for his obvious abilities but as a symbol for myself that I still carried a message for young people. It was an important psychological moment for me.[8]

Friday, after a press conference announcing new officers of the national committee, it was home to Waverly, Minnesota, as the Democratic nominee for President. In 1952, I had been the favorite-son candidate of the Minnesota delegation. In 1956, I had made a serious effort to become the vice-presidential candidate with Adlai Stevenson. In 1960, I had made a brief but determined run at the nomination in the primaries. Having lost all of those, I had given up my hopes for higher office until Lyndon Johnson picked me for the vice-presidential nomination in 1964. I was now the nominee for President. Yet, I knew I was behind. I had to begin to catch up, and fast.*

My immediate need was for a single campaign manager to replace the preconvention diffused leadership. I persuaded Larry O'Brien to take over. He had become a close friend, I liked him, he had the Kennedy connection, and he was a pro. By the time the convention was over, however, I doubt he really believed I could win. His enthusiasm seemed bruised, if not crushed.

He brought in another top professional, Joseph Napolitan, who was a political-campaign consultant. The two of them, Orville Freeman, Max Kampelman, Bill Connell, Ira Kapenstein (another associate of O'Brien's), Ted Van Dyk, Norman Sherman, and I met at Waverly to plan the campaign. The quiet lake and the still woods were so different from Chicago that our intense political talk seemed almost a violation of nature. We hastily drew up what plans we could in those two days. The convention had been so late that there was no time for healing the wounds, planning the finances, organizing the campaign, or preparing for the campaign.

The campaign started in Philadelphia. We stumbled through too thin crowds, with too little time for advance work and preparation. The press was irritated when phones or tables were not where they were supposed to be, and became more irritated when Frank Rizzo, then Philadelphia police commissioner, disdainfully gave them an inflated crowd estimate.

Partially, the cause of our bad beginning was bringing on too

---

* The 1968 Democratic convention was set by Lyndon Johnson to coincide with his birthday, on August 27. For an incumbent President, late is fine. For a non-incumbent it is awful. My nomination came later than any other Democratic non-incumbent's nomination during this century. I desperately needed time to heal wounds, build party organization, raise money, outline our advertising—in short, to build a tightly knit campaign. I had lost the month of August, and the campaign started on Labor Day, in September.

many new people too quickly who had too little knowledge of the working politics of the Democratic party and the country. But we had no other choice. The day the convention was over, the battle began.

I have already touched on the disarray within the Democratic party through the primary period. My nomination did not solve the problem. With a few exceptions, the Democratic party did not campaign for me with much enthusiasm until the very last days of the campaign. It was difficult to get anyone to really work and talk for the national ticket. Party leaders would be on hand, usually when I'd come to their city, but sometimes they were scarce, and after I left there was no real work done. The lack of enthusiasm on the part of governors and congressmen and others hurt us.

This disinterest was related directly to how we stacked up in the polls, which poses the question as to the effect of polling on a campaign. I think it had a tremendous effect. When those polls kept saying I was ten to fifteen points behind Nixon, it was politically predictable that many local Democratic officeholders would take care of themselves and forget about the Democratic nominees for President and Vice President. When, later, those polls began to show that we were closing the gap and moving up fast, we couldn't find space in our cars or on our stands for Democratic office seekers. They were hanging on and coming aboard. They were all with us then. But that was the last ten days of the campaign. What we needed were people who really went out front for us from the beginning.[9]

Among the many days of struggle and disappointment, one wonderful night stands out. I had gone to Detroit to address its Economic Club, an association of many of the community's business leaders. The meeting went more than well. I handled the questions briefly and persuasively, and the audience and press reflected what I felt.

When that meeting was over, I moved over to a nearby room in the same building, where dozens of black ministers had gathered. We had not asked them to meet; they had come at their own expense and because some of their own leaders had asked for the meeting. When I arrived, they treated me not as the Vice President, not as the candidate, but as a "brother."

There was electricity in the air, a mood of revival-meeting joy, and as I spoke, cries of "Amen!" rang out. At one point, the plate was passed, and this very special congregation donated several thousand dollars to my campaign. When the meeting was about to close, we joined hands on the podium and with our bodies swaying together we sang "We Shall Overcome" and "The Battle Hymn of the Republic." It was a wonderfully moving experience. Nevertheless, we lacked both time and enthusiastic support from too many powerful politicians. New Jersey, for example, was lost because of dissension in the Democratic ranks there and the feeling that Humphrey-Muskie just couldn't win. When I went there, it was often difficult to find any of the Democratic officeholders. Governor Hughes was always with me, trying to be helpful. He was a loyal, good man. But his organization was not delivering, a fact that was perfectly obvious every time I went there.

A similar situation existed in Illinois. I felt certain that we could win that state, too. As it was, everyone said things would come out all right in New Jersey and that we would lose Illinois regardless of what we did. Yet, two weeks before the election, a Lou Harris Poll showed me within a couple of points of winning in Illinois. We put together a trip into downstate Illinois—Rockford, Peoria, and Springfield—where we had friendly and large crowds.

We had written Illinois off too soon, and so apparently had Mayor Daley and his lieutenants. There was really no enthusiasm for us when I went among the political leaders. But when I went into Illinois, I found the people enthusiastic. Had we been there earlier, we would have carried it.

Virtually everywhere, Democratic leaders failed to accept the challenge. They never caught up to the voters. They thought we were beaten, and when it looks as if the head of the ticket can't win, people running for other offices take care of themselves.

I saw this in California, particularly in the Senate race, in which Alan Cranston had a substantial lead in his poll, some ten or twelve percentage points. As I was leaving for Los Angeles one day, I asked Alan to step inside the men's room in the airport terminal. I said, "Alan, you have your campaign won. Now

Muskie and I need your help. We aren't asking for glowing praise or lavish endorsements—just please mention our *names*."

The fact was that, in California and other areas, the names of Humphrey and Muskie were conspicuous by their absence from locally printed campaign literature as well as local radio and TV political ads. I appealed to Alan as a loyal Democrat, and he did some work on our behalf. But it was too late.

Seattle was a turning point in the campaign. For the first time, we had an overflow house filled with spirit. Seattle is what I had felt was coming. It's the blood and guts of a campaign. People moving you. You moving people. I looked out from the stage of the civic auditorium at the smiling faces, the noise, the political signs. The hall was packed. Many others, outside, were trying to get in.

But up in the balcony about one hundred protesters sat chanting, jeering, waving signs, amplifying their chants through a bull horn. Sometimes, on other occasions, the speakers who preceded me could handle the protesters in some fashion, so that by the time I took the microphone they were under control. But, that night, it didn't work. Both Gene Barry and Bill Dana, skilled show business professionals, tried. When I got up to speak, the small but noisy group was still at it. I watched the crowd's enthusiasm drain away, furious with the antics of the protesters. It was a replay of so many days that summer and fall. They would not let me speak. Finally, the local police moved in, quietly and with as little force as possible, to move out the protesters. The television cameras pivoted and turned away from the stage in a co-ordinated effort worthy of the Rockettes. We all watched—cameras, I, the guests on the stage, the fifteen thousand people—and the meeting died, recorded on film for the world to see.

In the balcony near the protesters were several TV correspondents. One, David Schoumacher then of CBS, who came to us from the McCarthy campaign, where he had been not only reporter but participant, turned to his camera crew on the floor and made the gesture, tips of thumb and forefinger together in a circle, that everything was fine. The pleasure in his face brought only sadness to mine.

I went back to my hotel room disappointed, angry, depressed.

Late at night, when guests had gone, I sat with some of my staff trying to make sense of it all. By two o'clock in the morning, as I listened and sometimes talked, my mind had sorted out my emotions. I was tired. I felt no one but my family and me was working. Muriel had consistently done well on television and in her interviews. As we had grown older she had grown more sure of herself in public and she had grown more photogenic. Her warmth and her decency, her compassion and her sincerity came through. My children were traveling the country and with their spouses doing an excellent job of campaigning.

I sipped a glass of beer and said to my staff: "I'm probably going to lose this election. Not much we do seems to come out right. But win or lose, I'm going to speak my mind, and I'm going to fight. I'm not going to be denied the right to be heard and I'm going to say what I feel."

I look back with both pride and disappointment in the campaign from that time on. I am proud that I said what I felt was right and true on the race question—both in the North and the South—and on fiscal policies and on international affairs.

I have no regret that I said what I thought, trying to deal with complex issues, but I have had time to think about three topics that Richard Nixon and I handled much differently from each other.

I went to the South and refused to play the cheap politics of saying we would slow down desegregation. I had no "secret plan" to get us out of Vietnam. I refused to play games with the oil industry on the oil depletion allowance. (A small group of oil men came to see me at Waverly one day. I assumed they had come to talk about contributing. I did not understand that they had come to bargain. We were broke and needed their money, but I said that no tax reform bill ought to pass without substantially reducing the oil depletion allowance. I kept my honor. They kept their money.)

I am disappointed that so much of the substantive material—developed by many bright and creative people around me—was lost in the noise and shouting of demonstrators, the inevitable static of a campaign, the understandable emphasis on the war.

I slept fitfully, the sounds of the bull horn and protesters not far out of my consciousness. But I awoke the next morning refreshed, my mind clearer than ever about what I must do. I looked forward to a relatively quiet Sunday, during which I could work on a speech on Vietnam to be televised from Salt Lake City on Monday.

For weeks, I had delayed a definitive statement, which my campaign badly needed. Virtually any statement that differed even a hair from Administration policy would have been played as a break with Johnson and could have jeopardized the Paris peace talks. I could not do that. Now, the chief negotiator, Averell Harriman, no longer raised that objection, having, I suppose, lost heart himself that the negotiations would really succeed. In any case, without his objection my dilemma was solved.

I could do what was long overdue: tell the American people what I proposed to do on Vietnam if elected. I could speak out without damaging negotiations.

Ted Van Dyk appeared with a handful of draft speeches, and he and I and Norman Sherman sat in a dining alcove in the suite talking about the various suggestions.[10] The major draft had been done by George Ball, who had been of immense help throughout the campaign. He had been in frequent contact with Averell Harriman in Paris. I depended on him for advice and counsel, recalling his independence and wisdom on the war in earlier arguments within the Adminstration.

Van Dyk showed me a telegram from Larry O'Brien that said in effect, "Ball speech a disaster." It was not that, but George had indeed emphasized Europe and its meaning in foreign relations, hoping to provide a broader context for whatever I said on Vietnam. O'Brien felt, probably correctly, that it would look like I was weaseling and not dealing directly with the central problem.

None of the drafts seemed quite right, and I had already decided in general terms what I wanted to say. Van Dyk and I reviewed my thoughts and I told him to draft a new speech. Using a task-force report we had prepared weeks earlier, he prepared a draft for a meeting scheduled for two o'clock that afternoon.

Van Dyk, Sherman, Connell, Jim Rowe, Edgar Berman, and Fred Harris joined me, and Larry O'Brien arrived later, having just flown in from Washington. We argued about the text as I marked it up. There was no consensus, and I hadn't expected or really wanted one. I knew what I wanted to say and used the arguments only to bring my own writing to as fine an edge as possible.

We flew later that day to Salt Lake City, and the speech was retyped while we were in the air. We met again that night to review the speech. In addition to the earlier group, there were Bill Welsh and John Bailey, who had come from Washington, and briefly, Senator Ted Moss of Utah.

One by one, people left—hungry, tired, or simply wanting a change of conversation and scenery. Finally, all were gone except for Connell, Van Dyk, Welsh, and Sherman. For them, loyal associates, hunger, boredom, fatigue could be set aside until the speech was done exactly as I wanted it. Very different from one another, with widely disparate views on the war and the speech, they shared with me the sense that this was a moment of truth—either the speech would be effective and we would move up, or it would not and our hope for success would be diminished.

We worked until about two in the morning, and once again sent the speech off for typing. The next morning, George Ball arrived and I went over the speech with him. His mere presence was reassuring, and while it was not the speech he would have given, he later briefed the press on its "significance." George called Averell Harriman, in Paris, to double check what I was planning to say. It was absolutely necessary that no statement of mine weaken or hinder the progress of negotiations with the North Vietnamese or Viet Cong. Harriman listened, made some suggestions, and said the speech was O.K. The press reaction to the written text was not particularly favorable, but George was able to persuade them that it was an important step beyond our previous statements, and their stories reflected his view.

During the day, I went on with my normal political activities. I met with Hugh Brown, one of the twelve apostles of the Mormon Church, who had been a friend and quiet supporter of mine. Many of his fellow apostles were much more conservative and did not approve of my candidacy, but Brown arranged for me to speak in the Mormon Tabernacle. It was a special, soothing break from partisan audiences and left me rather relaxed for my television appearance.

About fifteen minutes before I began my speech, I called President Johnson from the studio. I told him what I intended to say and he said curtly, "I gather you're not asking my advice." I said that was true, but that I felt that there was nothing embarrassing to him in the speech and certainly nothing that would jeopardize peace negotiations.[11] I said we had been in direct contact with Averell Harriman and that George Ball was there with me.

Johnson said tartly and finally, "Well, you're going to give the speech anyway. Thanks for calling, Hubert." And that was that.

The next day, I flew to Nashville and there were only two kinds of signs: Wallace signs and those that said, in variations, "If you mean it, we're for you." Except for the Wallace signs, the turmoil of pickets, heckling, and hostility diminished and virtually disappeared from that moment on.

A few days later, I was in Boston to address the National Association of Retail Druggists. As I approached the hotel where the association was holding its convention, I found myself surrounded by hundreds of students carrying signs that read, "We're for you, Hubert," or simply, "Humphrey for President." This was the same Boston that only a few weeks earlier had been the scene of noisy demonstrators who heckled both Ted Kennedy and me. Now they were for me, shouting and cheering, "Humphrey is our man."

Our theme of trust began to take hold, particularly since Nixon refused to debate. Our efforts in co-operation with the labor movement brought back some of the nominally Democratic vote that seemed destined for Wallace. Young people and Kennedy and McCarthy adults moved in large part back to my candidacy, though with something less, in many instances, than total enthusiasm.

Money started to come in again and we launched a limited, but first-rate, media campaign. Our message was getting through and the crowds reflected it. Candidates, one of the best bellwethers, who wouldn't get near me or my candidacy earlier, were suddenly clustered about.

Weeks of struggling, trying to catch up for lost time, frantically putting together an organization, always short of finances, error compounded by error, led suddenly to a building momentum, to larger and larger crowds, to excitement and enthusiasm, to a feel-

ing of possible success. The last weekend began in Suffolk
County, Long Island. We landed on Long Island at Islip, a
small, usually quiet airport. There was a crazy crowd of planes,
people, cameras. We drove fifty miles, stopping at shopping centers, climbing up on jerry-built platforms, speaking to cheering
crowds, ever larger, the highways between stops lined with people waving, young parents holding up little children. There were
no hostile signs. The hate of the earlier trips was gone, disappeared.

And then into the city, Queens, Brooklyn, Manhattan, the
Bronx. Street crowds—large, noisy, enthusiastic. It was a glorious
day.

While we were in New York, during October, though his
support was not so wholehearted, I had Ted Van Dyk call ahead
to the White House to set up an appointment with the President.
I hadn't seen him for a while, and my half-day visit to Washington was to be my last one of the campaign.

When we landed, I went first to a rally at a shopping center
in Maryland just outside of Washington. It was a rainy day and I
went home to put on dry clothes, running about ten minutes late.
During that time, Jim Jones, the President's aide, called my office
and said, "If the Vice President isn't here in five minutes, the
President is leaving for the weekend."

At the shopping center, a reporter asked Jack Limpert, an assistant press secretary of mine, whether there was a "lid" on for
the rest of the day since there was nothing public on my schedule. The term means that there is not going to be any news and
the reporters are free to leave. Limpert, being honest and not
wanting to deceive, said, equivocally, "There isn't a lid on, but
we don't expect any news. If there is any, we'll call."*

* Two reporters independently figured out that if there was no certain lid
on and no announced meetings, that I must be seeing the President secretly. They called the White House to confirm their suspicion. The meeting was denied, but the fact that the press had been calling infuriated the
President. Even though the White House could have reached me directly
at any time through the Secret Service communications, they did not, and
as I got out of my car at the White House, Jim Jones approached and said,
"The President is not going to see you. The meeting is canceled."

I told Jones in a fury that I was trying to run a presidential campaign as
the Democratic nominee and if Lyndon Johnson didn't care, that was fine
with me. Then I asked Jones if he would carry a message from me to the

But, the very next day, it was all different. On Sunday, we flew to Texas for a meeting in the Astrodome, a difficult place to fill for a sporting event and an impossible place to fill for a political rally. A month before, we would have had row after row of empty seats. That Sunday, the Astrodome was packed with people, over-flowing with enthusiasm and spirit. And there on that day was an uncomplicated, giving, supporting Lyndon Johnson, my friend and President of the United States.

We confidently walked the perimeter of the field. It was Babe Ruth, Joe DiMaggio, Mickey Mantle, taking the cheers of the crowd. Home plate to right field, to deep center, to left field, and back home. It was politics in the round. You could reach out to the crowd in any direction.

No ambiguity about Lyndon Johnson that day. He strongly supported me, and his message got across to the Texans. That afternoon, at least, we seemed to have resolved whatever difficulties we had.

I felt so good after those two days that there were moments when I was certain we could win. California topped off the weekend. We arrived in Los Angeles on the night of November 3, and we had a cheering mob at the airport to meet us. What a difference! Earlier visits always had been the same: several hundred dutiful supporters—one suspected many were employees of the campaign—virtually no political figures besides Kenneth Hahn, a Los Angeles County commissioner and devoted supporter, and a few of our Democratic faithful, particularly my friends of the labor movement. Now there were thousands of people. Even Jesse Unruh was there. They were all there.

Monday's meetings went very well. And the noon parade was an incredible political event. We were told a parade wouldn't work in Los Angeles because it didn't have the concrete canyons of New York City or Chicago, which lend themselves so well to crowds and parades. We were told Los Angeles was too spread out.

As we started, there was no question that the doubters had been wrong. What we found on Saturday in New York, on Sunday in Texas, we found also in California on Monday. Noise. Enthusiasm. Crowds. Thousands of people packing the streets. A

President. He agreed. And I described in terms that the President would understand what they could do with their meeting.

feeling of victory. Ed Muskie and I in the convertible, looking at one another from time to time, sensing that victory was possible. The crush so overwhelming that we feared that someone would be hurt. The moment carried me on a wave of euphoria through the afternoon and early evening to our final national television show.

Ed and I fielded questions from all over the nation, from anyone who wanted to call in. There was nothing false or phony about it. We took what came. Radio, television, and movie personalities answered the phone. We did the show twice—once for the East Coast and then for western states. It was unrehearsed and spontaneous. It had what I meant earlier when I spoke of the politics of joy: good spirit, serious fun. When it was over, I thought that no other television we had done was any better or conveyed as well what we were all about.

In contrast, I thought the Nixon show was posed and static. Bud Wilkinson, a good football coach but a dull political performer, lobbed soft questions. Nixon, with deep and solemn answers, handled it all with structured ease. He appeared on CBS, and we on ABC, with many fewer stations. I hoped that people would switch back and forth and compare us, but later surveys indicated that this didn't happen. Then there were the last political polls: Harris showed Humphrey 44 per cent to Nixon 43; Gallup showed Humphrey 43 per cent to Nixon's 44. The Sindlinger daily poll showed the race neck and neck, but Humphrey coming on strong. The key question: did we have enough time to reap the harvest of increasing support? Later on, Sindlinger said that had the election been eight hours later, I would have won.

When the results were in, the next day, Nixon had polled 31.8 million votes. Ed Muskie and I had 31.2 million. George Wallace registered less than 10 million votes.

We had come on fast and well, but we had not come far enough fast enough. My dreams and hopes were smashed in a year when so much more in America was destroyed.

36. THE BETTER PART OF BEING VICE PRESIDENT

Despite the immense miseries of the Vietnam years for our country, for the Johnson administration, and for me personally, I liked being Vice President.

There is a special kind of excitement, tension, and drama in being so close to executive power. You cannot escape the recurring thought that you could be President someday and, as elections draw near, possibly soon. But even when that is far from your mind, even while you realize a Vice President's "power" is for the most part derivative, you do have some authority, some political and governmental clout if used carefully. Further, the vice presidency can be a "bully pulpit" for persuasion.

I learned that a Vice President can, through his various co-ordinating roles, push public policy as a gadfly or a conciliator. So many federal programs cut across cabinet lines that it is imperative that disparate but related parts of government work together. While cabinet members resent others' (including their cabinet colleagues as well as the Vice President) interfering in their departments and are jealous of their own domains, the Vice President at least is elected—and is, in a sense, half a step up.

It is that fact that has led the Congress and the President to set up a number of councils with the Vice President as chairman. These vary by administration. I was chairman of President's councils on Equal Opportunity, on Youth Opportunity, on Indian Opportunity, on Marine Sciences, and on Recreation and Natural

Beauty. I was chairman of the National Aeronautics and Space Council and presided over the President's Council on Economic Opportunity. As the President's liaison with local government, I particularly liked the duty, and I took these opportunities seriously.

I studied subjects that were new to me. I learned more about subjects that weren't. I co-ordinated with a vengeance. Where "my" programs were involved, I persuaded legislators to appropriate money. I cajoled department heads into spending it.

In some of these areas, such as the space program, it was hard to have real influence through the co-ordinating role of the councils. But in others, particularly in the poverty-related efforts, I could and did play some useful part.

I started out hoping to have a major role in civil rights programs, feeling it was a logical extension of civil rights work in the Senate. There was much to be done as a result of the Civil Rights Act of 1964. Title VI, relating to the expenditure of federal funds, required a host of new activities by the federal government. I urged the President to establish a President's Council on Equal Opportunity. I hired a first-rate staff led by Wiley Branton, the original lawyer on the Little Rock desegregation case and a leader of the Southern Regional Council. We intended to co-ordinate federal civil rights activities, consulting with cabinet members, figuring out specifically how Title VI would be carried out, monitoring the success or failure of the federal government.

We met repeatedly with cabinet or subcabinet officials, mostly with Nick Katzenbach and Burke Marshall of Justice, Cy Vance (the under secretary of defense), Secretary of Labor Willard Wirtz, and Secretary of HEW John Gardner.

We had just begun what I thought was a crucial program to make the legal structure a human reality when the council was abolished. The President had brought in Joe Califano, one of Robert McNamara's whiz kids at Defense, to be co-ordinator of domestic programs in the White House. Joe was smart and able, liked power, and did not want to share it. He convinced the President that direction of federal civil rights efforts should flow from him. In the fall, the council disappeared, its staff and powers dispersed. The President would entertain no appeal, though many civil rights leaders outside government shared my concern that we had lost a valuable vehicle for giving life to the legislation. The only solace was that the President continued to solicit my views and help on civil rights.[1]

We turned our attention to the legislation that was reaching Congress, in a successful effort to get most of it passed. While I tried to keep a relatively "low profile" in order not to offend the majority leader, I was able to do what I liked so well, help guide progressive legislation through the Congress.

One bill gave us a particular problem. There had been developed a concept of dealing with central cities as an entity, trying to face many of the problems of the core of any major city in health, education, housing, and community organization. Just at the time when there were demonstrations, some of them resulting in confrontation and violence, in our cities, the bill we were pushing was titled the City Demonstration Act. We quickly changed the title to Model Cities, preventing its opponents from suggesting in derision that we were, indeed, funding demonstrations.

The bill was intended to start small funding projects in no more than ten cities. But support was thin. To get the votes we needed, we had to expand to include cities from very small ones to major metropolitan areas. By spreading the program so thin, we would not be able to concentrate money and effort in a major way in the few areas that most needed such an effort. Further, the compromise needed to pass the legislation would preclude our being able to adequately test the idea before moving out broadly.

The bill seemed doomed until Ed Muskie was involved. I asked Ed, who was from a small, non-urban state but had strong credentials in intergovernmental programs, to take the lead in pushing the bill. His intense efforts guaranteed its passage in the Senate. It still seemed destined to die in the House, until I could convince Chet Holifield of California to get it out of committee as a personal favor. Without Muskie and Holifield, regardless of its merits, the bill would never have passed. It once again demonstrated the importance of friendship and mutual respect in passing legislation.

The bill attracted hostility from mayors and other local government officials. Like the community action programs of the poverty bill, it seemed to create new power centers with new leadership unaccustomed to getting along with elected officials. The unknown challenge, as well as the complaints from people who felt left out, was disconcerting.

As the President's liaison with local government officials, I was able to lobby with them for support.* They gave it tentatively, grudgingly, but ultimately they gave it.

I think they accepted the idea that one of the most severe challenges of modern America was to make local government more responsive to the disadvantaged. Obviously, municipal government is closer to the people than the federal government, and it affects the daily lives of our citizens in more perceptible ways.

Possibly our most important and satisfying work was on the poverty program. My legislative interests had long been focused on improving the lot of the poor, and in 1964 I had written a book called *War on Poverty*. Further, much of the impetus for the programs had begun in the Kennedy years because of Walter Heller. Walter made a persuasive case that poverty was not only inhumane, it was a drag on the economy we could ill afford. He made his arguments not as a suspect social dreamer, but as a hard-nosed (but not hardhearted) economist. He convinced the President that he should do something about poverty on purely economic grounds, if not for moral ones alone.

Johnson accepted Heller's view that an investment in the people was economically sound, bringing in tax revenues, improving the economy generally, and cutting down costs for welfare and unemployment. The programs became Johnson's new initiative

* During my three years as liaison man, we helped vast numbers of the three thousand counties, eighteen thousand mayors and managers of municipalities, and twenty-one thousand school systems cut through the red tape of the federal bureaucracy. For the first time in U.S. history, we put together a catalogue of federal programs that was understandable and helpful in showing what was available and how to participate in the programs. Before that, a mayor looking for the help he needed was like a housewife in a supermarket where no cans were labeled. One of my staff, Neal Peterson, spent much of his time working with local officials, and we became virtually ombudsmen for them. Once again, I saw that a single staff person, dedicated to getting something done, can accomplish major things.

in government action, a significant change even from the New Deal and one too little acknowledged then and now.

That the programs did not ultimately reach all their goals is not surprising. What is surprising is how much was accomplished. The goals were high, the path difficult, the results hard to measure immediately.

With Kennedy's death, the Vietnam War diverting Johnson's attention, and the recessions and lack of interest of the Nixon and Ford administrations, an intelligent effort at making lives better, our society more stable, and our economy more expansive was prematurely buried. We had in large part achieved the legal base for making the abolition of poverty real, but its implementation was not easy. We knew how to break, at least in part, the cycle of poverty. It became a question of will, of commitment, of tolerance for change. We couldn't muster enough of any of those. We let the noise of critics overwhelm great beginnings.

In the six years between 1964 and 1970, the number of poor (measured on poverty level adjusted for price increases) decreased from 36 million to 26 million. That is quite simply *the most rapid decline in numbers of the poor in any nation in history*. Since 1970, the tide has been reversed and a million and a half people have slipped back.

Millions of Americans had their first health examinations—and lives were saved or enhanced. We cannot yet measure the value of Head Start programs for preschool youngsters, but we know that children were exposed to learning and ideas they would ordinarily never have had available—and lives were enriched. People were employed in the Job Corps and Neighborhood Youth Corps, many for the first time lifted out of a life of nothingness. A whole level of paraprofessional jobs serving great needs of our society was created, and people were trained to assist doctors, technicians, librarians, and teachers.

An entire new generation of black leadership otherwise destined to a life as "invisible" Americans came forward. That some of those leaders and some of their actions distressed some of white America was inevitable. But to deny them and their children a part of the American dream was intolerable.

The poverty program was not a program for blacks alone. It

gave hope to whites, Chicanos, Indians, to all who had been left out.

I found it immensely exciting, as Vice President, to be an advocate for these programs.† We had to deal not just with jobs or with schools, but with the entire range of conditions that either force or attract people into welfare and disadvantage. And, naturally, we had to deal with political opposition.

Once again, local officials across the country did not like what we were doing. Our efforts upset the status quo of municipal politics, raising new power centers to deal with. I spent much time in 1965 and 1966 mediating between mayors, other regional officials, and the poverty-program leadership. When any success came, I was exhilarated because democracy was working—as always, not perfectly, but partly.

Take employment, for instance. There is a kind of easy assumption by some affluent Americans that people can find work if they wish. It is just not that simple or easy. On one visit to Chicago, in a job-training center, I saw surprising things. Young adults were being trained in personal grooming, how to use a public washroom neatly, how to punch a time clock. One might ask: How could they *not* know those things? There are people in America who do not have money for food, much less soap. Routine cleanliness is almost irrelevant in lives in which hot water for a bath is unavailable.

It was a shock to visit a Job Corps camp and see adults who had been through some years of our public education system stare at a blackboard where a teacher was writing "cat" or helping them write their own names. In another room, men were learning to tell time. What are you to make of the strange apparatus of a time clock if you can't tell time?

The whole job question for young people was brought home by Willard Wirtz, one of the more decent men in politics. He came to me with a bleak report of youth unemployment, particularly black youth. With his guidance, I set out to develop a proposal for a summer-jobs program, working first with various

† I was a stronger advocate for the assistance and wisdom of Hyman Bookbinder. Once again, the devotion of a staff member permitted me to do more things better in a cause we both held dear—the abolition of poverty.

agencies of government. I shook loose money for jobs that they said wasn't there. We put people to work.[2]

It was clear, however, that government could not itself supply enough jobs, and so I moved into the private sector. John Stewart, who had been so involved in our 1964 civil rights work, insisted that we could not succeed without a prestigious businessman in the lead. I was able to prevail on Henry Ford II to become national chairman of the summer-jobs program.

It was successful, and once again the White House moved in, setting up the National Alliance of Businessmen to provide year-round employment, in addition to the summer jobs. Ford became its first chairman and contined to help.

The importance of that effort is strikingly underlined by conditions today, as I write, when we find in some cities up to 40 per cent unemployment among black youth, some of whom, because of high unemployment in the general economy, will reach their late twenties without *ever* having had a paying job. It need not be so, even under current conditions, but it seems to have become a matter of indifference to the administrations since 1969.

Though jobs and poverty seemed to be my specialty, I also found I was working from the bottoms of the oceans to the moon.

During the fifties, again through the interests of a staff member, Julius Cahn, I spoke in the Senate about our need to look to the seas for protein for the hungry as well as an energy source. It was not a very popular subject and I sometimes felt it was talking against the tides. But when Paul Rogers, a Florida congressman, and Senator Warren Magnuson of Washington began to promote a marine-sciences council, I moved to support them.

Legislation was passed to establish a Marine Sciences and Engineering Council with the Vice President as chairman.

As chairman, I needed to be educated further on the subject, and I needed a knowledgeable man to direct the council. We found him at the Library of Congress. Ed Wenk, now a professor at the University of Washington, was an engineer and scientist by training who, as head of the science section of the library, had become equally wise in the formulation of public policy in scientific areas.

Together we were able to get attention for federal programs related to the oceans and ultimately produced the first substantial overview of U.S. interest in them and their potential in oil, energy, fishing, and food protein.

Being chairman of the Space Council was as interesting, but more difficult. There were massive bureaucracies in the National Aeronautics and Space Agency and the Department of Defense which considered our efforts an intrusion on their programs. To some extent they were right, and I tried to be helpful without being a nuisance. I did what I could when they had problems on the Hill and became an advocate in public for their efforts.

I learned a great deal from visits to the lift-offs at Cape Kennedy and to other space installations and from the friendships I developed with a number of the astronauts.

Two became special favorites of mine. I had gone to Chicago with Ed White and James McDivitt, who had just come back from the first extra-vehicular trip in space. The public acclaim was impressive.

At one point, the Russians were absolutely dominating the Paris Air Show with a huge new aircraft and with Yuri Gagarin, the first Russian cosmonaut.[3] A member of the Space Council staff who accompanied me to Chicago suggested when we got home that American astronauts White and McDivitt be sent to Paris. His suggestion made sense and I carried the idea to the White House.

The next day, word came back through Bill Moyers that James Webb, the able administrator of NASA, opposed astronauts' travel for that purpose. I felt that the "official" position was wrong, so I went back to the President.

On Friday, about four days after the episode began, the President had scheduled a showing of films of the space walk, at the State Department Auditorium, for the diplomatic community. I was asked to be there and suspected nothing even when Johnson winked and smiled mischievously at me.

Without warning, he announced that the two astronauts, their wives, and the Vice President would be leaving that night for Paris. In a matter of hours, space suits and other gear were flown in from Houston; my staff and State Department and Space Agency officials gathered; and about two o'clock in the morning, we all took off from the White House lawn by helicopter for Andrews Air Force Base and the trip to Paris. It was a wonderful success, the astronauts heroes wherever they went, sophisticated Frenchmen rising in applause when we entered restaurants, crowds gathering wherever we were.

The President sent me as goodwill ambassador to Europe, Africa, and Asia. Goodwill is easy but, in each case, I was able to perform some functions of a substantive nature. In Europe, for example, I was able to help on negotiations for the Kennedy round of economic talks and on the nuclear non-proliferation treaty. In other countries, I announced AID or Food for Peace grants. I have written about the mission to Asia to survey and gain support for what we were trying to do in Vietnam.

Most of these things might have been done by others. The value for a Vice President of this travel (I visited thirty-four countries) rests on the personal relationships that develop, on the education that necessarily results, on the different perspective one gets. (It is not too different from the presidential candidate who learns by traveling within the United States. You don't see everyone or everything, but your vision broadens.)

While such trips almost always invited anti-American, anti-Vietnam War demonstrations, which were distressing, there were diverting moments. In Rome one night, as I got out of my car to attend the opera, a demonstrator threw a plastic bag of yellow paint at me. I was being introduced to the impresario of the opera, a distinguished, tall, gray-haired man. He bowed and the bag sailed past his head, against a wall, splattering paint over his head and down his suit. As the Secret Service shoved us through the door into the lobby, I tried to say something that would ease his dripping embarrassment, and managed to say, absurdly, "Does this happen to you often?" As much bewildered by the question as the event, he shook his jowly head and said something like, "Not in thirty years."

Unfortunately, the good things that were happening, the productive discussions, were lost in insistent coverage of yet another demonstration. (In 1969, I went to Oslo to attend former UN Secretary General Trygve Lie's funeral. No demonstrators showed up and the local United Press International representative received a message from New York that said, *What? No demonstrators? If any appear, should be ultra-up in story.*)

In France for a lunch with General de Gaulle, I was handed a toast written by one of my accompanying State Department escorts. It told of all the wonderful things we had done for France. It was banal and I tossed it away, ad libbing a brief toast that began with Lafayette, whose picture was on the wall, and ended up with a peroration to the glory of France and all the things she had done by us. De Gaulle's eyes filled with tears, and I figured the lunch had not harmed Franco-American relations.

In Britain, Muriel and I were invited to dinner with Queen Elizabeth and Prince Philip. We stayed overnight at Windsor Castle, awed by it all. It was a special sensation to be driven through the countryside and to suddenly find yourself at that historic gate. With us were Harold and Mary Wilson, who were friends of ours. Their presence made us relax a bit, and the tricycles and other toys in one of the massive hallways set us still more at ease.

Before dinner, Princess Anne came up to me alone and asked, "Mr. Vice President, you have coeducational schools and colleges in America? Well, we're just deciding now where I shall go to college and I want to go to a coeducational school, but my mother thinks I should go to a girls' school. Don't you believe that coeducational schools are much better for both men and women?" When I said that I thought so, she said, "Well, I wish you would speak to my mother and tell her that you think it would be good for me to go to one."

Dumfounded at the thought of advising the Queen on family matters, I must have registered a qualm on my face. Princess Anne continued, "She'll listen to you, since you've been a teacher. Would you do that for me?" Tempted and torn throughout the stay, I did not raise the question with the Queen. I believe that the young princess went to a girls' school.

After dinner, Muriel and I asked the Wilsons to join us for a nightcap in the apartment we had been assigned. The more formal part of the evening had limited personal political chatter. When we looked around, we saw there was nothing to drink, and I turned to Wilson, saying, "Harold, what ungrateful people you British are! Here I am, a guest of the royal household, the Vice

President of a country which has done so much for you, and there is not a bottle of whisky to be found." Wilson disappeared with a smile and returned with a bottle of scotch.

As we lifted our glasses, he said, "Well, Hubert, this is quite an evening, isn't it? Here we are, just a couple of ordinary fellows, one of us the son of an English schoolteacher, the other the son of a small-town druggist, and here we sit in Windsor Castle drinking the Queen's whisky. Not bad for a couple of boys trying to make good."

It was not bad at all.

One area of international policy in which I did play an active role was the Middle East, particularly during the Six Day War, in 1967. President Johnson, sympathetic to Israel, felt he could not completely rely on the State Department to carry out his support for Israel during and after the war.

Arthur Goldberg, Ambassador to the U.N., was the President's principal adviser and had the responsibility of negotiating with the Soviet Union, the Arab nations and our allies, but the President consulted with me frequently. My prime task beyond participating in the frequent National Security Council deliberations was to make certain the President's wishes were carried out. I asked Max Kampelman to serve as my liaison with the Israeli Embassy.

One morning during the National Security Council meeting, the President ordered immediate assistance to Israel. At noon, as I was about to open the Senate, Max arrived at my office with the Ambassador and the Minister of the Israeli Embassy, Avraham Harmon and Ephraim Evron, who was a special friend of the President. The President had personally called Evron that morning to tell him of his decision. Later that morning, the State Department called with a contrary message of no assistance. While the three of them stood by, I called the President, reaffirmed his decision, and indignantly called the State Department to straighten out any "misunderstanding." The Israelis got their help.

Israel has a special place in my heart. I find it hard to describe the satisfaction I have knowing there is a Hubert H. Humphrey Forest growing in that ancient land. Recently, Hebrew

University of Jerusalem named its entrance gardens of the Mt. Scopus campus after me.

I believe that our friendship serves both our international interests and the best interests of the free world.

From my first visit, in 1956, when I saw pioneers turning piles of rock into productive land, I was excited by the country. But Israel is somehow more than land and people, it is the essence of renewal, of rebirth. All of this has created a special closeness to its leadership and special respect for the courage of its people.

Sometimes I muse on what real peace in the Middle East could do for the peoples of Egypt, Jordan, Syria, Lebanon, as well as Israel. Within this cradle of civilization, this source of Christian, Moslem, and Jewish faiths, real understanding might bring not only peace for the people there, but an example of moral force for the rest of the world.

One trip I remember fondly was my visit to Puerto Rico to help honor Pablo Casals on his ninetieth birthday. Two dear friends, political supporters and renowned musicians, Eugene Istomin and Isaac Stern, had been involved in setting up the evening's program and asked me to join them.

The performance that evening was truly special. Stern, Istomin and Leonard Rose played as a surprise a piece of music written by Casals many years earlier. He had never played it because of political, not musical, reasons. I watched Casals' face as the music began. By the second bar, the joy of recognition covered his face and tears came to his eyes. He lifted slightly off his chair in a kind of involuntary reaction, then settled back and squeezed his wife's hand, obviously moved.

Afterward, I presented him a pipe as a birthday gift and we each made brief speeches. We went to dinner and Casals talked of his early concert tours in the United States, traveling west to play for cowboys wearing six-shooters in frontier towns. Casals told us that his favorite TV show was "Gunsmoke." I have often laughed thinking of this tiny, delicate, unique artist of immense spirit even at ninety watching a TV Western. When Lorne Greene and his wife, Nancy, campaigned with us in 1972, I thought often of Casals and that evening.

Burying the dead has become, not totally inappropriately, one of the accepted duties of Vice Presidents. Generally, a President is too busy with the living to attend, but diplomacy and protocol require representation from a relatively high-ranking official. So the duty devolves frequently upon the Vice President, and in a sober way, some good may come from this sort of mingling of national leaders.

I stood next to Eisenhower at the Kennedy gravesite and saw Charles de Gaulle, who was standing between Eisenhower and Truman, involve them both in a friendly, quiet conversation. There was no place for personal antagonism at that place and time, and the two former Presidents seemed to welcome the opportunity to talk. They walked away together chatting, and finally shook hands. I had the feeling that it was no accident; De Gaulle knew precisely what he was doing.

Soon after I became Vice President, Winston Churchill died and there was some expectation that I would be sent to the funeral. I, as a matter of fact, expected to go, but was not particularly disappointed when passed over. The press took the situation and built it into a significant slight and rejection by Johnson. The joke in Washington at the time was that I wasn't sent because I couldn't look serious. The serious comments and questions of the press succeeded in driving a small wedge between Johnson and me and also demeaned the importance of the man who was sent, Chief Justice Earl Warren, who had known Churchill personally, as I had not.

Johnson explained to me that he meant no slight and hoped that I would not become the number-one funeral attender for the Administration. Whether that was rationalization or real became irrelevant as the press played with the fact. It would have been better for me had Johnson sent me.

One night, about ten o'clock, I was at work in the Executive Office Building when a call came from the President saying he wanted me to leave immediately for New Delhi to attend the funeral of Prime Minister Shastri, who had died that day. This was no last-minute slight. Indian tradition required virtually immediate immolation on a funeral pyre. Johnson said he was trying to get all the former U.S. ambassadors to India to go along. In a matter of hours, John Kenneth Galbraith, George Allen, Senator John Sherman Cooper, and I were en route.

I stayed at the Governor's Palace, a huge old building used by the governor general when India was a colony of the British. It had all the architectural charm and warmth of a military barracks (which in part it had been). There was a communal toilet with ancient fixtures down the hall.

But it was surrounded by gardens, a lovely lagoon, and paths through the trees and flowers. The next morning, when I decided to take a walk, I saw laborers on their hands and knees clipping the grass by hand. In the distance, as I walked, I noticed a small group of people and recognized Alexei Kosygin. When our paths crossed, we stopped to talk. He was accompanied by his daughter and two or three security men. His daughter spoke fluent English and became our interpreter. Shortly after we began a rather cool and formal chat, mostly about Vietnam, one of the security men left and soon returned with a package, a gift which Kosygin gave me.

I was not prepared for the surprising gift and sent my associate, David Gartner, back to our suite to get a pair of cuff links.[4] I explained to Kosygin that they carried a reproduction of the vice-presidential seal. At first he said he wasn't sure he should accept them. But I insisted and he did. We talked on for about a half hour, Kosygin reiterating that we were terribly wrong in being in Vietnam, then continued our walks separately.

Later that day, we met again, at the Russian Embassy. The meeting included Secretary of State Rusk, Averell Harriman, and our ambassador to India, Chester Bowles. Again we focused on Vietnam in a largely stiff and unproductive meeting. At the end, to lighten it up a little, I said, "Mr. Secretary, I just want you to know that the Chairman and I exchanged gifts this morning, despite his reluctance, since we have such grave differences over the situation in Southeast Asia. I convinced him that he should keep the cuff links we gave him and use them when our relationships are more cordial."

Everyone looked at me strangely. I continued, "Mr. Secretary, keep your eyes on Chairman Kosygin's wrists in every picture of him in the future. If he is wearing those vice-presidential cuff links, you'll know that a new spirit of friendliness and co-operation has come over the Soviet leadership." The meeting ended on a cheerful note, though I was never to see the cuff links in a picture.

The Shastri funeral service itself was an eerie experience. On the way to the ceremony, our cars passed between massive numbers of people lining the streets. I had never seen such huge crowds surging forward, beaten back by police wielding sticks that made a normal billy club look like a toothpick, using techniques that made brutality look like an embrace. The people seemed to ignore the beatings, accepting them without protest or apparent complaint.

When we got to the speakers' platform, where I was to sit in the front row with Kosygin; Lord Mountbatten of Great Britain; and the President of India, the philosopher-politician Sarvepalli Radhakrishnan; I looked out over a sea of half a million faces standing or squatting in the sun as they had been for hours. Shastri's remains lay on top of a pile of timbers, surrounded by flowers and branches with leaves. Many of the Indians were still squatted down as the ceremony began, and Radhakrishnan turned to me and said, "That is what's wrong with my country: people on their haunches, just waiting."

Kosygin spoke first, and though we had been asked to speak briefly, he went on for about twenty-five minutes. Mountbatten, in a stage whisper, said to all in earshot, "These people will never conquer the world. They talk too long."

I spoke for five minutes, and when I got back Mountbatten and Radhakrishnan, who were old friends, were bantering without revealing in their faces what they were saying. Mountbatten was complaining about the fact that he hadn't had any sleep. He had been visiting with the Queen when word came that Shastri had died. He too had only had a few hours' notice before his departure. He said, "Radhi, if you don't stop these pagan rites of yours, it's going to be the death of all of us." The ceremony went on endlessly, but the climax, the lighting of the pyre, was, though in anticipation revolting, in fact not. In the strange surroundings of a different culture, it seemed suddenly appropriate and without shock.

When Adlai Stevenson died suddenly in London, Lyndon Johnson asked Muriel and me to fly there to escort Adlai's body back. I was not a passive representative performing an assigned role automatically. With the exception of deaths in my closest family, Adlai's death moved me more than any other. We were political contemporaries, he having been elected governor of Illinois the year I was first elected to the Senate. We had spent so much time together over the years, sharing the same concerns about our country and the world. What he had provided for so many people in his inspiring way, I had received doubly. I felt his loss as I had felt the loss of my father, a friend, a counselor, an inspiration.

I wept in London, in Washington at the National Cathedral (where memorial services were held), and even more at his graveside in Libertyville, Illinois, where Adlai Stevenson was laid to rest, his travels over.

37. A LESSON OR TWO

Are there lessons from the Vietnam experience? Will there be no more Vietnams? We all hope so. One wishes we could all answer with absolute assurance. I wish I could say to myself and the world that we have now learned enough and the world has moved enough to guarantee no further American military entanglement abroad.

Unfortunately, no man can in conscience and in honesty say, "Never again." For one thing, it doesn't always depend on us. For another, prophecy in foreign affairs is unreliable and deceptive.

Almost surely, we will not walk into an Asian mantrap the same way. But it remains possible that in Asia or elsewhere this nation could again slide into actions that go beyond our original intent. It is against that possibility that our nation, and its leaders, must guard.

The world is still a dangerous place. Our foreign conduct is seldom entirely of our own choosing. International affairs are not always rational. International prophecy is a hazardous trade with such factors as the People's Republic of China, the Soviet Union, the quarrelsome blood hatreds of the Middle East, and the incendiary potential of Latin America and Africa.

But there are a few hard-earned lessons of Vietnam on which reasonable people must agree:

1. We cannot be a full-world power (and we are whether we like it or not) with a half-world knowledge.

2. The "containment" of communism is an important theory that needs revision. Our basic containment policy was fashioned at a time when there was a very different Communist world.

3. The United States remains the "last, best hope of mankind," but we delude ourselves if we think we can export freedom and democratic ideals. We can encourage democracy to grow, but it is an arduous, long-term effort with inevitable setbacks, disappointments, and failure, as well as some inevitable successes.

4. We should not be ashamed to act in our own "self-interest," but we must define this self-interest carefully. And that definition cannot be the work of one man or just several. It requires honest consultation with many, including the elected representatives of the people.

5. Adequate military power is essential in today's world, but we have to understand that there are limits to that power. We must not become deeply involved where we have little at stake or where our own security can be protected by means other than military intervention.

6. Congress must find its way back to an effective sharing of power in foreign policy.

7. The President must find new and imaginative ways to institutionalize skepticism and dissent in his official ranks. Without that, there is no way for a President to save himself, and the country, from the costs of excessive "yesmanship." The President needs to have people in his policy entourage willing to disagree. The temptation to demand unanimity around him, particularly in foreign affairs, is a temptation that every President must avoid. It is the minimum that the American people can demand from a President.

8. A democracy cannot fight a war without substantial majority support.

Until recently, most people responsible for consequential decisions had only a modest understanding of the history, personalities, and culture of many parts of the world. They didn't know nearly enough about Asia and Africa. We know a great deal about Europe, but we've been, until quite recently, ill-informed, or not even truly interested, in the developing nations of the world.

We also acted in a tradition of American interventionism, always dangerous and costly, but not always bad. Certainly our assistance to the victims of Fascism and Nazism and our support for the war-torn economies were indispensable. But too often we have acted out of our experiences in Europe. Patterns and policies that make sense there do not necessarily work elsewhere.

As for containment, the U.S. policy toward communism worked for many years in providing some international stability. But the policy is too limiting and cannot assure peace today. It must be revised to meet the new realities. Unquestionably, the interventionist and aggressive policies and practices of the Soviet Union are still cause for serious concern and a continued need to remain alert. Certain measures were and remain necessary to meet them. Having an adequate military force and a carefully controlled intelligence service is basic in this world. But containment does not necessarily require American military intervention. Power is more than military might alone. We have political, economic and technological power, and we must learn to use them wisely and with discretion. There is power in ideas, in the faith of ideals. These are the elements of a new diplomacy.

Furthermore, it is one thing to agree that "appeasement only tempts aggression" and another to move our military and intelligence forces into action without a better idea of where, how long, and at what cost. In the case of Vietnam, our involvement became confused with containment, chauvinism, paternalism, wounded pride and self-justification.

While foreign policy has to be executed by the President and the Department of State, it cannot originate there exclusively. A countervailing force to the power of the presidency must reside in Congress, and it is a power that must be used.

These and other lessons of Vietnam do not teach us that we can turn our backs on international responsibility, in Asia or anywhere else. We need stability in the world, but the search for it will be fruitless and self-defeating unless we help bring about the economic, political and social changes needed to move a billion or more people out of deprivation, starvation and misery and into a process of development, self-help and hope. It is an age-old challenge.

We cannot be either the world's policeman or its Santa Claus. But if we can understand our motives, learn from our mistakes and excesses, and use the power that comes from the merger of our ideals and our strength, we can still set an example for people and countries who cherish and yearn for liberty, justice and the good life.

Otherwise, "No more Vietnams" will remain an empty political promise, a vain and cynical appeal without honor. We will have learned nothing from Vietnam.

And what of the lessons of the vice presidency?

There is an old story about a mother who has two sons; one goes to sea, and the other becomes Vice President of the United States. Neither is heard from again.

Another view of the vice presidency comes from the Constitution. It defines the job simply: the Vice President presides over the Senate, casting a vote in case of a tie, and becomes acting President or President upon the President's death or inability to serve.

The story may have somewhat more relevance than the Constitution. For the definition remains the same, but the role changes with each President. It depends on the personality of the President, his trust and regard for the Vice President, and shifting pressures upon the President.

What the Vice President can do and how he can do it are determined only by him, but even more so by what the President considers desirable. Let there be no question about this. No matter what the cast of characters: Truman-Barkley; Eisenhower-Nixon; Kennedy-Johnson; Johnson-Humphrey; Nixon-Agnew; Nixon-Ford; Ford-Rockefeller—if a President takes a dim view of the Vice President, his powers are extinguished, his influence thwarted; he fades into insignificance, forgotten and ignored, the object of cartooning and harpooning.

If a Vice President doesn't like the way he is treated or disagrees violently with a policy, he could make an open break with the President, fighting it out on an issue. He would lose. His weapons are few and feeble; the President has an arsenal. The one real vice-presidential weapon is resignation and public attack. Short of that, any disagreement that goes public is doomed.

The Vice President is clearly subordinate, his relationship to the President that of an auxiliary. He is not an innovator. He doesn't create new programs, unless the President allows it. He must be willing to stay a step or two behind the President, physically at times, and always in the news and in matters that relate to public policy.

His statutory responsibilities, largely co-ordinating in nature, bring with them little or no administrative authority. What he tries to effect through co-ordination cannot exceed what the President himself wants.

Even cabinet officers are not inclined to co-operate with the Vice President unless they are explicitly instructed to do so. The Vice President has responsibility but no inherent authority. Realistically, whatever authority the Vice President may have is delegated to him by the President, and the President can remove that authority at will—capriciously, spasmodically, entirely.

When a sitting Vice President becomes a candidate for President, as I did, all these things become important. While I have a very special feeling and sometime affection for the office, its possibilities, even the frustrations, in 1968 the vice presidency was both an asset and a liability—an asset in terms of preconvention political power and a liability when it came to freewheeling, self-assertive politics.

When I was frozen out, the symptoms were everywhere. The staff took their cues from the boss. It meant sitting outside Joe Califano's office, while he, pretentiously, went about his work inside at his own pace.[1] Or Marvin Watson instructed to cancel the use of a boat on the Potomac just before my guests were to arrive.

Sometimes I wasn't frozen, just forgotten. If I said something of interest in the course of work with the Space Council, the Youth Opportunity Program, in work on oceanography, trade, or travel, the President not only frustrated ordinary human desire for praise or recognition, he openly clamped down. I continued to work and tried to do my best.

He and the press were hardly in love, and he felt that my staff and I could add to the Administration's controversies. This made relationships with journalists, men and women with whom I had been open and honest all my years in Washington, newly awkward.

Johnson did not like my being interviewed. He decreed that we would carry no press on my journeys around the United States. Local press attention was acceptable, probably because it was unavoidable.

And yet, when it came to national radio or television shows such as "Meet the Press," "Face the Nation," or "Issues and Answers," Johnny Carson, Mike Douglas, Joey Bishop, or Dinah Shore, the President would be pleased and often generous in his praise. He sensed that the press would always try to find some conflict between him and me. He knew that any deviation by the Vice President, even inadvertent, would be headline news—played up and worked over.

The Vice President has to understand that there cannot be two major voices in an administration, and it is easy for the Vice President to find his remarks interpreted in a manner that makes it appear that there are serious differences between him and the President.

In a speech to the National Association of County Officials, in Detroit, as the President's liaison with local government, I called for a "Marshall Plan" for our cities. What I was talking about, of course, was a massive, well-co-ordinated program of urban revitalization, one with the vision and generosity and productive potential of our aid to war-ravaged Europe. The Washington *Star* ran an eight-column headline on the front page in an early edition. The Administration could have seized the idea. Instead they shot it, and me, down.

Before the late-afternoon editions of the paper appeared, the White House was asked about it, said there was no such thing being considered, that there wasn't going to be one, and the story sank slowly with the sunset into oblivion.

The vice-presidential life was colored by more than LBJ's temper. The temper of the times was no better. My visits to colleges and universities—about a hundred of them up to the time I became a candidate for the presidency—became more difficult as the war in Vietnam went on and protests began.

Except for the President, I had been the Administration's primary defender of the increasingly ugly and unpopular war. I may have been wrong, but I acted out of conviction and upon the information made available to me. I was under the impression for a long while that what I was reading of intelligence reports was precisely what the President was getting. I was told that that would be the case. As it turned out, it was not so.

I was picketed at almost every meeting. Generally, there were protesters outside the hall, but frequently, too, there would be some within the hall, heckling or walking out. In percentage terms, they were few, and the larger audience in the auditorium was generally at least polite and often enthusiastic. But every speech, every visit became emotionally draining. The harassment, the shouting, the interruptions became a little tough to take over a long period of time. By mid-term, I had an almost Pavlovian reaction every time students approached, a tightening up physically and psychologically. Hammered daily, it was easy to become defensive, aggressive, and strident.

I did not realize how much my resilience was shattered until the campaign of 1968 was over. Only then, with time to contemplate, did I know how tired I was. Only then did I clearly understand the effects of tension and harassment.

When 1968 drew to a close, I looked back on it with intense and often conflicting emotions. It had been a year with some moments of joy and pleasure and excitement. It had many more of another kind. As midnight struck on December 31, I went into the bathroom of my home and flushed the toilet. I knew it was a silly gesture, but it seemed appropriate.

Would I recommend the vice presidency to any other man or woman? Yes. With the understanding that it is important to talk out the arrangements with the President (or candidate) to start, that you can play well and in tune as second fiddle, that you take the job because the chances to serve the Lord and the land do come along.

38. THE PRIVILEGE

When I began this book, seven years ago, no longer Vice President, I had been out of public office for less than a month.* Since then, whatever we accomplished, whatever our problems, the events that followed cast a new light on them. The war in Vietnam went on, then struggled to a close. The episodes called "Watergate" and the resignation of a President and a Vice-President dominated the news for several years. An unelected President and Vice President oversee an economy in trouble.

I again became a teacher[1] and again a candidate for the Senate and for the presidency. But to recount those years would take another volume and more time than I am able to give. For, as I conclude this book, I am at home again, in the United States Senate.

Returning in 1971 like a freshman senator, I spent a year trying to find a proper role. Again it was not easy. The issues I might normally have taken up again as my prime domain—health, education, welfare, disarmament—now "belonged" to others. To have moved aggressively into any of these areas would have brought resistance.

Civil rights, our great unfinished business, was, however, no longer quite the central issue it was before the passage of the

* The contract was signed in 1967 for some later date, since I assumed I'd run again for Vice President. I did begin work in 1969 when I was out of office.

1964 and 1965 acts. I thought I might be productive in foreign affairs but was refused a seat on the Foreign Relations Committee.

I was, in short, in limbo—back but not yet at home. I reached tentatively for the levers of power I once held, but without success. The normal prerequisites of years of service in the Senate were simply not available. This is the normal pattern. Continuous service is what counts for seniority. I had no institutional power; I got a minimum of office space and staff. What friendship I had with Mike Mansfield had been damaged by my years as Vice President, when I worked the Hill arduously, pushing Lyndon Johnson's "Great Society" legislation, supporting the President on Vietnam, impinging, I'm sure, on the majority leader's prerogatives and power.

I had hoped to be treated as Barry Goldwater was when he returned to the Senate after a four-year absence, entering essentially at the same status as when he left, at least with the same committees. That was not to be the case.

The previous two years, the only time I had been out of public office since 1945, had been useful and productive for me. I had begun teaching at Macalester College and the University of Minnesota again and enjoyed the change of pace. Of course, some students retained and demonstrated their hostility over my Vietnam "connection." I understood that hostility as much as I didn't like it.

A few faculty members at both institutions resented my presence, as though twenty-five years in public service had made me incapable of teaching political science and government.

Had I not been elected to office in 1945, had I completed my Ph.D., had I written, as I undoubtedly would have, several slim books on serious subjects, I might have been considered an intellectual peer. I would have had to make no political decisions, no compromises with philosophical positions. I would not have been involved day to day with government and would, therefore, have been acceptable as a true professor of political science.[2] Well, so be it. Lord knows, whatever I had managed to achieve in creating the laws of the land for the benefit of its people could never be classified as scientific.

Despite that, most students and faculty members were friendly and welcomed me back to the campus. Without question, I learned more from the students than they learned from me. They helped me see America through their eyes, with a freshness that was emancipating. While I disagreed with some of what they said, some of what they were demanding, I grew less defensive, more receptive to new ideas. A kind of staleness of spirit was lifted from me.

While I traveled extensively around the country and the world, lecturing (on business, in some cases, as chairman of the board of the Encyclopaedia Britannica Educational Corporation, which was owned by my old friend William Benton), I still had time to spend with my family, to read and think about America and politics without the kind of pressure and activity that had dominated my life for the preceding twenty-five years. I expressed some of these thoughts in a weekly column—which was syndicated to over a hundred newspapers.

It was a special, mind-clearing opportunity to be not only my own man, but simply a private person again. Just Hubert Humphrey. I spent more time doing the things that people do in private life: traveling, fishing, playing with my grandchildren, catching up on conversations with my children (delayed for a decade), and earning more money than I ever had before. It was a wonderful time.

Almost immediately, questions arose about whether I would again seek some public role. In fact, shortly after the 1968 election, President-elect Nixon asked to see me in Florida, where we both would be vacationing. When my plane landed at the Opa-locka Coast Guard Station, just north of Miami, he was there to meet me. It was a hot day, but he was perspiring more than one would expect, and his hands shook perceptibly as he greeted me. I was struck by how ill at ease he seemed. He asked me to be Ambassador to the United Nations, and to sweeten the offer, proposed to grant me control over any Democratic appointments he was required to make. I had a special feeling about the United Nations, had enjoyed my stint there as a Congressional representative in 1956 and 1957, but I was not eager to go from Lyndon Johnson's Vice President to Richard Nixon's Ambassador. Because the UN Ambassador is limited by the Secretary of State and the President, I asked Nixon whom he intended to appoint as Secretary. When he said he hadn't made up his mind, I told him that it was impossible for me to consider the job.[3]

I am not sure why either of us went through the charade. There were really no conditions under which I would have accepted a post in the Nixon administration. I can't imagine that Mr. Nixon really wanted me except perhaps as a token of unity, a unity that did not exist.[4]

In any case, we were both relieved when that awkward interview was over. I could not deny that elected office eventually was as attractive as ever. The logical theme was to run for the Senate, but there were two Democratic senators from Minnesota, Walter Mondale and Eugene McCarthy. There was no incumbent Democratic governor, and when the desire for public life returned, I considered for a time running for governor.

But the pull of Washington, the need, I suppose, to resurrect my previous career and reputation, were too great. By the winter of 1969, I had begun to think of running for the Senate again, since by then Senator McCarthy, down to about 15 per cent approval in the Minnesota Poll had indicated that he would not seek re-election.

With Gene McCarthy out, it became inevitable that I would run again. But I moved slowly. I did not want to be embarrassed in Minnesota by rejection or defeat. In the spring of 1970, having tested public opinion by moving around the state, I decided I had a strong chance to win, and began, with renewed vigor, the old campaign pattern: from county fair to church basement to Farmers Union picnics to union halls.[5]

The campaign was the same grind and the same fun, but this time it was well planned, well financed, and well run—possibly the best campaign effort I had ever made on my own.

The campaign was managed by a young Minneapolis attorney, Jack Chestnut, who had been an advance man† for me, from time to time, since 1964. (In 1968, he was asked to help, "advance" the Chicago convention. He went there, spent one day

---

† Advance men are relatively new creatures in American politics, at least in number and importance. They check the details of a trip from hotel accommodations to motorcade routes to meeting sites to who gets to see the candidate. They also arrange the pleasantly hokey things like "spontaneous" crowds, and home-made signs. A major stop may have four or five advance men working several days to a week ahead of time.

looking around, and then called to say he was returning to Minneapolis immediately, since nothing could be done to prevent chaos. Later he took charge of our visits to Minneapolis during the campaign, including the huge problems of the final Election Day visit of hundreds of press, staff, and friends. At just the moment of our arrival on Election Day, his father died. Jack stayed until he was satisfied that plans for the day were in order and working. Only then did he leave to be with his grieving family.)

I won by 220,231 votes, my largest-percentage victory ever in a Senate race, defeating Clark MacGregor, a popular, six-term congressman who was a friend of both Richard Nixon and my friend Dwayne Andreas.[6]

I came back to Washington eager, refreshed, determined to end my public career with two useful, productive terms in the Senate. I had no intention, and only minimal interest at that point, in running for the presidency again. I was convinced, as were most people, that Ed Muskie would be the 1972 nominee,[7] and I was prepared to support him enthusiastically.

I did not think that Ted Kennedy either wanted to or could run in 1972, and while I like George McGovern personally and respect his abilities and humanitarianism, I quite honestly did not take him seriously as a presidential candidate. Henry Jackson was a man to be respected but, again, I did not take him seriously as a sufficiently charismatic personality to excite and lead our party.

George Wallace, I saw in another light. His slogan, "Send them a message" reflected the significant alienation of many people from much of what government had been doing. Some of the "message" was racist, some illogical and absurd, but some reflected a strong public undercurrent of dissatisfaction with the whole economic and social system. But, whatever the limited validity of his message, Wallace personally was a threat to what I considered the essence of the American experiment: goodwill, conciliation, justice for all. We had *his* message. We simply did not need his presidency.

When Muskie's campaign faltered, I decided to move into the presidential primaries. Before leaping, I did look. Ed Muskie and I talked in 1969 and 1970 about his moving into a position of national leadership in the Senate and in the country with the thought of pre-empting the presidential candidacy for 1972. It was becoming increasingly evident to me, however, that this was not working out. Many prominent Democrats and labor leaders were expressing their private doubts to me about Ed Muskie's being able to win in the primaries. His campaign was losing momentum. I did not believe that George McGovern could be the nominee and, as far as I could see, his campaign had no momentum either. By the fall of 1971, therefore, I was coming close to a decision to run. My campus experience had stimulated me. My return to the Senate made me feel that I had a great deal more to offer and could help the country. Furthermore, a private poll indicated that I could beat Nixon, and I desperately wanted to do that.

So I decided I would run. At first, I intended to announce as late as possible and save myself for the later primaries. But I had to run in Pennsylvania, because I felt I could win that important industrial state. When the Pennsylvania State Legislature changed its filing date to early January, I had to announce earlier than planned and then go on to prove myself a credible candidate in the Florida and Wisconsin races.

I ran second to Wallace in Florida, ahead of all the other Democrats, and surprised the media with that accomplishment. We were encouraged, but the Wisconsin campaign was coming up, and the money wasn't. We began to run the Wisconsin contest on credit, and we suffered for it. My vote there was disappointing, even though the New York *Times* reported that their survey showed me with more genuine Democratic votes than any other candidate in the Wisconsin primary. A heavy Republican cross-over vote gave both Wallace and McGovern a lead over me. Then came Pennsylvania, and organized labor once again came to my support: I won. Then came additional victories in Ohio, Indiana, and West Virginia.

I hoped that the financing for the climactic California primary would be forthcoming. My friend and financial chairman, S. Harrison "Sonny" Dogule, tried manfully to raise the money, but it was not possible. In the meantime, McGovern was accumulating a huge campaign war chest which he proceeded to spend in California.

California was to be, as expected, the crucial state. There,

McGovern had the organization and the money. I had less of both. Eugene Wyman, a long-time dear friend from Los Angeles, had raised a large amount for use in California, but a crisis drained it. About three weeks before primary-election day, I returned to our Los Angeles hotel suite at 2 A.M. after campaigning in the San Bernardino area. Gene Wyman, Jack Chestnut, Bill Connell, and Max Kampelman were waiting for me. They had sober faces. Trouble. Gene explained that the money he had raised in California was sufficient to help us win. He couldn't raise any more, but felt it was enough, even though we would be greatly outspent by McGovern. That evening, however, an urgent call had come from our Washington National Headquarters saying that some checks had been issued against expected funds that had never arrived. Those checks, coming to approximately three hundred thousand dollars, had to be covered immediately or they would bounce.

To transfer those funds East, Gene argued, could mean that we could lose the election. The decision had to be mine. I made it. We depleted our California resources. We cut back on our media and "turn out the vote" campaigns. Those sums were never replenished. We lost.

Our last hope would be at the Democratic National Convention. Had the California delegation followed proportional representation rules in force elsewhere, I might still have stopped McGovern and received the nomination. But when National Democratic Chairman Larry O'Brien ruled, in essence, for the McGovern delegates, any hope of my getting the nomination ended.

Just as Adlai Stevenson, John Kennedy, and Eugene McCarthy had brought people into the Democratic party, so did George McGovern. While most of us paid him little mind, he had put together a phenomenally successful coalition of people, many of whom had never before tasted political power. Its doom, however, was sealed in its success. The Democratic national convention once again displayed an unattractive image that did nothing to enhance his chances for election. Party regulars and labor felt excluded. As I campaigned for McGovern whenever and wherever I was asked, it could be seen that Richard Nixon would be re-elected easily.

For most people, the depths of the Nixon administration had

not yet become, in his own favorite term, perfectly clear. Watergate and its abominations were either unreported or unrecognized. But even without Watergate, there were flaws that should have been obvious.

Nixon's belief in corporations and corporate managers bordered on religion: if you did well in business, you were automatically capable, with skills that were applicable anywhere. That is true enough in some cases, but not always. Successful businessmen do not necessarily fit well into government posts (and vice versa). Government service requires something more than a "market place" mind, which too often does not understand that democracy functions to attain ideals through compromise and conciliation.

Nevertheless when Nixon could focus on international problems (and not on his own), he had done well in areas that surprised me: Russia, China, the Middle East. I wasn't surprised that he had done poorly in other fields—with the economy particularly, and in education and health.

But, from the time the campaign was over until Nixon's resignation, Washington, like the nation, was consumed with the details of a bankrupt administration—its lies, its distortions, its stupidities.

A real curse of the Nixon administration was that it too often let inept and unqualified men run the country. For all the time that Mr. Nixon was defending himself from various charges, there was almost no central direction in the government except from the Office of Management and Budget and Henry Kissinger.

First, there was Spiro Agnew. Whatever the miseries and inadequacies of the vice presidency, I had considered it an honored position, and to have been succeeded by Spiro Agnew did not please me.

Among the able Republicans Nixon might have chosen in 1964, Agnew's record and character had little to recommend him. Nothing in his behavior as Vice President seemed to lift him above a dubious level.

What bothered me most was the paranoid, anti-democratic spirit of those years and those people who surrounded Nixon. They were like a cloud of polluted air settling over the landscape, choking off the air and spirit of democracy.

When the transcripts of the White House tapes were released,

I was appalled at their emptiness, their lack of concern with public policy, their casual corruption of the democratic ideal.

I have talked with four Presidents during my career in Washington and to the people around them. I was not close enough to Eisenhower to know his private language, but Presidents Truman, Kennedy, and Johnson were as capable of similar crudities of language as Nixon. But all of them loved their country; their failures, ineptitudes, fallibilities were mitigated by a feeling for what America is all about. That love shone through; their concern for improving the condition of our people, however they conceived it, was real. They were democrats with a little "d," greater or lesser Presidents to whom the continuity of the American experiment was important.

It is that continuity, after two hundred years of our history, that fills my life with hope today. I remain an optimist about our country. Our democracy is the most exceptional attempt at popular governance in the history of the world, and to have a hand in it, even a small voice, is the privilege of being a public man.

ACKNOWLEDGMENTS

In writing this book, I have had editorial assistance from Norman Sherman, a friend and member of my staff for a number of years. I chose him in part because he had shared some of the experiences of my life, but more because he seemed to understand my midwestern roots and my national politics.

What he did most valuably was to insist that this book must be mine and only mine: "You must write it, or at least talk it, and I'll help get it in shape on paper." This I have done.

This advice was sensible because the book, like the life, is mine, and mine alone, for better or worse. Editing hours of transcripts of dictation into tape recorders could not have been easy—some have suggested it was inhumane—but Norman did it with skill, patience, and good humor.

Other key friends, advisers, and staff members have raised questions, offered recollections to refresh my memory, read all or parts of the manuscript to help assure its honesty. I have called on others for research and transcription. Listing everyone alphabetically seems the only way to justice:

Joan Barrone, Linda Blake, Sandra Carlson, Patricia Coleman, William Connell, Ken Gray, Thomas L. Hughes, Max Kampelman, Susan McCone, Neal Peterson, John Rielly, James Rowe, Virginia Sherman, Betty South, Dan Spiegel, John G. Stewart, Curt Suplee, Ted Van Dyk, Ruth Wallace, Herbert Waters, William Welsh, Nancy Wilson.

At Doubleday, I am grateful for the faith and patience of Nelson Doubleday; the experienced hand of Sam Vaughan, Publisher, and Kenneth McCormick, Senior Consulting Editor; and to their associates, including Mary Brandt, Raymond Davidson, Jere Denlinger, Alice Einhorn, Lois Eisenstein, Jack Grandin, Horace Havemeyer,

Betty Heller, Frank Hoffman, Pyke Johnson, Evelyn Metzger, Ellen Sargent, Joan Valentine, and Joan Ward.

There are, of course, hundreds of people who have helped me over the years. Some, of equal importance to those mentioned here and in the text, have fallen to the limitations of time, space, and editors. I apologize to them. Their absence is one of name only. I hope they recognize their contributions of spirit, ideas, and energy. This is primarily my journey, but once again it is really *our* story.

H.H.H.
March 1976.

NOTES

To the Reader:

The next few pages are a vital part of my story. I wanted most of the footnotes in the body of the book, but the publisher said, "No."

I hope you will find them interesting and enjoyable.

H.H.H.

28. As security officers keep a lookout, the author addresses students at San Jose State in 1968.

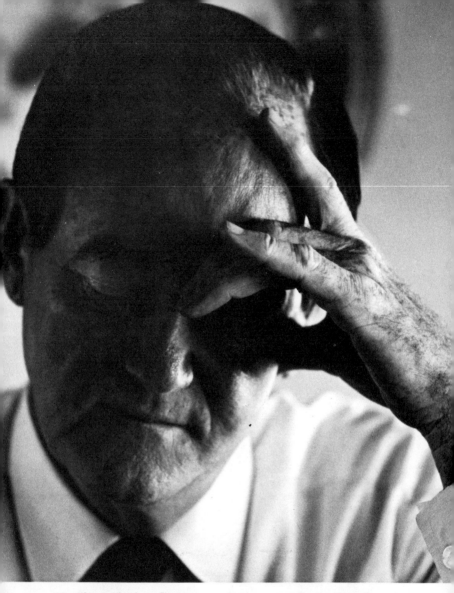

29. The author's reflections on the vice-presidency (here he returns from a trip to Europe, 1967) are a mixture of joy, pride, frustration, and behind-the-scenes maneuvers. "There is a special kind of excitement, tension, and drama in being so close to executive power. . . . But a Vice President's power is for the most part derivative. Still, you cannot escape the recurring thought that you could be President someday . . . possibly soon."

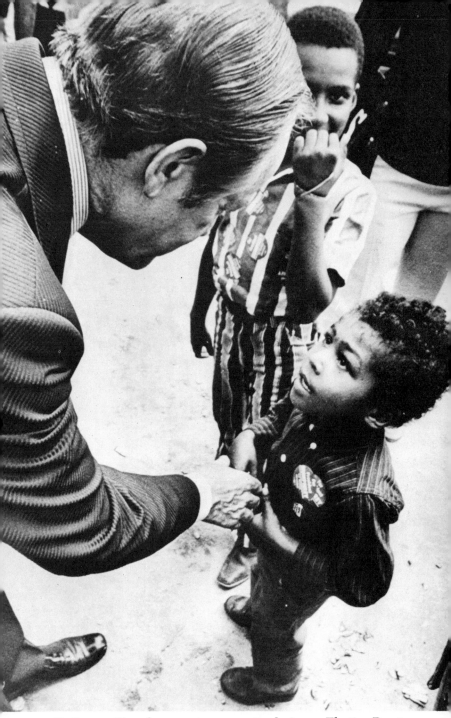

30. Senator Humphrey greets a youngster during an Election Day tour of Miami before the Florida Presidential Primary.

31. With Muriel, "without whom I could not have reached out. . . ."

BOOK I

CHAPTER 2, NOTE 1
South Dakota population went from 401,570 in 1900 to 583,888 in 1910, almost a 50 per cent increase. Sixty years later, in 1970, the population of South Dakota was only 650,000.

CHAPTER 2, NOTE 2
His need to instruct was not limited to the newspapers. At least twice a year after dinner he would pull out William Jennings Bryan's "Cross of Gold" speech and read it aloud to the family. From time to time, he'd put Frances and me on his lap and read us Woodrow Wilson's "Fourteen Points."

Wilson was his political hero, and he often read us passages from Wilson's *The New Freedom* and from Joseph P. Tumulty's *Woodrow Wilson As I Know Him*. He didn't just read books, he used them; and among the most used were *The Life of Thomas Paine,* by Moncure D. Conway, and *The Life and Public Services of Abraham Lincoln,* by Henry J. Raymond. And, of course, the Bible, though in early years that was more my mother's influence than my dad's.

CHAPTER 2, NOTE 3
Except for his brief pharmacy training, my dad had no education beyond the twelfth grade. But I never sensed any feelings of inferiority. Whatever intellectual pursuits he followed, seemed natural. Art and culture were not foreign to his family. His younger brother, Fortas, was an artist who died while painting a mural at Stanford University. His brother John was an unpublished poet and writer who was also an inventor and businessman. John invented a potato picker and as best I know was the originator of trading stamps. In 1915–16 he had an office in Wall Street from which he peddled "Green Market Basket" trading stamps. It was an idea before its time. We had huge wooden boxes of unused stamps in the basement of our store.

CHAPTER 2, NOTE 4

Utilities have a peculiar place in American history. Early on, they were the basis of fortunes for some "robber barons" and the source of corruption in many cities and states, where legislators and franchises were bought and manipulated.

Privately owned public utilities is a strange concept in any case. In Doland, it wasn't a question of corruption. It was empty promises that my dad objected to: promises of cheaper rates, greater efficiency, street lights. Years later, when I would return to Doland, people would insist on bringing up that old controversy to tell me that my father had been right.

CHAPTER 3, NOTE 1

There is a Federal Reserve bulletin written in 1930 that says blandly, "The effect of the crisis of 1920 was to eliminate unnecessary banks, marginal and unproductive lands, incompetent farmers and excess merchandising units." I didn't read the bulletin at the time, but we surely felt this "Establishment" attitude. I have never viewed the banking structure of the United States, and particularly the Federal Reserve System, without remembering that cold, inhuman, statistical approach to life.

CHAPTER 4, NOTE 1

That trip was the first that involved us personally, but my youthful interest had been piqued four years earlier, when my father and his friends argued about Calvin Coolidge and John W. Davis, the Democratic candidate.

Right after Mr. Coolidge had won, I came bounding into the drugstore overflowing with the enthusiasm and foolishness of a thirteen-year-old trying to be smart. I made a sarcastic remark about Republicans and President Coolidge at the moment my dad was waiting on one of the nicer women of Doland, who was—inevitably—a Republican. She suffered my impertinence in silence. My dad did not. He said, in effect, "Young man, the election is *over*. Mr. Coolidge has been elected and I want you to respect the office of the President of the United States."

Chastened, I listened later as he insisted that partisanship has limits and that the institutions of government in a democracy deserve respect whether one likes the incumbent or not.

CHAPTER 5, NOTE 1

Having a choice of movies was something new, too. As often as I could, I'd go to the Minnesota Theater, an elegant, overdone building of massive chandeliers, a huge central staircase, velvet drapes, and thick rugs.

(If Folwell Hall was Beer Barrel Renaissance, this was Prairie Baroque.) The palaces of the Medici could not have been more awe-inspiring to a Florentine peasant than the Minnesota Theater was to me.

CHAPTER 5, NOTE 2

By 1919, fewer than 2 per cent of the farms of America were electrified. During the next ten years, the figure crept up to 9.5 per cent, but with farm depression across the plains and prairies and the high cost of running the lines long distances, the pace slowed. In 1929, as I traveled back and forth, there were still very few long lines in Minnesota or South Dakota.

By 1935, only an additional 1 per cent of farms nationally had electricity. Then, in May of that year, President Franklin Roosevelt, by executive order, established the Rural Electrification Administration. Power generated for irrigation pumps meant that marginal land became productive. Conveyors, unloading equipment for silos, and barn cleaners run by electricity lifted some of the heavy work from the backs of farmers. Tools and machinery could be repaired after dark in lighted barns. Milkhouses and henhouses were lighted, permitting the farmer to work more effectively. By 1960, 97 per cent of American farms had electricity. About 1,000 REA systems, run co-operatively and locally, were in operation, overseeing 1.5 million miles of lines and serving 4.8 million people.

The national REA was and is simply a lending agency, which during its first twenty-five years lent over 6 billion dollars, of which 3 billion had been repaid by the end of that period.

The immediate effect of the REA was not just agricultural. It was social, too. Suddenly, with adequate light after sundown, families could read and write and study more conveniently. The wife could sew, and when there was money, she might buy a Sears Roebuck or Montgomery Ward washing machine, iron, or refrigerator.

In subsequent years, radio and television brought the farmer onto common ground of mass culture with city dwellers.

It is no wonder that people in rural areas still refer to "light" bills, rather than electric bills.

Politicians took advantage, too. In rural areas during a campaign period, they used early-morning radio to reach the farmer at work in his barn, milking or preparing for the day's labor in the fields.

CHAPTER 6, NOTE 1

Through the years, he became almost as close an adviser as my dad, particularly after my father's death, when I lived not far from Uncle Harry's home in Cabin John, Maryland. He had a strong influence on my life. His constant emphasis upon the importance of a college education—his deep respect for learning—inspired me.

CHAPTER 7, NOTE 1

When my sister Frances attended Huron College, tuition was paid in the form of merchandise to professors. They got IOU's or scrip, which in turn could be exchanged at stores owned by parents of the students. It was a primitive type of economy, but it was all we had.

CHAPTER 7, NOTE 2

Before my father died, he told my brother and me, "I don't care whether you have to pay more for merchandise or not. You buy from McKesson's and Minneapolis Drug. Whatever you can buy, you buy from them. When I needed them, they took care of me. I don't want you going around looking for a cheap price someplace. You buy from the people that helped us."

I've never forgotten that lesson in loyalty. Loyalty adulterated, as sometimes happens in politics, is cronyism. But genuine loyalty in politics or in business—the kind that grows from understanding, compassion, respect—is a precious virtue.

CHAPTER 8, NOTE 1

Muriel's dad sold his business to Fairmont Creameries—a big, interstate corporation—but he demanded in the terms of sale protection for the jobs of those who had faithfully worked for him over the years. He was a proud man.

CHAPTER 8, NOTE 2

For a couple of years, she and her dad also raised turkeys. There is no more smelly, temperamental, or dumb bird anywhere. A loud noise scares them into panic. They race about noisily, piling up on one another in a corner of the pen, suffocating those below, chewing on each other in a flutter of feathers and squawks as they try to get to the top. In fact, if they look up with their mouths open when it rains, they can drown just standing there. Fortunately, the turkey business didn't last long, since the slight profit was not equal to the great trouble.

CHAPTER 9, NOTE 1

There were others, too. Ben Lippincott, a very smooth and suave man, was somewhat older than the rest of us and quite unlike my midwestern colleagues. He was a provocative professor who moved me into the realm of political philosophy and theory. Asher Christensen had a great influence on me, too. He was not as scholarly as Lippincott or Kirkpatrick, but he made American government come alive. He gave it spirit and zest and taught me that government, among other things, could be both entertaining and serious. Elio Monachesi had a light but scholarly touch in sociology. My introduction to constitutional law was also exciting. Oliver P. Field, almost blind, was our professor; and what I learned from him did not quite make me the equal of later colleagues in the Senate like Sam Ervin of North Carolina, but it surely helped.

CHAPTER 9, NOTE 2

When Muriel's dad visited us, he asked where the fire escape was. When we said there was none, he got a coil of thick rope to tie to the radiator so that we could throw the other end out the window and climb down in case of fire. There are still small-town hotels in the Midwest with coils of rope in the corner.

CHAPTER 9, NOTE 3

Orville Freeman has remained a close and dear friend for all the years since then. That kind of extended relationship is rare enough in life, but even more rare when two men have separate political careers that sometimes conflict. Orv has been among the very best of public servants—tough-minded, bright, creative, and totally honest. His six years as governor of Minnesota and eight years as Secretary of Agriculture, both difficult and demanding jobs, were distinguished.

CHAPTER 10, NOTE 1

One day, a parade of flatbed trucks set up like jail cells, with the names of Huey Long associates identifying the "inmates," circled the campus. In one of them, a former president of the university was mocked in effigy, as James Jinglemoney Monroe, working on a rock pile. Middle initials were adapted by both sides to fit a useful epithet: James Applehead Noe, Gerald Lucifer Kodfish Smith, Sam Highhat Jones, Richard Walkingstick Lesh.

But the name game was mild compared to the rest of the campaign. I never really got used to one man calling another a crook or a thief. In Minnesota, about the worst I'd ever heard might be a political whisper that a man wasn't a Lutheran.

CHAPTER 10, NOTE 2

Virtually my only contact with blacks had been about seventeen years before, when I was eleven or twelve years old. Highway 22 was being built from Doland to Redfield, South Dakota, and most of the drivers and construction workers were black.

During the week, after school, I'd go out and ride the mule-drawn dump trucks with them, asking questions, learning from these strangers. My mother was shocked, but my dad never disapproved.

To my dad, every person was worthy of respect. He'd often say, "Treat people like people. If you treat them like dogs, expect to be bitten."

(Later, when white hobos drifted through town, my dad welcomed them, too. Most townspeople feared and hated them, calling them "wobblies," seeing them as radical and threatening men. My father apparently found them interesting and liked to visit with them.)

I knew no blacks well until much later. As a matter of fact, before going South, there was no black person, other than Horace Bell, a University of Minnesota student and football player, with whom I had ever had a serious conversation.

CHAPTER 10, NOTE 3

When I went to the Senate, almost ten years later, the Southerners seemed to feel that I was personally antagonistic. I wasn't. As a matter of fact, as a Midwesterner I found much in common with the South. Both regions were essentially agricultural in outlook and there had been an affinity of interest between the two regions going back to the time of Andrew Jackson. By then, too, I was not unaware of what went on in the North and particularly within the Populist tradition, which is my own heritage in American politics. It would be comfortable to claim that Populists and progressives had steadfastly fought against racism and white complacency through the years, but it isn't true.

CHAPTER 10, NOTE 4

I said, in my best graduate-student prose, "The New Deal, faced with an unprecedented economic collapse of the domestic and world economy, chose the course of moderation and rebuilding. It acted boldly to stabilize and to rehabilitate the economic mechanism. It religiously preserved the profit system. . . .

"The New Deal may be described as a changed concept of the duty and responsibility of government toward economic life. It has steadfastly adhered to the inseparability of economics and politics. It has manifested a willingness to accept change for granted and to take political action in terms of that change. The primary objective has been to regain and to secure economic liberty for the average man not by abrupt change and revolution, but by an experimental reordering of the profit system in order to provide economic security without sacrificing political liberty. There has been no concerted attack upon private enterprise but, rather, a positive effort to revive and restore competition. The New Deal has utilized the power of government to establish a balance between American class relations and a balance in the economic system.

"The readjustment cannot be termed revolutionary in the historical meaning of the term, but implicit in all of the program has been a call for a changed conception of economy and life. Exploitation and speculation are to be curbed in the interest of security and stabilization. Personal liberty is to be adjusted in terms of the common welfare and the social good. The task of government has been enlarged to the development of an economic declaration of rights, an economic constitutional order. Human values have been emphasized, and property values judged in light of their relationship to the common welfare.

"It appears that for the New Deal the essence of a liberal society is that it makes the common good available not to a privileged class but to all, insofar as the capacity of each permits him to share it.

"The democratic tradition in America is a long struggle to secure for every man the privilege of property and the liberty that attends it. The New Deal has adhered to this tradition. It regards the 'middle state' as the best state; one wherein government rests on a wide distribution of private property. It seeks to define property not merely as land, but as secure income. It goes back for its inspiration to the Jeffersonian formula of the right of every man to life, liberty, and the pursuit of happiness. All of the New Deal recovery measures are but a continuation and elaboration of the democratic tradition. They find their historical justification and precedent in the philosophy of Jefferson, the progressivism of Populism, the Square Deal, and the New Freedom."

CHAPTER 10, NOTE 5

All three of my committee members went on to distinguished careers in political science. Charles Hyneman served during the Second World War with the U. S. Intelligence Service and afterward was director for broadcasting for the Federal Communications Commission. Later he taught at Northwestern University and the University of Indiana, where he was named a distinguished professor of political science in 1961. He wrote and edited numerous books on government.

Robert Harris had an extremely successful academic career. Author and co-author of four books on government, he taught at Columbia, Vanderbilt, and the University of Virginia, where he became the James Hart professor of government in 1968.

Norton Long, whose special field of interest was urban affairs, served the U. S. Government in the Office of Price Administration and the National Housing Agency. He taught at a variety of universities, among them the University of Texas, Northwestern, Brandeis, and the universities of Illinois and of Missouri. He wrote several books and articles on the problems of cities.

CHAPTER 11, NOTE 1

There was an interesting mix of people in our group. Orville Freeman was to be governor of Minnesota from 1954 to 1960 and Secretary of Agriculture from 1961 to 1969. Arthur Naftalin, who was to work in my office when I was mayor of Minneapolis, was himself to be elected mayor in 1961. After several years, he was to return to the University of Minnesota to continue his teaching career. Herbert McCloskey, a young political scientist, has been at the University of California at Berkeley for many years.

Two men who were important in the formulation of the Democratic Farmer Labor party were William Kubicek and Frederick Kottke. They became professors of physical medicine at the University of Minnesota Medical School, and Kubicek for many years was secretary of the state DFL party and an important strategist in many campaigns.

William Anderson was a generation older than the rest of us and already an established scholar. He had tremendous influence on my attitudes and my development as a student of government.

Augustus Kelley, the first master of the Grange, farmed near Elk River. Ignatius Donnelly, author, politician, spokesman for Populism, dramatic and often derided for his style and personal excesses, lived near St. Paul.

Just before World War I, A. C. Townley, a North Dakota socialist, organized the Non-Partisan League, a fiery effort to elect men in either party who would support their program: state ownership of mills, grain elevators, and terminals; state inspection of grain; tax exemption for farm improvements; state hail insurance; and rural credit banks operating at cost. Its emotional appeal to the frustrated and alienated farmer was simple: it would protect him from the evils of the system personified in Big Business. The league was most successful in North Dakota, both in electing candidates and in getting parts of its program made law, but its role was significant, too, in Minnesota. Its membership grew from 40,000 in 1916 to almost 190,000 in 1918, most of them in Minnesota, the Dakotas, and Montana. In 1918 and 1919, in Minnesota, limited efforts were made to involve the laboring men as well. First, Charles Lindbergh, Sr., unsuccessfully running for governor of Minnesota, tried to put together an alliance of the two forces and, in 1919, under the leadership of Senator Henrik Shipstead, a Workingmen's Non-Partisan League was formed.

By the early twenties, the NPL's limited success waned, though some league candidates continued to run and be elected. More importantly, however, the philosophy of federal co-operation and concern for the farmer had been developed and articulated, and some sense of common interests had been nurtured between farmers and laborers, giving both a more effective political base than either would have been able to establish alone. None of these advances were ever again to be totally submerged. They would fluctuate in importance, but in large measure they were adopted into the programs of all subsequent liberal or progressive political movements as an integral part of their political platforms.

Minnesota's political independence is legendary. It cast its electoral vote for Theodore Roosevelt's Bull Moose party in the 1912 election, and third-party movements regularly drew relatively large support. The Farmer-Labor party, another manifestation of Minnesota's innovative politics, was a direct descendant of the Populist spirit, but a more politically sophisticated way of dealing with the pains attending the birth of midwestern industrialism.

While the NPL refused to become a third party, the Farmer-Labor party was one from its beginning. It has been called a "marriage of convenience" between the NPL and the Workingmen's NPL, which came into existence in August 1918 with Floyd Olson at its helm. Olson was a big, dramatic man, who characterized himself a "radical" and who became the political focus and indeed molder of the protest spirit in Minnesota during the late twenties and thirties. It is not too much of a simplification to say the party's political temperament fluctuated with Olson's—and finally died as a political organization when he did, in 1936.

In 1922 the Farmer-Labor party ran a full slate of candidates for state-wide offices, and in 1924, Olson himself was the candidate for governor. He ran a radical campaign, frightening the middle class as well as the conservatives, and lost. In 1930, he ran again for governor; and this time, toning down the rhetoric, he was elected.

Olson was succeeded on his death by his lieutenant governor, Hjalmar Petersen, but the left wing secured the nomination at the next election for Elmer Benson, who became governor in the fall of 1936. Benson lacked Olson's personal affability and political prowess and was unable, if he tried, to prevent destructive internal factional conflicts between the doctrinaire Marxists and the reform-minded Progressives.

Harold Stassen beat Benson in 1938, and the liberal, progressive forces floundered for years. But the Communists, despite their factions and their limited spheres, did well, having an inordinate strength in both labor matters and political parties. This was particularly true because of the phenomenal leadership of the Dunne brothers, Vincent Ray, Miles, and Grant. They were tough and bright and determined, and they organized and led the bloody truck drivers' strikes of 1934 and 1936. They broke the Yankee domination of Minneapolis, taking the city from an unorganized condition to one in which labor had a voice and structure.

The Dunnes were Trotskyites, and Vincent Ray particularly was a high priest of their movement. (Farrell Dobbs, one of the drivers, later, under Dunne's guidance, was subsequently to become their candidate for President several times.)

The Stalinist wing of the Communist party, again partially through indigenous leaders, but also with the help of the party in the East, worked diligently in Minnesota. In part they were fighting the Trotskyites wherever they appeared, but again, because of the peculiar strain and admixture of radicalism in our area, they were effective, particularly within the CIO.

CHAPTER 12, NOTE 1

The Smith Act, passed in 1940, made it a federal crime to advocate overthrow of the government. The maximum penalty was twenty years in jail and a twenty-thousand-dollar fine.

CHAPTER 12, NOTE 2

Cecil Newman, then editor and publisher of a small weekly, the Minneapolis *Spokesman,* helped me tremendously.

CHAPTER 12, NOTE 3

Our supporters in organized labor were extremely hard-working and very successful on our behalf. The group included Harold Seavey, our campaign manager for labor, Lester Covey of the railroad brotherhoods, Robley Cramer from the *Minneapolis Labor Review*, and, among others, George Matthews, Bob Wishart, Gene Larson, Harry Leonard, Rubin Latz, Mike Finkelstein, and Sander Genis.

CHAPTER 13, NOTE 1

Floyd Olson understood this in the thirties. He had arranged with the national Democratic party that Roosevelt would not vigorously support the Democratic candidate for governor, and that Olson, even as a third-party candidate, would support Roosevelt. This meant, of course, that the Democratic party was engaged primarily in handing out federal patronage after Roosevelt won, but was not likely to win many elections in Minnesota except for a couple of local offices.

Naftalin, Kirkpatrick, and I had discussed the fusion of the two parties with many people. Farmer-Labor leaders were skeptical, if not outright hostile. They said it had been tried before and was just a dream that couldn't be accomplished. I was both naïve and determined. A fusion was necessary if liberals were to win in Minnesota, and it was important if Roosevelt was to carry the state in 1944.

CHAPTER 13, NOTE 2

One particular class made news on the campus. It began in midafternoon, about three-thirty, and discussion went on excitedly and heatedly until around six in the evening. When no one wanted to stop, I suggested we recess for a spaghetti dinner at an inexpensive place and reconvene after dinner. We started class again about seven and ran on until about ten.

CHAPTER 13, NOTE 3

Once again the political science faculty provided me with friends and political allies. Dorothy Jacobson was a strongly anti-Communist liberal who had been raised on a Minnesota farm and had a Columbia University graduate degree. She later became DFL state chairwoman and executive assistant to Orville Freeman both while he was governor and while he was Secretary of Agriculture. She was involved in strategy and battles of fusion and then of making the DFL a power in state politics. Her husband, George, a leader of the farm co-operative movement, with contacts all over the state, was also of great help.

Theodore Mitau, a young German Jewish immigrant, was an exciting professor and friend who shared our hopes and work. He later became chancellor of the Minnesota State College system.

Later that year, Dr. Charles Turck, the president of Macalester, returned from military service. He was not active in the DFL fusion but was to be a lifelong friend.

CHAPTER 13, NOTE 4

Barney Allen was another important figure in putting the DFL together. Barney and his wife, Ilse, were and are genuinely warm and cheerful people who became our close personal friends. Barney had served in the Iowa legislature before moving to Minnesota, and he embodied a lighthearted and whimsical approach to politics that I found charming.

But beneath a kind of bucolic hayseed exterior there lay a shrewd political strategist and a wise man. He became DFL national committeeman, later Minnesota commissioner of agriculture, and then served in the U. S. Department of Agriculture, when Orville Freeman was Secretary.

CHAPTER 14, NOTE 1

The day of Fred's funeral, his home was burglarized while his family was at church. It was a strange burglary. His wall safe in the basement was professionally torn from the wall, and nothing else was taken. Cash and jewelry in sight in the bedrooms were left though drawers were dumped. Police in Minneapolis tell me that a safe taken in a "normal" burglary generally shows up in a field or dump. Fred's safe has never appeared. Considering the now public political burglaries of the time, one is left with lingering questions about the break-in.

CHAPTER 15, NOTE 1

Mintener was general counsel for Pillsbury, the flour company, and an almost singular exception to corporate indifference to police corruption.

CHAPTER 15, NOTE 2

Of the many commissions I instituted as mayor, perhaps none was as successful as the Community Self-Survey and the results that came out of it. It was an extremely innovative program—especially in the mid-forties—and could still be applied with much profit today.

Minneapolis, like most other cities, had troubled race relations. In particular, we had problems with discrimination against blacks and with an often angry anti-Semitism. Fortunately, at about that same time, the American Council on Race Relations had just been formed, with its main office in Chicago.

Serving in that office was L. Howard Bennett, a black man with a long and distinguished record in civil rights and race relations. A woman from St. Paul had come to his office to inform him of the anti-Semitism she had experienced in Minneapolis, and Bennett came to the Twin Cities in the fall of 1945 to study the scope of the problem.

He researched the situation and discovered that Jewish children were being beaten on their way home from school and that some faculty and school newspapers were blatantly anti-Semitic. In fact, it was even the case that the American Automobile Association of Minneapolis would not accept Jewish members. As well, there were some problems in police relations with blacks.

I was running for mayor by that time, and when I learned that Bennett was in town, I asked to have a meeting with him. We talked for six hours and then had dinner.

I asked him what he would do about the problems he had found in our city, and he was quick to reply with an articulate and sensible five-point plan for change.

I thought that it was an excellent program, and I asked Bennett to write it up as a memorandum so that we could use it in the campaign. He was willing to do so, and we included it in our platform. After I was inaugurated, I asked Bennett and his organization to return and help us, and they did—with Bennett assigned as chief consultant to Minneapolis and to me as mayor.

With his help, and later with Herman Long (of the Race Relations Department at Fisk University), and with the devoted support of many community leaders, we began to look at our city. We used a research questionnaire designed by Bennett which gave us a solid base of information.

It was a self-survey, intended to tell us about ourselves as a community, about our attitudes toward one another and among the races. Because it was a *self*-survey, it avoided potential criticism that it was conducted by hostile "outsiders" who were trying to impose foreign notions on a local town. Instead, it provided our local people with a way to learn about themselves in their own way.

We followed that survey—which was probably the most comprehensive and intensive in the nation—with a vigorous program of social action developed along the lines of what Bennett had proposed before the campaign and Long afterward.

It wasn't business as usual, by any means, and there were many citizens who deeply resented and resisted our efforts. But we did it, and I am still proud of what we were able to accomplish.

CHAPTER 16, NOTE 1

For almost thirty years, I have benefited from Max Kampelman's friendship and advice. On a different level, but like Fred Gates and Dwayne Andreas, he has been intimately involved in my career. When I first met him, in 1946, he had only recently finished his role as a conscientious-objector subject in starvation-diet experiments and had become an instructor of political science.

He had been a pacifist and socialist, but slowly evolved into a more pragmatic liberal and ultimately an advocate of a strong defense system, as many anti-Communist socialists did. He was a student and scholar and an intellectual with a flair for politics. He had done his Ph.D. thesis on the CIO and Communist infiltration there, and out of that had contacts with the labor movement that became important for me.

After getting his doctorate in political science, he went off to teach at Bennington College in Vermont, but joined me in Washington as my legislative assistant when I was elected to the Senate. He was immensely creative and helpful then in areas of labor law and public welfare, in health care and education, as well as in politics.

He had been active on his own and alongside me in the formative days of the Americans for Democratic Action and later, through his efforts, I became a vice president of the American Political Science Association. It was through him and these groups that I met many liberal intellectuals, particularly in economics and political science.

A man in public life needs people around him with a sense of outreach, someone who can bring in others to implant new ideas, to challenge old ones—simply to stretch one's mind. Max has done that for me better than anyone else during my public career. And he does it to this day.

Though he has long since left my staff (he did so in 1955), he remains a loyal and constant friend. But in neither role—staff nor friend —has he ever let loyalty keep him from arguing with me when he has thought me wrong. He does it diplomatically and without being abrasive, offering as the good lawyer he is, alternatives with the logic for the various positions. He has a crucial talent for separating his own position from the argument, viewing with dispassion other's points of view—in this case, mine.

Max has come in for his share of criticism because the public perception of him is distorted by his success as a lawyer. When a failure or somewhat inadequate person is close to an elected politician not much is said, but when a talented, successful, hard working person is, he invariably is seen as self-serving.

The fact, of course, is that had I left the Senate the same day Max left my staff, he would today be no less successful than he is. His abilities would have carried him just as far.

His interests are broad, his leadership recognized. He helped organize, and was the long-time chairman, of the public television station in Washington, was the first president of the Friends of the National Zoo, an officer of the American Political Science Association, a trustee of a college, and president of the American Friends of Hebrew University.

I marvel sometimes at the willingness of people like Max to devote so much of their time and energy to politicians' lives. Obviously, they love politics and the power to do things as much as politicians themselves, but their motives are always suspect to cynics among the press and public. They are never pure enough and always fair game for darts and gossip. Their mammoth commitment to working for a good society is largely ignored, their flaws magnified beyond reason.

CHAPTER 16, NOTE 2

It attracted, to some degree, a segment of the intellectuals and some radical ideologues who did, indeed, want a new and, in their eyes, better economic and political system. It was more middle class than working or lower class (a fact that continues to be true about American radicalism).

CHAPTER 16, NOTE 3

Eugenie Anderson had been active in the League of Women Voters and a member of the school board of the Burnside Consolidated Schools in Red Wing—a small town just south of Minneapolis, where she lived with her husband, John. She was different from most of the rest of us since she came from a family of some wealth.

In later years, she became our DFL national committeewoman and subsequently served as the first U.S. woman ambassador, appointed by President Truman to be our Ambassador to Denmark. Later, she was a friend and foreign policy adviser to Adlai Stevenson, U. S. Minister to Bulgaria, and a U.S. delegate to the United Nations.

Dean Acheson once called her one of the most able diplomats ever to serve America.

CHAPTER 16, NOTE 4

Since I had no power within the CIO, Murray sent two men to Minnesota to effect the changes. One, Smaile Chatek, was a close friend of Murray. He spoke broken English and was an organizer straight out of the Pennsylvania coal mines. He was an artful labor politician who could not be pushed around either intellectually or physically. He had a kind of primitive eloquence which moved people, and he used it to isolate and then defeat the Communist leadership.

The second man, Darrel Smith, was a staff man who also understood labor politics. Between the two of them, with what help we could muster from Minnesota, they straightened out the CIO and helped us clean up the DFL. Both continued to be active in our politics for many more years.

A third man, George L. P. Weaver, who was the assistant to CIO Secretary-Treasurer James Carey, was active as a trouble shooter during this period, although he did not work full time. He was a truly remarkable man who, in the course of his career, worked his way up from being a sleeping-car porter to assistant secretary of labor.

CHAPTER 16, NOTE 5

We derived support from many quarters, some of them unusual. Father Dunphy, of Ascension parish, was addressing his congregation on the Sunday before Election Day. He said, in his rich Irish brogue, "You know the position of the Church on matters political.

"But I want all of you to know that on Tuesday morning I shall be voting for a fine young man running for mayor—Hubert Humphrey."

I carried the precinct 587 to 67.

CHAPTER 16, NOTE 6

Though it may surprise some of my contemporaries, the suggestion that I run for President came from friends and was far from my mind in 1948. Many friends urged me to run for governor of Minnesota rather than the Senate. Their logic was that senators did not get nominated for the presidency and governors did. I rejected the suggestion because it seemed so irrelevant and because my interests were in national legislation and international affairs.

CHAPTER 17, NOTE 1

The ADA became the vehicle for the Democratic left to speak out, fighting Communist influence and Communist domination of liberal organizations and labor unions. Its leadership included men of great ability and dedication to democratic ideals: Leon Henderson, Reinhold Niebuhr, Wilson Wyatt, Walter Reuther, David Dubinsky, Emil Rieve, Hugo Ernst, and Jim Loeb.

Jim, who became the executive director of ADA, was a remarkable human being, always kind and considerate, a truly liberal social democrat with a brilliant mind and capacity for organization.

Shortly after being elected to the Senate in 1948, I decided to accept the national chairmanship of ADA. That decision made me the spokesman for a national constituency which, if not large, was nonetheless important, containing as it did a large number of the liberal, anti-Communist left and the academic and labor communities. With that base to represent, the Senate became more than a place to exist as a quiet freshman representing a medium-sized midwestern state. It was a forum to expound a point of view. It was really only after I left the chairmanship of ADA that I began to study the rules of the Senate and to focus on my life there.

CHAPTER 17, NOTE 2

While my association with the ADA was important in my political education, it was also important for the people I got to meet and who became friends. One man whom I met frequently in those days was Marvin Rosenberg, a big, tall, shy New York City businessman. He was successful, but not rich. He was widely respected as a selfless person with a tireless dedication to liberal causes. He became not only a good friend but a valuable fund-raiser in my campaigns.

He has given of his own time, energy, and money—never asking for anything in return except a commitment to liberal principles and programs. And he has brought in only the cleanest kind of campaign money. The people who have given contributions to Marvin for national candidates know that they were buying nothing: no patronage jobs, no power, and no influence.

Through the years of my career, no one has been more loyal and helpful than Marvin. He was deeply troubled by my support of President Johnson and our national policy in Vietnam. And yet, although he was saddened by it all, he remained loyal. He is a true friend and I am proud to know him.

Another New Yorker who deserves special note is Mary Lasker. When in recent years people talk harshly of political contributors as though they are all venal, I think of Mary—the most altruistic "giver" I know.

Mary Lasker is a wealthy New Yorker, bright, charming, sophisticated, dedicated to improving the quality of life. She has donated immense amounts of money for everything from health-research projects to beautification efforts. She has contributed frequently to me as she has to other politicians who share her interest in a better America.

CHAPTER 17, NOTE 3

I delivered the following text before the Democratic National Convention in Philadelphia, July 14, 1948, in support of my civil rights plank to the party platform:

I realize that I am dealing with a charged issue—with an issue which has been confused by emotionalism on all sides. I realize that there are those here—friends and colleagues of mine, many of them—who feel as deeply as I do about this issue and who are yet in complete disagreement with me.

My respect and admiration for these men and their views was great when I came here.

It is now far greater because of the sincerity, the courtesy and the forthrightness with which they have argued in our discussions.

Because of this very respect—because of my profound belief that we have a challenging task to do here—because good conscience demands it—I feel I must rise at this time to support this report—a report that spells out our democracy, a report that the people will understand and enthusiastically acclaim.

Let me say at the outset that this proposal is made with no single region, no single class, no single racial or religious group in mind.

All regions and all states have shared in the precious heritage of American freedom. All states and all regions have at least some infringements of that freedom—all people, all groups have been the victims of discrimination.

The masterly statement of our keynote speaker, the distinguished United States senator from Kentucky, Alben Barkley, made that point with great force. Speaking of the founder of our party, Thomas Jefferson, he said:

"He did not proclaim that all white, or black, or red, or yellow men are equal; that all Christian or Jewish men are equal; that all Protestant and Catholic men are equal; that all rich or poor men are equal; that all good or bad men are equal.

"What he declared was that all men are equal; and the equality which he proclaimed was equality in the right to enjoy the blessings of free government in which they may participate to which they have given their consent."

We are here as Democrats. But more important, as Americans—and I firmly believe that as men concerned with our country's future, we must specify in our platform the guarantees which I have mentioned.

Yes, this is far more than a party matter. Every citizen has a stake in the emergence of the United States as the leader of the free world. That world is being challenged by the world of slavery. For us to play our part effectively, we must be in a morally sound position.

We cannot use a double standard for measuring our own and other people's policies. Our demands for democratic practices in other lands will be no more effective than the guarantees of those practiced in our own country.

We are God-fearing men and women. We place our faith in the brotherhood of man under the fatherhood of God.

I do not believe that there can be any compromise of the guarantees of civil rights which I have mentioned.

In spite of my desire for unanimous agreement on the platform there are some matters which I think must be stated without qualification. There can be no hedging—no watering down.

There are those who say to you—we are rushing this issue of civil rights. I say we are 172 years late.

There are those who say—this issue of civil rights is an infringement on states' rights. The time has arrived for the Democratic party to get out of the shadow of states' rights and walk forthrightly into the bright sunshine of human rights.

People—human beings—this is the issue of the twentieth century. People—all kinds and sorts of people—look to America for leadership—for help—for guidance.

My friends—my fellow Democrats—I ask you for a calm consideration of our historic opportunity. Let us forget the evil passions, the blindness of the past. In these times of world economic, political, and spiritual—above all spiritual, crisis, we cannot—we must not, turn from the path so plainly before us.

That path has already led us through many valleys of the shadow of death. Now is the time to recall those who were left on that path of American freedom.

For all of us here, for the millions who have sent us, for the whole two billion members of the human family—our land is now, more than ever, the last best hope on earth. I know that we can—I know that we shall—begin here the fuller and richer realization of that hope—that promise of a land where all men are free and equal, and each man uses his freedom and equality wisely and well.

CHAPTER 17, NOTE 4

We had elected our first DFL official in 1946. John Blatnik was elected to the U. S. Congress from the Duluth-Iron Range district. In 1948, when I was elected to the Senate, Eugene McCarthy, a young college professor, was elected to the House of Representatives from St. Paul, Roy Weir (labor movement) from the Third District, in Minneapolis and suburbs, and Fred Marshall (farmer) in the Sixth District, of north-central Minnesota.

BOOK II

CHAPTER 18, NOTE 1

In 1974, Cyril King was elected governor of the Virgin Islands. He had grown up there and at my urging had been appointed Government Secretary, the second-highest office in the islands, by President Kennedy.

One of the comments frequently repeated about me is that I always have a lousy staff. I have found that criticism a little strange for a couple of reasons. For one thing, when men and women leave my staff, they are eagerly seized by other senators, become successful businessmen and lawyers, heads of foundations and intellectual organizations, college professors. Beyond that, they are the very people who have made it possible for me to be involved in everything from dairy support programs to the technical aspects of nuclear disarmament, from civil rights legislation to tax reform, from oceanography to space programs.

My staff, I suspect, works harder than almost any other on the Hill, longer hours, more days, fewer vacations, and frequently at less salary. That leaves them little time for the kind of social life and reputation building that is so much a part of Washington.

Bill Connell, who served me well from 1955 to 1969, is a case in point. He was often picked out by the press and political opponents as someone to attack if they wanted to attack me but didn't quite have the courage to do so.

As a youngster, Bill had traveled around the world with his dad, who was a Public Health Service officer, and when Bill and I first met, he was just nineteen and had already been a naval officer at the end of World War II. In the years that followed, he got a master's degree from the University of Minnesota, became an accomplished radio and TV writer, and had written and produced four short films by his mid-twenties.

He was a speech writer for the president of the University of Minnesota when I hired him, in 1955, to be my "Mr. Minnesota"—caring for constituent requests, staying on top of projects for our state—and to back up Herb Waters as press secretary. His background and interests carried him beyond those limits, however, into many legislative matters. In 1961 he became my chief aide and ran an office of several dozen people who answered many thousands of letters and requests annually. Bill's guidance protected my reputation for taking good care of my constituents and permitted me to take on increased legislative responsibility in the Kennedy and early Johnson years. That was no mean assignment, and he performed well and loyally.

Bill also directed the 1964 preconvention maneuvering for the vice-presidential nomination and has been involved intimately in each of my campaigns since.

He remains a trusted friend who speaks up even when his views oppose mine—a quality always desperately needed in Washington.

CHAPTER 18, NOTE 2

Bill Simms had worked with me in the mayor's office. He had been a special investigator in the Hennepin County Attorney's office and knew politicians and other people back home. Bill performed an immensely important function. Like Fred Gates, he never let me lose touch with my base. He made sure every letter was answered, and quickly. He watched over every constituent request. He, possibly more than anyone else, helped me establish a reputation in Minnesota for getting things done. He never worried about policy, never intruded his views on legislative matters. He was content to be an assistant, never aspired to be an alter ego.

CHAPTER 18, NOTE 3

It was a courteous act that I never forgot. Our relationship from that day until he left the Senate was a friendly one, through issues on which we differed as well as when we were allies.

CHAPTER 18, NOTE 4

My father's fatal cerebral hemorrhage struck as he sat at home working on a sermon he was to deliver on laymen's Sunday at the Methodist Church in Huron.

CHAPTER 18, NOTE 5

At one point, Senator William Fulbright suggested that Truman resign to permit a Republican to take over.

CHAPTER 18, NOTE 6

The NAM fought, with everything at its command, any talk of fair employment practices. The Chamber of Commerce ardently opposed increase in the minimum wage, anything that helped collective bargaining, any kind of federal aid to education. Both supported the Taft-Hartley Law, which labor found oppressive.

Not twenty years later, the NAM was conducting seminars to teach businessmen how to comply with the Fair Employment Practices Law, which they praised. At the same time, the Chamber of Commerce was educating its members about the need for job opportunities for minorities, for developing the inner city.

They had been dragged, as Adlai Stevenson once described it, kicking and screaming into the twentieth century. But the American Medical Association resisted the twentieth century even more strenuously. They attacked a serious study, *The Nation's Health,* as "purely politically inspired." They spoke of "compulsory health insurance" and "compulsory sickness insurance" as though it were leprosy—to be avoided at any cost. Those programs, as limited as they were, were "the forerunners of a socialist state" which would bring about the "enslavement of the medical profession."

CHAPTER 19, NOTE 1

If Lyndon Johnson had listened to Russell, we might well have avoided our extensive involvement in Vietnam. It is true Russell was a supporter of strong military defense and was considered a friend of the Pentagon, but he even more strongly opposed overextension of American power.

CHAPTER 19, NOTE 2

I introduced the first bill on health care under Social Security in 1949. Medicare passed in 1964. The first aid-to-education effort I made was in 1949; the National Defense Education Act, a kind of federal aid, was passed in 1958 and, the same year, the Primary and Secondary Education Act became law. The same sort of pattern exists in civil rights legislation: 1957, 1960, 1964, 1965.

The Peace Corps, Food for Peace, and the Youth Opportunity Act became realities only after repeated efforts to pass similar legislation.

CHAPTER 19, NOTE 3

Time magazine of November 22, 1963, carried an article about student sentiment in its education section that said in part:

"Campus disenchantment with President Kennedy now spreads far and wide. At conservative Georgia Tech, the complaint is that 'he's interfering with my personal life' through Big Government. At liberal Reed, where 'he doesn't inspire respect as Stevenson did,' the gripe is Kennedy's caution on the civil rights bill. At exuberant Wisconsin, 'he's liked in a negative way,' faulted for lack of political conviction. 'We're sick of him,' say dissidents at Jesuit Georgetown."

CHAPTER 19, NOTE 4

There is an interesting historical irony here. At the time that the Bricker Amendment was introduced, it was the conservative element of the Senate that feared and wished to curtail presidential power—at that time in the hands of a Democrat.

Some two decades later, when Congressional efforts were again being directed against the powers of that office, held by a Republican, the liberals were leading the fight.

Changes like these remind us that it is a fact of American life that politics is not a static discipline. It shifts and alters its preoccupations to correspond with new ideas, new events, and new perceptions in the greater society that surrounds it. And that is as it should be.

CHAPTER 19, NOTE 5

In 1954, when Joe McCarthy was at his raging peak, I sponsored a bill, that later was damaging to me in some liberal circles. McCarthy implied frequently that liberals and Communists were the same and unfortunately sold the idea to many Americans. It was outrageous, since liberal democracy and communism are diametrically opposed, but it was difficult to deal with McCarthy frontally.

The witch-hunting he led damaged many absolutely loyal Americans, and some governmental and industrial practices that came into being violated the civil liberties of many people by denying them the right to counsel, the right to face an accuser, the right to know and respond to adverse evidence, and in many cases the right to a fair trial. Something had to be done.

I tried to do it in terms of legislation. I believed from student days that democracy has a right to defend itself from internal as well as external enemies. The courts, following an eloquent opinion of Judge Learned Hand, had increasingly found that the Communist Party was part of an international conspiracy to undermine our government by force and violence.

In 1954, there was on the floor of the Senate a bill sponsored by Senator McCarran that was being opposed by labor and civil-liberties groups. To replace it, Tom Harris of the CIO and Max Kampelman prepared a bill fashioned carefully along the lines of Judge Hand's opinion.

The bill made membership in the Communist Party a crime and permitted anyone accused of being a Communist to sue for libel if the accusation was false. There would be procedures that guaranteed the right to confront accusing witnesses, refute adverse evidence and ensure a fair trial.

I took the draft to Wayne Morse, a respected lawyer and civil libertarian. He refined it and joined as a cosponsor. When Paul Douglas joined us, we proposed it as a substitute for the McCarran bill.

We did not have the votes to win, and McCarran shrewdly added our proposal as an amendment to his bill. By looking more liberal, he thwarted some opposition and then gutted the amendment in conference committee. Most of our basic concepts disappeared and what came out was barely recognizable.

The bill was defended in a law-review article by an old friend and ADA associate, Carl Auerbach, but his arguments have never persuaded many who have not forgiven me for what they saw as a transgression against civil liberties.

CHAPTER 20, NOTE 1

One night, we went to a party at a fancy home where I was lionized as the "bright, new liberal senator." I liked the attention, the adulation, and my pleasure must have been excessively obvious. As we drove home, Muriel said, "Hubert, you have to make a choice. Now." Puzzled, I asked, "What do you mean?" "Well, you can turn into a social butterfly, a Washington phony, or you can skip this sort of evening and become a good senator. You have the choice."

CHAPTER 20, NOTE 2

Ordinarily, since I did not serve on a committee—Finance or Appropriations—that was concerned with taxation, I should not, in Senate protocol, have been so involved. To step outside normal procedures was chancy but, as it turned out, a good thing to do.

CHAPTER 20, NOTE 3

Most tax bills are passed with a few senators intimately involved, the rest dependent on what they say is in the bill. It is complex legislation, whose nuances may escape even careful reading. Max Kampelman gathered a group of people to provide a quick course in the politics and economics of tax policy. He brought two men—Joseph Pechman and Charlie Davis—to me. Davis was then staff director of the House Ways and Means Committee and later general counsel of the Internal Revenue Service. He, in particular, was extremely helpful. Pechman was an economist and tax expert at the Treasury Department. The two of them also brought in a number of tax lawyers, including Louis Oberdorfer and Carl Price, who during the day took advantage of tax loopholes for their clients but studied with us at night on ways to close those same loopholes.

CHAPTER 21, NOTE 1

Without doubt one of the most powerful and influential men in Washington, his power often rivaled the President's. Had he not been from Texas he might very well have been nominated for President. In 1948, when the Democratic party was torn by factional fights, his name frequently was raised as a possible nominee and then dropped, since the cliché of the time was that a Southerner could not be elected.

CHAPTER 21, NOTE 2

When a piece of legislation is passed in different forms by the Senate and the House, its differences are resolved in a conference committee with members from both houses. The bill then goes back to the separate bodies for final passage.

By tradition, the members of conference committees are drawn from the House and Senate committees that report the bill out or have jurisdiction over its subject. The committee chairmen customarily submit a list of names (cleared with ranking members) which are announced by the presiding officer.

CHAPTER 22, NOTE 1

What it meant then and later was that such men as Albert Gore and Estes Kefauver of Tennessee, and Paul Douglas, could build up seniority on the Finance Committee, where tax-reform and social-security legislation, including Medicare, were considered; that Philip Hart of Michigan, Quentin Burdick of North Dakota, and Herbert Lehman of New York could serve on Judiciary, where civil rights bills were written; that such as Gale McGee of Wyoming and Mike Mansfield and I could serve on Appropriations, where funds for social welfare programs were allocated and appropriated. In general, Senate liberals always asked for service in labor-related committees—and the leadership was happy to go along.

These assignments and others like them over the years changed the political ideology from conservative to moderately liberal on major committees. Much of the legislation passed during the past decade would have been blocked in committee except for the new directions Johnson set through appointments while he was majority leader. And legislation approved in committee has an infinitely better chance of passing the full Senate than legislation and amendments proposed on the floor. By seeing to it that liberals had a voice on the steering and policy committees, he assured further assignments of liberals after he had given up the reins as majority leader. All of these things diluted the power of the southern bloc in controlling the Senate and influencing the content of legislation.

Johnson did all this out of altruism as well as pragmatism. He felt it was wasteful for freshman senators to sit out their early years at the edge of Senate work. He also realized he enhanced his own power by breaking the system. All of us who benefited owed him something.

CHAPTER 23, NOTE 1

One of the charges that attached itself to the Truman administration was cronyism. Whether the complaint was true or not in most cases, it certainly does not describe Charlie Murphy.

He had been a career government lawyer before becoming President Truman's special counsel, and was a gentleman who carried himself with great dignity. He was a very knowledgeable and thorough legal scholar.

After the Truman years, when he went into successful private practice, Charlie Murphy continued to be active in the Democratic party and in politics generally.

CHAPTER 23, NOTE 2

But there had been trouble before the bill, too. Having watched what chain stores and discount houses have been able to do to independent merchants with their vast economic power, I think the bill served a useful function. In recent years, consumer advocates, joined by some manufacturers, have attacked the fair-trade concept as an expensive one for consumers, viewing low prices as the sole measure of importance, and the bill has now been repealed. Individual state laws, of course, are still in force.

CHAPTER 23, NOTE 3

One evening, when I was still very new to Washington, I was invited out to an important dinner at a large hotel. While I was there, I met an aide to former President Herbert Hoover, who was staying in the hotel at the time. I wanted to see Mr. Hoover, and after a phone call I went up to his rooms.

I remember being impressed with the physical presence of the man: the big, muscular arms and hands. I had made a lot of political hay out of attacking Hoover and his administration, and I wanted to make sure that he did not take it personally.

I said, "Mr. President, in my campaign I spent a lot of time attacking you and your policies."

Hoover said, "Did it help you politically?"

I said that I supposed that it had—perhaps a great deal.

"Well," Hoover said, "then it's all right."

CHAPTER 23, NOTE 4

Years later, after President Truman's death, Bess Truman sent me his cane, noting that Truman had wanted me to have some token of his affection.

CHAPTER 23, NOTE 5

At that point, Max Kampelman called. I picked up the phone, laughed, and said, "Max, are you thinking what I'm thinking?"

He said that he was.

I said, "Well, don't worry—I've already called the White House."

CHAPTER 23, NOTE 6

Reuben was the pastor of Mt. Olivet Lutheran Church—one of the largest Lutheran congregations in the country. As mayor, I had appointed him chairman of the Mayor's Council on Human Relations.

CHAPTER 23, NOTE 7

Ultimately, my pleasure, largely political at that moment, was enhanced by the nature of Luther Youngdahl's subsequent career on the bench. He has proved to be a superb judge, and has earned the respect of the bar. His has been a liberal voice, particularly in the area of civil liberties.

We have remained good friends over the years, although I haven't been able to see him as often as I would like; and when John Kennedy took office as President, I recommended Youngdahl enthusiastically for appointment to the U. S. Court of Appeals.

So, as it turned out, my motives may have been self-serving at the time—but the results were in the public interest.

CHAPTER 24, NOTE 1

Our mail often got mixed up, and I frequently would receive letters commenting on some speech he made. Finally, I made a speech in the Senate about the two Humphreys.

I suggested that the differences between us might be made clear if people remembered him as "Trickle-down George" and me as "Percolate-up Hubert." His theory seemed to be if you made the rich richer some crumbs might trickle down from the table to those below. My concept was that if you increased the economic power of the mass of the population that profits would percolate up to the business community.

CHAPTER 24, NOTE 2

The Republicans barely controlled the Senate in 1953–54, and committees reflected the relative strength. Foreign Relations split eight to seven under the relatively weak chairmanship of Alexander Wiley. According to Johnson, strong Democratic voices could, beyond mere numbers, influence the committee's direction.

CHAPTER 24, NOTE 3

In 1956, Herb Waters drafted what became Adlai Stevenson's farm speeches. Stevenson never wanted to go quite as far as we, but he moved as far as he did primarily because of Herb's work.

Herb performed a similar role, under similar conditions, during the Kennedy campaign. As a result, he later became assistant administrator of the Agency for International Development (AID), a rank equivalent to assistant secretary of state. He devoted most of his time and talent to overseas economic development, with particular emphasis on food and nutrition.

He left AID when allegations were made that he had accepted personal favors, not involving money, from AID contractors. After a complete grand jury investigation, no charges were ever brought and even the Nixon administration subsequently approved his appointment as a U.S. delegate to world food conferences.

CHAPTER 24, NOTE 4

When Herb began to plan for the 1954 campaign, he insisted that I list the five most likely attacks or charges the Republicans would level at me. I refused at first, thinking it a silly exercise. Herb kept after me until I did. The first one said, "Humphrey talks too much." I've forgotten the other four.

After my re-election, Herb became my administrative assistant, continuing his guidance on agriculture. But his quick and bright mind absorbed the complexities of other issues, and he was as creative in education, for example, as in agriculture. In addition to running the office, he watched over my political welfare.

CHAPTER 24, NOTE 5

A variation on the program was a food-for-work concept. People in developing nations were paid for certain kinds of work with food. In Indonesia, for example, as Vice President I visited a massive project where irrigation ditches were being built virtually by hand—pick and shovel. The ditches, connected to a huge dam we had helped build, made the area much closer to food self-sufficiency.

On visits like that one, there is a traditional exchange of gifts. Instead of the usual teapot or Steuben glass, I thought I would do something out of the ordinary. I ordered a two-and-one-half-horsepower pump from Sears, Roebuck, to be the official gift, pumping water from a primary to a secondary ditch. The State Department objected, considering it slightly ridiculous. I insisted, but when it arrived in Indonesia there was a Tiffany sterling silver plaque on it, explaining it was a gift from the United States. The plaque, soon dusty and illegible, cost about three times what the pump did.

CHAPTER 24, NOTE 6

In fiscal year 1974, for example, almost half of the commodities shipped under the Food for Peace program went to Cambodia and Vietnam. The administration planned to ship two thirds of the program commodities to Southeast Asia, the Middle East, or to other countries, such as Chile, to which the Department of State had made special foreign-policy commitments.

CHAPTER 24, NOTE 7

Thatcher felt that farmers must have power, both marketing and political, centralized since they were so weak individually. He developed sophisticated political education through a weekly newspaper and periodic conferences for thousands of his members, when "participatory democracy" was a slogan yet to become the catch phrase of people who thought they had invented the concept.

Over the years, GTA has handled hundreds of millions of bushels of wheat, corn, and other grains grown in Kansas, North and South Dakota, Montana, Wyoming, Iowa, and Minnesota. Through marketing, financing, and political education, M. W. Thatcher has improved the lives of hundreds of thousands of people.

CHAPTER 24, NOTE 8

Lyndon Johnson had taken an active role in the dinner and put together a temporary alliance of conservatives and liberals in a tremendous display of unity. Senator Walter George was the chairman, and the evening was a love fest of Northerners and Southerners, of liberals and conservatives.

CHAPTER 24, NOTE 9

In 1940, the city of Minneapolis had virtually the same number and percentage of representatives in the state legislature as it had had in 1910. During the same period, the population of Minneapolis had increased from around three hundred thousand to five hundred thousand, its percentage of the state population from 14.5 to 17.6. As mayor, I found I could expect little co-operation from either the state legislature or government. And, of course, our city's relations with the state were not different from other city-state relations around the country, probably better than most.

CHAPTER 24, NOTE 10

The Budget Control Act of 1974 may change this. It is too early to tell. The Budget Act at last made multiyear budget planning—which I had before advocated—a matter of law. But it did not require the kind of public consultation I feel is necessary.

CHAPTER 25, NOTE 1

I was convinced at the time that it was in these areas that we would find the key to eventually break down the "iron curtain" and reduce Cold War hostilities. Mutual needs and interests, exchange of people and ideas, I hoped, would overwhelm political hostility.

CHAPTER 25, NOTE 2

Khrushchev was a politician who enjoyed politics, which were played in a very limited circle of upper-echelon Communists.

He spoke with genuine delight of the way he had outwitted Molotov, Zhukov, Bulganin, Kaganovich, Malenkov, and others whom he had publicly denounced as "anti-party" scoundrels. Stalin would probably have had them killed, and I thought Khrushchev would have done the same thing if he figured he had to.

But I got the impression he truly enjoyed the party infighting, preferring to outtalk and outsmart his opponents rather than exile or liquidate them.

CHAPTER 26, NOTE 1

I had known Jim Rowe for a long time, but I had never been close to him. He had had a distinguished career in government. He served as Justice Frankfurter's clerk in the Supreme Court (although Jim was originally from Montana, he had graduated from Harvard Law School); and when Franklin Roosevelt asked Congress for permission and money to expand the White House staff, Jim was one of the first persons hired. He fit FDR's specification—"a passion for anonymity."

Jim and Lyndon Johnson became very good friends during the '30s, and they were to remain close friends over the years.

One day in 1958, Jim and Max Kampelman, who were neighbors, were talking. Jim said that if Johnson was not going to run for the presidency in 1960—and he didn't think that Johnson would—then he would back me for the nomination.

That exchange led to a meeting of myself, Herb Waters, Max, and Jim at a downtown Washington restaurant to discuss my chances and campaign. Jim said that he would talk to Johnson about whether or not he would run. A few days later, he called Max and said, "The coast is clear."

When Johnson later did decide to enter the contest, Jim Rowe stayed with us.

CHAPTER 26, NOTE 2

The Washington group, in addition to Jim Rowe, included Max Kampelman, who was then in private law practice, having left my staff in 1955; Herb Waters, my administrative assistant; Joe Rauh, a liberal attorney with whom I had worked closely in the ADA; and Robert Barrie, a Minnesotan who had become administrative assistant to Senator Harrison Williams of New Jersey. Marvin Rosenberg, less a strategist than a fund-raiser, worked closely with us from his New York base. Also with us was Jim Loeb, a founder of ADA and later its executive director. Jim published a newspaper in Saranac Lake, New York, and was a close friend of Reinhold Niebuhr. He worked for us full-time, without pay.

The main responsibility remained with Minnesotans in Minnesota: Eugenie Anderson, Orville Freeman, Karl Rolvaag, Ray Hemenway (who was then state DFL chairman and who knew many of his counterparts around the country), Congressman John Blatnik, Walter Mondale, Barney Allen, Miles Lord, and Gerald Heaney (an exceptionally bright and talented political operative who was our national committeeman).

Miles Lord, now a federal judge, has been a special friend. He and his family and I and mine have shared many happy times. He is an exuberant man, a people's judge, who takes the concept of justice for all seriously.

On Miles Lord: One day, years ago, when Miles and I took our kids fishing, we were on a narrow road in northern Minnesota and found ourselves blocked by a disabled bus. Miles was then attorney general of Minnesota and I was senator. Both of us were unshaven, dressed sloppily, and Miles went up to find out what the trouble was.

When he came back, he told me that the bus was filled with people on tour from California and encouraged me to go up and greet them.

What he didn't tell me was that he himself had gone aboard the bus, welcomed the stranded visitors, and told them there was a "harmless nut" in the area who looked like Hubert Humphrey and often introduced himself as Humphrey. He had suggested that they humor the man if he got aboard, assuring them that that was the best thing to do. I went up to the bus, boarded it, and proceeded to announce that I was Senator Hubert Humphrey. Laughter rolled through the bus, though I didn't think I had said anything funny.

As I stood there trying to figure out what was going on, a voice from the back of the bus said, "Yeah, and I'm Governor Pat Brown."

CHAPTER 26, NOTE 3

Yet it is not even the amount of money that is the problem, but whether it comes early enough. Five thousand dollars early may be worth ten thousand dollars later. There is a terrible waste in campaigning when financing is inadequate or delayed. One of the clichés of politics is that 50 per cent of everything spent is wasted. Unfortunately, it is impossible to know which 50 per cent.

Every campaign is filled with some realistic, some grandiose, plans which are stopped and started, or sometimes just stopped. It is an absurd and costly system, which public financing, much too long in coming, may now rectify.

CHAPTER 26, NOTE 4

Of that group, only Senator William Proxmire was a real disappointment.

When Joe McCarthy died, in 1957, a special election was held to fill his Senate seat. Proxmire was running for the office. My staff and I spent a good deal of time and energy raising funds and generally aiding his campaign. And he won.

Later I intervened with Lyndon Johnson to get Proxmire some important committee positions—a move Johnson was reluctant to make but which he did as a favor to me.

But three years later, when I was in Wisconsin running a tough race against tough competition, Proxmire was nowhere to be seen. He could have given us the kind of help and influence we needed to combat the Kennedy campaign.

One man who did was the lieutenant governor, Philleo Nash, an anthropologist, a guitar playing, folk-song-singing scholar, and a public servant.

CHAPTER 26, NOTE 5

I got more than my "hundred votes." I carried the city.

CHAPTER 26, NOTE 6

It upset the Kennedys. Just before the election, Gene McCarthy met Jack Kennedy in a Detroit hotel corridor during a Democratic conference. Kennedy pulled our brochure from his pocket, brandished it at McCarthy, and said angrily, "This is outrageous." McCarthy, deadpan, and ignoring the point of Kennedy's remark, responded, "Jack, it's not so bad a record for a man from Massachusetts."

CHAPTER 26, NOTE 7

In Wisconsin, the Kennedy campaign refined the use of public-opinion polls. Money and people are attracted to the likely winner.

Success breeds success. The polls seem to have a life of their own; they live off themselves and they create their own momentum. Journalists watch them, write some people off, project others as possible or likely winners. If you are leading in the polls, your organization points that out, attracting waverers, convincing the unconvinced.

I have never seen them more effectively used than in 1959 and 1960 by the Kennedy forces. Larry O'Brien and Kenny O'Donnell were masters. First, they would slip the polls to selected reporters and columnists, who would race to their typewriters, vehicles for the propaganda, fascinated by the seeming inside "scoop."

Then the polls *and* the articles were fed to wavering politicians. The message was clear: "Look, Kennedy is the leader, he is going to be the winner, and you had better join up early rather than be left out after the final victory comes." It was, to say the least, effective campaign strategy. It is a circular system, which feeds upon itself. The Kennedy organization used it more adroitly and cleverly than anyone before or since, though both Lyndon Johnson and Richard Nixon became almost fixated, in the President's office, on their polls.

CHAPTER 26, NOTE 8

Some felt that if I must consider another state it ought to be Nebraska, an agricultural state with a closed primary, in which, unlike Wisconsin, only Democrats could vote for either Kennedy or me.

CHAPTER 27, NOTE 1

The Ku Klux Klan had been active and strong in West Virginia.

CHAPTER 27, NOTE 2

Our campaign in West Virginia was brightened by the presence of Jimmy Wofford, a native West Virginia folk singer. Karl Rolvaag heard him sing and recruited him to travel with us. He picked up his guitar and sang our campaign songs at rally after rally, warming up the crowd, his enthusiasm as infectious as it was ingenuous. When we lost, Jimmy cried.

Later that year, he hitchhiked to Los Angeles for the Democratic convention. One night at a Minnesota party, we all sang and laughed and cried together as Jimmy sang. We passed the hat to raise money for Jimmy's hotel room and food, and he did not have to hitchhike home.

Right after the West Virginia primary, Max Kampelman brought Alex Rose and Arthur Goldberg to my office at their request. They said they spoke not only for themselves but for Walter Reuther and David Dubinsky and wanted to do what was necessary to minimize any hostility between Kennedy and me. I was not in a particularly conciliatory mood, particularly irritated with Arthur, who had been a long-time friend and whose support I had expected until he became a close adviser to Jack Kennedy. I, not Kennedy, had been their liberal colleague for a dozen years. We had stood together on the issues, and Kennedy had been to the right of us all. Yet, when the crunch came they moved, shamelessly I thought, to Kennedy.

I said only that I would respond if Kennedy were to make the first move on the floor of the Senate. A day or two later, word came through Max that Kennedy would make the approach, and when he did, our reconciliation began.

At that first meeting with Goldberg and Rose, they thought that a Kennedy-Humphrey ticket would be the strongest one possible and urged me to consider it. I was not really interested but told them I would consider it and let them know through Max what I decided. In the meantime, Goldberg called Max to report that a number of other labor leaders had approached Kennedy about my being on the ticket and that he had responded favorably.

As the convention approached, I met with them again and expressed a less negative view. We agreed once more to keep in touch. They soon told Max that a deal had been struck between Kennedy and the labor leaders and that the nomination was mine if I wanted it. Tempted to accept, I flew home to discuss it with Muriel before we went on to Los Angeles for the convention.

When we arrived in L.A., Max was among the large delegation who greeted us at the airport. I drew him aside and said, "Tell our friends that it is all off. Muriel is against it, and that swings the vote."

When Max conveyed that message to Goldberg, Rose, Reuther and Dubinsky, they were furious as well as disappointed and asked to see me personally. I had little desire to see them, since I felt they had let me down in Wisconsin and West Virginia. Now to have them beseech me to take the nomination for Vice President seemed to be not second prize, but last prize. I met with them only long enough to reaffirm the decision Muriel and I had made.

A little later, George Meany spoke to me, indicating that he also thought that Kennedy would take me as Vice President, and encouraged me to accept. I told him there were more vice-presidential commitments around than a mangy dog had fleas and that I supposed I was considered with all the rest of those who thought they had commitments—Henry Jackson, Robert Docking, Herschel Loveless, Orville Freeman—but that I was not going to be used and my answer was no.

CHAPTER 27, NOTE 4

I remain unforgiving about only one aspect of the West Virginia campaign. Among the many outsiders they brought in, most of them able and tough politicians, was Franklin Roosevelt, Jr. The Roosevelt name was revered in West Virginia, and President Roosevelt remained an untarnished hero, a presence as forceful as though he were still alive.

Young Franklin was the image of his father, tall, good-looking, with a voice that seemed a precise echo of fireside chats heard on crystal sets and Emerson radios. Beneath the image, however, there are no beneficent comparisons.

This Roosevelt was the carrier of libelous tripe about my lack of military service. He labeled me a draft dodger among the patriotic people of West Virginia, and he continued to do so even after we had made repeated contacts with the Kennedys demonstrating the untruth of the allegations. They believed me, but never shut FDR, Jr., up, as they easily could have. It was a dishonest and politically unnecessary thing to do, but it persisted. Months later, Roosevelt came to my office to apologize.

CHAPTER 27, NOTE 5

I have, in the course of a long public life, sometimes been accused of long-windedness. Part of this, I freely admit, derives from a simple love of talk. But part also comes from learning to speak to midwestern audiences, who actually want to hear a speech of sizable length.

Moreover, anyone who has spent a great deal of his or her youth in the formal discipline of debate has been shaped, to some degree, by the ancient adage: "Tell them what you're going to tell them; tell them; and then tell them what you've told them." It is a theory calculated to promote clarity at the expense of patience.

CHAPTER 27, NOTE 6

I made it my business to bring Kennedy and the Farmers Union leaders together. The first step was a conference I arranged between Kennedy and John Baker, their Washington legislative representative. After that, I urged a series of other meetings.

Kennedy listened to them: James Patton, a distinguished, tall man whose presence was enhanced by a black eye patch; Tony DeChant, who succeeded Patton as president; and Robert Lewis, Baker's Washington colleague. All of them were knowledgeable, wise, and liberal advocates who significantly changed Kennedy's unformed view of American agriculture. Lewis and Baker later became assistant secretaries of agriculture.

CHAPTER 28, NOTE 1

Tom Kuchel was defeated by the right wing of his own party in the primary of 1968.

CHAPTER 28, NOTE 2

President Kennedy's choice of Sargent Shriver to head the Peace Corps was a fortuitous one. He gathered around him people who shared his enthusiasm: Bill Moyers, Frank Mankiewicz, Franklin Williams, William Haddad, Harris Wofford, Jack Vaughn. And they in turn excited the altruistic vision of thousands of young Americans.

CHAPTER 29, NOTE 1

Earlier that day, President Johnson asked me to find out if Max would join the White House staff. Max did not want to, but said that he would not turn down a request from the President. He asked me to stop the request as diplomatically as I could. I did.

It was understandable that Johnson would want Max on board. He had come to know him personally and well during the fifties, when, as my legislative counsel and a moderate voice in liberal Senate discussions, Max had worked hard to bridge the gap between conservatives like Georgia's Walter George and those of us on the liberal side.

CHAPTER 29, NOTE 2

One was by Horace Busby, one by Ted Sorensen, and one apparently by Adlai Stevenson.

CHAPTER 30, NOTE 1

Because I had been able, as mayor, to win passage of the nation's first municipal statute on fair employment practices, I made that one of my prime objectives in the Senate. I should have known better, I suppose, since Harry Truman had been submitting a federal FEP bill since 1945, only to see it die a yearly death. When an FEP bill actually passed the House, in 1950, it was filibustered to death in the Senate.

This did not necessarily occur because all those senators blocking our efforts were the embodiment of evil or hatred. On their side, they had a powerful mistrust of Northerners who were backing civil rights legislation. They felt that we were insincere, simply political opportunists who were making a play for black votes. We, on our side, felt that *they* were insincere, that some of them saw the injustice of racial discrimination but obstinately stood in the way of progress. Some, of course, were sincere in their bigotry.

This two-way misunderstanding gradually began to decline. One day, Walter George was overheard talking to some of his colleagues in the Senate cloakroom. "You know," he said, in a hushed tone of wonder and almost disbelief, "this fellow Humphrey is actually *sincere* about civil rights!"

CHAPTER 30, NOTE 2

At the beginning, its funds came largely from the National Association for the Advancement of Colored People and the United Auto Workers.

I continued:

"They are coming to exercise their constitutional rights of petition, assembly, and speech in a fashion wholly within the American traditions of liberty. In fact, they are conducting themselves in a manner quite reminiscent of the spirit which must have motivated and inspired the Founding Fathers of this nation.

"These people—both white and Negro—are coming to Washington out of a deep personal sense of commitment to the struggle for civil rights that is underway in this land. They are coming because they share the belief that second-class citizenship must be banished without delay. They are coming to Washington because their consciences will permit them no other course.

"I suppose that tomorrow's demonstration will be largely composed of people who have never before demonstrated for or against anything. There will be housewives, manual laborers, doctors, lawyers, the unemployed, churchmen, stage and screen personalities, government workers, blue-collar workers, and white-collar workers. I have spoken with these people, and their enthusiasm and expectancy for this demonstration is remarkable—and contagious. These are not troublemakers or rabble-rousers; these are responsible and concerned American citizens who are determined to speak out in favor of full freedom and equality for their fellow citizens. That is why they are coming to Washington.

"In a world in which the people of so many areas are denied the opportunity of freedom of petition, in a world in which tyranny seems to rule so many people, what a blessed and wonderful experience it is to know that in the United States of America the voice of the people can and will be heard in a democratic meeting.

"Of course, there are certain risks in bringing so many thousands of people together to support a matter that is charged with emotion and feeling. But there are few things in this world that are worth accomplishing which do not also entail a certain degree of risk. I am convinced and confident that the marchers themselves will not initiate any public disorder. Should certain agitators attempt to subvert the objectives of the demonstration, I am confident that the district police will enforce the law and maintain order.

"Regardless of the risk, I support this demonstration because it serves as a unique vehicle whereby thousands of Americans can express their deep personal convictions that the time for equal justice is now. This is a totally voluntary outpouring of the human spirit in behalf of freedom and liberty, an outpouring that has not been seen in this country for many generations. As such, I believe the feelings of the marchers will be transmitted across this land to all Americans and across the seas to people everywhere.

"When this demonstration has been concluded, we will have evidence in abundance that the lamp of liberty still burns on these shores. We will learn again the age-old lesson of liberty that America first learned nearly two hundred years ago and has been teaching the rest of mankind ever since.

"As one senator from Minnesota, I rise to welcome the many thousands of Americans who will come to Washington tomorrow. I intend to participate fully in their activities. I am confident that their effort will be successful and that the entire nation will be reached by the dedication and enthusiasm which the demonstrators bring with them."

CHAPTER 30, NOTE 4

Nicholas Katzenbach, then deputy attorney general, was later to become Attorney General. Burke Marshall was the assistant attorney general in charge of the Civil Rights Division.

CHAPTER 30, NOTE 5

Senator Willis Robertson of Virginia was one of the stalwart southern opponents of the civil rights bill. He was always good for an hour speech, but it was a strain for him at his advanced age. Occasionally, to make it easier for him, I would interrupt to ask questions. He would smile and respond, acknowledging without words my gesture. Afterward, we might share his Virginia sour-mash whiskey.

It may seem strange to help and socialize with an opponent in such a crucial legislative battle. In Senate terms, it was not. On those rare occasions when a liberal colleague had slipped the traces and we were shy a body for a quorum call, I'd find Willis and he would come to the Senate floor, never letting me down when I needed him.

CHAPTER 30, NOTE 6

Senators Clark, Magnuson, Hart, Pastore, Morse, Douglas, Long of Missouri, and Dodd were made team captains for particular titles of the bill. Each team, learned in the niceties of its title, would discuss it as the debate began.

CHAPTER 30, NOTE 7

Senators Roman Hruska of Nebraska and Norris Cotton of New Hampshire were two who felt they could not be captains.

CHAPTER 30, NOTE 8

I had not fought alone since 1948, and the success in 1964 was happily shared with old allies. Andrew Biemiller, the chief AFL-CIO lobbyist, was with us throughout that spring, helping to finish what we had started in 1948, as were Joe Rauh, the ADA leader, and Clarence Mitchell of the NAACP.

CHAPTER 30, NOTE 9

I was confident about the outcome. I called President Johnson the night before to assure him that we would win. We had delayed any effort to enact cloture until we were virtually certain we could win. To have tried and failed would have been a devastatingly serious setback, creating almost irresistible pressures to dilute the bill and compromise with the opposition. Yet, for all my confidence, I spent the evening pursuing, by phone, three Democratic senators—Howard Edmondson of Oklahoma, Ralph Yarborough of Texas, and Howard Cannon of Nevada—whose votes were not certain.

CHAPTER 30, NOTE 10

Philip Hart worked long and well on this bill. He, along with Paul Douglas and Herbert Lehman, must rank among the most principled, compassionate voices ever to serve in the United States Senate, or at least during my career.

CHAPTER 30, NOTE 11

Working alongside Clarence through much of the battle for civil rights legislation was another very special person, Joe Rauh. Joe had been a law clerk for Felix Frankfurter and was one of the founders of Americans for Democratic Action. He was a brilliant, emotional, devoted fighter for liberal causes who was close to Walter Reuther and the United Auto Workers.

Because we shared so many common interests in issues and legislation, Joe was also one of my most ardent and consistent supporters politically. He worked hard for me in the 1960 presidential primaries and in my efforts for the vice-presidential nomination in 1964. Our friendship was severely strained by the Vietnam War and my support for it. In 1968 he did not support my candidacy—and that break in our political association was of particular sadness for me.

Joe was not always easy to deal with, but we always knew where he stood. He was an unbending advocate of what he believed in and found compromise difficult to accept. There were few liberal programs that came out of the past twenty-five years that did not benefit from his involvement.

CHAPTER 30, NOTE 12

Mitchell did another shrewd thing in that walking conversation. He pointed out, in more delicate terms, that the shibboleth of the Southerners that civil rights was too often "judge-made law," that is, the product primarily of the Supreme Court, was no longer true. Now we had a Civil Rights Act that was the product of Congress, an act by elected officials. Mitchell also told Lyndon Johnson of that conversation, subtly suggesting that Johnson talk to his friend Russell in those terms. I don't know if Johnson did or not, but several days later, at home in Georgia, Russell did speak, however grudging, of the Civil Rights Act as the result of the legislative process. That helped.

CHAPTER 30, NOTE 13

It was too late on Friday to get a flight to Minneapolis. My fears for

Bob blocked out my pleasure through a sleepless night. Finally, on Saturday morning, I made it to his side.

In the intervening eleven years there has been no recurrence. He is, in medical statistics, cured.

CHAPTER 31, NOTE 1

"Larger than life" is a label constantly applied to Johnson, and rightly. It is not a description that is generally applied to other Presidents I have known: Truman, Eisenhower, Kennedy, Nixon, Ford. Their virtues and flaws are in a human dimension. Smart, honest, charming, handsome, or their opposites, but never "larger than life."

CHAPTER 31, NOTE 2

One good example might be legislation concerning soybeans. Dwayne Andreas made part of his fortune in soybeans, and I was a consistent supporter of bills that benefited soybean farmers.

If Dwayne Andreas had never existed, I still would have enthusiastically backed the same legislation, if for no other reason than that it is a primary crop in Minnesota.

I knew that Dwayne was never out to corrupt me or anyone else with campaign contributions and *quid pro quo* deals. That is why I was so deeply pained when he was later brought to court on an information by a U.S. attorney concerning the possibility of an illegal corporate contribution to my 1968 campaign. It was a real blow to the man who was and is my close friend.

Too few people remember that the judge found Dwayne entirely innocent and fully exonerated him of all charges.

CHAPTER 31, NOTE 3

In 1969, a friend of mine who had raised funds for us in the 1968 campaign was soliciting contributions to Hebrew University in Israel. In the course of his rounds, he called on Dwayne, hoping that he might send them something in the neighborhood of five thousand dollars.

Instead, Dwayne sent the university a check for twenty-five thousand dollars, along with a request for complete anonymity. And he has continued to send them the same amount every year since, with the same request, and has never received any public recognition for his generosity until the publication of this book.

CHAPTER 31, NOTE 4

Basic questions concerning equality in the delegate-selection process were involved, not the kind of questions that would quietly fade away. Frequently, the white delegates who came from Mississippi did not support the national ticket. Blacks and whites who did were systematically excluded by state party procedures.

CHAPTER 31, NOTE 5

Later, the President said that if I hadn't had sense enough to know that I was going to be his running mate a lot earlier than that night in Atlantic City, I didn't deserve to be on the ticket. That may possibly have been so and I suppose that he believed it, but it was truly impossible to know what he would do in a political situation like that. In his own, oft-repeated term, he liked to keep his options open.

CHAPTER 31, NOTE 6

Once, we docked in front of the house he had built for Jack and Mary Margaret Valenti. He marched several of us into it, to show it off. In the kitchen, he opened the refrigerator door to show that it was properly filled with oranges and eggs and juice and soda pop.

CHAPTER 31, NOTE 7

That label had, of course, originally been applied to Al Smith in the 1928 presidential campaign. I liked it and it seemed appropriate. Later, when the Vietnam War grew intense, political opponents turned it on me and it became an embarrassment.

BOOK III

CHAPTER 32, NOTE 1

An associate of Lansdale's, Rufus Phillips, worked closely with Bill Connell. The two of them, together and separately, prepared memoranda that described the dangers of concentrating on a military solution and offered alternative, political approaches.

CHAPTER 32, NOTE 2

One staff member, my foreign-policy assistant, John Rielly, objected to my carrying the Lansdale message on an entirely different basis. He said Lansdale gave priority to Southeast Asia that it didn't deserve. He encouraged me to use what influence I had to turn American attention to other areas.

In the spring of 1964, his first draft of an article on U.S. policy in Latin America began with a line that said that, compared to Brazil, Vietnam's importance to our foreign policy was like a pebble on the beach. I rejected the comparison as being gratuitous, but the point remains that John could seriously make the case even then.

CHAPTER 32, NOTE 3

In June 1964 (when we had about twenty-one thousand Americans in Vietnam), President Johnson had asked for my views, and I had sent him a memorandum which, in a generally pessimistic appraisal, urged a middle course between pulling out and "launching . . . a Korea-type conventional war in the area."

I hoped for an independent and free Southeast Asia but said, "The Vietnamese must be skillfully and firmly guided, but it is they (not we) who must win their war."

I continued, "The two most urgent fundamental needs in Vietnam are: stabilizing the Vietnamese leadership and giving some hope to which the Vietnamese people can rally. . . . A political base is needed to support all other actions. . . . No amount of additional military involvement can be successful without accomplishing this task."

I concluded, "Direct U.S. military action against North Vietnam, U.S.

assumption of command roles, or the participation in combat of U.S. troop units is unnecessary and undesirable."

CHAPTER 32, NOTE 4

The article appeared in the New York *Times Magazine*. I said that we should help the South Vietnamese defend themselves against the Viet Cong, but that we must realize in the long run there was no real defense against communism in Asia without "an Asian coalition of powers with India as its main force."

The article continued: "While aiding the South Vietnamese, we must make it clear that the primary responsibility for preserving independence and achieving peace in Vietnam remains with the Vietnamese people and their government."

I warned, ". . . we must be careful as a nation to avoid fluctuations between extremes. First there was isolation and now the tendency is that everything everywhere is our business. Let us have a prudent posture. We do not aspire to a Pax Americana."

I think it was good advice.

CHAPTER 32, NOTE 5

Dean Rusk was one of my favorite people in Washington during the Kennedy and Johnson administrations. He was a southern gentleman in its finest sense—learned, soft-spoken, of quiet dignity and great integrity. He had deep feelings and understanding of the working of democracy, with a special sense of constitutional roles. That his excellence should have been mired in Vietnam is yet another tragedy of the whole event.

CHAPTER 32, NOTE 6

It may be that what Bundy cabled, moved Johnson more than would have been normal. Bundy was an impressive man. Ordinarily, he was factual, never tried to plead a personal point of view. He was not Secretary of Defense, he was not Secretary of State, and he never presumed to be either. He had clearly defined his role, and that was to present the President with a thoughtful analysis of options. At Pleiku, however, he became, for the moment, an advocate.

Walt Rostow, who was also bright and able, was generally much more an advocate for a point of view. He weighed in on one side or the other; Bundy did not.

My view of Bundy changed over the years I knew him. I did not like him at first. He seemed cold, smug, and distant. I did not expect him to be co-operative or helpful. I was quite wrong about him. He always treated me decently, sharing his knowledge and wisdom to the limit that conditions—and the President—permitted.

CHAPTER 32, NOTE 7

Pietro Nenni, the Italian Socialist leader, planned to attend the Pacem in Terris conference and would have welcomed an invitation to come to

Washington. The State Department made it immediately clear that he would not be invited. I had hoped to see him in New York, because he was a friend, but was asked not to.

Pietro Nenni was one of Italy's most powerful and distinguished political leaders in the early sixties.

At an East-West parliamentary conference in Rome, I sought him out, and in the course of our meeting the subect of the new coalition government was discussed.

One of our government's deep concerns about Italy at this point was that the Socialists in the coalition would mean that Italy would no longer support the NATO alliance.

I asked Nenni directly if this were so, and he replied firmly that if he entered the coalition not only would he support NATO, but that he was prepared to split his party, the Socialists, if that was required.

Our ambassador was astonished. They had not had a hint that Nenni would take such a position, and President Kennedy was delighted when I reported the Nenni conversation to him back in Washington.

CHAPTER 32, NOTE 8

Through my friends Bill Boggs and Harry Ashmore, who were at the Center for the Study of Democratic Institutions, I had been involved in discussions about the conference virtually from its inception many months before. I was disappointed that the President would not accept the invitation. One can only wonder what might have been had he said "no" to the bombing of the north and "yes" to Pacem in Terris, where he could have defined America's goals for peace.

CHAPTER 32, NOTE 9

Senator Fulbright said in July, "It is ironic that at the same time that the vestiges of the Monroe Doctrine are being fitfully liquidated, the United States should be formulating a similar doctrine of pre-eminent responsibility for Asia. One wonders whether the Asian doctrine will reap for the United States as rich a harvest of affection for democracy as has the Monroe Doctrine. One wonders whether China will accept American hegemony as gracefully as Cuba and the Dominican Republic have accepted it, and one wonders whether anyone ever thought of asking the Asians if they really want to join the Great Society."

CHAPTER 32, NOTE 10

That spring, about six weeks after I returned from Vietnam, Senator Fulbright held hearings on U.S. policy on China, and one of the academic experts, Doak Barnett, of Columbia at the time, used the expression "containment without isolation." The idea and the phrase both appealed to me, and I used the phrase subsequently in speeches, specifically on "Meet the Press" in late March. Bill Bundy called afterward, indicating his distress at my talking in those terms, feeling that it encouraged other countries to believe that our attitude on China was changing. As assistant secretary of state for far eastern affairs, he probably reflected not only his own, but the Administration, view.

CHAPTER 32, NOTE 11

Harold Wilson was a steadfast friend of the United States during those difficult years. It was not easy for him; indeed, it was an immense political burden. His own constituency within the British Labour Party was not at all sympathetic to the American position in Vietnam.

CHAPTER 32, NOTE 12

Charts and maps became necessary props. They are useful, of course, but McNamara and the military and Johnson all seemed to love them unduly.

Several years later, when I watched President Nixon explain on television why we were moving on Cambodia, I thought I recognized charts I had seen. I recalled the day when the Joint Chiefs presented to Johnson a plan to bomb Cambodia—charts, rationale, the whole bit.

Johnson leaned wearily forward, elbows spread on the table, and said in his broad Texas drawl, "General, Ah got one _____ war; Ah don't need uhnother one."

CHAPTER 32, NOTE 13

Under JFK, the trainers and advisers moved out from the side of the South Vietnamese lieutenants and took the point at the head of the column. When the trainer-adviser role changed radically, it became a precedent for the heavier investment of troops later.

CHAPTER 32, NOTE 14

On several occasions that month, I told the President that I did not think the North Vietnamese would ever come to the conference table. They would surely gain less there than they might on the battlefield, unless we were able to subject them to increased pressure. To do that, we had to expect, and accept, more intense criticism, knowing (or believing, at least) that greater military action could bring that about.

My real hope was that, if we were adamant and strong, they might decide to retire from the battlefield, explaining to their people that withdrawal was not defeat but a strategic move permitting them to come back at a later time.

CHAPTER 32, NOTE 15

The recommendation to bomb North Vietnam had been made before, and Johnson had refused to permit it. One day when we were alone, he said, "Look, Hubert, if I follow the advice of my military on this Haiphong thing, here's what's going to happen: There's going to be a plane made in Texas piloted by a Texan with a bomb made in Texas, and no matter how good the pilot, one bomb he drops is going to miss

the harbor and the docks and fall right down the smokestack of a Soviet freighter. And then I am going to have one hell of a bigger war on
my hands."

CHAPTER 32, NOTE 16

Komer continued to have the difficult assignment of making order out
of domestic chaos in Vietnam, some of it indigenous, but much the result of our presence there. He became the "pacification" chief, running
what came to be called the "other war," that is, rural development, domestic economic matters, and the semblance of democratic government
on the province and village levels.

The Evans and Novak column of October 1, 1967, said, ". . . the
big news here this year is that Bunker, pacification chief Robert Komer,
and Deputy Ambassador Edwin Locke are trying for the first time to
use the full weight of U.S. power to convince Thieu and his new government (not yet selected) that U.S. patience is not inexhaustible."

CHAPTER 32, NOTE 17

It is quite possible that a kind of racism was behind all this, including
that of self-styled and real liberals. It might have been easier to convince people of the validity of our battle if the beneficiaries had been
English, French, or German. It was easy for critics to accuse our military of having disdain for Asians, repeating the canard, as they sometimes did, that Asians have a different view of life. But had the war
been in Italy, for example, or Greece, some of our doves would have
molted quickly and grown the feathers of hawks.

CHAPTER 32, NOTE 18

The reporters were not of a single mind on American involvement in
Asia. They included men who might be considered hawks, such as
Keyes Beech of the Chicago *Daily News,* an old Asia hand and terribly
wise, and younger men with differing views, such as Ronald Ross of the
Minneapolis *Tribune,* Murray Fromson of CBS, and Peter Arnett of the
Associated Press.

Whatever their private views on whether the United States should be
in Vietnam, they were unanimous in saying it was not going well. I did
not want to believe them, but they were so unemotionally firm in their
descriptions of corruption, failures, and official lies and distortions, that
I began to hear what they were saying.

CHAPTER 32, NOTE 19

On this trip there had been time for briefing. I learned from government documents dated 1964, but that I had never seen before, that we
had great reservation about Thieu. The reports read: "Thieu is considered to be loyal to only one ideal—*his* own personal aggrandizement. It
is felt that Thieu will stoop to anything, stop at nothing, in his drive for
self-advancement. It is further believed that Thieu has no basic loyalty

to either the Government of the Republic of Vietnam (GRVN) or to the Republic of Vietnam and that his ambition is so overriding that he is believed capable of joining the People's Army of Vietnam if he were assured of the top position in that army. Thieu is considered loyal to the current GRVN only to the extent that the fact of his loyalty is not detrimental to his own self-interests.

"Not only is Thieu extremely ambitious and unscrupulous, but he is also highly egotistical. When in the presence of American military officers, Thieu talks of only one subject—coups d'etat. He considers himself and refers to himself as a 'coup expert.' He has stated on one occasion, 'If you want to have a coup, just come to see me.' He loves to talk of his roles in the coups d'etat of 1 November 1963 and 30 January 1964. He has claimed unto himself a major portion of the credit for the successful planning and execution of both the above mentioned coups."

The report also said: "Thieu is an extremely capable, well qualified officer."

CHAPTER 32, NOTE 20

Shortly after that speech, I got a letter from Richard Nixon, then practicing law in New York. My speech, he said, was the best exposition he had seen on the subject of Vietnam. I thought I recognized parts of it in his 1968 acceptance speech in Miami Beach.

CHAPTER 32, NOTE 21

At the time we were spending $30 billion a year in Vietnam, we were spending a total of $25.6 billion in programs at home for health care and research, urban revitalization, foreign economic assistance, and encouragement of the arts.

People talked easily then of a "peace dividend," as though it would automatically happen when the war ended. But "guns *or* butter" was never realistically the question, and I was not surprised, when Vietnam was over, that money did not flow into other areas.

CHAPTER 33, NOTE 1

Labor unions and labor leaders come in for a lot of abuse these days. They don't rate highly with many people, but they do with me.

The labor movement has been essential to improving the quality of American life in my time. No legislative accomplishment that fills me with pride or satisfaction lacked labor support. Steady, determined, courageous, effective—they've stood up against totalitarianism, they've lifted up vast segments of the poor and downtrodden.

As I look back over my thirty years of public life—three races for mayor, four Senate campaigns, four national campaigns, countless legislative struggles—I can only report that labor has been steadfast in good times and bad.

My career began with a labor endorsement. It gained momentum with the early support of such men as Philip Murray of the CIO, Bill Green of the AFL, Al Whitney of the railroad brotherhoods, Sidney Hillman, and David Dubinsky.

In recent years, George Meany has been an immensely powerful ally, though he has not always agreed with what I have done or said. To list all the men and women of labor who have fought the good fights with me would take pages and pages.

CHAPTER 33, NOTE 2

I suppose one of the truly exciting parts of my life has been to work for and with the black community in America to reach for social justice. The thirty years of my public life have coincided with a period of rapid change in the status and role of blacks in American society.

As a result, personally, politically, and legislatively, I have enjoyed the friendship of leaders of the black community during that whole period. In Minnesota, Cecil Newman, William Seabron, and Judge L. Howard Bennett were with me at the beginning of my career. (Bill Leland, a lifelong fighter for equal rights, who was white, was intensely involved then, too.) At various later times, I have worked closely with such national leaders as Walter White, Roy Wilkins, Clarence Mitchell, Whitney Young, Jim Farmer, A. Philip Randolph, Bayard Rustin, George L. P. Weaver and Jim Jones. They have all added to a precious part of my life.

CHAPTER 34, NOTE 1

Among these friends were Minnesotans who have been important parts of my political life for a long time and helped immensely in the 1968 campaign.

Geri Joseph became vice-chairman of the Democratic National Committee when I got the nomination. She had been an award-winning journalist and state DFC chairwoman and national committeewoman before assuming the national office. She and her husband, Burton, have been my friends for twenty years, and her father-in-law, I. S. Joseph, one of my earliest supporters and a leader in the Minneapolis Jewish community. Burton, like his dad, is an honored philanthropist and leader.

Three other men, Pat O'Connor, Jeno Paulucci, and Robert Short, are successful Minnesotans who have been personal friends and fund-raisers for years.

CHAPTER 34, NOTE 2

Not that this was at all surprising. We had consistently led Kennedy in the polls. The Gallup and Harris polls for May of 1968 showed the following results:

	Gallup	Harris
Humphrey	40	38
Kennedy	31	27
McCarthy	19	25
No opinion	10	10

CHAPTER 34, NOTE 3

My strong feelings about Jesse Unruh derive from his elusive support and calculating positions. Unruh was the speaker of the state house of representatives, a powerful political boss, and later an unsuccessful candidate for governor.

In 1968, I felt that he was snubbing not only me but the national Democratic party as well, which was contending with Richard Nixon— a man Unruh should have known particularly well, as a fellow Californian.

When it seemed reasonable and politically acceptable, Jesse had been a hawk on Vietnam. He had, as a matter of fact, approached Max Kampelman and Jim Rowe to make a deal with President Johnson that would have helped Jesse politically. He offered to support Johnson (and his war position) if he could control federal patronage in California, thus putting Unruh people into important jobs. Johnson, however, was not about to make a deal.

Shortly after his offer was rejected, Jesse surprised many people by appearing in "love beads." He had become an ardent dove. I do not ascribe this change of position merely to his rejection by Johnson. It is possible that he, like others honestly changed views on the war. His posturing in 1968, however, made it appear that he had always been anti-war, and gave at least the appearance of hypocrisy.

CHAPTER 34, NOTE 4

In 1948, 2.4 million students were enrolled in America's colleges and universities. That was about 14.2 per cent of the 18–24-year-old population. By 1968, the figures had grown to 6.9 million students—30.3 per cent of that age group.

However, it is instructive to remember that two out of every three young people were not in college; and yet, very little attention was paid to them by the media. In general, the national news organizations interpreted the mood of the nation's youth only on its college campuses— and even then, only at the larger state universities and private institutions. The degree to which the average American youth, students included, was radicalized during the protest period will remain unknown until historians and sociologists have studied it.

Whatever the over-all effect of the protest movement, we carried Cambridge, Massachussetts (which contains Harvard University), and Princeton, New Jersey.

CHAPTER 34, NOTE 5

If Gene McCarthy's challenging Lyndon Johnson saved even one life by forcing the war to come to a close sooner than it otherwise would, he made a valuable contribution. I think, however, the most lasting impact of his campaign was in his challenge to executive power. He suggested, "We must return to the founding fathers' concept of the presidency as an office of significant but limited power. It must again be an office that shares both power and responsibility with the other branches of government and with the people." This suggestion is one that must be taken seriously. It is something the next President of the United States ought to consider. It would be exciting to have those changes come from a President honestly working with the Congress rather than have the changes come through contention.

CHAPTER 34, NOTE 6

That kind of alliance can still be produced, even today, if people are willing to take the time and the energy to meet and organize. In September of 1968, I spent an entire day and night at the Rice Hotel in Houston, Texas, meeting with such leaders as Ralph Yarborough, Barbara Jordan, and Jim Wright, our campaign chairman in Texas, along with leaders from the AFL-CIO, the Farmers Union, the Mexican-American community, and the more conservative elements of the party, represented by John Connally.

Evans and Novak wrote a column about that meeting, about how much time I had wasted when I should have been out on the road campaigning. But the fact is that that time was not wasted; we carried the state, and without that meeting, we very likely would not have.

One of my most dedicated supporters at that meeting was Ralph Yarborough, a dove and dedicated anti-war spokesman. Despite his profound objections to both President Johnson and his administration's war policies, Ralph nonetheless went all out for our campaign, in an extraordinary display of loyalty.

CHAPTER 34, NOTE 7

During the middle of September, 1968, the Gallup Poll showed Wallace with 21 per cent of the voter preference. During a previous week, the Harris Poll had found the same number.

But when the voters actually cast their ballots, Wallace received only 13.5 per cent, some 9.9 million votes.

CHAPTER 35, NOTE 1

As a matter of fact, three persons died in Miami in protest battles with the police. They were out of sight of the cameras, but their deaths were no less real.

CHAPTER 35, NOTE 2

I have always liked Nelson Rockefeller personally, and when he was suggested to me as a vice-presidential running mate, the idea was intriguing. He was a Republican, of course, and it would have been difficult to sell him to a Democratic convention. But it was worth considering, and I permitted two separate contacts to be made to see if he was interested.

A friend of Max Kampelman who was also a close friend of both David and Nelson Rockefeller and raised the question directly with Nelson. The report came back that Rockefeller, despite his hostility toward Richard Nixon and his respect and affection for me, felt he had to remain a Republican.

Later, though Rockefeller's answer had been clear and unequivocal, Endicott Peabody, the former governor of Massachusetts, asked whether he could approach Rockefeller about the vice presidency. When he insisted, just before the convention, I reluctantly agreed to a second approach, which Rockefeller, of course, turned down.

CHAPTER 35, NOTE 3

I saw relatively little of the convention on television compared to most interested citizens. Meetings, negotiations, caucuses, phone calls took up most of my time.

CHAPTER 35, NOTE 4

Ginsberg had stopped Gene McCarthy in the lobby of the hotel and told him of the Vietnam plank, asking if he would read it. McCarthy sloughed him off, saying offhandedly: "It doesn't matter. Why don't you just show it to Dick Goodwin."

CHAPTER 35, NOTE 5

I seriously considered Sargent Shriver. Earlier, Ken O'Donnell and Larry O'Brien had made it clear that this would be looked on as an unfriendly act by the Kennedy forces. Since they were not talking to each other at the time, I was sure that they had independently confirmed the family point of view. Thursday morning, I checked once again and the answer was the same.

CHAPTER 35, NOTE 6

I called my friends in the labor movement: George Meany, I. W. Abel of the Steelworkers, Joe Beirne of the Communications Workers, Walter Reuther, Jack Jorgensen of the Teamsters. I talked to other political leaders: Mayor Daley and some of the southern governors, John Connally of Texas, Bob McNair of South Carolina, Buford Ellington of Tennessee, Hulett Smith of West Virginia.

Outside the South, I called on other public officeholders and Democratic party figures.

CHAPTER 35, NOTE 7

Vi Williams Biglane has been my personal secretary for more than twenty years. Her loyalty and hard work for long days through all those years have been impressive, and infinitely valuable.

My appointments secretary deserves a special note, too. The scheduling of appointments is a sensitive job in any political or governmental office. Deciding what invitations to accept, whom to see, how to do everything that has to be done, becomes complicated and demands skills that are beyond the time and energy of any single person. Ten years ago, a young woman, Ursula Culver, started in my office as a secretary. She soon demonstrated that she had both the political sensitivity and the toughness the job requires, and has since run my appointments and scheduling. What order there is in my public life these days is the result of her excellence in a thankless job.

CHAPTER 35, NOTE 8

I suffered most of the verbal abuse of the protesters in silence. The shouts of "Dump the Hump" and the gutter vulgarities were so constant that I became almost used to them. But there were some things I never got used to.

One day, I was riding on a cable car in San Francisco's Chinatown with Mayor Joseph Alioto, other local politicians, staff, and press. The car crept slowly up the hill through a large and mostly friendly crowd. Behind the crowd, which was reaching up to shake hands, there was a young man in his twenties or early thirties carrying a child of two or three on his shoulders.

The man's face was horribly contorted in anger as he screamed, "Murderer! . . . Burner of babies!" over and over again as he kept pace with the moving car. The child he was carrying was rigid with terror of the jostling crowd and the screaming. I leaned out from the cable car and called to the man, "You have a face filled with love!" He abruptly stopped yelling, moved back, and left.

Shortly after that, we were in Michigan, and our motorcade moved slowly through a group of Wallace pickets who were shouting and waving their fists at us. One face in the crowd, a man shouting "Nigger lover," was an almost perfect duplication of the contorted features on the man in San Francisco. It was an eerie coincidence, and was noted by several people besides myself.

CHAPTER 35, NOTE 9

The impact of public-opinion polls in 1968 was immense on our fund-raising and political activity. We came out of the Chicago convention—its chaos depicted on TV throughout America—down twenty-two points in the polls. Activists, potential contributors, and press shared a single view: Humphrey-Muskie could not win.

The activists stopped working. The contributors, for the most part, never started contributing. And the press just wrote over and over that we couldn't win.

Bill Connell and Joe Napolitan turned up data in the fall indicating a switch in favor of the Democrats. Using their poll material, they had limited success with contributors and party activists, but virtually none with the press, who continued to write us off.

On our flight into California the last weekend of the campaign, Connell rode the press plane and, using his statistics as background, told the press we would carry New York, Pennsylvania, and Massachusetts and that we had a 50-50 chance in California, Texas, and Illinois.

The press hooted and laughed. When we landed, two of their members came as representatives to complain that Connell was treating them like children and was lying to them. Even when results proved him essentially correct, many remained hostile toward him.

We too often forget the transitory nature of polls. They describe a particular moment of time and attitude.

CHAPTER 35, NOTE 10

Other drafts were prepared by many people, including Bill Welsh, Ben Reed, and Norman Cousins. Cousins had been a good and loyal friend for many years. A pre-eminent liberal, severely torn by the Vietnam War, he nonetheless worked with us constantly, and his help was extremely valuable.

CHAPTER 35, NOTE 11

The Salt Lake City speech read, in part:

"As President, I would stop the bombing of the North as an acceptable risk for peace, because I believe it could lead to success in the negotiations and thereby shorten the war. This would be the best protection for our troops.

"In weighing that risk—and before taking action—I would place key importance on evidence—direct or indirect, by deed or word—of Communist willingness to restore the demilitarized zone between North and South Vietnam.

"If the government of North Vietnam were to show bad faith, I would reserve the right to resume the bombing.

"Secondly, I would take the risk that the South Vietnamese would meet the responsibilities they say they are now ready to assume in their own self-defense.

"I would move, in other words, toward de-Americanization of the war.

"I would sit down with the leaders of South Vietnam to set a specific timetable by which American forces could be systematically reduced while South Vietnamese forces took over more and more of the burden.

"The schedule must be a realistic one—one that would not weaken the over-all allied defense posture. I am convinced such action would be as much in South Vietnam's interest as in ours."

CHAPTER 36, NOTE 1

At the time of the confrontation between Martin Luther King, Jr., and his followers, and the police in Selma, Alabama, I urged the President to speak out deploring the violence, and encouraged him to go before a joint session of Congress. Johnson asked me to work on his speech; mostly, I urged him to follow his own decent instincts. In a moving speech, particularly for a man viewed as a "southern president," Johnson himself declared, echoing Dr. King, "We shall overcome."

CHAPTER 36, NOTE 2

One of the most challenging opportunities as Vice President was the development of our youth programs. Each year, over one million jobs were provided for disadvantaged youth in public and private employment. Additional millions of young people were in sports and recreation programs sponsored by local government and private groups. The program has since been allowed to die by White House inertia.

CHAPTER 36, NOTE 3

For some odd reason, our embassy officials tried to keep our astronauts from meeting Gagarin. The Soviet officials seemed just as nervous. I ignored them both and marched McDivitt and White down to where Gagarin sat. I like to think that their conversations there in the bleachers at the air show paved the way for our combined efforts in space.

CHAPTER 36, NOTE 4

David does not like to travel, hates airplanes, and would have preferred to stay at home. But he had become, since he first began working on agricultural problems for me in the whip office, more than a staff member. He is a loyal friend, and Muriel and I enjoy having him with us on our travels and at home in Waverly. While I used to depend on him almost entirely for his knowledge of agriculture, he now is my chief assistant, having gone to law school after 1968.

CHAPTER 37, NOTE 1

By contrast, one White House staff person with whom I had close and friendly associations was John Roche. John, a witty, and profound, political scientist at Brandeis University then and Tufts now, was chairman of ADA for a while and served in the Johnson White House. There were others in the White House who were friendly and helpful, too, but John was a special friend.

CHAPTER 38, NOTE 1

I retained one quasi-governmental role. Just before my term as Vice President ended, I asked President Johnson to consider nominating me as a trustee of the Woodrow Wilson International Center for Scholars, the nation's memorial to the former President which Congress had established in 1968. In one of his final acts as President, Johnson went even further, by nominating me as the first board chairman of the Wilson Center.

Because Wilson was my boyhood hero, and the hero of my father's adult life, I took special pride as a private citizen in launching this center of governmental study and research in the nation's capital.

CHAPTER 38, NOTE 2

As it was, my appointment was not in the Political Science Department, though that is what I taught.

CHAPTER 38, NOTE 3

Although Richard Nixon and I have had serious political and philosophical differences through all the days of our service in Washington, I must in all fairness record that he was always personally thoughtful and considerate.

When Muriel and I had to pack up our belongings and move back to Minnesota in January 1969, he provided an airplane, permitting our departure to be dignified and private. There was a bouquet of roses with a handwritten note of good wishes from him and Pat on the plane, too.

In 1972 after the Democratic convention, he sent me another handwritten note, warmly philosophical about political defeat.

CHAPTER 38, NOTE 4

Obviously, I could have been useful in that respect. The meeting had been set up at the suggestion of Tom Dewey, who was the friend and attorney of my friend Dwayne Andreas.

CHAPTER 38, NOTE 5

I no longer needed Freddy Gates's car, since I frequently used a helicopter or, at other times, hired a driver. I no longer swallowed a cheese sandwich into a lump in my stomach, lubricated by gulps of a chocolate malted milk. Nonetheless, Freddy, though ill, was there by my side, looking after me and my campaign. I think he resolved to live long enough to see me back in the Senate. He died a month after I returned.

CHAPTER 38, NOTE 6

MacGregor's friendship for Nixon was later abused when he was named to head the Committee to Re-elect the President and put out front to defend the Watergate charges while he was being lied to, as we all were.

CHAPTER 38, NOTE 7

In mid 1971, I was certain that Ed Muskie would be the next President. In public opinion polls, President Nixon had only a 50 per cent favorable rating, not particularly good for an incumbent President. I reasoned that all Muskie had to do was carry the states we had in 1968, plus California and New Jersey, and that a united Democratic party could do that.

INDEX

and civil rights, 66, 267, 268–87, 289, 408–9; and civil rights plank (Democratic National Convention, 1948), 111–16, 124; and death of JFK, 257–65; and debating, 39, 61, 220, 475; decision to run for presidency (1968), 369; and domestic programs and legislation, 407–14, 427, 428; earliest contact with blacks, 447; early interest and involvement in politics, 26, 27, 28, 31, 34–36, 58, 59, 61, 68, 89–93, 94–101, 103–9; education, 36, 37–40, 41–44, 45–46, 56, 57ff., 61, 62–66, 67–72; elected to first term in Senate, 117, 122; on foreign policy and lessons of Vietnam, 255, 423–26; and friendships and relationships, 368 (see also specific individuals); and Honolulu conference and declaration, 329, 335, 337–38; influence of father on, 19, 23–25, 26–28, 29, 33, 34, 58, 59, 68 (see also Humphrey, Hubert H., Sr.); influence of Hayden on, 152–54; influence of South Dakota on, 19, 23, 170; and JFK and his presidency, 229–43 passim, 244–58 passim; and JFK and presidential primaries (1960), 195–96, 204–12, 213–25ff.; and liberalism, 147–48, 169ff., 195; and LBJ and his presidency, 259–61, 262–63, 264, 265–66, 267–87 passim, 288ff.; as majority whip in the Senate, 242–43, 245ff., 267–87, 290ff., 316; marriage, 51–55; as mayor of Minneapolis, 89–93, 94–101, 102–9; meeting with Khrushchev in Moscow,

196–203; memorandum on Vietnam to LBJ, 320–24; in Mexico, 358; on Nixon, 436–38; and presidential campaign (1968), 3–15, 354–68, 369–80, 381–406, 427, 429; and presidential campaign (1972), 434–36; and presidential nomination acceptance speech (1968), 393–95; and re-election to the Senate (1954), 173–74, 175, 180; relations with LBJ, 342–43 (see also under Johnson, Lyndon B.); religion, 29; and return to Senate (1971), 430–31, 433–34; in Soviet Union, 196–203, 253–56; and Stevenson in 1956 campaign, 187–89; and teaching, 62, 67, 68–72, 83–84, 431–32; teen-age years, 31–32, 33–36; and trip to Paris with astronauts, 414–15; trips abroad, 157–58, 184, 196–203, 253–55, 329–38, 347–49, 358, 414–22; trips to Asia, 329–38, 347–49; trips as goodwill ambassador for LBJ, 414–21; and Truman, 125–26, 152, 166, 168, 169–70, 171–75, 178–79 (see also Truman, Harry S); as Vice President, 309, 354ff., 407–22; and vice-presidential campaign (1964), 289–309; and Vietnam, 313–53, 354–64, 384–90, 415, 423–26, 428, 430–31 (see also Vietnam); and Vietnam and 1968 campaign, 354–64, 385, 387–90, 395, 400–2, 428–29; and World War II period, 73ff., 85–86; writes syndicated column, 432

Humphrey, Hubert H., Sr. (father), 19, 22, 23–24, 25–28, 29, 36, 37, 38, 41, 42,